Study Guide & Working Papers
for use with

College Accounting

CHAPTERS 1–32
ELEVENTH EDITION

John Ellis Price

M. David Haddock

Horace R. Brock

 McGraw-Hill Irwin

Boston   Burr Ridge, IL   Dubuque, IA   Madison, WI   New York   San Francisco   St. Louis
Bangkok   Bogotá   Caracas   Kuala Lumpur   Lisbon   London   Madrid   Mexico City
Milan   Montreal   New Delhi   Santiago   Seoul   Singapore   Sydney   Taipei   Toronto

McGraw-Hill
Irwin

Study Guide & Working Papers for use with
COLLEGE ACCOUNTING, Eleventh Edition
Chapters 1–32
John Ellis Price, M. David Haddock, Jr., and Horace R. Brock

Published by McGraw-Hill/Irwin, a business unit of The McGraw-Hill Companies, Inc., 1221
Avenue of the Americas, New York, NY 10020. Copyright © 2007 by The McGraw-Hill
Companies, Inc.
All rights reserved.

1 2 3 4 5 6 7 8 9 0 QPD/QPD 0 9 8 7 6 5

ISBN-13:   978-0-07-303059-3 (chapters 1–32)
ISBN-10:   0-07-303059-7 (chapters 1–32)
ISBN-13:   978-0-07-303058-6 (chapters 14–25)
ISBN-10:   0-07-303058-9 (chapters 14–25)
ISBN-13:   978-0-07-320348-5 (chapters 1–13)
ISBN-10:   0-07-320348-3 (chapters 1–13)

www.mhhe.com

Contents

CHAPTER 1

Accounting: The Language of Business

STUDY GUIDE

Understanding the Chapter

Objectives
1. Define accounting. **2.** Identify and discuss career opportunities in accounting. **3.** Identify the users of financial information. **4.** Compare and contrast the three types of business entities. **5.** Describe the process used to develop generally accepted accounting principles. **6.** Define the accounting terms new to this chapter.

Reading Assignment
Read Chapter 1 in the textbook. Complete the textbook Section Self Review as you finish reading each section of the chapter, and the Comprehensive Self Review at the end of the chapter. Refer to the Chapter 1 Glossary or to the Glossary at the end of the book to find definitions for terms that are not familiar to you.

Activities

❏ **Thinking Critically**
Answer the *Thinking Critically* questions for Yahoo and Managerial Implications.

❏ **Discussion Questions**
Answer each assigned discussion question in Chapter 1.

❏ **Critical Thinking Problem**
Complete the critical thinking problem as assigned.

❏ **Business Connections**
Complete the Business Connections activities as assigned to gain a deeper understanding of Chapter 1 concepts.

Practice Tests

Complete the Practice Tests, which cover the main points in your reading assignment. Compare your answers with those in the Practice Test Answer Key for Chapter 1 at the end of this chapter. If you have answered any questions incorrectly, review the related section of the text.

Part A True-False *For each of the following statements, circle T in the answer column if the answer is true or F if the answer is false.*

T   F   **1.** Passing a test called the Uniform CPA Examination is required for one to become a certified public accountant.

T   F   **2.** The Securities and Exchange Commission has a great deal of power to dictate accounting methods used by companies whose stock is traded on the stock exchanges.

T   F   **3.** The Securities and Exchange Commission often relies on pronouncements of the Financial Accounting Standards Board.

T   F   **4.** The Financial Accounting Standards Board issues income tax rules.

T   F   **5.** Because of the separate entity assumption, the personal financial activities of the owner of a sole proprietorship are combined with the financial affairs of his or her business in the accounting records of the business.

T   F   **6.** All accounting principles are established by law.

T   F   **7.** Because of the difference in the structures of the three types of business entities, certain aspects of their financial affairs are accounted for in different ways.

T   F   **8.** A sole proprietorship is a form of business entity owned by two or more people.

T   F   **9.** There is little difference between a corporation and other forms of business entities.

T   F   **10.** Shares of stock represent ownership in a corporation.

T   F   **11.** Employees should have no particular interest in the financial information about the business for which they work.

T   F   **12.** The American Institute of Certified Public Accountants is a governmental agency.

T   F   **13.** In a large company, the auditing process is completed by bookkeepers.

Part B Completion   *In the answer column, supply the missing word or words needed to complete each of the following statements.*

_____   1. The _____ and other tax authorities are interested in financial information about a firm.

_____   2. Corporate owners are called _____.

_____   3. Ownership in a corporation is evidenced by _____.

_____   4. The three major types of business entities are sole proprietorships, corporations, and _____.

_____   5. An economic entity is an organization whose major purpose is to produce a profit, whereas a(n) _____ is a nonprofit organization.

_____   6. The accounting process involves _____, summarizing, interpreting, and communicating financial information about an economic or social entity.

_____   7. Many people call accounting the _____.

_____   8. Periodic reports prepared from accounting records are called _____.

_____   9. _____ is the study of accounting principles used by different countries.

_____ 10. The IRS and the _____ have large numbers of accountants on their staff and use them to uncover possible violations of the law.

_____ 11. Major areas of accounting are public accounting, managerial accounting, and _____.

_____ 12. The _____ is an organization of accounting educators.

_____ 13. The _____ is a national association of professional accountants.

_____ 14. _____ are developed by the Financial Accounting Standards Board.

_____ 15. The _____ was created to review and oversee the accounting methods of publicly owned corporations.

Name _____

_____

_____

_____

_____

_____

_____

_____

_____

_____

_____

_____

_____

_____

_____

_____

_____

_____

_____

_____

Chapter 1 Practice Test Answer Key

Part A True-False	Part B Completion
1. T	1. IRS
2. T	2. stockholders or shareholders
3. T	3. shares of stock
4. F	4. partnerships
5. F	5. social entity
6. F	6. recording, classifying
7. T	7. language of business
8. F	8. financial statements
9. F	9. International accounting
10. T	10. FBI
11. F	11. government accounting
12. F	12. AAA
13. F	13. AICPA
	14. Generally accepted accounting principles
	15. SEC

CHAPTER 2

Analyzing Business Transactions

STUDY GUIDE

Understanding the Chapter

Objectives
1. Record in equation form the financial effects of a business transaction. 2. Define, identify, and understand the relationship between asset, liability, and owner's equity accounts. 3. Analyze the effects of business transactions on a firm's assets, liabilities, and owner's equity and record these effects in accounting equation form. 4. Prepare an income statement. 5. Prepare a statement of owner's equity and a balance sheet 6. Define the accounting terms new to this chapter.

Reading Assignment
Read Chapter 2 in the textbook. Complete the textbook Section Self Review as you finish reading each section of the chapter, and the Comprehensive Self Review at the end of the chapter. Refer to the Chapter 2 Glossary or to the Glossary at the end of the book to find definitions for terms that are not familiar to you.

Activities

❑ **Thinking Critically**
Answer the *Thinking Critically* questions for Southwest Airlines, Accounting on the Job, and Managerial Implications.

❑ **Internet Application**
Complete the activity for Accounting on the Job.

❑ **Discussion Questions**
Answer each assigned discussion question in Chapter 2.

❑ **Exercises**
Complete each assigned exercise in Chapter 2. Use the forms provided in this SGWP. The objectives covered by an exercise are given after the exercise number. If you need help with an exercise, review the portion of the chapter related to the objective(s) covered.

❑ **Problems A/B**
Complete each assigned problem in Chapter 2. Use the forms provided in this SGWP. The objectives covered by a problem are given after the problem number. If you need help with a problem, review the portion of the chapter related to the objective(s) covered.

❑ **Challenge Problem**
Complete the challenge problem as assigned. Use the forms provided in this SGWP.

❑ **Critical Thinking Problem**
Complete the critical thinking problem as assigned. Use the forms provided in this SGWP.

❑ **Business Connections**
Complete the Business Connections activities as assigned to gain a deeper understanding of Chapter 2 concepts.

Practice Tests
Complete the Practice Tests, which cover the main points in your reading assignment. Compare your answers with those in the Practice Test Answer Key for Chapter 2 at the end of this chapter. If you have answered any questions incorrectly, review the related section of the text.

Part A True-False
For each of the following statements, circle T in the answer column if the answer is true or F if the answer is false.

T   F   **1.** When equipment is purchased for cash, there is no change in the total value of the firm's property.

T   F   **2.** The balance sheet is prepared at the end of the accounting period to show the results of operations.

T   F   **3.** A net loss results if total expenses exceed total revenue.

T   F   **4.** Profit and loss statement is another name for the income statement.

T   F   **5.** The balance sheet shows the financial position of a business on a specific date.

T   F   **6.** The net income or net loss for the period is shown in the Assets section of the balance sheet.

T   F   **7.** The net income or net loss for the period is shown on both the income statement and the statement of owner's equity.

T   F   **8.** The collection of cash from accounts receivable increases owner's equity.

T   F   **9.** Expenses decrease owner's equity.

T   F   **10.** Revenue decreases owner's equity.

Part B Matching
For each numbered item, choose the matching term from the box and write the identifying letter in the answer column.

_____   **1.** Amounts owed by charge account customers

_____   **2.** Amount remaining when total revenue is more than total expenses

_____   **3.** Those to whom money is owed

_____   **4.** Owner's financial interest in the business

_____   **5.** Property owned by a business

_____   **6.** A business obligation or debt

_____   **7.** An expression of the relationship in which assets equal liabilities plus owner's equity

_____   **8.** Inflows of money or other assets resulting from sales of goods or service

a. Accounts Receivable
b. Assets
c. Creditors
d. Revenue
e. Owner's equity
f. Liability
g. Net income
h. Fundamental accounting equation

Part C Completion *In the answer column, supply the missing word or words needed to complete each of the following statements.*

_____ **1.** Accountants must _____ each business transaction before they can intelligently record, report, and interpret it.

_____ **2.** The purchase of new equipment on account creates a debt that is called a(n) _____.

_____ **3.** When property values and financial interest increase or decrease, the sum of the items on both sides of the equation always remains _____.

_____ **4.** The basic reason for starting a business is the possibility of making a _____.

_____ **5.** Accounts receivable result when goods are sold or services are performed on _____.

_____ **6.** When expenses are paid, the owner's equity is _____.

_____ **7.** Regardless of the number and variety of transactions, liabilities plus owner's equity always equal _____.

_____ **8.** When supplies are first purchased for use in operations, they are considered a type of _____.

Demonstration Problem

The account balances for Kawonza Carter, CPA, for the month of January 2007 are shown below in random order.

Rent Expense	$ 8,000	Advertising Expense	$ 5,000
Fees Earned	138,240	Office Equipment	51,120
Accounts Payable	29,824	K. Carter, Drawing	15,156
Salaries Expense	23,780	Accounts Receivable	29,800
Cash	182,276	K. Carter, Capital 1/1	?

Instructions
1. Determine the balance for **Kawonza Carter, Capital,** on January 1, 2007.
2. Prepare an income statement, a statement of owner's equity, and a balance sheet as of January 31, 2007.

SOLUTION

Determine the balance for Kawonza Carter, Capital, on January 1, 2007.
Let Kawonza Carter, Capital = X. Solving for X:

	Assets			=	Liabilities +		Owner's Equity			
	Accts.		Office		Accounts	K. Carter,				
Cash	+ Rec.	+	Equip.	=	Pay.	+ Capital	− Drawing	+ Revenue	− Expenses
182,276	+ 29,800	+	51,120	=	29,824	+ X	− 15,156	+ 138,240	− 36,780
			263,196	=	116,128	+ X			
	263,196	−	116,128	=	X				
			147,068	=	X				

Kawonza Carter, Capital, January 1, 2007 = **$147,068**

Total Expenses:

Rent Expense	$ 8,000
Salaries Expense	23,780
Advertising Expense	5,000
	$36,780

Kawonza Carter, CPA
Income Statement
Month Ended January 31, 2007

Revenue			
Fees Earned			138 2 4 0 00
Expenses			
Rent Expense	8 0 0 0 00		
Salaries Expense	23 7 8 0 00		
Advertising Expense	5 0 0 0 00		
Total Expenses		36 7 8 0 00	
Net Income		101 4 6 0 00	

Kawonza Carter, CPA
Statement of Owner's Equity
Month Ended January 31, 2007

Kawonza Carter, Capital, January 1, 2007			147 0 6 8 00
Net Income	101 4 6 0 00		
Less Withdrawals	15 1 5 6 00		
Increase in Capital			86 3 0 4 00
Kawonza Carter, Capital, January 31, 2007			233 3 7 2 00

SOLUTION (continued)

Kawonza Carter, CPA

Balance Sheet

January 31, 2007

Assets					Liabilities					
Cash	182	2	7	6	00	Accounts Payable		29	8	2	4	00
Accounts Receivable	29	8	0	0	00	Owner's Equity					
Office Equipment	51	1	2	0	00	Kawonza Carter, Capital	233	3	7	2	00
Total Assets	263	1	9	6	00	Total Liabilities and Owner's Equity	263	1	9	6	00

WORKING PAPERS

Name _____

EXERCISE 2.1

1. _____
2. _____
3. _____
4. _____
5. _____

EXERCISE 2.2

Assets _____

Liabilities _____

Owner's Equity _____

EXERCISE 2.3

	Assets	=	Liabilities	+	Owner's Equity
1.	_____	=	_____	+	_____
2.	_____	=	_____	+	_____
3.	_____	=	_____	+	_____
4.	_____	=	_____	+	_____
5.	_____	=	_____	+	_____

EXERCISE 2.4

Transaction	Assets	=	Liabilities	+	Owner's Equity
1.	____ + ____	=	_____	+	____ + ____
2.	_____	=	_____	+	_____
3.	_____	=	_____	+	_____
4.	_____	=	_____	+	_____
5.	_____	=	_____	+	_____
6.	_____	=	_____	+	_____
7.	_____	=	_____	+	_____
8.	_____	=	_____	+	_____
9.	_____	=	_____	+	_____
10.	_____	=	_____	+	_____

EXERCISE 2.5

	Cash	+	Accounts Receivable	+	Equipment	=	Accounts Payable	+	Inez Owens Capital	+	Revenue	−	Expenses
			Assets			=	Liabilities +				Owner's Equity		
1.													
2.													
3.													
4.													
5.													
6.													
7.													
8.													
Totals		+		+		=		+		+		−	

EXERCISE 2.6

1. _____
2. _____
3. _____
4. _____
5. _____
6. _____
7. _____

EXERCISE 2.7

_____

Revenue

_____

Expenses

_____

_____

_____

_____

_____

_____

EXERCISE 2.8

Revenue

Expenses

EXERCISE 2.9

EXERCISE 2.10

PROBLEM 2.1A or 2.1B

	Cash	+	Accounts Receivable	+	Supplies	+	Equipment	=	Accounts Payable	+	Owner's Capital
							Assets	=	Liabilities	+	Owner's Equity
1.											
2.											
3.											
4.											
5.											
6.											
7.											
8.											
9.											
10.											
11.											
Totals		+		+		+		=		+	

$$=$$

Analyze: _____
_____

PROBLEM 2.2A or 2.2B

	Assets				= Liabilities +		Owner's Equity		
	Cash	+ Accounts Receivable +		+	= Accounts Payable	+ Capital	+ Revenue	− Expenses	

	Cash		Accounts Receivable				Accounts Payable	Capital	Revenue	Expenses
Beginning Balances	_____	+	_____	+	_____	+	_____ =	_____ +	_____ +	_____ − _____
1.	_____		_____		_____					
New Balances	_____	+	_____	+	_____	+	_____ =	_____ +	_____ +	_____ − _____
2.	_____		_____		_____					
New Balances	_____	+	_____	+	_____	+	_____ =	_____ +	_____ +	_____ − _____
3.	_____		_____		_____					
New Balances	_____	+	_____	+	_____	+	_____ =	_____ +	_____ +	_____ − _____
4.	_____		_____		_____					
New Balances	_____	+	_____	+	_____	+	_____ =	_____ +	_____ +	_____ − _____
5.	_____		_____		_____					
New Balances	_____	+	_____	+	_____	+	_____ =	_____ +	_____ +	_____ − _____
6.	_____		_____		_____					
New Balances	_____	+	_____	+	_____	+	_____ =	_____ +	_____ +	_____ − _____
7.	_____		_____		_____					
New Balances	_____	+	_____	+	_____	+	_____ =	_____ +	_____ +	_____ − _____
8.	_____		_____		_____					
New Balances	_____	+	_____	+	_____	+	_____ =	_____ +	_____ +	_____ − _____
9.	_____		_____		_____					
New Balances	_____	+	_____	+	_____	+	_____ =	_____ +	_____ +	_____ − _____
10.	_____		_____		_____					
New Balances	_____	+	_____	+	_____	+	_____ =	_____ +	_____ +	_____ − _____
							=			

Analyze: _____

_____

PROBLEM 2.3A or 2.3B

Analyze:

PROBLEM 2.4A or 2.4B

PROBLEM 2.4A or 2.4B (continued)

Analyze: _____

CHAPTER 2 CHALLENGE PROBLEM

Determine the balance for **French Taylor, Capital**, April 1, 2007.

	Assets			= Liabilities +		Owner's Equity			
Cash	+ Accounts Receivable	+ Machinery	=	Accounts Payable	+ French Taylor Capital	− French Taylor Drawing	+ Revenue	− Expenses
$6,500 +	$2,800 +	$8,500 =		$3,200 +	?	− $1,200 +	$9,500 −	$5,000

Let French Taylor, Capital = X.

Solving for X:

French Taylor, Capital, April 1, 2007, = _____

Advertising Expense	$ 900
Maintenance Expense	1,100
Salaries Expense	3,000
Total Expenses	═══

CHAPTER 2 CHALLENGE PROBLEM (continued)

Analyze: _____

CHAPTER 2 CRITICAL THINKING PROBLEM

_____

_____

Chapter 2 Practice Test Answer Key

Part A True-False		Part B Matching		Part C Completion	
1. T	6. F	1. a	5. b	1. analyze	5. credit or on account
2. F	7. T	2. g	6. f	2. accounts payable or liability	6. reduced or decreased
3. T	8. F	3. c	7. h	3. equal	7. assets
4. T	9. T	4. e	8. d	4. profit	8. asset or property
5. T	10. F				

CHAPTER 3

Analyzing Business Transactions Using T Accounts

STUDY GUIDE

Understanding the Chapter

Objectives

1. Set up T accounts for assets, liabilities, and owner's equity. **2.** Analyze business transactions and enter them in the accounts. **3.** Determine the balance of an account. **4.** Set up T accounts for revenue and expenses. **5.** Prepare a trial balance from T accounts. **6.** Prepare an income statement, a statement of owner's equity, and a balance sheet. **7.** Develop a chart of accounts. **8.** Define the accounting terms new to this chapter.

Reading Assignment

Read Chapter 3 in the textbook. Complete the textbook Section Self Review as you finish reading each section of the chapter, and the Comprehensive Self Review at the end of the chapter. Refer to the Chapter 3 Glossary or to the Glossary at the end of the book to find definitions for terms that are not familiar to you.

Activities

❏ **Thinking Critically**

Answer the *Thinking Critically* questions for Johnson & Johnson, Computers in Accounting, and Managerial Implications.

❏ **Internet Application**

Complete the activity for Computers in Accounting.

❏ **Discussion Questions**

Answer each assigned discussion question in Chapter 3.

❏ **Exercises**

Complete each assigned exercise in Chapter 3. Use the forms provided in this SGWP. The objectives covered by an exercise are given after the exercise number. If you need help with an exercise, review the portion of the chapter related to the objective(s) covered.

❏ **Problems A/B**

Complete each assigned problem in Chapter 3. Use the forms provided in this SGWP. The objectives covered by a problem are given after the problem number. If you need help with a problem, review the portion of the chapter related to the objective(s) covered.

❏ **Challenge Problem**

Complete the challenge problem as assigned. Use the forms provided in this SGWP.

❏ **Critical Thinking Problem**

Complete the critical thinking problem as assigned. Use the forms provided in this SGWP.

❏ **Business Connections**

Complete the Business Connections activities as assigned to gain a deeper understanding of Chapter 3 concepts.

Practice Tests

Complete the Practice Tests, which cover the main points in your reading assignment. Compare your answers with those in the Practice Test Answer Key for Chapter 3 at the end of this chapter. If you have answered any questions incorrectly, review the related section of the text.

Part A True-False *For each of the following statements, circle T in the answer column if the answer is true or F if the answer is false.*

T F **1.** The **Accounts Payable** account is decreased by a debit entry.

T F **2.** Increases in expense accounts are recorded by credit entries.

T F **3.** Accountants keep a separate record for each asset, liability, and owner's equity item.

T F **4.** The T account allows increases and decreases to be separated and recorded on different sides.

T F **5.** Increases in assets are recorded on the debit side of an account.

T F **6.** Decreases in assets are recorded on the left side of an account.

T F **7.** The owner's beginning investment is entered as a debit in the owner's capital account.

T F **8.** Increases in liabilities are recorded on the debit side of an account.

T F **9.** A cash payment by a business is recorded as a debit entry in the **Cash** account.

T F **10.** Decreases in liabilities are credited to the liability account.

T F **11.** An increase in the owner's investment is recorded by crediting the owner's capital account.

T F **12.** Revenue accounts are increased by credits.

T F **13.** An entry on the left side of any account is called a debit.

T F **14.** A reduction in the equity of the owners is recorded by making a debit entry in the **Owner's Capital** account.

T F **15.** The receipt of cash is recorded by a debit entry to the **Cash** account.

Part B Matching

For each numbered item, choose the matching item from the box and write the identifying letter in the answer column.

_____ **1.** An operating cost that decreases owner's equity.

_____ **2.** The system of accounting that requires equality of the entries on each side of the equation.

_____ **3.** Accounts whose balances are carried forward to start a new period.

_____ **4.** An entry on the left side of an account.

_____ **5.** A system for arranging accounts in logical order.

_____ **6.** An entry on the right side of an account.

_____ **7.** Accounts whose balances are transferred to a summary account at the end of the accounting period.

_____ **8.** A subdivision of owner's equity that is used to record various types of income of a business.

_____ **9.** A separate written record that is kept for each asset, liability, and owner's equity item.

> **a.** Account
>
> **b.** Double-entry system
>
> **c.** Credit
>
> **d.** Permanent accounts
>
> **e.** Temporary accounts
>
> **f.** Expense
>
> **g.** Revenue
>
> **h.** Chart of accounts
>
> **i.** Debit

Part C Completion

In the answer column, supply the missing word or words needed to complete each of the following statements.

_____ **1.** The _____ of an account is where increases in the account are recorded and where the balance is recorded.

_____ **2.** The _____ is a statement prepared to test the accuracy of the figures recorded in the accounts.

_____ **3.** A(n) _____ is an error where the decimal point is misplaced.

_____ **4.** A(n) _____ is an error where the digits of a number are switched.

_____ **5.** A(n) _____ is the total of several entries on either side of an account that is entered in small pencil.

Demonstration Problem

Adiam Ghirmai is an investment broker who operates her own business, Ghirmai Investment Counseling.

Instructions

1. Analyze the transactions for the month of January 2007, and record each in the appropriate T accounts. Use plus and minus signs to show increases and decreases. Identify each entry in the T accounts by writing the number of the transaction next to the entry.

2. Determine the balance for each T account. Prepare a trial balance.

Transactions

1. Adiam Ghirmai invested $25,000 in cash to start the business.

2. Ghirmai Investment Counseling purchased office furniture for $4,500 on account.

3. Paid $1,500 for one month's rent.

4. Sold an investment portfolio to the Inez Family and received fees of $25,000.

5. Purchased a computer for $2,000, paying $1,000 in cash and putting the balance on account for 60 days.

6. Paid $4,200 for employee salaries.

7. Purchased office equipment for $3,750 with credit terms of 60 days.

8. Sold an investment portfolio to the Reed Family and will receive commission fees of $10,500 in 30 days.

9. Issued a check for $1,875 for partial payment of the amount for office equipment.

10. Adiam Ghirmai withdrew $2,500 in cash for personal use.

11. Issued a check for $520 to pay the utility bill.

SOLUTION

Cash			
(1)	+ 25,000	(3)	− 1,500
(4)	+ 25,000	(5)	− 1,000
		(6)	− 4,200
		(9)	− 1,875
	50,000	(10)	− 2,500
		(11)	− 520
Bal.	38,405		11,595

Accounts Receivable	
(8)	+ 10,500

Office Furniture	
(2)	+ 4,500

Office Equipment	
(5)	+ 2,000
(7)	+ 3,750
Bal.	5,750

Accounts Payable			
(9)	− 1,875	(2)	+ 4,500
		(5)	+ 1,000
		(7)	+ 3,750
		Bal.	7,375

Adiam Ghirmai, Capital			
		(1)	+ 25,000

Adiam Ghirmai, Drawing	
(10)	+ 2,500

Fees Income			
		(4)	+ 25,000
		(8)	+ 10,500
		Bal.	35,500

Rent Expense	
(3)	+ 1,500

Salaries Expense	
(6)	+ 4,200

Utilities Expense	
(11)	+ 520

SOLUTION (continued)

Ghirmai Investment Counseling
Trial Balance
January 31, 2007

ACCOUNT NAME	DEBIT	CREDIT
Cash	38 4 0 5 00	
Accounts Receivable	10 5 0 0 00	
Office Furniture	4 5 0 0 00	
Office Equipment	5 7 5 0 00	
Accounts Payable		7 3 7 5 00
Adiam Ghirmai, Capital		25 0 0 0 00
Adiam Ghirmai, Drawing	2 5 0 0 00	
Fees Income		35 5 0 0 00
Rent Expense	1 5 0 0 00	
Salaries Expense	4 2 0 0 00	
Utilities Expense	5 2 0 00	
Totals	67 8 7 5 00	67 8 7 5 00

WORKING PAPERS

EXERCISE 3.1

EXERCISE 3.2

EXERCISE 3.3

1. _____
2. _____
3. _____
4. _____
5. _____

EXERCISE 3.4

1. _____   5. _____
2. _____   6. _____
3. _____   7. _____
4. _____   8. _____

EXERCISE 3.5

_____   _____

_____   _____

_____   _____

_____   _____

_____   _____

EXERCISE 3.6

_____

_____

ACCOUNT NAME	DEBIT	CREDIT

EXERCISE 3.6 (continued)

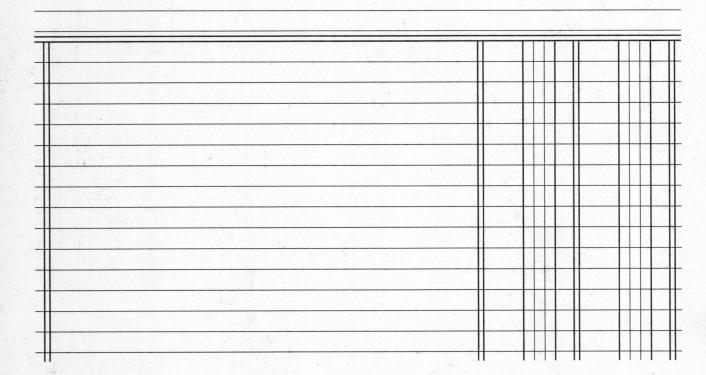

EXERCISE 3.7

EXERCISE 3.7 (continued)

EXERCISE 3.8

PROBLEM 3.1A or 3.1B

1. _____|_____   _____|_____

2. _____|_____   _____|_____

3. _____|_____   _____|_____

4. _____|_____   _____|_____

5. _____|_____   _____|_____

6. _____|_____   _____|_____

7. _____|_____   _____|_____

8. _____|_____   _____|_____

Analyze: _____

_____

PROBLEM 3.2A or 3.2B

1. _____|_____   _____|_____

2. _____|_____   _____|_____

3. _____|_____   _____|_____

4. _____|_____   _____|_____

5. _____|_____   _____|_____

6. _____|_____   _____|_____

7. _____|_____   _____|_____

8. _____|_____   _____|_____

Analyze: _____

_____

PROBLEM 3.3A or 3.3B

1. _____ | _____   _____ | _____

2. _____ | _____   _____ | _____

3. _____ | _____   _____ | _____

4. _____ | _____   _____ | _____

5. _____ | _____   _____ | _____

6. _____ | _____   _____ | _____

7. _____ | _____   _____ | _____

8. _____ | _____   _____ | _____

9. _____ | _____   _____ | _____

10. _____ | _____   _____ | _____

11. _____ | _____   _____ | _____

12. _____ | _____   _____ | _____

Analyze: _____
_____

PROBLEM 3.4A or 3.4B

Analyze: _____
_____

PROBLEM 3.5A or 3.5B

_____
_____

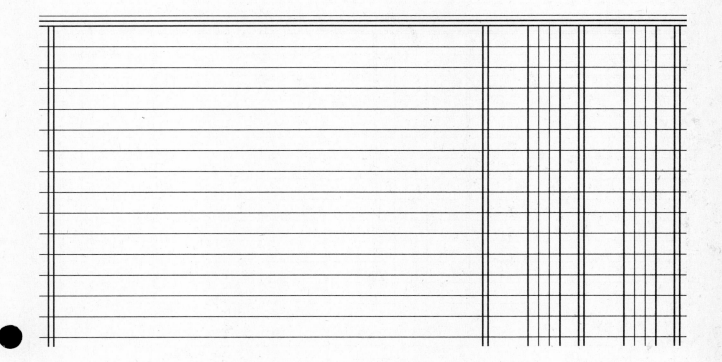

ACCOUNT NAME	DEBIT	CREDIT

	DEBIT	CREDIT

PROBLEM 3.5A or 3.5B (continued)

CHAPTER 3 CHALLENGE PROBLEM

CHAPTER 3 CHALLENGE PROBLEM (continued)

ACCOUNT NAME	DEBIT	CREDIT

CHAPTER 3 CHALLENGE PROBLEM (continued)

Analyze:

CHAPTER 3 CRITICAL THINKING PROBLEM

CHAPTER 3 CRITICAL THINKING PROBLEM (continued)

CHAPTER 3 CRITICAL THINKING PROBLEM (continued)

_____
_____
_____
_____
_____
_____
_____
_____
_____
_____
_____
_____
_____
_____
_____
_____

Chapter 3 Practice Test Answer Key

Part A True-False	Part B Matching
1. T	1. f
2. F	2. b
3. T	3. d
4. T	4. i
5. T	5. h
6. F	6. c
7. F	7. e
8. F	8. g
9. F	9. a
10. F	
11. T	**Part C Completion**
12. T	1. normal balance
13. T	2. trial balance
14. T	3. slide
15. T	4. transposition
	5. footing

The General Journal and the General Ledger

STUDY GUIDE

Understanding the Chapter

Objectives

1. Record transactions in the general journal. **2.** Prepare compound journal entries. **3.** Post journal entries to general ledger accounts. **4.** Correct errors made in the journal or ledger. **5.** Define the accounting terms new to this chapter.

Reading Assignment

Read Chapter 4 in the textbook. Complete the textbook Section Self Review as you finish reading each section of the chapter, and the Comprehensive Self Review at the end of the chapter. Refer to the Chapter 4 Glossary or to the Glossary at the end of the book to find definitions for terms that are not familiar to you.

Activities

❑ **Thinking Critically**

Answer the *Thinking Critically* questions for Caterpillar, Inc., Accounting on the Job, and Managerial Implications.

❑ **Internet Application**

Complete the activity for Accounting on the Job.

❑ **Discussion Questions**

Answer each assigned discussion question in Chapter 4.

❑ **Exercises**

Complete each assigned exercise in Chapter 4. Use the forms provided in this SGWP. The objectives covered by an exercise are given after the exercise number. If you need help with an exercise, review the portion of the chapter related to the objective(s) covered.

❑ **Problems A/B**

Complete each assigned problem in Chapter 4. Use the forms provided in this SGWP. The objectives covered by a problem are given after the problem number. If you need help with a problem, review the portion of the chapter related to the objective(s) covered.

❑ **Challenge Problem**

Complete the challenge problem as assigned. Use the forms provided in this SGWP.

❑ **Critical Thinking Problem**

Complete the critical thinking problem as assigned. Use the forms provided in this SGWP.

❑ **Business Connections**

Complete the Business Connections activities as assigned to gain a deeper understanding of Chapter 4 concepts.

Practice Tests

Complete the Practice Tests, which cover the main points in your reading assignment. Compare your answers with those in the Practice Test Answer Key for Chapter 4 at the end of this chapter. If you have answered any questions incorrectly, review the related section of the text.

Part A Matching *For each numbered item, choose the matching term from the box and write the identifying letter in the answer column.*

_____ 1. A ledger account form that always shows the current balance of an account.

_____ 2. A journal entry that consists of more than one debit or more than one credit.

_____ 3. A permanent, classified record of all accounts used by a business.

_____ 4. Used to analyze transactions but not used to maintain financial records.

_____ 5. The process of transferring information from the journal to the ledger.

_____ 6. An entry that is made when there is an error in data that has been journalized and posted.

_____ 7. Record of original entry.

_____ 8. The process of recording transactions in the journal.

_____ 9. Invoices and other business forms that contain the original data about transactions.

_____ 10. A chain of references that makes it possible to trace information about transactions through an accounting system.

a. journal
b. source documents
c. posting
d. general ledger
e. T accounts
f. journalizing
g. correcting entry
h. compound entry
i. balance ledger form
j. audit trail

Part B Completion *In the answer column, supply the missing word or words needed to complete each of the following statements.*

_____ 1. The accountant always records the _____ items first in the Description column of the journal.

_____ 2. The _____ is always entered at the top of the Date column.

_____ 3. The accountant enters transactions in the general journal in _____ order.

_____ 4. The pages in the ledger are usually organized so that the _____ come first.

_____ 5. If an error is discovered in a journal before the entry is _____, the error can be neatly crossed out and the correct data written above it.

_____ 6. All the accounts together constitute a(n) _____, or a record of final entry.

_____ 7. Notations that allow the data in journals and ledgers to be easily traced are called _____.

_____ 8. Descriptions in the general journal should be complete but _____.

_____ 9. On the balance ledger form the second money column is used to record _____ amounts.

_____ 10. On the balance ledger form the first money column is used to record _____ amounts.

Demonstration Problem

On January 1, 2007, Patricia King opened her consulting office and began business as King Consulting Services. Selected transactions for the first month of operations follow.

Instructions

1. Journalize the transactions on page 1 of a general journal. Write the year at the top of the Date column; include an explanation for each entry.

2. Post to the general ledger accounts.

3. Prepare a trial balance.

DATE	TRANSACTIONS
January 1	Patricia King invested $40,000 cash in the business.
2	Issued Check 101 for $3,500 to pay the January rent.
5	Purchased office equipment for $20,500 from Kerry Office Supply, Invoice 4507; issued Check 102 for $5,500 down payment with the balance due in 30 days.
12	Wrote a lease contract for Pamela Davis for $2,000 cash.
15	Performed consulting services for a client, Zant Supply Company, for $15,000 to be received in 30 days.
28	Issued Check 103 for $7,000 for payment to Kerry Office Supply.
29	Issued Check 104 for $3,000 to Patricia King for personal use.
31	Received $9,000 from Zant Supply Company for partial payment of their account.

SOLUTION

GENERAL JOURNAL

PAGE ___1___

	DATE		DESCRIPTION	POST. REF.	DEBIT	CREDIT	
1	2007						1
2	Jan.	1	Cash	101	40 0 0 0 00		2
3			Patricia King, Capital	301		40 0 0 0 00	3
4			Investment to start business				4
5							5
6		2	Rent Expense	514	3 5 0 0 00		6
7			Cash	101		3 5 0 0 00	7
8			Issued Check 101 for January rent				8
9							9
10		5	Office Equipment	131	20 5 0 0 00		10
11			Cash	101		5 5 0 0 00	11
12			Accounts Payable	202		15 0 0 0 00	12
13			Issued Check 102 for office equipment,				13
14			balance due in 30 days.				14
15							15
16		12	Cash	101	2 0 0 0 00		16
17			Fees Income	401		2 0 0 0 00	17
18			Performed services for cash.				18
19							19
20		15	Accounts Receivable	111	15 0 0 0 00		20
21			Fees Income	401		15 0 0 0 00	21
22			Performed services on account.				22
23							23
24		28	Accounts Payable	202	7 0 0 0 00		24
25			Cash	101		7 0 0 0 00	25
26			Paid Invoice 4507, Check 103				26
27							27
28		29	Patricia King, Drawing	302	3 0 0 0 00		28
29			Cash	101		3 0 0 0 00	29
30			Issued Check 104 to owner for personal use.				30
31							31
32		31	Cash	101	9 0 0 0 00		32
33			Accounts Receivable	111		9 0 0 0 00	33
34			Received partial payment				34
35			from Zant Supply Company				35

44 ■ Chapter 4

SOLUTION (continued)

GENERAL LEDGER

ACCOUNT __Cash__   ACCOUNT NO. ____101

DATE		DESCRIPTION	POST. REF.	DEBIT	CREDIT	BALANCE DEBIT	BALANCE CREDIT
2007							
Jan.	1		J1	40 0 0 0 00		40 0 0 0 00	
	2		J1		3 5 0 0 00	36 5 0 0 00	
	5		J1		5 5 0 0 00	31 0 0 0 00	
	12		J1	2 0 0 0 00		33 0 0 0 00	
	28		J1		7 0 0 0 00	26 0 0 0 00	
	29		J1		3 0 0 0 00	23 0 0 0 00	
	31		J1	9 0 0 0 00		32 0 0 0 00	

ACCOUNT __Accounts Receivable__   ACCOUNT NO. ____111

DATE		DESCRIPTION	POST. REF.	DEBIT	CREDIT	BALANCE DEBIT	BALANCE CREDIT
2007							
Jan.	15		J1	15 0 0 0 00		15 0 0 0 00	
	31		J1		9 0 0 0 00	6 0 0 0 00	

ACCOUNT __Office Equipment__   ACCOUNT NO. ____131

DATE		DESCRIPTION	POST. REF.	DEBIT	CREDIT	BALANCE DEBIT	BALANCE CREDIT
2007							
Jan.	5		J1	20 5 0 0 00		20 5 0 0 00	

ACCOUNT __Accounts Payable__   ACCOUNT NO. ____202

DATE		DESCRIPTION	POST. REF.	DEBIT	CREDIT	BALANCE DEBIT	BALANCE CREDIT
2007							
Jan.	5		J1		15 0 0 0 00		15 0 0 0 00
	28		J1	7 0 0 0 00			8 0 0 0 00

ACCOUNT __Patricia King, Capital__   ACCOUNT NO. ____301

DATE		DESCRIPTION	POST. REF.	DEBIT	CREDIT	BALANCE DEBIT	BALANCE CREDIT
2007							
Jan.	1		J1		40 0 0 0 00		40 0 0 0 00

SOLUTION (continued)

ACCOUNT __Patricia King, Drawing__   ACCOUNT NO. ____302____

DATE		DESCRIPTION	POST. REF.	DEBIT	CREDIT	BALANCE	
						DEBIT	CREDIT
2007							
Jan.	29		J1	3 0 0 0 00		3 0 0 0 00	

ACCOUNT __Fees Income__   ACCOUNT NO. ____401____

DATE		DESCRIPTION	POST. REF.	DEBIT	CREDIT	BALANCE	
						DEBIT	CREDIT
2007							
Jan.	12		J1		2 0 0 0 00		2 0 0 0 00
	15		J1		15 0 0 0 00		17 0 0 0 00

ACCOUNT __Rent Expense__   ACCOUNT NO. ____514____

DATE		DESCRIPTION	POST. REF.	DEBIT	CREDIT	BALANCE	
						DEBIT	CREDIT
2007							
Jan.	2		J1	3 5 0 0 00		3 5 0 0 00	

King Consulting Services
Trial Balance
January 31, 2007

ACCOUNT NAME	DEBIT	CREDIT
Cash	32 0 0 0 00	
Accounts Receivable	6 0 0 0 00	
Office Equipment	20 5 0 0 00	
Accounts Payable		8 0 0 0 00
Patricia King, Capital		40 0 0 0 00
Patricia King, Drawing	3 0 0 0 00	
Fees Income		17 0 0 0 00
Rent Expense	3 5 0 0 00	
Totals	65 0 0 0 00	65 0 0 0 00

WORKING PAPERS

Name _____

EXERCISE 4.1

	Debit	Credit			Debit	Credit			Debit	Credit
1.	_____			**5.**	_____			**8.**	_____	
2.	_____			**6.**	_____			**9.**	_____	
3.	_____			**7.**	_____			**10.**	_____	
4.	_____									

EXERCISE 4.2

GENERAL JOURNAL

PAGE _____

	DATE	DESCRIPTION	POST. REF.	DEBIT	CREDIT	
1						1
2						2
3						3
4						4
5						5
6						6
7						7
8						8
9						9
10						10
11						11
12						12
13						13
14						14
15						15
16						16
17						17
18						18
19						19
20						20
21						21
22						22
23						23
24						24
25						25
26						26
27						27
28						28
29						29
30						30

EXERCISE 4.2 (continued)

GENERAL JOURNAL   PAGE _____

	DATE		DESCRIPTION	POST. REF.	DEBIT	CREDIT	
1							1
2							2
3							3
4							4
5							5
6							6
7							7
8							8
9							9
10							10
11							11
12							12
13							13
14							14
15							15
16							16
17							17

EXERCISE 4.3

GENERAL LEDGER

ACCOUNT _____   ACCOUNT NO. _____

DATE		DESCRIPTION	POST. REF.	DEBIT	CREDIT	BALANCE	
						DEBIT	CREDIT

EXERCISE 4.3 (continued)

GENERAL LEDGER

ACCOUNT _____ ACCOUNT NO. _____

	DATE	DESCRIPTION	POST. REF.	DEBIT	CREDIT	BALANCE	
						DEBIT	CREDIT

ACCOUNT _____ ACCOUNT NO. _____

	DATE	DESCRIPTION	POST. REF.	DEBIT	CREDIT	BALANCE	
						DEBIT	CREDIT

ACCOUNT _____ ACCOUNT NO. _____

	DATE	DESCRIPTION	POST. REF.	DEBIT	CREDIT	BALANCE	
						DEBIT	CREDIT

ACCOUNT _____ ACCOUNT NO. _____

	DATE	DESCRIPTION	POST. REF.	DEBIT	CREDIT	BALANCE	
						DEBIT	CREDIT

ACCOUNT _____ ACCOUNT NO. _____

	DATE	DESCRIPTION	POST. REF.	DEBIT	CREDIT	BALANCE	
						DEBIT	CREDIT

EXERCISE 4.3 (continued)

GENERAL LEDGER

ACCOUNT _____ ACCOUNT NO. _____

DATE	DESCRIPTION	POST. REF.	DEBIT	CREDIT	BALANCE	
					DEBIT	CREDIT

ACCOUNT _____ ACCOUNT NO. _____

DATE	DESCRIPTION	POST. REF.	DEBIT	CREDIT	BALANCE	
					DEBIT	CREDIT

ACCOUNT _____ ACCOUNT NO. _____

DATE	DESCRIPTION	POST. REF.	DEBIT	CREDIT	BALANCE	
					DEBIT	CREDIT

ACCOUNT _____ ACCOUNT NO. _____

DATE	DESCRIPTION	POST. REF.	DEBIT	CREDIT	BALANCE	
					DEBIT	CREDIT

ACCOUNT _____ ACCOUNT NO. _____

DATE	DESCRIPTION	POST. REF.	DEBIT	CREDIT	BALANCE	
					DEBIT	CREDIT

ACCOUNT _____ ACCOUNT NO. _____

DATE	DESCRIPTION	POST. REF.	DEBIT	CREDIT	BALANCE	
					DEBIT	CREDIT

EXERCISE 4.4

GENERAL JOURNAL

PAGE _____

	DATE	DESCRIPTION	POST. REF.	DEBIT	CREDIT	
1						1
2						2
3						3
4						4
5						5
6						6
7						7
8						8
9						9
10						10
11						11
12						12
13						13
14						14
15						15
16						16
17						17
18						18
19						19
20						20
21						21
22						22
23						23
24						24
25						25
26						26
27						27
28						28
29						29
30						30
31						31
32						32
33						33
34						34
35						35
36						36
37						37

EXERCISE 4.5

GENERAL JOURNAL

PAGE _____

	DATE		DESCRIPTION	POST. REF.	DEBIT	CREDIT	
1							1
2							2
3							3
4							4
5							5
6							6

EXERCISE 4.6

GENERAL JOURNAL

PAGE _____

	DATE		DESCRIPTION	POST. REF.	DEBIT	CREDIT	
1							1
2							2
3							3
4							4
5							5
6							6

EXTRA FORM

GENERAL JOURNAL

PAGE _____

	DATE		DESCRIPTION	POST. REF.	DEBIT	CREDIT	
1							1
2							2
3							3
4							4
5							5
6							6
7							7
8							8
9							9
10							10
11							11
12							12
13							13

PROBLEM 4.1A or 4.1B

GENERAL JOURNAL   PAGE _____

	DATE	DESCRIPTION	POST. REF.	DEBIT	CREDIT	
1						1
2						2
3						3
4						4
5						5
6						6
7						7
8						8
9						9
10						10
11						11
12						12
13						13
14						14
15						15
16						16
17						17
18						18
19						19
20						20
21						21
22						22
23						23
24						24
25						25
26						26
27						27
28						28
29						29
30						30
31						31
32						32
33						33
34						34
35						35
36						36
37						37
38						38

PROBLEM 4.1A or 4.1B (continued)

GENERAL JOURNAL   PAGE _____

	DATE	DESCRIPTION	POST. REF.	DEBIT	CREDIT	
1						1
2						2
3						3
4						4
5						5
6						6
7						7
8						8
9						9
10						10
11						11
12						12
13						13
14						14
15						15
16						16
17						17
18						18
19						19
20						20
21						21
22						22
23						23
24						24
25						25
26						26
27						27
28						28
29						29
30						30
31						31
32						32
33						33
34						34
35						35
36						36
37						37

Analyze: _____

PROBLEM 4.2A or 4.2B

GENERAL JOURNAL

PAGE _____

DATE	DESCRIPTION	POST. REF.	DEBIT	CREDIT	
1					1
2					2
3					3
4					4
5					5
6					6
7					7
8					8
9					9
10					10
11					11
12					12
13					13
14					14
15					15
16					16
17					17
18					18
19					19
20					20
21					21
22					22
23					23
24					24
25					25
26					26
27					27
28					28
29					29
30					30
31					31
32					32
33					33
34					34
35					35
36					36
37					37

Name _____

PROBLEM 4.2A or 4.2B (continued)

GENERAL JOURNAL   PAGE _____

	DATE		DESCRIPTION	POST. REF.	DEBIT	CREDIT	
1							1
2							2
3							3
4							4
5							5
6							6
7							7
8							8
9							9
10							10
11							11
12							12
13							13
14							14
15							15
16							16
17							17
18							18
19							19
20							20
21							21
22							22
23							23
24							24
25							25
26							26
27							27
28							28
29							29
30							30
31							31
32							32
33							33
34							34
35							35
36							36
37							37

56 ■ Chapter 4

PROBLEM 4.2A or 4.2B (continued)

GENERAL LEDGER

ACCOUNT _____ ACCOUNT NO. _____

DATE	DESCRIPTION	POST. REF.	DEBIT	CREDIT	BALANCE	
					DEBIT	CREDIT

ACCOUNT _____ ACCOUNT NO. _____

DATE	DESCRIPTION	POST. REF.	DEBIT	CREDIT	BALANCE	
					DEBIT	CREDIT

ACCOUNT _____ ACCOUNT NO. _____

DATE	DESCRIPTION	POST. REF.	DEBIT	CREDIT	BALANCE	
					DEBIT	CREDIT

ACCOUNT _____ ACCOUNT NO. _____

DATE	DESCRIPTION	POST. REF.	DEBIT	CREDIT	BALANCE	
					DEBIT	CREDIT

PROBLEM 4.2A or 4.2B (continued)

GENERAL LEDGER

ACCOUNT _____ ACCOUNT NO. _____

DATE	DESCRIPTION	POST. REF.	DEBIT	CREDIT	BALANCE	
					DEBIT	CREDIT

ACCOUNT _____ ACCOUNT NO. _____

DATE	DESCRIPTION	POST. REF.	DEBIT	CREDIT	BALANCE	
					DEBIT	CREDIT

ACCOUNT _____ ACCOUNT NO. _____

DATE	DESCRIPTION	POST. REF.	DEBIT	CREDIT	BALANCE	
					DEBIT	CREDIT

ACCOUNT _____ ACCOUNT NO. _____

DATE	DESCRIPTION	POST. REF.	DEBIT	CREDIT	BALANCE	
					DEBIT	CREDIT

ACCOUNT _____ ACCOUNT NO. _____

DATE	DESCRIPTION	POST. REF.	DEBIT	CREDIT	BALANCE	
					DEBIT	CREDIT

PROBLEM 4.2A or 4.2B (continued)

GENERAL LEDGER

ACCOUNT _____ ACCOUNT NO. _____

DATE	DESCRIPTION	POST. REF.	DEBIT	CREDIT	BALANCE	
					DEBIT	CREDIT

ACCOUNT _____ ACCOUNT NO. _____

DATE	DESCRIPTION	POST. REF.	DEBIT	CREDIT	BALANCE	
					DEBIT	CREDIT

ACCOUNT _____ ACCOUNT NO. _____

DATE	DESCRIPTION	POST. REF.	DEBIT	CREDIT	BALANCE	
					DEBIT	CREDIT

ACCOUNT _____ ACCOUNT NO. _____

DATE	DESCRIPTION	POST. REF.	DEBIT	CREDIT	BALANCE	
					DEBIT	CREDIT

ACCOUNT _____ ACCOUNT NO. _____

DATE	DESCRIPTION	POST. REF.	DEBIT	CREDIT	BALANCE	
					DEBIT	CREDIT

Analyze: _____

_____

PROBLEM 4.3A or 4.3B

_____
_____
_____
_____
_____
_____

Analyze: _____
_____

PROBLEM 4.4A or 4.4B

GENERAL JOURNAL   PAGE _____

	DATE	DESCRIPTION	POST. REF.	DEBIT	CREDIT	
1						1
2						2
3						3
4						4
5						5
6						6
7						7
8						8
9						9
10						10
11						11
12						12
13						13
14						14
15						15
16						16
17						17
18						18
19						19
20						20
21						21
22						22
23						23
24						24
25						25
26						26

Name _____

PROBLEM 4.4A or 4.4B (continued)

GENERAL LEDGER

ACCOUNT _____ ACCOUNT NO. _____

DATE	DESCRIPTION	POST. REF.	DEBIT	CREDIT	BALANCE DEBIT	CREDIT

ACCOUNT _____ ACCOUNT NO. _____

DATE	DESCRIPTION	POST. REF.	DEBIT	CREDIT	BALANCE DEBIT	CREDIT

ACCOUNT _____ ACCOUNT NO. _____

DATE	DESCRIPTION	POST. REF.	DEBIT	CREDIT	BALANCE DEBIT	CREDIT

ACCOUNT _____ ACCOUNT NO. _____

DATE	DESCRIPTION	POST. REF.	DEBIT	CREDIT	BALANCE DEBIT	CREDIT

ACCOUNT _____ ACCOUNT NO. _____

DATE	DESCRIPTION	POST. REF.	DEBIT	CREDIT	BALANCE DEBIT	CREDIT

Name _____

PROBLEM 4.4A or 4.4B (continued)

GENERAL LEDGER

ACCOUNT _____ ACCOUNT NO. _____

DATE	DESCRIPTION	POST. REF.	DEBIT	CREDIT	BALANCE DEBIT	BALANCE CREDIT

ACCOUNT _____ ACCOUNT NO. _____

DATE	DESCRIPTION	POST. REF.	DEBIT	CREDIT	BALANCE DEBIT	BALANCE CREDIT

ACCOUNT _____ ACCOUNT NO. _____

DATE	DESCRIPTION	POST. REF.	DEBIT	CREDIT	BALANCE DEBIT	BALANCE CREDIT

ACCOUNT _____ ACCOUNT NO. _____

DATE	DESCRIPTION	POST. REF.	DEBIT	CREDIT	BALANCE DEBIT	BALANCE CREDIT

Analyze: _____

_____

EXTRA FORM

GENERAL LEDGER

ACCOUNT _____ ACCOUNT NO. _____

DATE	DESCRIPTION	POST. REF.	DEBIT	CREDIT	BALANCE DEBIT	BALANCE CREDIT

CHAPTER 4 CHALLENGE PROBLEM

GENERAL JOURNAL   PAGE _____

	DATE	DESCRIPTION	POST. REF.	DEBIT	CREDIT	
1						1
2						2
3						3
4						4
5						5
6						6
7						7
8						8
9						9
10						10
11						11
12						12
13						13
14						14
15						15
16						16
17						17
18						18
19						19
20						20
21						21
22						22
23						23
24						24
25						25
26						26
27						27
28						28
29						29
30						30
31						31
32						32
33						33
34						34
35						35
36						36
37						37

CHAPTER 4 CHALLENGE PROBLEM (continued)

GENERAL JOURNAL PAGE _____

	DATE	DESCRIPTION	POST. REF.	DEBIT	CREDIT	
1						1
2						2
3						3
4						4
5						5
6						6
7						7
8						8
9						9
10						10
11						11
12						12
13						13
14						14
15						15
16						16
17						17
18						18
19						19
20						20
21						21
22						22
23						23
24						24
25						25
26						26
27						27
28						28
29						29
30						30
31						31
32						32
33						33
34						34
35						35
36						36
37						37

Name _____

CHAPTER 4 CHALLENGE PROBLEM (continued)

GENERAL JOURNAL

PAGE _____

	DATE	DESCRIPTION	POST. REF.	DEBIT	CREDIT	
1						1
2						2
3						3
4						4
5						5
6						6
7						7
8						8
9						9
10						10
11						11
12						12
13						13
14						14

GENERAL LEDGER

ACCOUNT _____ ACCOUNT NO. _____

DATE	DESCRIPTION	POST. REF.	DEBIT	CREDIT	BALANCE DEBIT	BALANCE CREDIT

Name _____

CHAPTER 4 CHALLENGE PROBLEM (continued)

GENERAL LEDGER

ACCOUNT _____ ACCOUNT NO. _____

DATE	DESCRIPTION	POST. REF.	DEBIT	CREDIT	BALANCE DEBIT	BALANCE CREDIT

ACCOUNT _____ ACCOUNT NO. _____

DATE	DESCRIPTION	POST. REF.	DEBIT	CREDIT	BALANCE DEBIT	BALANCE CREDIT

ACCOUNT _____ ACCOUNT NO. _____

DATE	DESCRIPTION	POST. REF.	DEBIT	CREDIT	BALANCE DEBIT	BALANCE CREDIT

ACCOUNT _____ ACCOUNT NO. _____

DATE	DESCRIPTION	POST. REF.	DEBIT	CREDIT	BALANCE DEBIT	BALANCE CREDIT

ACCOUNT _____ ACCOUNT NO. _____

DATE	DESCRIPTION	POST. REF.	DEBIT	CREDIT	BALANCE DEBIT	BALANCE CREDIT

CHAPTER 4 CHALLENGE PROBLEM (continued)

GENERAL LEDGER

ACCOUNT _____ ACCOUNT NO. _____

DATE	DESCRIPTION	POST. REF.	DEBIT	CREDIT	BALANCE DEBIT	BALANCE CREDIT

ACCOUNT _____ ACCOUNT NO. _____

DATE	DESCRIPTION	POST. REF.	DEBIT	CREDIT	BALANCE DEBIT	BALANCE CREDIT

ACCOUNT _____ ACCOUNT NO. _____

DATE	DESCRIPTION	POST. REF.	DEBIT	CREDIT	BALANCE DEBIT	BALANCE CREDIT

ACCOUNT _____ ACCOUNT NO. _____

DATE	DESCRIPTION	POST. REF.	DEBIT	CREDIT	BALANCE DEBIT	BALANCE CREDIT

ACCOUNT _____ ACCOUNT NO. _____

DATE	DESCRIPTION	POST. REF.	DEBIT	CREDIT	BALANCE DEBIT	BALANCE CREDIT

CHAPTER 4 CHALLENGE PROBLEM (continued)

GENERAL LEDGER

ACCOUNT _____ ACCOUNT NO. _____

	DATE	DESCRIPTION	POST. REF.	DEBIT	CREDIT	BALANCE	
						DEBIT	CREDIT

ACCOUNT _____ ACCOUNT NO. _____

	DATE	DESCRIPTION	POST. REF.	DEBIT	CREDIT	BALANCE	
						DEBIT	CREDIT

ACCOUNT _____ ACCOUNT NO. _____

	DATE	DESCRIPTION	POST. REF.	DEBIT	CREDIT	BALANCE	
						DEBIT	CREDIT

EXTRA FORMS

GENERAL LEDGER

ACCOUNT _____ ACCOUNT NO. _____

	DATE	DESCRIPTION	POST. REF.	DEBIT	CREDIT	BALANCE	
						DEBIT	CREDIT

ACCOUNT _____ ACCOUNT NO. _____

	DATE	DESCRIPTION	POST. REF.	DEBIT	CREDIT	BALANCE	
						DEBIT	CREDIT

CHAPTER 4 CHALLENGE PROBLEM (continued)

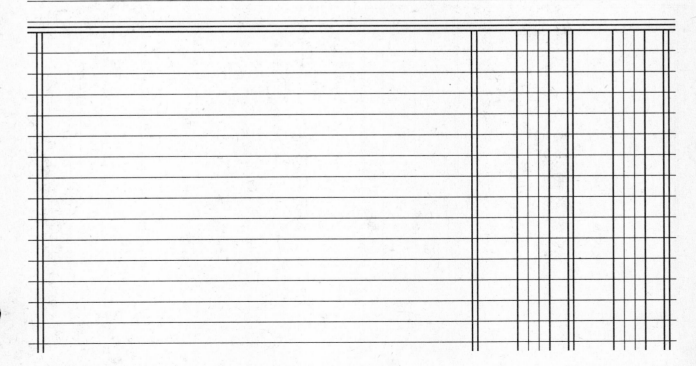

ACCOUNT NAME	DEBIT	CREDIT

	DEBIT	CREDIT

CHAPTER 4 CHALLENGE PROBLEM (continued)

Analyze: _____

_____

CHAPTER 4 CRITICAL THINKING PROBLEM

Name _____

CHAPTER 4 CRITICAL THINKING PROBLEM (continued)

Chapter 4 Practice Test Answer Key

Part A Matching	Part B Completion
1. i	1. debit
2. h	2. year
3. d	3. chronological or date
4. e	4. assets or balance sheet accounts
5. c	5. posted
6. g	6. ledger
7. a	7. posting references
8. f	8. brief or concise
9. b	9. credit
10. j	10. debit

CHAPTER 5 Adjustments and the Worksheet

STUDY GUIDE

Understanding the Chapter

Objectives

1. Complete a trial balance on a worksheet. **2.** Prepare adjustments for unrecorded business transactions. **3.** Complete the worksheet. **4.** Prepare an income statement, statement of owner's equity, and balance sheet from the completed worksheet. **5.** Journalize and post the adjusting entries. **6.** Define the accounting terms new to this chapter.

Reading Assignment

Read Chapter 5 in the textbook. Complete the textbook Section Self Review as you finish reading each section of the chapter, and the Comprehensive Self Review at the end of the chapter. Refer to the Chapter 5 Glossary or to the Glossary at the end of the book to find definitions for terms that are not familiar to you.

Activities

❑ **Thinking Critically**
Answer the *Thinking Critically* questions for Boeing, Computers in Accounting, and Managerial Implications.

❑ **Internet Application**
Complete the activity for Computers in Accounting.

❑ **Discussion Questions**
Answer each assigned discussion question in Chapter 5.

❑ **Exercises**
Complete each assigned exercise in Chapter 5. Use the forms provided in this SGWP. The objectives covered by an exercise are given after the exercise number. If you need help with an exercise, review the portion of the chapter related to the objective(s) covered.

❑ **Problems A/B**
Complete each assigned problem in Chapter 5. Use the forms provided in this SGWP. The objectives covered by a problem are given after the problem number. If you need help with a problem, review the portion of the chapter related to the objective(s) covered.

❑ **Challenge Problem**
Complete the challenge problem as assigned. Use the forms provided in this SGWP.

❑ **Critical Thinking Problem**
Complete the critical thinking problem as assigned. Use the forms provided in this SGWP.

❑ **Business Connections**
Complete the Business Connections activities as assigned to gain a deeper understanding of Chapter 5 concepts.

Practice Tests
Complete the Practice Tests, which cover the main points in your reading assignment. Compare your answers with those in the Practice Test Answer Key for Chapter 5 at the end of this chapter. If you have answered any questions incorrectly, review the related section of the text.

Part A True-False
For each of the following statements, circle T in the answer column if the statement is true or F if the statement is false.

T   F   1. The balances of the expense accounts are normally transferred to the Income Statement Debit column of the worksheet.

T   F   2. When the Balance Sheet columns of the worksheet are first added, the total of the Debit column should equal the total of the Credit column.

T   F   3. After the net income (or net loss) is computed in the Income Statement section of the worksheet, this amount is transferred to the Balance Sheet section of the worksheet.

T   F   4. On a worksheet, the difference between the Debit and Credit Column totals in the Income Statement section must equal the difference between the Debit and Credit column totals in the Balance Sheet section.

T   F   5. The Income Statement columns and Balance Sheet columns provide the figures for preparing the financial statements.

T   F   6. The ledger must be in balance before financial statements are prepared.

T   F   7. Accountants use a worksheet as a means of organizing their figures quickly.

T   F   8. The first two money columns of the worksheet contain a trial balance of the general ledger accounts.

T   F   9. Asset account balances from the trial balance are normally transferred to the Income Statement Debit column of the worksheet.

T   F   10. Liability account balances from the trial balance are normally transferred to the Balance Sheet credit column of the worksheet.

Part B Matching   *For each numbered item, choose the matching term from the box and write the identifying letter in the answer column.*

_____ 1. A form used to organize the amounts needed to prepare the financial statements

_____ 2. The term used when referring to an account in which there is an excess of credits over debits

_____ 3. The term used when the total of the debit amounts in the general ledger and the total of the credit amounts are equal

_____ 4. The term used for an account with an excess of debits over credits

_____ 5. A way to test the accuracy of the figures recorded in the general ledger

_____ 6. Assets = Liabilities + Owner's Equity

a. Worksheet

b. Trial balance

c. Debit balance

d. Fundamental accounting equation

e. Credit balance

f. In balance

Demonstration Problem

The general ledger accounts listed on the worksheet for the Environmental Design Company on January 31, 2007, show the results of the first month of operation.

Instructions

1. Record the following adjustments in the Adjustments section of the worksheet using the information below.

   a. Supplies used during the month, $1,475.

   b. The amount in the **Prepaid Rent** account represents a payment made on January 1 for the rent for 12 months.

   c. The equipment, purchased in January, has an estimated useful life of 10 years with no salvage value. The firm uses the straight-line method of depreciation.

2. Complete the worksheet.

3. Journalize and post the adjusting entries. Use journal page number 2.

SOLUTION

Environmental Design Company

Worksheet

Month Ended January 31, 2007

ACCOUNT NAME	TRIAL BALANCE DEBIT	TRIAL BALANCE CREDIT	ADJUSTMENTS DEBIT	ADJUSTMENTS CREDIT	ADJUSTED TRIAL BALANCE DEBIT	ADJUSTED TRIAL BALANCE CREDIT	INCOME STATEMENT DEBIT	INCOME STATEMENT CREDIT	BALANCE SHEET DEBIT	BALANCE SHEET CREDIT
Cash	12,450.00				12,450.00				12,450.00	
Accounts Receivable	16,900.00				16,900.00				16,900.00	
Supplies	2,900.00			(a)1,475.00	1,425.00				1,425.00	
Prepaid Rent	42,000.00			(b)3,500.00	38,500.00				38,500.00	
Equipment	42,000.00				42,000.00				42,000.00	
Accum. Depr.—Equipment				(c)350.00		350.00				350.00
Accounts Payable		26,800.00				26,800.00				26,800.00
John Peoples, Capital		49,200.00				49,200.00				49,200.00
John Peoples, Drawing	3,000.00				3,000.00				3,000.00	
Fees Income		75,505.00				75,505.00		75,505.00		
Advertising Expense	3,800.00				3,800.00		3,800.00			
Insurance Expense	4,000.00				4,000.00		4,000.00			
Salaries Expense	22,500.00				22,500.00		22,500.00			
Supplies Expense			(a)1,475.00		1,475.00		1,475.00			
Rent Expense			(b)3,500.00		3,500.00		3,500.00			
Telephone Expense	875.00				875.00		875.00			
Utilities Expense	1,080.00				1,080.00		1,080.00			
Depr. Expense—Equipment			(c)350.00		350.00		350.00			
Totals	151,505.00	151,505.00	5,325.00	5,325.00	151,855.00	151,855.00	37,580.00	75,505.00	114,275.00	76,350.00
Net Income							37,925.00			37,925.00
							75,505.00	75,505.00	114,275.00	114,275.00

SOLUTION (continued)

GENERAL JOURNAL

PAGE ___2___

	DATE		DESCRIPTION	POST. REF.	DEBIT	CREDIT	
1			**Adjusting Entries**				1
2	2007						2
3	Jan.	31	**Supplies Expense**	518	1 4 7 5 00		3
4			**Supplies**	121		1 4 7 5 00	4
5							5
6		31	**Rent Expense**	519	3 5 0 0 00		6
7			**Prepaid Rent**	131		3 5 0 0 00	7
8							8
9		31	**Depreciation Expense—Equipment**	524	3 5 0 00		9
10			**Accumulated Depreciation—Equipment**	142		3 5 0 00	10
11							11

GENERAL LEDGER (PARTIAL)

ACCOUNT __Supplies__   ACCOUNT NO. ____121____

DATE		DESCRIPTION	POST. REF.	DEBIT	CREDIT	BALANCE DEBIT	BALANCE CREDIT
2007							
Jan.	3		J1	2 9 0 0 00		2 9 0 0 00	
	31	Adjusting	J2		1 4 7 5 00	1 4 2 5 00	

ACCOUNT __Prepaid Rent__   ACCOUNT NO. ____131____

DATE		DESCRIPTION	POST. REF.	DEBIT	CREDIT	BALANCE DEBIT	BALANCE CREDIT
2007							
Jan.	2		J1	42 0 0 0 00		42 0 0 0 00	
	31	Adjusting	J2		3 5 0 0 00	38 5 0 0 00	

ACCOUNT __Accumulated Depreciation—Equipment__   ACCOUNT NO. ____142____

DATE		DESCRIPTION	POST. REF.	DEBIT	CREDIT	BALANCE DEBIT	BALANCE CREDIT
2007							
Jan.	31	Adjusting	J2		3 5 0 00		3 5 0 00

SOLUTION (continued)

GENERAL LEDGER (PARTIAL)

ACCOUNT __Supplies Expense__   ACCOUNT NO. ____518____

DATE		DESCRIPTION	POST. REF.	DEBIT	CREDIT	BALANCE	
						DEBIT	CREDIT
2007							
Jan.	31	Adjusting	J2	1 4 7 5 00		1 4 7 5 00	

ACCOUNT __Rent Expense__   ACCOUNT NO. ____519____

DATE		DESCRIPTION	POST. REF.	DEBIT	CREDIT	BALANCE	
						DEBIT	CREDIT
2007							
Jan.	31	Adjusting	J2	3 5 0 0 00		3 5 0 0 00	

ACCOUNT __Depreciation Expense—Equipment__   ACCOUNT NO. ____524____

DATE		DESCRIPTION	POST. REF.	DEBIT	CREDIT	BALANCE	
						DEBIT	CREDIT
2007							
Jan.	31	Adjusting	J2	3 5 0 00		3 5 0 00	

WORKING PAPERS

Name _____

EXERCISE 5.1

1. _____
   _____
   _____
   _____

2. _____
   _____
   _____
   _____

3. _____
   _____
   _____
   _____

EXERCISE 5.2

1. _____
   _____
   _____
   _____

2. _____
   _____
   _____
   _____

EXERCISE 5.3

EXERCISE 5.4

_____
_____
_____
_____
_____
_____
_____
_____
_____
_____
_____
_____
_____
_____

EXERCISE 5.5

GENERAL JOURNAL

PAGE _____

DATE	DESCRIPTION	POST. REF.	DEBIT	CREDIT	
					1
					2
					3
					4
					5
					6
					7
					8
					9
					10
					11

GENERAL LEDGER

ACCOUNT __Supplies__   ACCOUNT NO. ____121

DATE	DESCRIPTION	POST. REF.	DEBIT	CREDIT	BALANCE	
					DEBIT	CREDIT

ACCOUNT __Prepaid Insurance__   ACCOUNT NO. ____131

DATE	DESCRIPTION	POST. REF.	DEBIT	CREDIT	BALANCE	
					DEBIT	CREDIT

ACCOUNT __Accumulated Depreciation—Equipment__   ACCOUNT NO. ____142

DATE	DESCRIPTION	POST. REF.	DEBIT	CREDIT	BALANCE	
					DEBIT	CREDIT

EXERCISE 5.5 (continued)

GENERAL LEDGER

ACCOUNT **Depreciation Expense—Equipment** _____ ACCOUNT NO. **517**

DATE	DESCRIPTION	POST. REF.	DEBIT	CREDIT	BALANCE	
					DEBIT	CREDIT

ACCOUNT **Insurance Expense** _____ ACCOUNT NO. **521**

DATE	DESCRIPTION	POST. REF.	DEBIT	CREDIT	BALANCE	
					DEBIT	CREDIT

ACCOUNT **Supplies Expense** _____ ACCOUNT NO. **523**

DATE	DESCRIPTION	POST. REF.	DEBIT	CREDIT	BALANCE	
					DEBIT	CREDIT

EXTRA FORMS

ACCOUNT _____ ACCOUNT NO. _____

DATE	DESCRIPTION	POST. REF.	DEBIT	CREDIT	BALANCE	
					DEBIT	CREDIT

ACCOUNT _____ ACCOUNT NO. _____

DATE	DESCRIPTION	POST. REF.	DEBIT	CREDIT	BALANCE	
					DEBIT	CREDIT

PROBLEM 5.1A or 5.1B

	ACCOUNT NAME	TRIAL BALANCE		ADJUSTMENTS	
		DEBIT	CREDIT	DEBIT	CREDIT
1					
2					
3					
4					
5					
6					
7					
8					
9					
10					
11					
12					
13					
14					
15					
16					
17					
18					
19					
20					
21					
22					
23					
24					
25					
26					
27					
28					
29					
30					
31					
32					

PROBLEM 5.1A or 5.1B (continued)

_____
_____

ADJUSTED TRIAL BALANCE		INCOME STATEMENT		BALANCE SHEET		
DEBIT	CREDIT	DEBIT	CREDIT	DEBIT	CREDIT	
						1
						2
						3
						4
						5
						6
						7
						8
						9
						10
						11
						12
						13
						14
						15
						16
						17
						18
						19
						20
						21
						22
						23
						24
						25
						26
						27
						28
						29
						30
						31
						32

Analyze: _____

_____

PROBLEM 5.2A or 5.2B

_____

_____

	ACCOUNT NAME	TRIAL BALANCE		ADJUSTMENTS	
		DEBIT	CREDIT	DEBIT	CREDIT
1					
2					
3					
4					
5					
6					
7					
8					
9					
10					
11					
12					
13					
14					
15					
16					
17					
18					
19					
20					
21					
22					
23					
24					
25					
26					
27					
28					
29					
30					
31					
32					

PROBLEM 5.2A or 5.2B (continued)

_____

_____

ADJUSTED TRIAL BALANCE		INCOME STATEMENT		BALANCE SHEET		
DEBIT	CREDIT	DEBIT	CREDIT	DEBIT	CREDIT	
						1
						2
						3
						4
						5
						6
						7
						8
						9
						10
						11
						12
						13
						14
						15
						16
						17
						18
						19
						20
						21
						22
						23
						24
						25
						26
						27
						28
						29
						30
						31
						32

Analyze: _____

_____

PROBLEM 5.3A or 5.3B

PROBLEM 5.3A or 5.3B (continued)

Analyze: _____

PROBLEM 5.4A or 5.4B

	ACCOUNT NAME	TRIAL BALANCE		ADJUSTMENTS	
		DEBIT	CREDIT	DEBIT	CREDIT
1					
2					
3					
4					
5					
6					
7					
8					
9					
10					
11					
12					
13					
14					
15					
16					
17					
18					
19					
20					
21					
22					
23					
24					
25					
26					
27					
28					
29					
30					
31					
32					

PROBLEM 5.4A or 5.4B (continued)

	ADJUSTED TRIAL BALANCE		INCOME STATEMENT		BALANCE SHEET		
	DEBIT	CREDIT	DEBIT	CREDIT	DEBIT	CREDIT	
							1
							2
							3
							4
							5
							6
							7
							8
							9
							10
							11
							12
							13
							14
							15
							16
							17
							18
							19
							20
							21
							22
							23
							24
							25
							26
							27
							28
							29
							30
							31
							32

PROBLEM 5.4A or 5.4B (continued)

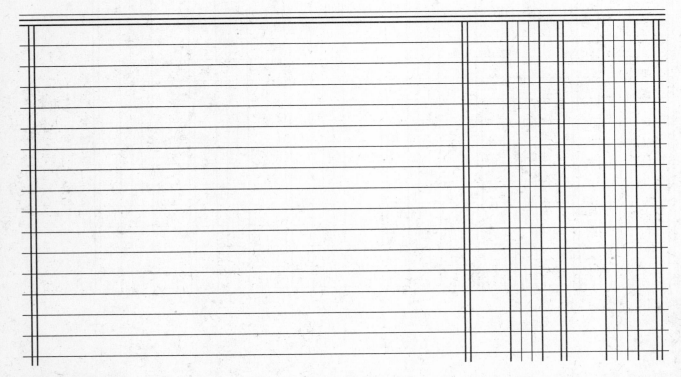

PROBLEM 5.4A or 5.4B (continued)

PROBLEM 5.4A or 5.4B (continued)

GENERAL JOURNAL   PAGE _____

	DATE	DESCRIPTION	POST. REF.	DEBIT	CREDIT	
1						1
2						2
3						3
4						4
5						5
6						6
7						7
8						8
9						9
10						10
11						11
12						12
13						13
14						14

GENERAL LEDGER

ACCOUNT _____   ACCOUNT NO. _____

DATE	DESCRIPTION	POST. REF.	DEBIT	CREDIT	BALANCE	
					DEBIT	CREDIT

ACCOUNT _____   ACCOUNT NO. _____

DATE	DESCRIPTION	POST. REF.	DEBIT	CREDIT	BALANCE	
					DEBIT	CREDIT

ACCOUNT _____   ACCOUNT NO. _____

DATE	DESCRIPTION	POST. REF.	DEBIT	CREDIT	BALANCE	
					DEBIT	CREDIT

PROBLEM 5.4A or 5.4B (continued)

GENERAL LEDGER

ACCOUNT _____ ACCOUNT NO. _____

	DATE	DESCRIPTION	POST. REF.	DEBIT	CREDIT	BALANCE	
						DEBIT	CREDIT

ACCOUNT _____ ACCOUNT NO. _____

	DATE	DESCRIPTION	POST. REF.	DEBIT	CREDIT	BALANCE	
						DEBIT	CREDIT

ACCOUNT _____ ACCOUNT NO. _____

	DATE	DESCRIPTION	POST. REF.	DEBIT	CREDIT	BALANCE	
						DEBIT	CREDIT

ACCOUNT _____ ACCOUNT NO. _____

	DATE	DESCRIPTION	POST. REF.	DEBIT	CREDIT	BALANCE	
						DEBIT	CREDIT

ACCOUNT _____ ACCOUNT NO. _____

	DATE	DESCRIPTION	POST. REF.	DEBIT	CREDIT	BALANCE	
						DEBIT	CREDIT

Analyze: _____
_____

CHAPTER 5 CHALLENGE PROBLEM

	ACCOUNT NAME	TRIAL BALANCE		ADJUSTMENTS	
		DEBIT	CREDIT	DEBIT	CREDIT
1					
2					
3					
4					
5					
6					
7					
8					
9					
10					
11					
12					
13					
14					
15					
16					
17					
18					
19					
20					
21					
22					
23					
24					
25					
26					
27					
28					
29					
30					
31					
32					

CHAPTER 5 CHALLENGE PROBLEM (continued)

_____
_____
_____

	ADJUSTED TRIAL BALANCE		INCOME STATEMENT		BALANCE SHEET		
	DEBIT	CREDIT	DEBIT	CREDIT	DEBIT	CREDIT	
							1
							2
							3
							4
							5
							6
							7
							8
							9
							10
							11
							12
							13
							14
							15
							16
							17
							18
							19
							20
							21
							22
							23
							24
							25
							26
							27
							28
							29
							30
							31
							32

CHAPTER 5 CHALLENGE PROBLEM (continued)

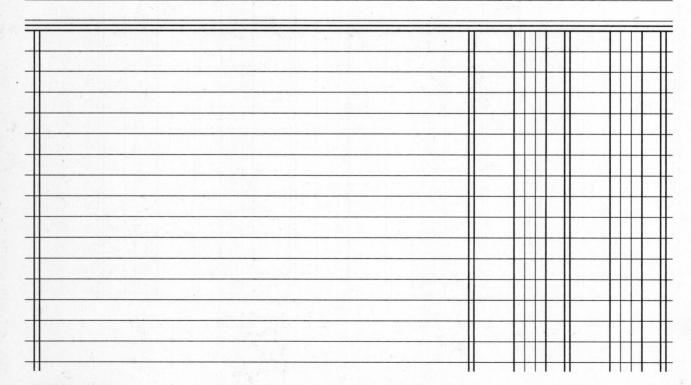

CHAPTER 5 CHALLENGE PROBLEM (continued)

CHAPTER 5 CHALLENGE PROBLEM (continued)

GENERAL JOURNAL
PAGE _____

	DATE	DESCRIPTION	POST. REF.	DEBIT	CREDIT	
1						1
2						2
3						3
4						4
5						5
6						6
7						7
8						8
9						9
10						10
11						11

GENERAL LEDGER

ACCOUNT _____ ACCOUNT NO. _____

DATE	DESCRIPTION	POST. REF.	DEBIT	CREDIT	BALANCE	
					DEBIT	CREDIT

ACCOUNT _____ ACCOUNT NO. _____

DATE	DESCRIPTION	POST. REF.	DEBIT	CREDIT	BALANCE	
					DEBIT	CREDIT

ACCOUNT _____ ACCOUNT NO. _____

DATE	DESCRIPTION	POST. REF.	DEBIT	CREDIT	BALANCE	
					DEBIT	CREDIT

CHAPTER 5 CHALLENGE PROBLEM (continued)

GENERAL LEDGER

ACCOUNT _____ ACCOUNT NO. _____

DATE	DESCRIPTION	POST. REF.	DEBIT	CREDIT	BALANCE	
					DEBIT	CREDIT

ACCOUNT _____ ACCOUNT NO. _____

DATE	DESCRIPTION	POST. REF.	DEBIT	CREDIT	BALANCE	
					DEBIT	CREDIT

ACCOUNT _____ ACCOUNT NO. _____

DATE	DESCRIPTION	POST. REF.	DEBIT	CREDIT	BALANCE	
					DEBIT	CREDIT

Analyze: _____

_____

EXTRA FORMS

ACCOUNT _____ ACCOUNT NO. _____

DATE	DESCRIPTION	POST. REF.	DEBIT	CREDIT	BALANCE	
					DEBIT	CREDIT

ACCOUNT _____ ACCOUNT NO. _____

DATE	DESCRIPTION	POST. REF.	DEBIT	CREDIT	BALANCE	
					DEBIT	CREDIT

CHAPTER 5 CRITICAL THINKING PROBLEM

TO: _____

FROM: _____

DATE: _____

SUBJECT: _____

_____

_____

_____

_____

_____

_____

_____

_____

_____

_____

_____

_____

_____

_____

_____

_____

_____

_____

_____

_____

_____

_____

_____

Chapter 5 Practice Test Answer Key

Part A True-False		Part B Matching	
1. T	6. T	1. a	4. c
2. F	7. T	2. e	5. b
3. T	8. T	3. f	6. d
4. T	9. F		
5. T	10. T		

CHAPTER 6

Closing Entries and the Postclosing Trial Balance

STUDY GUIDE

Understanding the Chapter

Objectives

1. Journalize and post closing entries. **2.** Prepare a postclosing trial balance. **3.** Interpret financial statements. **4.** Review the steps in the accounting cycle. **5.** Define the accounting terms new to this chapter.

Reading Assignment

Read Chapter 6 in the textbook. Complete the textbook Section Self Review as you finish reading each section of the chapter, and the Comprehensive Self Review at the end of the chapter. Refer to the Chapter 6 Glossary or to the Glossary at the end of the book to find definitions for terms that are not familiar to you.

Activities

❏ **Thinking Critically**

Answer the *Thinking Critically* questions for Carnival Corporation, Accounting on the Job, and Managerial Implications.

❏ **Internet Application**

Complete the activity for Accounting on the Job.

❏ **Discussion Questions**

Answer each assigned discussion question in Chapter 6.

❏ **Exercises**

Complete each assigned exercise in Chapter 6. Use the forms provided in this SGWP. The objectives covered by an exercise are given after the exercise number. If you need help with an exercise, review the portion of the chapter related to the objective(s) covered.

❏ **Problems A/B**

Complete each assigned problem in Chapter 6. Use the forms provided in this SGWP. The objectives covered by a problem are given after the problem number. If you need help with a problem, review the portion of the chapter related to the objective(s) covered.

❏ **Challenge Problem**

Complete the challenge problem as assigned. Use the forms provided in this SGWP.

❏ **Critical Thinking Problem**

Complete the critical thinking problem as assigned. Use the forms provided in this SGWP.

❏ **Business Connections**

Complete the Business Connections activities as assigned to gain a deeper understanding of Chapter 6 concepts.

Practice Tests

Complete the Practice Tests, which cover the main points in your reading assignment. Compare your answers with those in the Practice Test Answer Key for Chapter 6 at the end of this chapter. If you have answered any questions incorrectly, review the related section of the text.

Part A True-False
For each of the following statements, circle T in the answer column if the statement is true or F if the statement is false.

T   F   1. The general ledger is a continuing record.

T   F   2. The postclosing trial balance will show figures for asset, liability, owner's equity, revenue, and expense accounts.

T   F   3. The total of all expenses appears on the credit side of the **Income Summary** account.

T   F   4. To close a revenue account, the accountant debits that account and credits the **Income Summary** account.

T   F   5. All asset accounts are closed into the **Income Summary** account.

T   F   6. The balance of the **Income Summary** account—net income or net loss—is transferred to the owner's capital account.

T   F   7. The Income Summary is a financial statement prepared at the end of each accounting period.

T   F   8. Adjusting entries create a permanent record of any changes in account balances that are shown on the worksheet.

T   F   9. If an adjustment is not made for supplies used, the net income for the period will be understated.

T   F   10. Closing entries reduce the balance of revenue and asset accounts to zero so that they are ready to receive data for the next period.

Part B Matching
For each numbered item, choose the matching term from the box and write the identifying letter in the answer column.

_____   **1.** The procedure of journalizing and posting the results of operations at the end of an accounting period.

_____   **2.** Journal entries used to transfer the balances of the revenue and expense accounts to the summary accounts as part of the end-of-period procedures.

_____   **3.** Special account in the general ledger used for combining data about revenue and expenses.

_____   **4.** Term used when referring to an account after its balance has been transferred out.

_____   **5.** The last step in the end-of-period procedure, which shows the accountant that it is safe to proceed with entries for the new period.

a. Closing the accounting records
b. Closing entries
c. Closed account
d. Postclosing trial balance
e. Income Summary

Demonstration Problem

The Income Statement and Balance Sheet sections of the worksheet for George Burke for the period ended December 31, 2007 are shown below.

Instructions

1. Journalize the closing entries on page 24 of a general journal.

2. Determine the new balance for Capital once the closing entries have been posted.

George Burke

Worksheet

Month Ended December 31, 2007

	ACCOUNT NAME	INCOME STATEMENT DEBIT	INCOME STATEMENT CREDIT	BALANCE SHEET DEBIT	BALANCE SHEET CREDIT
1	Cash			96 0 0 0 00	
2	Accounts Receivable			6 0 0 0 00	
3	Supplies			12 0 0 0 00	
4	Prepaid Rent			9 0 0 0 00	
5	Equipment			60 0 0 0 00	
6	Accumulated Depreciation—Equipment				1 4 4 0 00
7	Accounts Payable				15 0 0 0 00
8	George Burke, Capital				109 5 0 0 00
9	George Burke, Drawing			6 0 0 0 00	
10	Fees Income		90 0 0 0 00		
11	Salaries Expense	14 4 0 0 00			
12	Utilities Expense	2 1 0 0 00			
13	Supplies Expense	4 8 0 0 00			
14	Advertising Expense	4 2 0 0 00			
15	Depreciation Expense—Equipment	1 4 4 0 00			
16	Totals	26 9 4 0 00	90 0 0 0 00	189 0 0 0 00	125 9 4 0 00
17	Net Income	63 0 6 0 00			63 0 6 0 00
18		90 0 0 0 00	90 0 0 0 00	189 0 0 0 00	189 0 0 0 00
19					

SOLUTION

	DATE		DESCRIPTION	POST. REF.	DEBIT	CREDIT	
1			**Closing Entries**				1
2	2007						2
3	Dec.	31	Fees Income	401	90 0 0 0 00		3
4			Income Summary	399		90 0 0 0 00	4
5							5
6		31	Income Summary	399	26 9 4 0 00		6
7			Salaries Expense	511		14 4 0 0 00	7
8			Utilities Expense	514		2 1 0 0 00	8
9			Supplies Expense	517		4 8 0 0 00	9
10			Advertising Expense	522		4 2 0 0 00	10
11			Depreciation Expense—Equipment	523		1 4 4 0 00	11
12							12
13		31	Income Summary	399	63 0 6 0 00		13
14			George Burke, Capital	301		63 0 6 0 00	14
15							15
16		31	George Burke, Capital	301	6 0 0 0 00		16
17			George Burke, Drawing	302		6 0 0 0 00	17
18							18

New Capital Balance:

George Burke, Capital, December 1, 2007		$109,500.00
Add: Net Income	63,060.00	
Less Withdrawals for December	(6,000.00)	
Increase in Capital		57,060.00
George Burke, Capital, December 31, 2007		$166,560.00

WORKING PAPERS

Name _____

EXERCISE 6.1

GENERAL JOURNAL   PAGE _____

	DATE		DESCRIPTION	POST. REF.	DEBIT	CREDIT	
1							1
2							2
3							3
4							4
5							5
6							6
7							7
8							8
9							9
10							10
11							11
12							12
13							13
14							14
15							15
16							16
17							17
18							18
19							19
20							20
21							21

EXERCISE 6.2

1. _____

2. _____

3. _____

4. _____

5. _____

6. _____

7. _____

8. _____

9. _____

EXERCISE 6.3

1. _____   5. _____
2. _____   6. _____
3. _____   7. _____
4. _____

EXERCISE 6.4

1. _____   6. _____   11. _____
2. _____   7. _____   12. _____
3. _____   8. _____   13. _____
4. _____   9. _____   14. _____
5. _____   10. _____   15. _____

EXERCISE 6.5

1. Total revenue for the period is _____ .

2. Total expenses for the period are _____ .

3. Net income for the period is _____ .

4. Owner's withdrawals for the period are _____ .

EXERCISE 6.6

GENERAL JOURNAL

PAGE _____

	DATE		DESCRIPTION	POST. REF.	DEBIT	CREDIT	
1							1
2							2
3							3
4							4
5							5
6							6
7							7
8							8
9							9
10							10
11							11
12							12
13							13
14							14
15							15
16							16
17							17
18							18
19							19
20							20
21							21
22							22
23							23
24							24
25							25
26							26
27							27
28							28
29							29
30							30
31							31
32							32
33							33
34							34
35							35
36							36
37							37

Name _____

EXERCISE 6.6 (continued)

GENERAL LEDGER

ACCOUNT __Dennis Ortiz, Capital__   ACCOUNT NO. ___301___

DATE	DESCRIPTION	POST. REF.	DEBIT	CREDIT	BALANCE DEBIT	BALANCE CREDIT
2007						
Mar. 31	Balance	✔				58 8 0 0 00

ACCOUNT __Dennis Ortiz, Drawing__   ACCOUNT NO. ___302___

DATE	DESCRIPTION	POST. REF.	DEBIT	CREDIT	BALANCE DEBIT	BALANCE CREDIT
2007						
Mar. 31	Balance	✔			3 0 0 0 00	

ACCOUNT __Income Summary__   ACCOUNT NO. ___399___

DATE	DESCRIPTION	POST. REF.	DEBIT	CREDIT	BALANCE DEBIT	BALANCE CREDIT

ACCOUNT __Fees Income__   ACCOUNT NO. ___401___

DATE	DESCRIPTION	POST. REF.	DEBIT	CREDIT	BALANCE DEBIT	BALANCE CREDIT
2007						
Mar. 31	Balance	✔				138 0 0 0 00

ACCOUNT __Depreciation Expense—Equipment__   ACCOUNT NO. ___510___

DATE	DESCRIPTION	POST. REF.	DEBIT	CREDIT	BALANCE DEBIT	BALANCE CREDIT
2007						
Mar. 31	Balance	✔			5 0 4 0 00	

EXERCISE 6.6 (continued)

GENERAL LEDGER

ACCOUNT __Insurance Expense__ **ACCOUNT NO.** __511__

DATE		DESCRIPTION	POST. REF.	DEBIT	CREDIT	BALANCE	
						DEBIT	CREDIT
2007							
Mar.	31	Balance	✔			4 8 0 0 00	

ACCOUNT __Rent Expense__ **ACCOUNT NO.** __514__

DATE		DESCRIPTION	POST. REF.	DEBIT	CREDIT	BALANCE	
						DEBIT	CREDIT
2007							
Mar.	31	Balance	✔			14 4 0 0 00	

ACCOUNT __Salaries Expense__ **ACCOUNT NO.** __517__

DATE		DESCRIPTION	POST. REF.	DEBIT	CREDIT	BALANCE	
						DEBIT	CREDIT
2007							
Mar.	31	Balance	✔			70 8 0 0 00	

ACCOUNT __Supplies Expense__ **ACCOUNT NO.** __518__

DATE		DESCRIPTION	POST. REF.	DEBIT	CREDIT	BALANCE	
						DEBIT	CREDIT
2007							
Mar.	31	Balance	✔			1 9 5 0 00	

ACCOUNT __Telephone Expense__ **ACCOUNT NO.** __519__

DATE		DESCRIPTION	POST. REF.	DEBIT	CREDIT	BALANCE	
						DEBIT	CREDIT
2007							
Mar.	31	Balance	✔			2 7 0 0 00	

EXERCISE 6.6 (continued)

GENERAL LEDGER

ACCOUNT __Utilities Expense__ ACCOUNT NO. __523__

DATE		DESCRIPTION	POST. REF.	DEBIT	CREDIT	BALANCE	
						DEBIT	CREDIT
2007							
Mar.	31	Balance	✔			3 6 0 0 00	

EXTRA FORMS

ACCOUNT _____ ACCOUNT NO. _____

DATE	DESCRIPTION	POST. REF.	DEBIT	CREDIT	BALANCE	
					DEBIT	CREDIT

ACCOUNT _____ ACCOUNT NO. _____

DATE	DESCRIPTION	POST. REF.	DEBIT	CREDIT	BALANCE	
					DEBIT	CREDIT

ACCOUNT _____ ACCOUNT NO. _____

DATE	DESCRIPTION	POST. REF.	DEBIT	CREDIT	BALANCE	
					DEBIT	CREDIT

EXERCISE 6.7

	DATE		DESCRIPTION	POST. REF.	DEBIT	CREDIT	
1							1
2							2
3							3
4							4
5							5
6							6
7							7
8							8

GENERAL JOURNAL   PAGE _____

EXERCISE 6.8

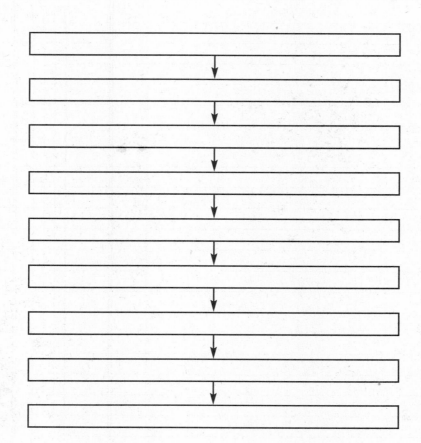

PROBLEM 6.1A or 6.1B

GENERAL JOURNAL

PAGE _____

	DATE	DESCRIPTION	POST. REF.	DEBIT	CREDIT	
1						1
2						2
3						3
4						4
5						5
6						6
7						7
8						8
9						9
10						10
11						11

GENERAL JOURNAL

PAGE _____

	DATE	DESCRIPTION	POST. REF.	DEBIT	CREDIT	
1						1
2						2
3						3
4						4
5						5
6						6
7						7
8						8
9						9
10						10
11						11
12						12
13						13
14						14
15						15
16						16
17						17
18						18
19						19
20						20

Analyze: _____

_____

PROBLEM 6.2A or 6.2B

GENERAL JOURNAL   PAGE _____

	DATE	DESCRIPTION	POST. REF.	DEBIT	CREDIT	
1						1
2						2
3						3
4						4
5						5
6						6
7						7
8						8
9						9
10						10
11						11

GENERAL JOURNAL   PAGE _____

	DATE	DESCRIPTION	POST. REF.	DEBIT	CREDIT	
1						1
2						2
3						3
4						4
5						5
6						6
7						7
8						8
9						9
10						10
11						11
12						12
13						13
14						14
15						15
16						16
17						17
18						18

PROBLEM 6.2A or 6.2B (continued)

GENERAL LEDGER

ACCOUNT __Supplies__   ACCOUNT NO. ____121____

DATE	DESCRIPTION	POST. REF.	DEBIT	CREDIT	BALANCE	
					DEBIT	CREDIT

ACCOUNT __Prepaid Advertising__   ACCOUNT NO. ____131____

DATE	DESCRIPTION	POST. REF.	DEBIT	CREDIT	BALANCE	
					DEBIT	CREDIT

ACCOUNT __Accumulated Depreciation—Equipment__   ACCOUNT NO. ____142____

DATE	DESCRIPTION	POST. REF.	DEBIT	CREDIT	BALANCE	
					DEBIT	CREDIT

ACCOUNT _____Capital_____   ACCOUNT NO. ____301____

DATE	DESCRIPTION	POST. REF.	DEBIT	CREDIT	BALANCE	
					DEBIT	CREDIT

ACCOUNT _____Drawing_____   ACCOUNT NO. ____302____

DATE	DESCRIPTION	POST. REF.	DEBIT	CREDIT	BALANCE	
					DEBIT	CREDIT

PROBLEM 6.2A or 6.2B (continued)

GENERAL LEDGER

ACCOUNT __Income Summary__   ACCOUNT NO. ___399___

DATE	DESCRIPTION	POST. REF.	DEBIT	CREDIT	BALANCE DEBIT	BALANCE CREDIT

ACCOUNT __Fees Income__   ACCOUNT NO. ___401___

DATE	DESCRIPTION	POST. REF.	DEBIT	CREDIT	BALANCE DEBIT	BALANCE CREDIT

GENERAL LEDGER

ACCOUNT __Salaries Expense__   ACCOUNT NO. ___511___

DATE	DESCRIPTION	POST. REF.	DEBIT	CREDIT	BALANCE DEBIT	BALANCE CREDIT

ACCOUNT __Utilities Expense__   ACCOUNT NO. ___514___

DATE	DESCRIPTION	POST. REF.	DEBIT	CREDIT	BALANCE DEBIT	BALANCE CREDIT

ACCOUNT __Supplies Expense__   ACCOUNT NO. ___517___

DATE	DESCRIPTION	POST. REF.	DEBIT	CREDIT	BALANCE DEBIT	BALANCE CREDIT

Name _____

PROBLEM 6.2A or 6.2B (continued)

ACCOUNT __Advertising Expense_____ ACCOUNT NO. ___526___

DATE	DESCRIPTION	POST. REF.	DEBIT	CREDIT	BALANCE	
					DEBIT	CREDIT

ACCOUNT __Depreciation Expense—Equipment_____ ACCOUNT NO. ___523___

DATE	DESCRIPTION	POST. REF.	DEBIT	CREDIT	BALANCE	
					DEBIT	CREDIT

ACCOUNT NAME	DEBIT	CREDIT

Analyze: _____

_____

Name _____

PROBLEM 6.3A or 6.3B

GENERAL JOURNAL   PAGE _____

	DATE	DESCRIPTION	POST. REF.	DEBIT	CREDIT	
1						1
2						2
3						3
4						4
5						5
6						6
7						7
8						8
9						9
10						10
11						11
12						12
13						13
14						14
15						15
16						16
17						17
18						18
19						19
20						20
21						21
22						22
23						23
24						24
25						25
26						26
27						27
28						28
29						29
30						30
31						31
32						32
33						33
34						34
35						35
36						36
37						37

PROBLEM 6.3A or 6.3B (continued)

GENERAL LEDGER

ACCOUNT _____**Capital**_____ ACCOUNT NO. ___**301**___

DATE	DESCRIPTION	POST. REF.	DEBIT	CREDIT	BALANCE DEBIT	CREDIT

ACCOUNT _____**Drawing**_____ ACCOUNT NO. ___**302**___

DATE	DESCRIPTION	POST. REF.	DEBIT	CREDIT	BALANCE DEBIT	CREDIT

ACCOUNT _**Income Summary**_ ACCOUNT NO. ___**399**___

DATE	DESCRIPTION	POST. REF.	DEBIT	CREDIT	BALANCE DEBIT	CREDIT

ACCOUNT _**Fees Income**_ ACCOUNT NO. ___**401**___

DATE	DESCRIPTION	POST. REF.	DEBIT	CREDIT	BALANCE DEBIT	CREDIT

Name _____

PROBLEM 6.3A or 6.3B (continued)

GENERAL LEDGER

ACCOUNT _Advertising Expense_   **ACCOUNT NO.** __511__

DATE	DESCRIPTION	POST. REF.	DEBIT	CREDIT	BALANCE DEBIT	BALANCE CREDIT

ACCOUNT _Depreciation Expense—Equipment_   **ACCOUNT NO.** __514__

DATE	DESCRIPTION	POST. REF.	DEBIT	CREDIT	BALANCE DEBIT	BALANCE CREDIT

ACCOUNT _Rent Expense_   **ACCOUNT NO.** __517__

DATE	DESCRIPTION	POST. REF.	DEBIT	CREDIT	BALANCE DEBIT	BALANCE CREDIT

ACCOUNT _Salaries Expense_   **ACCOUNT NO.** __519__

DATE	DESCRIPTION	POST. REF.	DEBIT	CREDIT	BALANCE DEBIT	BALANCE CREDIT

ACCOUNT _Utilities Expense_   **ACCOUNT NO.** __523__

DATE	DESCRIPTION	POST. REF.	DEBIT	CREDIT	BALANCE DEBIT	BALANCE CREDIT

Analyze: _____

PROBLEM 6.3A or 6.3B (continued)

GENERAL LEDGER

ACCOUNT _____ ACCOUNT NO. _____

DATE	DESCRIPTION	POST. REF.	DEBIT	CREDIT	BALANCE	
					DEBIT	CREDIT

ACCOUNT _____ ACCOUNT NO. _____

DATE	DESCRIPTION	POST. REF.	DEBIT	CREDIT	BALANCE	
					DEBIT	CREDIT

ACCOUNT _____ ACCOUNT NO. _____

DATE	DESCRIPTION	POST. REF.	DEBIT	CREDIT	BALANCE	
					DEBIT	CREDIT

ACCOUNT _____ ACCOUNT NO. _____

DATE	DESCRIPTION	POST. REF.	DEBIT	CREDIT	BALANCE	
					DEBIT	CREDIT

ACCOUNT _____ ACCOUNT NO. _____

DATE	DESCRIPTION	POST. REF.	DEBIT	CREDIT	BALANCE	
					DEBIT	CREDIT

PROBLEM 6.3A or 6.3B (continued)

GENERAL LEDGER

ACCOUNT _____ ACCOUNT NO. _____

	DATE	DESCRIPTION	POST. REF.	DEBIT	CREDIT	BALANCE	
						DEBIT	CREDIT

ACCOUNT _____ ACCOUNT NO. _____

	DATE	DESCRIPTION	POST. REF.	DEBIT	CREDIT	BALANCE	
						DEBIT	CREDIT

ACCOUNT _____ ACCOUNT NO. _____

	DATE	DESCRIPTION	POST. REF.	DEBIT	CREDIT	BALANCE	
						DEBIT	CREDIT

ACCOUNT _____ ACCOUNT NO. _____

	DATE	DESCRIPTION	POST. REF.	DEBIT	CREDIT	BALANCE	
						DEBIT	CREDIT

ACCOUNT _____ ACCOUNT NO. _____

	DATE	DESCRIPTION	POST. REF.	DEBIT	CREDIT	BALANCE	
						DEBIT	CREDIT

PROBLEM 6.4A or 6.4B

ACCOUNT NAME	TRIAL BALANCE		ADJUSTMENTS	
	DEBIT	CREDIT	DEBIT	CREDIT
1				
2				
3				
4				
5				
6				
7				
8				
9				
10				
11				
12				
13				
14				
15				
16				
17				
18				
19				
20				
21				
22				
23				
24				
25				
26				
27				
28				
29				
30				
31				
32				

Name _____

PROBLEM 6.4A or 6.4B (continued)

	ADJUSTED TRIAL BALANCE		INCOME STATEMENT		BALANCE SHEET		
	DEBIT	CREDIT	DEBIT	CREDIT	DEBIT	CREDIT	
							1
							2
							3
							4
							5
							6
							7
							8
							9
							10
							11
							12
							13
							14
							15
							16
							17
							18
							19
							20
							21
							22
							23
							24
							25
							26
							27
							28
							29
							30
							31
							32

PROBLEM 6.4A or 6.4B (continued)

GENERAL JOURNAL PAGE _____

DATE	DESCRIPTION	POST. REF.	DEBIT	CREDIT
1				
2				
3				
4				
5				
6				
7				
8				
9				
10				
11				
12				
13				

GENERAL JOURNAL PAGE _____

DATE	DESCRIPTION	POST. REF.	DEBIT	CREDIT
1				
2				
3				
4				
5				
6				
7				
8				
9				
10				
11				
12				
13				
14				
15				
16				
17				
18				

PROBLEM 6.4A or 6.4B (continued)

GENERAL LEDGER

ACCOUNT __Supplies__   ACCOUNT NO. __121__

DATE	DESCRIPTION	POST. REF.	DEBIT	CREDIT	BALANCE DEBIT	CREDIT

ACCOUNT __Prepaid Advertising__   ACCOUNT NO. __131__

DATE	DESCRIPTION	POST. REF.	DEBIT	CREDIT	BALANCE DEBIT	CREDIT

ACCOUNT __Accumulated Depreciation—__   ACCOUNT NO. __142__

DATE	DESCRIPTION	POST. REF.	DEBIT	CREDIT	BALANCE DEBIT	CREDIT

ACCOUNT __Capital__   ACCOUNT NO. __301__

DATE	DESCRIPTION	POST. REF.	DEBIT	CREDIT	BALANCE DEBIT	CREDIT

ACCOUNT __Drawing__   ACCOUNT NO. __302__

DATE	DESCRIPTION	POST. REF.	DEBIT	CREDIT	BALANCE DEBIT	CREDIT

PROBLEM 6.4A or 6.4B (continued)

GENERAL LEDGER

ACCOUNT __Income Summary__   ACCOUNT NO. ___399___

	DATE		DESCRIPTION	POST. REF.	DEBIT	CREDIT	BALANCE	
							DEBIT	CREDIT

ACCOUNT __Fees Income__   ACCOUNT NO. ___401___

	DATE		DESCRIPTION	POST. REF.	DEBIT	CREDIT	BALANCE	
							DEBIT	CREDIT

GENERAL LEDGER

ACCOUNT __Salaries Expense__   ACCOUNT NO. ___511___

	DATE		DESCRIPTION	POST. REF.	DEBIT	CREDIT	BALANCE	
							DEBIT	CREDIT

ACCOUNT __Utilities Expense__   ACCOUNT NO. ___514___

	DATE		DESCRIPTION	POST. REF.	DEBIT	CREDIT	BALANCE	
							DEBIT	CREDIT

ACCOUNT __Supplies Expense__   ACCOUNT NO. ___517___

	DATE		DESCRIPTION	POST. REF.	DEBIT	CREDIT	BALANCE	
							DEBIT	CREDIT

PROBLEM 6.4A or 6.4B (continued)

ACCOUNT __Advertising Expense__ _____ ACCOUNT NO. ___526___

DATE	DESCRIPTION	POST. REF.	DEBIT	CREDIT	BALANCE	
					DEBIT	CREDIT

ACCOUNT __Depreciation Expense—__ _____ ACCOUNT NO. ___523___

DATE	DESCRIPTION	POST. REF.	DEBIT	CREDIT	BALANCE	
					DEBIT	CREDIT

ACCOUNT NAME	DEBIT	CREDIT

Analyze: _____

_____

CHAPTER 6 CHALLENGE PROBLEM

The Barber Shop

Worksheet

Month Ended December 31, 2007

	ACCOUNT NAME	TRIAL BALANCE DEBIT	TRIAL BALANCE CREDIT	ADJUSTMENTS DEBIT	ADJUSTMENTS CREDIT
1	Cash	40 8 0 0 00			
2	Accounts Receivable	9 0 0 0 00			
3	Supplies	7 2 0 0 00			(a) 3 6 0 0 00
4	Prepaid Insurance	10 8 0 0 00			(b) 2 4 0 0 00
5	Machinery	84 0 0 0 00			
6	Accumulated Depreciation—Machinery				(c) 1 2 0 0 00
7	Accounts Payable		13 5 0 0 00		
8	Tommy Brooks, Capital		74 5 8 0 00		
9	Tommy Brooks, Drawing	6 0 0 0 00			
10	Fees Income		82 5 0 0 00		
11	Supplies Expense			(a) 3 6 0 0 00	
12	Insurance Expense			(b) 2 4 0 0 00	
13	Salaries Expense	11 1 0 0 00			
14	Depreciation Expense—Machinery			(c) 1 2 0 0 00	
15	Utilities Expense	1 6 8 0 00			
16	Totals	170 5 8 0 00	170 5 8 0 00	7 2 0 0 00	7 2 0 0 00
17	Net Income				
18					
19					
20					
21					
22					
23					
24					
25					
26					
27					
28					
29					
30					
31					
32					

CHAPTER 6 CHALLENGE PROBLEM (continued)

	ADJUSTED TRIAL BALANCE		INCOME STATEMENT		BALANCE SHEET		
	DEBIT	CREDIT	DEBIT	CREDIT	DEBIT	CREDIT	
							1
							2
							3
							4
							5
							6
							7
							8
							9
							10
							11
							12
							13
							14
							15
							16
							17
							18
							19
							20
							21
							22
							23
							24
							25
							26
							27
							28
							29
							30
							31
							32

CHAPTER 6 CHALLENGE PROBLEM (continued)

CHAPTER 6 CHALLENGE PROBLEM (continued)

GENERAL JOURNAL   PAGE _____

	DATE		DESCRIPTION	POST. REF.	DEBIT	CREDIT	
1							1
2							2
3							3
4							4
5							5
6							6
7							7
8							8
9							9
10							10
11							11
12							12
13							13
14							14
15							15
16							16

CHAPTER 6 CHALLENGE PROBLEM (continued)

GENERAL JOURNAL

PAGE _____

	DATE	DESCRIPTION	POST. REF.	DEBIT	CREDIT	
1						1
2						2
3						3
4						4
5						5
6						6
7						7
8						8
9						9
10						10
11						11
12						12
13						13
14						14
15						15
16						16
17						17
18						18

ACCOUNT NAME	DEBIT	CREDIT

Analyze: _____

_____

CHAPTER 6 CRITICAL THINKING PROBLEM

1. _____

_____

_____

_____

_____

_____

_____

_____

_____

_____

2.

GENERAL JOURNAL   PAGE _____

	DATE		DESCRIPTION	POST. REF.	DEBIT	CREDIT	
1							1
2							2
3							3
4							4
5							5
6							6

3. _____

_____

_____

_____

_____

_____

_____

_____

_____

_____

_____

_____

_____

_____

_____

_____

_____

CHAPTER 6 CRITICAL THINKING PROBLEM (continued)

_____
_____
_____
_____
_____
_____
_____
_____
_____
_____
_____
_____
_____
_____
_____
_____
_____
_____
_____
_____
_____
_____
_____
_____

Chapter 6 Practice Test Answer Key

Part A True-False	Part B Matching
1. T	1. a
2. F	2. b
3. F	3. e
4. T	4. c
5. F	5. d
6. T	
7. F	
8. T	
9. F	
10. F	

Name _____

GENERAL JOURNAL

PAGE _____

	DATE		DESCRIPTION	POST. REF.	DEBIT	CREDIT	
1							1
2							2
3							3
4							4
5							5
6							6
7							7
8							8
9							9
10							10
11							11
12							12
13							13
14							14
15							15
16							16
17							17
18							18
19							19
20							20
21							21
22							22
23							23
24							24
25							25
26							26
27							27
28							28
29							29
30							30
31							31
32							32
33							33
34							34

Name _____

GENERAL JOURNAL

PAGE _____

	DATE	DESCRIPTION	POST. REF.	DEBIT	CREDIT	
1						1
2						2
3						3
4						4
5						5
6						6
7						7
8						8
9						9
10						10
11						11
12						12
13						13
14						14
15						15
16						16
17						17
18						18
19						19
20						20
21						21
22						22
23						23
24						24
25						25
26						26
27						27
28						28
29						29
30						30
31						31
32						32
33						33
34						34
35						35
36						36
37						37
38						38
39						39

Name

GENERAL JOURNAL

PAGE

	DATE		DESCRIPTION	POST. REF.	DEBIT	CREDIT	
1							1
2							2
3							3
4							4
5							5
6							6
7							7
8							8
9							9
10							10
11							11
12							12
13							13
14							14
15							15
16							16
17							17
18							18
19							19
20							20
21							21
22							22
23							23
24							24
25							25
26							26
27							27
28							28
29							29
30							30
31							31
32							32
33							33
34							34
35							35
36							36
37							37
38							38
39							39

Name _____

GENERAL JOURNAL

PAGE _____

	DATE		DESCRIPTION	POST. REF.	DEBIT	CREDIT	
1							1
2							2
3							3
4							4
5							5
6							6
7							7
8							8
9							9
10							10
11							11
12							12
13							13
14							14
15							15
16							16
17							17
18							18
19							19
20							20
21							21
22							22
23							23
24							24
25							25
26							26
27							27
28							28
29							29
30							30
31							31
32							32
33							33
34							34
35							35
36							36
37							37
38							38
39							39

Name _____

GENERAL LEDGER

ACCOUNT _____ ACCOUNT NO. _____

DATE	DESCRIPTION	POST. REF.	DEBIT	CREDIT	BALANCE	
					DEBIT	CREDIT

ACCOUNT _____ ACCOUNT NO. _____

DATE	DESCRIPTION	POST. REF.	DEBIT	CREDIT	BALANCE	
					DEBIT	CREDIT

Name _____

GENERAL LEDGER

ACCOUNT _____ ACCOUNT NO. _____

DATE	DESCRIPTION	POST. REF.	DEBIT	CREDIT	BALANCE	
					DEBIT	CREDIT

ACCOUNT _____ ACCOUNT NO. _____

DATE	DESCRIPTION	POST. REF.	DEBIT	CREDIT	BALANCE	
					DEBIT	CREDIT

ACCOUNT _____ ACCOUNT NO. _____

DATE	DESCRIPTION	POST. REF.	DEBIT	CREDIT	BALANCE	
					DEBIT	CREDIT

ACCOUNT _____ ACCOUNT NO. _____

DATE	DESCRIPTION	POST. REF.	DEBIT	CREDIT	BALANCE	
					DEBIT	CREDIT

ACCOUNT _____ ACCOUNT NO. _____

DATE	DESCRIPTION	POST. REF.	DEBIT	CREDIT	BALANCE	
					DEBIT	CREDIT

Name _____

GENERAL LEDGER

ACCOUNT _____ ACCOUNT NO. _____

DATE	DESCRIPTION	POST. REF.	DEBIT	CREDIT	BALANCE	
					DEBIT	CREDIT

ACCOUNT _____ ACCOUNT NO. _____

DATE	DESCRIPTION	POST. REF.	DEBIT	CREDIT	BALANCE	
					DEBIT	CREDIT

ACCOUNT _____ ACCOUNT NO. _____

DATE	DESCRIPTION	POST. REF.	DEBIT	CREDIT	BALANCE	
					DEBIT	CREDIT

ACCOUNT _____ ACCOUNT NO. _____

DATE	DESCRIPTION	POST. REF.	DEBIT	CREDIT	BALANCE	
					DEBIT	CREDIT

Name _____

GENERAL LEDGER

ACCOUNT _____ ACCOUNT NO. _____

DATE	DESCRIPTION	POST. REF.	DEBIT	CREDIT	BALANCE DEBIT	BALANCE CREDIT

ACCOUNT _____ ACCOUNT NO. _____

DATE	DESCRIPTION	POST. REF.	DEBIT	CREDIT	BALANCE DEBIT	BALANCE CREDIT

ACCOUNT _____ ACCOUNT NO. _____

DATE	DESCRIPTION	POST. REF.	DEBIT	CREDIT	BALANCE DEBIT	BALANCE CREDIT

ACCOUNT _____ ACCOUNT NO. _____

DATE	DESCRIPTION	POST. REF.	DEBIT	CREDIT	BALANCE DEBIT	BALANCE CREDIT

ACCOUNT _____ ACCOUNT NO. _____

DATE	DESCRIPTION	POST. REF.	DEBIT	CREDIT	BALANCE DEBIT	BALANCE CREDIT

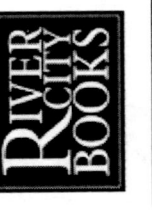

River City Books, LLC
20170 SW Avery Court, Tualatin, OR 97062
sales@rivercitybooks.com

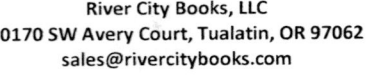

Our Order Number

1661146

165

Ship To

Sharon Ho
724 SEQUOIA DR

SUNNYVALE, CA 94086-8227
USA

Marketplace

Amazon

Marketplace's Order Number

105-1568466-4829023

Shipping Method

STANDARD

Order Received

11/11/2014 8:50:00 PM

LOCATION	SKU #	ISBN/ASIN/UPC #	CONDITION	TYPE	UNIT PRICE
FU-05-08-07	0214JD-203051	9780073030593	Used - Good	Paperback	0.81

TITLE: Study Guide & Working Papers Ch 1-32 to accompany College Accounting

COMMENTS: GOOD with average wear to cover, pages and binding. We ship quickly and work hard to earn your confidence. Order are generally shipped no later than next business day. We offer a no hassle guarantee on all our items.

LOCATION	SKU #	ISBN/ASIN/UPC #	CONDITION	TYPE	UNIT PRICE

TITLE:

COMMENTS:

GENERAL LEDGER

ACCOUNT _____ ACCOUNT NO. _____

DATE	DESCRIPTION	POST. REF.	DEBIT	CREDIT	BALANCE	
					DEBIT	CREDIT

ACCOUNT _____ ACCOUNT NO. _____

DATE	DESCRIPTION	POST. REF.	DEBIT	CREDIT	BALANCE	
					DEBIT	CREDIT

ACCOUNT _____ ACCOUNT NO. _____

DATE	DESCRIPTION	POST. REF.	DEBIT	CREDIT	BALANCE	
					DEBIT	CREDIT

ACCOUNT _____ ACCOUNT NO. _____

DATE	DESCRIPTION	POST. REF.	DEBIT	CREDIT	BALANCE	
					DEBIT	CREDIT

ACCOUNT _____ ACCOUNT NO. _____

DATE	DESCRIPTION	POST. REF.	DEBIT	CREDIT	BALANCE	
					DEBIT	CREDIT

Name

	ACCOUNT NAME	TRIAL BALANCE		ADJUSTMENTS	
		DEBIT	CREDIT	DEBIT	CREDIT
1					
2					
3					
4					
5					
6					
7					
8					
9					
10					
11					
12					
13					
14					
15					
16					
17					
18					
19					
20					
21					
22					
23					
24					
25					
26					
27					
28					
29					
30					
31					
32					
33					
34					
35					
36					
37					

Name _____

	ADJUSTED TRIAL BALANCE		INCOME STATEMENT		BALANCE SHEET		
	DEBIT	CREDIT	DEBIT	CREDIT	DEBIT	CREDIT	
							1
							2
							3
							4
							5
							6
							7
							8
							9
							10
							11
							12
							13
							14
							15
							16
							17
							18
							19
							20
							21
							22
							23
							24
							25
							26
							27
							28
							29
							30
							31
							32
							33
							34
							35
							36
							37

Name

ACCOUNT NAME	DEBIT	CREDIT

Analyze:

CHAPTER 7

Accounting for Sales and Accounts Receivable

STUDY GUIDE

Understanding the Chapter

Objectives
1. Record credit sales in a sales journal. 2. Post from the sales journal to the general ledger accounts. 3. Post from the sales journal to the customers' accounts in the accounts receivable subsidiary ledger. 4. Record sales returns and allowances in the general journal. 5. Post sales returns and allowances. 6. Prepare a schedule of accounts receivable. 7. Compute trade discounts. 8. Record credit card sales in appropriate journals. 9. Prepare the state sales tax return. 10. Define the accounting terms new to this chapter.

Reading Assignment
Read Chapter 7 in the textbook. Complete the textbook Section Self Review as you finish reading each section of the chapter, and the Comprehensive Self Review at the end of the chapter. Refer to the Chapter 7 Glossary or to the Glossary at the end of the book to find definitions for terms that are not familiar to you.

Activities

❏ **Thinking Critically**
Answer the *Thinking Critically* questions for Wal-Mart, Computers in Accounting, and Managerial Implications.

❏ **Internet Application**
Complete the activity for Computers in Accounting.

❏ **Discussion Questions**
Answer each assigned discussion question in Chapter 7.

❏ **Exercises**
Complete each assigned exercise in Chapter 7. Use the forms provided in this SGWP. The objectives covered by an exercise are given after the exercise number. If you need help with an exercise, review the portion of the chapter related to the objective(s) covered.

❏ **Problems A/B**
Complete each assigned problem in Chapter 7. Use the forms provided in this SGWP. The objectives covered by a problem are given after the problem number. If you need help with a problem, review the portion of the chapter related to the objective(s) covered.

❏ **Challenge Problem**
Complete the challenge problem as assigned. Use the forms provided in this SGWP.

❏ **Critical Thinking Problem**
Complete the critical thinking problem as assigned. Use the forms provided in this SGWP.

❏ **Business Connections**
Complete the Business Connections activities as assigned to gain a deeper understanding of Chapter 7 concepts.

Practice Tests
Complete the Practice Tests, which cover the main points in your reading assignment. Compare your answers with those in the Practice Test Answer Key for Chapter 7 at the end of this chapter. If you have answered any questions incorrectly, review the related section of the text.

Part A True-False

For each of the following statements, circle T in the answer column if the statement is true and F if the statement is false.

T F **1.** The amount of a sales allowance is debited to the Sales account because the revenue from sales has been reduced.

T F **2.** The larger the volume of credit sales, the more desirable it is to use a special sales journal.

T F **3.** The use of a special sales journal enables more than one person to work on the journals of a business at the same time.

T F **4.** The Sales Slip Number column in the sales journal shows where to look when more information is needed.

T F **5.** The use of a special sales journal makes posting to accounts in the general ledger unnecessary.

T F **6.** The columns and headings in the sales journal eliminate the need for a description of each entity.

T F **7.** The special sales journal is used for recording both cash sales and sales on credit.

T F **8.** The Sales account may be credited for a sale only when cash is received.

T F **9.** Sales on credit require debits to **Accounts Receivable.**

T F **10.** Special journals are needed when the transactions of a business include groups of repetitive entries.

T F **11.** A credit sale made on a credit card issued by a credit card company is accounted for in the same manner as a credit sale made on a bank credit card.

T F **12.** The accountant must keep an individual record of dealings with each customer to answer questions received from managers and salespeople of the company, from the customers themselves, and from banks and credit bureaus.

T F **13.** As proof of accuracy, the total of all customers' accounts in the accounts receivable ledger is compared with the balance of the **Accounts Receivable** account in the general ledger.

T F **14.** The **Accounts Receivable** account in the general ledger is known as a control account because it contains a summary of all activities involving accounts receivable.

T F **15.** When the balance-form ledger sheet is used in the accounts receivable ledger, the accountant figures the running balance of each account after each posting during the month.

T F **16.** The basic procedure for posting totals from the sales journal to the general ledger is not affected by the use of an accounts receivable ledger.

T F **17.** The amount of each credit sale is posted daily to the customer's account in the accounts receivable ledger.

T F **18.** The accounts receivable ledger is called a subsidiary ledger because it is only a part of the general ledger.

T F **19.** The **Accounts Receivable** account in the general ledger must be individually debited for each credit sale as it is made.

T F **20.** When a customer returns goods on which sales tax was charged, the firm gives credit for the price of goods and the sales tax.

152 ■ **Chapter 7**

Part B Matching

For each numbered item, choose the matching term from the box and write the identifying letter in the answer column.

_____ 1. A special journal for recording only the credit sales of a company.

_____ 2. A liability account for recording a tax levied by some states on certain retail sales.

_____ 3. A reduction in the amount charged to a customer who has received defective goods or services.

_____ 4. A reduction in price, based on volume purchased, given by wholesalers to retailers who buy goods for resale.

_____ 5. The type of credit usually given by a business on the basis of the personal knowledge of the customer.

_____ 6. Identification cards given by some businesses to their customers who have established credit.

_____ 7. Identification cards used by some banks to individuals for use in making credit card purchases at participating businesses.

> **a.** Trade discount
>
> **b.** Sales return or allowance
>
> **c.** Business credit card
>
> **d.** Sales tax payable
>
> **e.** Open-account credit
>
> **f.** Sales journal
>
> **g.** Bank credit cards

Part C Exercise

Answer each question about the accounts receivable subsidiary ledger account shown below.

ACCOUNTS RECEIVABLE SUBSIDIARY LEDGER

NAME __Charles O'Brien__   TERMS _____

ADDRESS __1891 Windsor Drive, Dallas, TX 75623-6998__

DATE		DESCRIPTION	POST. REF.	DEBIT	CREDIT	BALANCE DEBIT	BALANCE CREDIT
2007							
Jan.	1	Balance	✔			4 0 0 00	
	4	Sales Slip 101	S1	6 0 00		4 6 0 00	
	7	Sales Slip 167	S1	9 0 00		5 5 0 00	
	17		J1		7 5 00	4 7 5 00	

1. Where did the $400 entry come from?

_____

_____

2. How could you find a complete description of the $60 charge on January 4?

_____

_____

3. What was the probable reason for the $75.00 entry? How can you find out for sure?

_____

_____

Demonstration Problem

Twin City Auto Supply sells tires and auto supplies to retail stores. The firm offers a trade discount of 40 percent on tires and 20 percent on auto supplies. Transactions involving credit sales and sales returns and allowances for the month of April 2007 follow, along with the general ledger accounts used to record these transactions. Account balances shown are for the beginning of April 2007.

Instructions

1. Open the general ledger accounts; enter the balance for **Accounts Receivable**.
   - 111   Accounts Receivable $61,020
   - 401   Sales
   - 451   Sales Returns and Allowances

2. Set up the accounts receivable subsidiary ledger. Open an account for each credit customer and enter the balances as of April 1, 2007. All customers have terms of n/45.
Auto Mart	$14,790
Auto Discount Supply Center	
Jazzy Wheels and Window Tint Center	$42,000
Mike's Car Care Center	$4,230
City Auto Accessories Express	

3. Record the transactions on page 6 of a sales journal and on page 16 of the general journal. (Be sure to enter each sale at its net price.)

4. Post individual entries from the sales journal and the general journal to the appropriate ledger accounts.

5. Total and rule the sales journal as of April 30, 2007.

6. Post from the sales journal to the appropriate general ledger accounts.

7. Prepare a schedule of accounts receivable for April 30, 2007.

8. Compare the total of the schedule of accounts receivable to the balance of the **Accounts Receivable** account. The two should be equal.

DATE	TRANSACTIONS
April 1	Sold tires to Auto Discount Supply Center; issued invoice 6701 with a list price of $37,200.
5	Sold auto supplies to Mike's Car Care Center; issued invoice 6702 with a list price of $50,700.
9	Sold auto supplies to Jazzy Wheels and Window Tint Center; issued invoice 6703 with a list price of $19,800.
14	Sold tires to Auto Mart, issued invoice 6704 with a list price of $49,200.
18	Accepted a return of all auto supplies damaged in shipment to Jazzy Wheels and Window Tint Center; issued Credit Memorandum 251. The original sale was made on Invoice 6703 on April 9.
22	Sold auto supplies to Auto Discount Supply Center; issued Invoice 6705 with a list price of $93,480.
29	Sold tires to Mike's Car Care Center; issued Invoice 6706 with a list price of $82,230.
30	Sold tires to City Auto Accessories Express; issued Invoice 6707 with a list price of $43,230.

SOLUTION

SALES JOURNAL
PAGE ___6___

	DATE		INVOICE NO.	CUSTOMER'S NAME	POST. REF.	ACCOUNTS RECEIVABLE/ DR. SALES CR.	
1	2007						1
2	April	1	6701	Auto Discount Supply Center	✔	22 3 2 0 00	2
3		5	6702	Mike's Car Care Center	✔	40 5 6 0 00	3
4		9	6703	Jazzy Wheels and Window Tint Center	✔	15 8 4 0 00	4
5		14	6704	Auto Mart	✔	29 5 2 0 00	5
6		22	6705	Auto Discount Supply Center	✔	74 7 8 4 00	6
7		29	6706	Mike's Car Care Center	✔	49 3 3 8 00	7
8		30	6707	City Auto Accessories Express	✔	25 9 3 8 00	8
9						258 3 0 0 00	9
10						(1 1 1 /4 01)	10
11							11

GENERAL JOURNAL
PAGE ___16___

	DATE		DESCRIPTION	POST. REF.	DEBIT	CREDIT	
1	2007						1
2	April	18	Sales Returns and Allowances	451	15 8 4 0 00		2
3			Accounts Rec./Jazzy Wheels	111 ✔		15 8 4 0 00	3
4			and Window Tint Center				4
5			Accepted return of damaged supplies,				5
6			Credit Memo 251; original sale				6
7			made on Invoice 6703 of April 9				7
8							8

GENERAL LEDGER

ACCOUNT __Accounts Receivable__   ACCOUNT NO. ___111___

DATE		DESCRIPTION	POST. REF.	DEBIT	CREDIT	BALANCE DEBIT	BALANCE CREDIT
2007							
April	1	Balance	✔			61 0 2 0 00	
	18		J16		15 8 4 0 00	45 1 8 0 00	
	30		S6	258 3 0 0 00		303 4 8 0 00	

SOLUTION (continued)

GENERAL LEDGER

ACCOUNT __Sales__   ACCOUNT NO. ___401___

DATE		DESCRIPTION	POST. REF.	DEBIT	CREDIT	BALANCE DEBIT	BALANCE CREDIT
2007							
April	30		S6		258 3 0 0 00	258 3 0 0 00	

ACCOUNT __Sales Returns and Allowances__   ACCOUNT NO. ___451___

DATE		DESCRIPTION	POST. REF.	DEBIT	CREDIT	BALANCE DEBIT	BALANCE CREDIT
2007							
April	18		J16	15 8 4 0 00		15 8 4 0 00	

ACCOUNTS RECEIVABLE SUBSIDIARY LEDGER

NAME __Auto Discount Supply Center__   TERMS ___n/45___

DATE		DESCRIPTION	POST. REF.	DEBIT	CREDIT	BALANCE DEBIT	BALANCE CREDIT
2007							
April	1		S6	22 3 2 0 00		22 3 2 0 00	
	22		S6	74 7 8 4 00		97 1 0 4 00	

NAME __Auto Mart__   TERMS ___n/45___

DATE		DESCRIPTION	POST. REF.	DEBIT	CREDIT	BALANCE DEBIT	BALANCE CREDIT
2007							
April	1	Balance	✔			14 7 9 0 00	
	14		S6	29 5 2 0 00		44 3 1 0 00	

NAME __City Auto Accessories Express__   TERMS ___n/45___

DATE		DESCRIPTION	POST. REF.	DEBIT	CREDIT	BALANCE DEBIT	BALANCE CREDIT
2007							
April	30		S6	25 9 3 8 00		25 9 3 8 00	

SOLUTION (continued)

ACCOUNTS RECEIVABLE SUBSIDIARY LEDGER

NAME   **Jazzy Wheels and Window Tint Center**   TERMS ____ **n/45**

DATE		DESCRIPTION	POST. REF.	DEBIT	CREDIT	BALANCE DEBIT	BALANCE CREDIT
2007							
April	**1**	**Balance**	✔			42 0 0 0 00	
	9		S6	15 8 4 0 00		57 8 4 0 00	
	18		J16		15 8 4 0 00	42 0 0 0 00	

NAME   **Mike's Car Care Center**   TERMS ____ **n/45**

DATE		DESCRIPTION	POST. REF.	DEBIT	CREDIT	BALANCE DEBIT	BALANCE CREDIT
2007							
April	**1**		✔			4 2 3 0 00	
	5		S6	40 5 6 0 00		44 7 9 0 00	
	29		S6	49 3 3 8 00		94 1 2 8 00	

Twin City Auto Supply

Schedule of Accounts Receivable

April 30, 2007

Auto Discount Supply Center	97 1 0 4 00
Auto Mart	44 3 1 0 00
City Auto Accessories Express	25 9 3 8 00
Jazzy Wheels and Window Tint Center	42 0 0 0 00
Mike's Car Care Center	94 1 2 8 00
Total	303 4 8 0 00

WORKING PAPERS

Name _____

EXERCISE 7.1

1. _____
2. _____
3. _____
4. _____

5. _____
6. _____
7. _____
8. _____

EXERCISE 7.2

	Dr.	Cr.		Dr.	Cr.
1.	_____	_____	4.	_____	_____
2.	_____	_____	5.	_____	_____
3.	_____	_____	6.	_____	_____

EXERCISE 7.3

SALES JOURNAL

PAGE _____

	DATE	SALES SLIP NO.	CUSTOMER'S NAME	POST. REF.	ACCOUNTS RECEIVABLE DEBIT	SALES TAX PAYABLE CREDIT	SALES CREDIT	
1								1
2								2
3								3
4								4
5								5

EXERCISE 7.4

GENERAL JOURNAL   PAGE _____

	DATE		DESCRIPTION	POST. REF.	DEBIT	CREDIT	
1							1
2							2
3							3
4							4
5							5
6							6
7							7
8							8
9							9
10							10
11							11
12							12
13							13
14							14
15							15

EXERCISE 7.5

1. _____
_____
_____

2. _____
_____
_____

3. _____
_____
_____

4. _____
_____
_____

EXERCISE 7.6

1. _____
2. _____
3. _____

EXERCISE 7.7

1. _____
2. _____
3. _____

EXERCISE 7.8

GENERAL JOURNAL   PAGE _____

	DATE	DESCRIPTION	POST. REF.	DEBIT	CREDIT	
1						1
2						2
3						3
4						4
5						5

EXERCISE 7.9

Balance of Accounts Receivable: _____

EXERCISE 7.10

GENERAL LEDGER

ACCOUNT _____ ACCOUNT NO. _____

DATE	DESCRIPTION	POST. REF.	DEBIT	CREDIT	BALANCE	
					DEBIT	CREDIT

ACCOUNT _____ ACCOUNT NO. _____

DATE	DESCRIPTION	POST. REF.	DEBIT	CREDIT	BALANCE	
					DEBIT	CREDIT

ACCOUNT _____ ACCOUNT NO. _____

DATE	DESCRIPTION	POST. REF.	DEBIT	CREDIT	BALANCE	
					DEBIT	CREDIT

ACCOUNTS RECEIVABLE SUBSIDIARY LEDGER

NAME _____ TERMS _____

DATE	DESCRIPTION	POST. REF.	DEBIT	CREDIT	BALANCE

NAME _____ TERMS _____

DATE	DESCRIPTION	POST. REF.	DEBIT	CREDIT	BALANCE

PROBLEM 7.1A or 7.1B

SALES JOURNAL
PAGE _____

	DATE	SALES SLIP NO.	CUSTOMER'S NAME	POST. REF.	ACCOUNTS RECEIVABLE DEBIT	SALES TAX PAYABLE CREDIT	SALES CREDIT	
1								1
2								2
3								3
4								4
5								5
6								6
7								7
8								8
9								9
10								10
11								11
12								12

GENERAL LEDGER

ACCOUNT _____ ACCOUNT NO. _____

DATE	DESCRIPTION	POST. REF.	DEBIT	CREDIT	BALANCE DEBIT	BALANCE CREDIT

ACCOUNT _____ ACCOUNT NO. _____

DATE	DESCRIPTION	POST. REF.	DEBIT	CREDIT	BALANCE DEBIT	BALANCE CREDIT

ACCOUNT _____ ACCOUNT NO. _____

DATE	DESCRIPTION	POST. REF.	DEBIT	CREDIT	BALANCE DEBIT	BALANCE CREDIT

Analyze: _____

PROBLEM 7.2A or 7.2B

SALES JOURNAL   PAGE _____

	DATE	SALES SLIP NO.	CUSTOMER'S NAME	POST. REF.	ACCOUNTS RECEIVABLE DEBIT	SALES TAX PAYABLE CREDIT	SALES CREDIT	
1								1
2								2
3								3
4								4
5								5
6								6
7								7
8								8
9								9
10								10
11								11
12								12

GENERAL JOURNAL   PAGE _____

	DATE	DESCRIPTION	POST. REF.	DEBIT	CREDIT	
1						1
2						2
3						3
4						4
5						5
6						6
7						7
8						8
9						9
10						10
11						11
12						12
13						13
14						14
15						15
16						16
17						17
18						18
19						19
20						20
21						21

Name _____

PROBLEM 7.2A or 7.2B (continued)

GENERAL LEDGER

ACCOUNT _____ ACCOUNT NO. _____

DATE	DESCRIPTION	POST. REF.	DEBIT	CREDIT	BALANCE	
					DEBIT	CREDIT

ACCOUNT _____ ACCOUNT NO. _____

DATE	DESCRIPTION	POST. REF.	DEBIT	CREDIT	BALANCE	
					DEBIT	CREDIT

ACCOUNT _____ ACCOUNT NO. _____

DATE	DESCRIPTION	POST. REF.	DEBIT	CREDIT	BALANCE	
					DEBIT	CREDIT

ACCOUNT _____ ACCOUNT NO. _____

DATE	DESCRIPTION	POST. REF.	DEBIT	CREDIT	BALANCE	
					DEBIT	CREDIT

PROBLEM 7.2A or 7.2B (continued)

_____

_____

_____

Analyze: _____

_____

PROBLEM 7.3A or 7.3B

SALES JOURNAL   PAGE _____

	DATE	SALES SLIP NO.	CUSTOMER'S NAME	POST. REF.	ACCOUNTS RECEIVABLE DEBIT	SALES TAX PAYABLE CREDIT	SALES CREDIT	
1								1
2								2
3								3
4								4
5								5
6								6
7								7
8								8
9								9
10								10
11								11
12								12

PROBLEM 7.3A or 7.3B (continued)

GENERAL JOURNAL

PAGE _____

	DATE	DESCRIPTION	POST. REF.	DEBIT	CREDIT	
1						1
2						2
3						3
4						4
5						5
6						6
7						7
8						8
9						9
10						10
11						11
12						12
13						13
14						14
15						15

GENERAL LEDGER

ACCOUNT _____   ACCOUNT NO. _____

DATE	DESCRIPTION	POST. REF.	DEBIT	CREDIT	BALANCE	
					DEBIT	CREDIT

ACCOUNT _____   ACCOUNT NO. _____

DATE	DESCRIPTION	POST. REF.	DEBIT	CREDIT	BALANCE	
					DEBIT	CREDIT

PROBLEM 7.3A or 7.3B (continued)

GENERAL LEDGER

ACCOUNT _____ ACCOUNT NO. _____

DATE	DESCRIPTION	POST. REF.	DEBIT	CREDIT	BALANCE	
					DEBIT	CREDIT

ACCOUNT _____ ACCOUNT NO. _____

DATE	DESCRIPTION	POST. REF.	DEBIT	CREDIT	BALANCE	
					DEBIT	CREDIT

ACCOUNTS RECEIVABLE SUBSIDIARY LEDGER

NAME _____ TERMS _____

DATE	DESCRIPTION	POST. REF.	DEBIT	CREDIT	BALANCE

NAME _____ TERMS _____

DATE	DESCRIPTION	POST. REF.	DEBIT	CREDIT	BALANCE

NAME _____ TERMS _____

DATE	DESCRIPTION	POST. REF.	DEBIT	CREDIT	BALANCE

PROBLEM 7.3A or 7.3B (continued)

ACCOUNTS RECEIVABLE SUBSIDIARY LEDGER

NAME _____ TERMS _____

	DATE	DESCRIPTION	POST. REF.	DEBIT	CREDIT	BALANCE

NAME _____ TERMS _____

	DATE	DESCRIPTION	POST. REF.	DEBIT	CREDIT	BALANCE

NAME _____ TERMS _____

	DATE	DESCRIPTION	POST. REF.	DEBIT	CREDIT	BALANCE

NAME _____ TERMS _____

	DATE	DESCRIPTION	POST. REF.	DEBIT	CREDIT	BALANCE

NAME _____ TERMS _____

	DATE	DESCRIPTION	POST. REF.	DEBIT	CREDIT	BALANCE

NAME _____ TERMS _____

	DATE	DESCRIPTION	POST. REF.	DEBIT	CREDIT	BALANCE

PROBLEM 7.3A or 7.3B (continued)

Balance of Accounts Receivable account: _____

Analyze: _____
_____

PROBLEM 7.4A or 7.4B

SALES JOURNAL

PAGE _____

	DATE	INVOICE NO.	CUSTOMER'S NAME	POST. REF.	ACCOUNTS RECEIVABLE DR./ SALES CR.	
1						1
2						2
3						3
4						4
5						5
6						6
7						7
8						8
9						9
10						10
11						11
12						12

PROBLEM 7.4A or 7.4B (continued)

GENERAL JOURNAL

PAGE_____

	DATE	DESCRIPTION	POST. REF.	DEBIT	CREDIT	
1						1
2						2
3						3
4						4
5						5
6						6
7						7
8						8
9						9
10						10
11						11
12						12
13						13

GENERAL LEDGER

ACCOUNT_____ ACCOUNT NO. _____

DATE	DESCRIPTION	POST. REF.	DEBIT	CREDIT	BALANCE	
					DEBIT	CREDIT

ACCOUNT_____ ACCOUNT NO. _____

DATE	DESCRIPTION	POST. REF.	DEBIT	CREDIT	BALANCE	
					DEBIT	CREDIT

ACCOUNT_____ ACCOUNT NO. _____

DATE	DESCRIPTION	POST. REF.	DEBIT	CREDIT	BALANCE	
					DEBIT	CREDIT

PROBLEM 7.4A or 7.4B (continued)

ACCOUNTS RECEIVABLE SUBSIDIARY LEDGER

NAME _____ TERMS _____

DATE	DESCRIPTION	POST. REF.	DEBIT	CREDIT	BALANCE

NAME _____ TERMS _____

DATE	DESCRIPTION	POST. REF.	DEBIT	CREDIT	BALANCE

NAME _____ TERMS _____

DATE	DESCRIPTION	POST. REF.	DEBIT	CREDIT	BALANCE

NAME _____ TERMS _____

DATE	DESCRIPTION	POST. REF.	DEBIT	CREDIT	BALANCE

NAME _____ TERMS _____

DATE	DESCRIPTION	POST. REF.	DEBIT	CREDIT	BALANCE

PROBLEM 7.4A or 7.4B (continued)

ACCOUNTS RECEIVABLE SUBSIDIARY LEDGER

NAME _____ TERMS _____

	DATE	DESCRIPTION	POST. REF.	DEBIT	CREDIT	BALANCE

Balance of Accounts Receivable account: _____

Analyze: _____

CHAPTER 7 CHALLENGE PROBLEM

SALES JOURNAL   PAGE _____

	DATE	INVOICE NO.	CUSTOMER'S NAME	POST. REF.	ACCOUNTS RECEIVABLE DR./ SALES CR.	
1						1
2						2
3						3
4						4
5						5
6						6
7						7
8						8
9						9
10						10
11						11

Name _____

CHAPTER 7 CHALLENGE PROBLEM (continued)

GENERAL JOURNAL

PAGE _____

	DATE	DESCRIPTION	POST. REF.	DEBIT	CREDIT	
1						1
2						2
3						3
4						4
5						5
6						6
7						7

GENERAL LEDGER

ACCOUNT _____ ACCOUNT NO. _____

DATE	DESCRIPTION	POST. REF.	DEBIT	CREDIT	BALANCE DEBIT	BALANCE CREDIT

ACCOUNT _____ ACCOUNT NO. _____

DATE	DESCRIPTION	POST. REF.	DEBIT	CREDIT	BALANCE DEBIT	BALANCE CREDIT

ACCOUNT _____ ACCOUNT NO. _____

DATE	DESCRIPTION	POST. REF.	DEBIT	CREDIT	BALANCE DEBIT	BALANCE CREDIT

CHAPTER 7 CHALLENGE PROBLEM (continued)

ACCOUNTS RECEIVABLE SUBSIDIARY LEDGER

NAME _____ TERMS _____

	DATE	DESCRIPTION	POST. REF.	DEBIT	CREDIT	BALANCE

NAME _____ TERMS _____

	DATE	DESCRIPTION	POST. REF.	DEBIT	CREDIT	BALANCE

NAME _____ TERMS _____

	DATE	DESCRIPTION	POST. REF.	DEBIT	CREDIT	BALANCE

NAME _____ TERMS _____

	DATE	DESCRIPTION	POST. REF.	DEBIT	CREDIT	BALANCE

NAME _____ TERMS _____

	DATE	DESCRIPTION	POST. REF.	DEBIT	CREDIT	BALANCE

CHAPTER 7 CHALLENGE PROBLEM (continued)

ACCOUNTS RECEIVABLE SUBSIDIARY LEDGER

NAME _____ TERMS _____

DATE	DESCRIPTION	POST. REF.	DEBIT	CREDIT	BALANCE

Balance of Accounts Receivable account: _____

Analyze: _____

_____

CHAPTER 7 CRITICAL THINKING PROBLEM

1. _____
   _____
   _____
   _____
   _____

2. _____
   _____
   _____
   _____
   _____
   _____
   _____

3. _____
   _____
   _____
   _____
   _____

4. _____
   _____
   _____
   _____
   _____
   _____

Chapter 7 Practice Test Answer Key

Part A True-False		Part B Matching	Part C Exercises
1. F	11. F	1. f	1. The balance was carried over from December 2006.
2. T	12. T	2. d	2. By referring to a copy of Sales Slip 101.
3. T	13. T	3. b	3. It was most likely a sales return or allowance. Refer to the January 17 entry on page 1 of the general journal.
4. T	14. T	4. a	
5. F	15. T	5. e	
6. T	16. T	6. c	
7. F	17. T	7. g	
8. F	18. F		
9. T	19. F		
10. T	20. T		

CHAPTER 8   Accounting for Purchases and Accounts Payable

STUDY GUIDE

Understanding the Chapter

Objectives

1. Record purchases of merchandise on credit in a three-column purchases journal. 2. Post from the three-column purchases journal to the general ledger accounts. 3. Post credit purchases from the purchases journal to the accounts payable subsidiary ledger. 4. Record purchases returns and allowances in the general journal and post them to the accounts payable subsidiary ledger. 5. Prepare a schedule of accounts payable. 6. Compute the net delivered cost of purchases. 7. Demonstrate a knowledge of the procedures for effective internal control of purchases. 8. Define the accounting terms new to this chapter.

Reading Assignment

Read Chapter 8 in the textbook. Complete the textbook Section Self Review as you finish reading each section of the chapter, and the Comprehensive Self Review at the end of the chapter. Refer to the Chapter 8 Glossary or to the Glossary at the end of the book to find definitions for terms that are not familiar to you.

Activities

❏ **Thinking Critically**

Answer the *Thinking Critically* questions for Pier 1 Imports, Accounting on the Job, and Managerial Implications.

❏ **Internet Applications**

Complete the activity for Accounting on the Job.

❏ **Discussion Questions**

Answer each assigned discussion question in Chapter 8.

❏ **Exercises**

Complete each assigned exercise in Chapter 8. Use the forms provided in this SGWP. The objectives covered by an exercise are given after the exercise number. If you need help with an exercise, review the portion of the chapter related to the objective(s) covered.

❏ **Problems A/B**

Complete each assigned problem in Chapter 8. Use the forms provided in this SGWP. The objectives covered by a problem are given after the problem number. If you need help with a problem, review the portion of the chapter related to the objective(s) covered.

❏ **Challenge Problem**

Complete the challenge problem as assigned. Use the forms provided in this SGWP.

❏ **Critical Thinking Problem**

Complete the critical thinking problem as assigned. Use the forms provided in this SGWP.

❏ **Business Connections**

Complete the Business Connections activities as assigned to gain a deeper understanding of Chapter 8 concepts.

Practice Tests

Complete the Practice Tests, which cover the main points in your reading assignment. Compare your answers with those in the Practice Test Answer Key for Chapter 8 at the end of this chapter. If you have answered any questions incorrectly, review the related section of the text.

Part A True-False *For each of the following statements, circle T in the answer column if the statement is true or F if the statement is false.*

T F **1.** A receiving report is prepared to show the quantity of goods received and their condition.

T F **2.** The special purchases journal is used to record all transactions in which merchandise or equipment is purchased on credit.

T F **3.** When properly designed, a purchases journal makes posting to the general ledger unnecessary.

T F **4.** The provision in the purchases journal of special columns for the invoice number, the invoice date, and the credit terms is intended to ensure payment of the bill when it is due.

T F **5.** An account called **Purchases** is charged with the cost of the merchandise as it is sold.

T F **6.** One of the basic advantages of the purchases journal is that the posting to **Accounts Receivable** is simplified.

T F **7.** Each purchase of merchandise on credit should be recorded in the purchases journal as it occurs during the month.

T F **8.** The balance of each creditor's account in the accounts payable ledger is not computed until the end of the accounting period.

T F **9.** At the end of the month, the total of the Accounts Payable column in the purchases journal is debited to the **Accounts Payable** control account.

T F **10.** Payments made to creditors are recorded in the cash payments journal.

T F **11.** At the end of the month, the total of the payments made to creditors is debited to the **Purchases** account.

T F **12.** The use of the balance ledger form makes each creditor's balance readily available.

T F **13.** Within the accounts payable ledger, the accounts for creditors are arranged alphabetically or by account number.

T F **14.** After all postings for a period are completed, the total of the individual balances in the accounts payable ledger should be equal to the balance of the **Accounts Payable** control account in the general ledger.

T F **15.** As soon as it is recorded in the **Purchases** journal, the amount of a purchase is posted as a credit to the supplier's account in the accounts payable ledger.

T F **16.** A payment is first recorded in the cash payments journal and then debited immediately to the supplier's account in the accounts payable ledger.

T F **17.** The procedure for posting totals from the purchases journal remains the same, whether or not an accounts payable ledger is used.

T F **18.** Freight In becomes part of the cost of purchases shown in the Cost of Goods Sold section of the income statement.

Part B Exercise *Answer each of the following in the space provided. Make your answers complete but as brief as possible.*

A firm uses a multicolumn purchases journal with the following money columns: Accounts Payable Credit, Purchases Debit, and Freight In Debit

1. Where is the **Freight In** account shown on the income statement?

_____
_____
_____
_____

2. The figures of which column are used to update the accounts payable ledger?

_____
_____
_____
_____

3. Where would you record the purchase of office equipment on open account credit terms?

_____
_____
_____
_____

4. If the buyer pays freight charges directly to the carrier on a purchase of merchandise, where is the freight transaction recorded?

_____
_____
_____
_____

5. How is the accuracy of the totals verified at the end of the month?

_____
_____
_____
_____

6. Which columns are totaled and summary posted to the general ledger?

_____
_____
_____
_____

7. How is the **Purchases** account classified?

_____
_____
_____

Demonstration Problem

Frontier Office Supply is a retail business that sells office equipment, furniture, and office supplies. Its credit purchases and purchases returns and allowances for the month of October 2007 follow. The general ledger accounts used to record these transactions are given below.

Instructions

1. Open the general ledger accounts and enter the balance of Accounts Payable for October 1, 2007.

2. Using the list of creditors that follows, open the accounts in the accounts payable subsidiary ledger and enter the account balances for October 1, 2007.

3. Record the transactions in a purchases journal, page 12, and a general journal, page 30.

4. Post individual entries from the purchases journal to the accounts payable subsidiary ledger, then post from the general journal to the general ledger and accounts payable subsidiary ledger.

5. Total, prove, and rule the purchases journal as of October 31, 2007.

6. Post the column totals from the purchases journal to the appropriate general ledger accounts.

7. Compute the net delivered cost of the firm's purchases for the month.

8. Prepare a schedule of accounts payable for October 31, 2007.

9. Check the total of the schedule of accounts payable against the balance of the **Accounts Payable** account in the general ledger. The two amounts should be equal.

GENERAL LEDGER ACCOUNTS

205 Accounts Payable	$18,900 Cr.
501 Purchases	
502 Freight In	
503 Purchases Returns and Allowances	

CREDITORS

Name	Terms	Balance
Essential Office Supplies	n/30	
Dallas Office Supply	n/60	$2,320
Davis Office Products	n/30	
Metroplex Office Center	2/10, n/30	5,670
Thomas Copy and Paper	1/10, n/30	10,910

DATE	TRANSACTIONS
October 4	Purchased desks for $9,160 plus a freight charge of $280 from Davis Office Products, Invoice 3124 dated September 30, terms payable in 30 days.
9	Purchased computers for $6,550 from Essential Office Supplies, Invoice 7129 dated October 4, net due and payable in 30 days.
11	Received Credit Memo 165 for $600 from Davis Office Products as an allowance for slightly damaged but usable desks purchased on Invoice 3124 of September 30.
16	Purchased file cabinets for $2,720 plus a freight charge of $124 from Dallas Office Supply, Invoice 9088 dated October 11, terms of 60 days.
21	Purchased electronic calculators for $2,200 from Essential Office Supplies, Invoice 2765 dated October 16, net due and payable in 30 days.
24	Purchased laser printer paper for $3,350 plus a freight charge of $320 from Thomas Copy and Paper on Invoice 4891 dated October 19, terms of 1/10, n/30.
29	Received Credit Memo 629 for $440 from Essential Office Supplies for defective calculators that were returned. The calculators were originally purchased on Invoice 2765 of October 16.
31	Purchased office chairs for $3,900 plus a freight charge of $136 from Metroplex Office Center, Invoice 966 dated October 26, terms of 2/10, n/30.

SOLUTION

PURCHASES JOURNAL

PAGE __12__

DATE		CUSTOMER'S NAME	INVOICE NUMBER	INVOICE DATE	TERMS	POST. REF.	ACCOUNTS PAYABLE CREDIT	PURCHASES DEBIT	FREIGHT IN DEBIT
2007									
Oct.	4	Davis Office Products	3124	9/30	n/30		9 4 4 0 00	9 1 6 0 00	2 8 0 00
	9	Essential Office Supplies	7129	10/4	n/30		6 5 5 0 00	6 5 5 0 00	
	16	Dallas Office Supply	9088	10/11	n/60		2 8 4 4 00	2 7 2 0 00	1 2 4 00
	21	Essential Office Supplies	2765	10/16	n/30		2 2 0 0 00	2 2 0 0 00	
	24	Thomas Copy & Paper							
		Company	4891	10/19	1/10, n/30		3 6 7 0 00	3 3 5 0 00	3 2 0 00
	31	Metroplex Office Center	966	10/26	2/10, n/30		4 0 3 6 00	3 9 0 0 00	1 3 6 00
	31						28 7 4 0 00	27 8 8 0 00	8 6 0 00

GENERAL JOURNAL

PAGE __30__

	DATE		DESCRIPTION	POST. REF.	DEBIT	CREDIT	
1	2007						1
2	Oct.	11	Accounts Payable/Davis Office Products	205 ✓	6 0 0 00		2
3			Purchases Returns and Allowances	503		6 0 0 00	3
4			Received Credit Memo 165 for				4
5			damaged merchandise; original				5
6			purchase was made on Invoice 3124,				6
7			September 30, 2007				7
8							8
9		29	Accounts Payable/Essential Office Supplies	205 ✓	4 4 0 00		9
10			Purchases Returns & Allowances	503		4 4 0 00	10
11			Received Credit Memo 629 for damaged				11
12			merchandise that was returned;				12
13			original purchase was made on				13
14			Invoice 2765, October 16.				14
15							15

SOLUTION (continued)

GENERAL LEDGER

ACCOUNT __Accounts Payable__   ACCOUNT NO. ___205___

DATE		DESCRIPTION	POST. REF.	DEBIT	CREDIT	BALANCE DEBIT	BALANCE CREDIT
2007							
Oct.	1	Balance	✔				18 9 0 0 00
	11		J30	6 0 0 00			18 3 0 0 00
	29		J30	4 4 0 00			17 8 6 0 00
	31		P12		28 7 4 0 00		46 6 0 0 00

ACCOUNT __Purchases__   ACCOUNT NO. ___501___

DATE		DESCRIPTION	POST. REF.	DEBIT	CREDIT	BALANCE DEBIT	BALANCE CREDIT
2007							
Oct.	31		P12	27 8 8 0 00		27 8 8 0 00	

ACCOUNT __Freight In__   ACCOUNT NO. ___502___

DATE		DESCRIPTION	POST. REF.	DEBIT	CREDIT	BALANCE DEBIT	BALANCE CREDIT
2007							
Oct.	31		P12	8 6 0 00		8 6 0 00	

ACCOUNT __Purchases Returns and Allowances__   ACCOUNT NO. ___503___

DATE		DESCRIPTION	POST. REF.	DEBIT	CREDIT	BALANCE DEBIT	BALANCE CREDIT
2007							
Oct.	11		J30		6 0 0 00		6 0 0 00
	29		J30		4 4 0 00		1 0 4 0 00

Purchases	$27,880
Freight In	860
Delivered Cost of Purchases	$28,740
Less Purchases Returns and Allowances	1,040
Net Delivered Cost of Purchases	$27,700

SOLUTION (continued)

ACCOUNTS PAYABLE SUBSIDIARY LEDGER

NAME __Essential Office Supplies__   TERMS __n/30__

DATE		DESCRIPTION	POST. REF.	DEBIT	CREDIT	BALANCE
2007						
Oct.	9	Invoice 7129, 10/4/07	P12		6 5 5 0 00	6 5 5 0 00
	21	Invoice 2765, 10/16/07	P12		2 2 0 0 00	8 7 5 0 00
	29	CM 629	J30	4 4 0 00		8 3 1 0 00

NAME __Dallas Office Supply__   TERMS __n/60__

DATE		DESCRIPTION	POST. REF.	DEBIT	CREDIT	BALANCE
2007						
Oct.	1	Balance	✔			2 3 2 0 00
	16	Invoice 9088, 10/11/07	P12		2 8 4 4 00	5 1 6 4 00

NAME __Davis Office Products__   TERMS __n/30__

DATE		DESCRIPTION	POST. REF.	DEBIT	CREDIT	BALANCE
2007						
Oct.	4	Invoice 3124, 9/30/07	P12		9 4 4 0 00	9 4 4 0 00
	11	CM 165	J30	6 0 0 00		8 8 4 0 00

NAME __Metroplex Office Center__   TERMS __2/10, n/30__

DATE		DESCRIPTION	POST. REF.	DEBIT	CREDIT	BALANCE
20-07						
Oct.	1	Balance	✔			5 6 7 0 00
	31	Invoice 966, 10/26/07	P12		4 0 3 6 00	9 7 0 6 00

NAME __Thomas Copy and Paper Company__   TERMS __1/10, n/30__

DATE		DESCRIPTION	POST. REF.	DEBIT	CREDIT	BALANCE
2007						
Oct.	1	Balance	✔			10 9 1 0 00
	24	Invoice 4891, 10/19/07	P12		3 6 7 0 00	14 5 8 0 00

SOLUTION (continued)

Frontier Office Supply
Schedule of Accounts Payable
October 31, 2007

Essential Office Supplies		8	3	1	0	00
Dallas Office Supply		5	1	6	4	00
Davis Office Products		8	8	4	0	00
Metroplex Office Center		9	7	0	6	00
Thomas Copy and Paper Company	14	5	8	0	00
Total	46	6	0	0	00

WORKING PAPERS

Name _____

EXERCISE 8.1

1. _____   4. _____

2. _____   5. _____

3. _____   6. _____

EXERCISE 8.2

	Dr.	Cr.		Dr.	Cr.
1.	_____	_____	4.	_____	_____
2.	_____	_____	5.	_____	_____
3.	_____	_____	6.	_____	_____

EXERCISE 8.3

PURCHASES JOURNAL   PAGE _____

DATE	PURCHASED FROM	INVOICE NUMBER	INVOICE DATE	TERMS	POST. REF.	ACCOUNTS PAYABLE CREDIT	PURCHASES DEBIT	FREIGHT IN DEBIT

EXERCISE 8.4

GENERAL JOURNAL   PAGE _____

	DATE	DESCRIPTION	POST. REF.	DEBIT	CREDIT	
1						1
2						2
3						3
4						4
5						5
6						6
7						7
8						8
9						9
10						10

EXERCISE 8.5

GENERAL JOURNAL   PAGE _____

	DATE	DESCRIPTION	POST. REF.	DEBIT	CREDIT	
1						1
2						2
3						3
4						4
5						5
6						6
7						7

EXERCISE 8.6

_____

_____

_____

_____

_____

_____

EXERCISE 8.7

a. _____

_____

b. _____

_____

c. _____

d. _____

_____

EXERCISE 8.8

a. _____

b. _____

c. _____

d. _____

PROBLEM 8.1A or 8.1B

PURCHASES JOURNAL

PAGE _____

DATE	PURCHASED FROM	INVOICE NUMBER	INVOICE DATE	TERMS	POST. REF.	ACCOUNTS PAYABLE CREDIT	PURCHASES DEBIT	FREIGHT IN DEBIT

GENERAL JOURNAL

PAGE _____

	DATE	DESCRIPTION	POST. REF.	DEBIT	CREDIT	
1						1
2						2
3						3
4						4
5						5
6						6
7						7
8						8
9						9
10						10
11						11
12						12
13						13
14						14
15						15
16						16
17						17
18						18
19						19

Name _____

PROBLEM 8.1A or 8.1B (continued)

GENERAL LEDGER

ACCOUNT _____ ACCOUNT NO. _____

DATE	DESCRIPTION	POST. REF.	DEBIT	CREDIT	BALANCE DEBIT	CREDIT

ACCOUNT _____ ACCOUNT NO. _____

DATE	DESCRIPTION	POST. REF.	DEBIT	CREDIT	BALANCE DEBIT	CREDIT

ACCOUNT _____ ACCOUNT NO. _____

DATE	DESCRIPTION	POST. REF.	DEBIT	CREDIT	BALANCE DEBIT	CREDIT

ACCOUNT _____ ACCOUNT NO. _____

DATE	DESCRIPTION	POST. REF.	DEBIT	CREDIT	BALANCE DEBIT	CREDIT

Analyze: _____

PROBLEM 8.2A or 8.2B

ACCOUNTS PAYABLE SUBSIDIARY LEDGER

NAME _____ TERMS _____

	DATE	DESCRIPTION	POST. REF.	DEBIT	CREDIT	BALANCE

NAME _____ TERMS _____

	DATE	DESCRIPTION	POST. REF.	DEBIT	CREDIT	BALANCE

NAME _____ TERMS _____

	DATE	DESCRIPTION	POST. REF.	DEBIT	CREDIT	BALANCE

NAME _____ TERMS _____

	DATE	DESCRIPTION	POST. REF.	DEBIT	CREDIT	BALANCE

NAME _____ TERMS _____

	DATE	DESCRIPTION	POST. REF.	DEBIT	CREDIT	BALANCE

PROBLEM 8.2A or 8.2B (continued)

Analyze: _____

EXTRA FORM

Name _____

PROBLEM 8.3A or 8.3B

PURCHASES JOURNAL

PAGE _____

DATE	PURCHASED FROM	INVOICE NUMBER	INVOICE DATE	TERMS	POST. REF.	ACCOUNTS PAYABLE CREDIT	PURCHASES DEBIT	FREIGHT IN DEBIT

GENERAL JOURNAL

PAGE _____

	DATE	DESCRIPTION	POST. REF.	DEBIT	CREDIT	
1						1
2						2
3						3
4						4
5						5
6						6
7						7
8						8
9						9
10						10
11						11
12						12
13						13
14						14
15						15

PROBLEM 8.3A or 8.3B (continued)

GENERAL LEDGER

ACCOUNT _____   ACCOUNT NO. _____

DATE		DESCRIPTION	POST. REF.	DEBIT	CREDIT	BALANCE	
						DEBIT	CREDIT

ACCOUNT _____   ACCOUNT NO. _____

DATE		DESCRIPTION	POST. REF.	DEBIT	CREDIT	BALANCE	
						DEBIT	CREDIT

ACCOUNT _____   ACCOUNT NO. _____

DATE		DESCRIPTION	POST. REF.	DEBIT	CREDIT	BALANCE	
						DEBIT	CREDIT

ACCOUNT _____   ACCOUNT NO. _____

DATE		DESCRIPTION	POST. REF.	DEBIT	CREDIT	BALANCE	
						DEBIT	CREDIT

_____

_____

_____

_____

_____

PROBLEM 8.3A or 8.3B (continued)

ACCOUNTS PAYABLE SUBSIDIARY LEDGER

NAME _____ TERMS _____

	DATE	DESCRIPTION	POST. REF.	DEBIT	CREDIT	BALANCE

NAME _____ TERMS _____

	DATE	DESCRIPTION	POST. REF.	DEBIT	CREDIT	BALANCE

NAME _____ TERMS _____

	DATE	DESCRIPTION	POST. REF.	DEBIT	CREDIT	BALANCE

NAME _____ TERMS _____

	DATE	DESCRIPTION	POST. REF.	DEBIT	CREDIT	BALANCE

NAME _____ TERMS _____

	DATE	DESCRIPTION	POST. REF.	DEBIT	CREDIT	BALANCE

PROBLEM 8.3A or 8.3B (continued)

_____
_____

Analyze: _____
_____

EXTRA FORMS

NAME _____ TERMS _____

	DATE		DESCRIPTION	POST. REF.	DEBIT	CREDIT	BALANCE

NAME _____ TERMS _____

	DATE		DESCRIPTION	POST. REF.	DEBIT	CREDIT	BALANCE

PROBLEM 8.4A or 8.4B

PURCHASES JOURNAL
PAGE _____

DATE		PURCHASED FROM	INVOICE NUMBER	INVOICE DATE	TERMS	POST. REF.	ACCOUNTS PAYABLE CREDIT	PURCHASES DEBIT	FREIGHT IN DEBIT

GENERAL JOURNAL
PAGE _____

	DATE		DESCRIPTION	POST. REF.	DEBIT	CREDIT	
1							1
2							2
3							3
4							4
5							5
6							6
7							7
8							8
9							9
10							10
11							11
12							12
13							13
14							14
15							15

PROBLEM 8.4A or 8.4B (continued)

GENERAL LEDGER

ACCOUNT _____ ACCOUNT NO. _____

DATE	DESCRIPTION	POST. REF.	DEBIT	CREDIT	BALANCE	
					DEBIT	CREDIT

ACCOUNT _____ ACCOUNT NO. _____

DATE	DESCRIPTION	POST. REF.	DEBIT	CREDIT	BALANCE	
					DEBIT	CREDIT

ACCOUNT _____ ACCOUNT NO. _____

DATE	DESCRIPTION	POST. REF.	DEBIT	CREDIT	BALANCE	
					DEBIT	CREDIT

ACCOUNT _____ ACCOUNT NO. _____

DATE	DESCRIPTION	POST. REF.	DEBIT	CREDIT	BALANCE	
					DEBIT	CREDIT

Net Delivered Cost of Purchases

_____

_____

_____

_____

_____

PROBLEM 8.4A or 8.4B (continued)

ACCOUNTS PAYABLE SUBSIDIARY LEDGER

NAME _____ TERMS _____

	DATE	DESCRIPTION	POST. REF.	DEBIT	CREDIT	BALANCE

NAME _____ TERMS _____

	DATE	DESCRIPTION	POST. REF.	DEBIT	CREDIT	BALANCE

NAME _____ TERMS _____

	DATE	DESCRIPTION	POST. REF.	DEBIT	CREDIT	BALANCE

NAME _____ TERMS _____

	DATE	DESCRIPTION	POST. REF.	DEBIT	CREDIT	BALANCE

NAME _____ TERMS _____

	DATE	DESCRIPTION	POST. REF.	DEBIT	CREDIT	BALANCE

PROBLEM 8.4A or 8.4B (continued)

Analyze: _____

EXTRA FORM

CHAPTER 8 CHALLENGE PROBLEM

PURCHASES JOURNAL

PAGE _____

DATE		PURCHASED FROM	INVOICE NUMBER	INVOICE DATE	TERMS	POST. REF.	ACCOUNTS PAYABLE CREDIT	PURCHASES DEBIT	FREIGHT IN DEBIT

SALES JOURNAL

PAGE _____

	DATE		SALES SLIP NO.	CUSTOMER'S NAME	POST. REF.	ACCOUNTS RECEIVABLE DEBIT	SALES TAX PAYABLE CREDIT	SALES CREDIT	
1									1
2									2
3									3
4									4
5									5
6									6
7									7
8									8
9									9
10									10
11									11
12									12
13									13
14									14
15									15

CHAPTER 8 CHALLENGE PROBLEM (continued)

ACCOUNTS PAYABLE SUBSIDIARY LEDGER

NAME _____ TERMS _____

DATE	DESCRIPTION	POST. REF.	DEBIT	CREDIT	BALANCE

NAME _____ TERMS _____

DATE	DESCRIPTION	POST. REF.	DEBIT	CREDIT	BALANCE

NAME _____ TERMS _____

DATE	DESCRIPTION	POST. REF.	DEBIT	CREDIT	BALANCE

NAME _____ TERMS _____

DATE	DESCRIPTION	POST. REF.	DEBIT	CREDIT	BALANCE

NAME _____ TERMS _____

DATE	DESCRIPTION	POST. REF.	DEBIT	CREDIT	BALANCE

NAME _____ TERMS _____

DATE	DESCRIPTION	POST. REF.	DEBIT	CREDIT	BALANCE

CHAPTER 8 CHALLENGE PROBLEM (continued)

ACCOUNTS PAYABLE SUBSIDIARY LEDGER

NAME _____ TERMS _____

DATE	DESCRIPTION	POST. REF.	DEBIT	CREDIT	BALANCE

NAME _____ TERMS _____

DATE	DESCRIPTION	POST. REF.	DEBIT	CREDIT	BALANCE

ACCOUNTS RECEIVABLE SUBSIDIARY LEDGER

NAME _____ TERMS _____

DATE	DESCRIPTION	POST. REF.	DEBIT	CREDIT	BALANCE

NAME _____ TERMS _____

DATE	DESCRIPTION	POST. REF.	DEBIT	CREDIT	BALANCE

NAME _____ TERMS _____

DATE	DESCRIPTION	POST. REF.	DEBIT	CREDIT	BALANCE

CHAPTER 8 CHALLENGE PROBLEM (continued)

ACCOUNTS RECEIVABLE SUBSIDIARY LEDGER

NAME _____ TERMS _____

	DATE	DESCRIPTION	POST. REF.	DEBIT	CREDIT	BALANCE

NAME _____ TERMS _____

	DATE	DESCRIPTION	POST. REF.	DEBIT	CREDIT	BALANCE

NAME _____ TERMS _____

	DATE	DESCRIPTION	POST. REF.	DEBIT	CREDIT	BALANCE

NAME _____ TERMS _____

	DATE	DESCRIPTION	POST. REF.	DEBIT	CREDIT	BALANCE

NAME _____ TERMS _____

	DATE	DESCRIPTION	POST. REF.	DEBIT	CREDIT	BALANCE

NAME _____ TERMS _____

	DATE	DESCRIPTION	POST. REF.	DEBIT	CREDIT	BALANCE

CHAPTER 8 CHALLENGE PROBLEM (continued)

ACCOUNTS RECEIVABLE SUBSIDIARY LEDGER

NAME _____ TERMS _____

DATE	DESCRIPTION	POST. REF.	DEBIT	CREDIT	BALANCE

NAME _____ TERMS _____

DATE	DESCRIPTION	POST. REF.	DEBIT	CREDIT	BALANCE

GENERAL LEDGER

ACCOUNT _____ ACCOUNT NO. _____

DATE	DESCRIPTION	POST. REF.	DEBIT	CREDIT	BALANCE DEBIT	BALANCE CREDIT

ACCOUNT _____ ACCOUNT NO. _____

DATE	DESCRIPTION	POST. REF.	DEBIT	CREDIT	BALANCE DEBIT	BALANCE CREDIT

ACCOUNT _____ ACCOUNT NO. _____

DATE	DESCRIPTION	POST. REF.	DEBIT	CREDIT	BALANCE DEBIT	BALANCE CREDIT

ACCOUNT _____ ACCOUNT NO. _____

DATE	DESCRIPTION	POST. REF.	DEBIT	CREDIT	BALANCE DEBIT	BALANCE CREDIT

CHAPTER 8 CHALLENGE PROBLEM (continued)

GENERAL LEDGER

ACCOUNT _____ ACCOUNT NO. _____

DATE	DESCRIPTION	POST. REF.	DEBIT	CREDIT	BALANCE	
					DEBIT	CREDIT

ACCOUNT _____ ACCOUNT NO. _____

DATE	DESCRIPTION	POST. REF.	DEBIT	CREDIT	BALANCE	
					DEBIT	CREDIT

CHAPTER 8 CHALLENGE PROBLEM (continued)

Analyze: _____

Name _____

CHAPTER 8 CRITICAL THINKING PROBLEM

_____
_____
_____
_____
_____
_____
_____
_____
_____
_____
_____
_____
_____
_____
_____
_____
_____
_____
_____
_____
_____
_____
_____
_____
_____
_____
_____
_____

Chapter 8 Practice Test Answer Key

Part A True-False

1. T	10. T
2. F	11. F
3. F	12. T
4. T	13. T
5. F	14. T
6. F	15. T
7. T	16. T
8. F	17. T
9. F	18. T

Part B Exercises

1. In the Cost of Goods Sold Section.
2. The Accounts Payable Column.
3. The General Journal.
4. It is not recorded in the purchases journal at all; it is entered in the cash payments journal.
5. Accounts Payable Credit = Purchases Debit + Freight In Debit.
6. All Columns.
7. An Expense.

206 ■ **Chapter 8**

Copyright © 2007 The McGraw-Hill Companies, Inc. All rights reserved.

CHAPTER 9

Cash Receipts, Cash Payments, and Banking Procedures

STUDY GUIDE

Understanding the Chapter

Objectives	**1.** Record cash receipts in a cash receipts journal. **2.** Account for cash short or over. **3.** Post from the cash receipts journal to subsidiary and general ledgers. **4.** Record cash payments in a cash payments journal. **5.** Post from the cash payments journal to subsidiary and general ledgers. **6.** Demonstrate a knowledge of procedures for a petty cash fund. **7.** Demonstrate a knowledge of internal control routines for cash. **8.** Write a check, endorse checks, prepare a bank deposit slip, and maintain a checkbook balance. **9.** Reconcile the monthly bank statement. **10.** Record any adjusting entries required from the bank reconciliation. **11.** Define accounting terms new to this chapter.
Reading Assignment	Read Chapter 9 in the textbook. Complete the Section Self Review as you finish reading each section of the chapter, and the Comprehensive Self Review at the end of the chapter. Refer to the Chapter 9 Glossary or to the Glossary at the end of the book to find definitions for terms that are not familiar to you.

Activities

❑ **Thinking Critically**	Answer the *Thinking Critically* questions for H&R Block, Computers in Accounting, and Managerial Implications
❑ **Internet Application**	Complete the activity for Computers in Accounting.
❑ **Discussion Questions**	Answer each assigned review question in Chapter 9.
❑ **Exercises**	Complete each assigned exercise in Chapter 9. Use the forms provided in this SGWP. The objectives covered by an exercise are given after the exercise number. If you need help with an exercise, review the portion of the chapter related to the objective(s) covered.
❑ **Problems A/B**	Complete each assigned problem in Chapter 9. Use the forms provided in this SGWP. The objectives covered by a problem are given after the problem number. If you need help with a problem review the portion of the chapter related to the objective(s) covered.
❑ **Challenge Problem**	Complete the challenge problem as assigned. Use the forms provided in this SGWP.
❑ **Critical Thinking Problem**	Complete the critical thinking problem as assigned. Use the forms provided in this SGWP.
❑ **Business Connections**	Complete the Business Connections activities as assigned to gain a deeper understanding of Chapter 9 concepts.

Practice Tests

Complete the Practice Tests, which cover the main points in your reading assignment. Compare your answers with those in the Practice Test Answer Key for Chapter 9 at the end of this chapter. If you have answered any questions incorrectly, review the related section of the text.

Part A True-False *For each of the following statements, circle T in the answer column if the statement is true or F if the statement is false.*

T F **1.** The abbreviation "CP5" in the Posting Reference column of a ledger account indicates that the posting was made from the cash payments journal on the fifth day of the month.

T F **2.** When posting from the cash payments journal at the end of the month, the accountant posts the total cash payments as a single credit to cash.

T F **3.** The check to replenish the petty cash fund is written for an amount sufficient to restore the fund to its established balance.

T F **4.** The petty cash analysis sheet is a memorandum record of petty cash payments rather than a record of original entry.

T F **5.** Each petty cash payment is entered separately in the cash payments journal.

T F **6.** An adequate system of internal control over cash will provide for safeguarding both incoming and outgoing funds.

T F **7.** Correct internal control procedures require that the approval for paying all bills, writing all checks, and signing all checks should be the responsibility of the same person.

T F **8.** Except for petty cash payments, all payments should be made by check.

T F **9.** Internal controls are not necessary if payments are made by check.

T F **10.** The best form of endorsement for business purposes is the restrictive endorsement, which limits the use of the check to a stated purpose.

T F **11.** The money represented by deposited checks becomes available for use as soon as the deposit is made.

T F **12.** Checks made payable to cash or to bearer need not be endorsed when deposited.

T F **13.** Checks can be identified on a deposit slip by the use of the American Bankers Association transit numbers.

T F **14.** Only checks are listed on the deposit slip.

T F **15.** Cash received by mail should be deposited by a person other than the one who accepts and lists it.

T F **16. Cash Short or Over** is a general ledger account that normally has a debit balance because cash tends to be short more often than over.

T F **17.** The **Sales Tax Payable** account represents an expense of the business.

T F **18.** The title of a special journal makes it possible to omit much of the explanation that would be needed in a general journal entry.

T F **19.** A cash investment by the owner in a business should not be recorded in the cash receipts journal.

T F **20.** Account numbers are recorded below the totals of each column as each summary posting from the cash payments journal is completed.

T F **21.** The Other Accounts Debit column of a cash payments journal is used to record the debits that are to be posted individually.

Part B Matching *For each numbered item, choose the matching term from the box and write the identifying letter in the answer column.*

_____ **1.** The process by which a single amount is posted instead of each entry being posted separately.

_____ **2.** A written promise to pay a specific amount at a specific time.

_____ **3.** A system designed to safeguard assets and to help ensure the accuracy and reliability of accounting records.

_____ **4.** A form received from the bank showing all transactions recorded in the depositor's account during the month.

_____ **5.** Receipts that have been deposited and entered in the firm's accounting records but have not yet been entered on the bank's records.

_____ **6.** A form on which all cash and cash items are listed before they are placed in the bank.

_____ **7.** Checks issued and recorded that have not been paid by the bank.

_____ **8.** A check on which payment has been refused because of too few funds in the issuer's account.

_____ **9.** The person or firm from whose account a check is to be paid.

_____ **10.** The form that contains all the information necessary for journalizing a transaction paid by check.

_____ **11.** The firm or person designated on the check to receive payment.

_____ **12.** The process of determining why a difference exists between the firm's accounting records and the bank records and bringing them into balance.

a. NSF Check

b. Deposit in Transit

c. Outstanding checks

d. Bank reconciliation

e. Bank statement

f. Stub

g. Payee

h. Drawer

i. Deposit slip

j. Promissory note

k. Summary posting

l. Internal control

Demonstration Problem

On June 2, 2007, Seymore Realty received its May bank statement. Enclosed with the bank statement, shown below, was a debit memorandum for $140 for a NSF check issued by Calvin Reed. The firm's checkbook contained the information shown below about deposits made and checks issued during May. The balance of the **Cash** account and the checkbook on May 31 was $36,860.

Instructions

1. Prepare a bank reconciliation statement for Seymore Realty as of May 31, 2007.

2. Record general journal entries for any items on the bank reconciliation statement that must be journalized. Date the entries June 2, 2007.

May 1	Balance	$40,592
1	Check 177	400
1	Check 178	800
7	Deposit	2,600
8	Check 180	900
12	Check 181	6,000
17	Check 182	720
19	Deposit	680
22	Check 183	88
23	Check 184	592
26	Deposit	1,748
29	Check 185	60
30	Deposit	800
		$36,860

First Texas National Bank

Seymore Realty
4312 Pauline Street
Dallas, TX 75632-0989

ACCOUNT NO. 77546798
PERIOD ENDING: May 31, 2007

CHECK NO.	AMOUNT	DATE	DESCRIPTION	BALANCE
			Balance last statement	40,592.00
177	400.00	6/1		40,192.00
178	800.00	6/4		39,392.00
	2,600.00	6/7	Deposit	41,992.00
180	900.00	6/8		41,092.00
181	6,000.00	6/12		35,092.00
	140.00	6/12	Debit Memorandum	34,952.00
182	720.00	6/17		34,232.00
	680.00	6/19	Deposit	34,912.00
183	88.00	6/22		34,824.00
	1,748.00	6/26	Deposit	36,572.00
	10.00	6/29	Service Charge	36,562.00

SOLUTION

Seymore Realty

Bank Reconciliation Statement

May 31, 2007

Balance on Bank Statement			36 5 6 2 00
Additions:			
Deposit of May 30 in Transit			8 0 0 00
			37 3 6 2 00
Deductions for Outstanding Checks:			
Check 184 of May 23	5 9 2 00		
Check 185 of May 29	6 0 00		
Total Checks Outstanding		6 5 2 00	
Adjusted Bank Balance			36 7 1 0 00
Balance in Books			36 8 6 0 00
Deductions:			
NSF Check	1 4 0 00		
Bank Service Charge	1 0 00	1 5 0 00	
Adjusted Book Balance			36 7 1 0 00

GENERAL JOURNAL

PAGE __17__

	DATE		DESCRIPTION	POST. REF.	DEBIT	CREDIT	
1	2007						1
2	June	2	Accounts Receivable/Calvin Reed		1 4 0 00		2
3			Cash			1 4 0 00	3
4			To record NSF check Returned by bank				4
5							5
6		3	Miscellaneous Expense		1 0 00		6
7			Cash			1 0 00	7
8			To record bank service charge for May				8
9							9

EXERCISE 9.1

CASH RECEIPTS JOURNAL

PAGE _____

DATE	DESCRIPTION	POST. REF.	ACCOUNTS RECEIVABLE CREDIT	SALES TAX PAYABLE CREDIT	SALES CREDIT	OTHER ACCOUNTS CREDIT			CASH DEBIT
						ACCOUNT NAME	POST. REF.	AMOUNT	

EXERCISE 9.2

CASH PAYMENTS JOURNAL

PAGE _____

DATE	CK. NO.	DESCRIPTION	POST. REF.	ACCOUNTS PAYABLE DEBIT	OTHER ACCOUNTS DEBIT			PURCHASES DISCOUNT CREDIT	CASH CREDIT
					ACCOUNT NAME	POST. REF.	AMOUNT		

EXERCISES 9.3, 9.4

EXERCISE 9.3

CASH PAYMENTS JOURNAL

PAGE _____

DATE	CK. NO.	DESCRIPTION	POST. REF.	ACCOUNTS PAYABLE DEBIT	OTHER ACCOUNTS DEBIT			PURCHASES DISCOUNT CREDIT	CASH CREDIT
					ACCOUNT NAME	POST. REF.	AMOUNT		

EXERCISE 9.4

CASH PAYMENTS JOURNAL

PAGE _____

DATE	CK. NO.	DESCRIPTION	POST. REF.	ACCOUNTS PAYABLE DEBIT	OTHER ACCOUNTS DEBIT			PURCHASES DISCOUNT CREDIT	CASH CREDIT
					ACCOUNT NAME	POST. REF.	AMOUNT		

EXERCISE 9.5

GENERAL JOURNAL PAGE _____

	DATE		DESCRIPTION	POST. REF.	DEBIT	CREDIT	
1							1
2							2
3							3
4							4
5							5
6							6
7							7
8							8
9							9
10							10
11							11
12							12
13							13
14							14

EXERCISE 9.6

	Bank Balance	Book Balance	Accounting Entry
1.			
2.			
3.			
4.			
5.			
6.			
7.			

EXERCISE 9.7

EXERCISE 9.7 (continued)

GENERAL JOURNAL   PAGE _____

	DATE		DESCRIPTION	POST. REF.	DEBIT	CREDIT	
1							1
2							2
3							3
4							4
5							5
6							6
7							7
8							8
9							9
10							10
11							11

PROBLEM 9.1A or 9.1B

PAGE ___

CASH RECEIPTS JOURNAL

DATE	DESCRIPTION	POST. REF.	ACCOUNTS RECEIVABLE CREDIT	SALES TAX PAYABLE CREDIT	SALES CREDIT	OTHER ACCOUNTS CREDIT			CASH DEBIT
						ACCOUNT NAME	POST. REF.	AMOUNT	

PROBLEM 9.1A or 9.1B (continued)

GENERAL LEDGER

ACCOUNT _____ ACCOUNT NO. _____

	DATE	DESCRIPTION	POST. REF.	DEBIT	CREDIT	BALANCE DEBIT	CREDIT

ACCOUNT _____ ACCOUNT NO. _____

	DATE	DESCRIPTION	POST. REF.	DEBIT	CREDIT	BALANCE DEBIT	CREDIT

ACCOUNT _____ ACCOUNT NO. _____

	DATE	DESCRIPTION	POST. REF.	DEBIT	CREDIT	BALANCE DEBIT	CREDIT

ACCOUNT _____ ACCOUNT NO. _____

	DATE	DESCRIPTION	POST. REF.	DEBIT	CREDIT	BALANCE DEBIT	CREDIT

ACCOUNT _____ ACCOUNT NO. _____

	DATE	DESCRIPTION	POST. REF.	DEBIT	CREDIT	BALANCE DEBIT	CREDIT

PROBLEM 9.1A or 9.1B (continued)

GENERAL LEDGER

ACCOUNT _____ ACCOUNT NO. _____

DATE	DESCRIPTION	POST. REF.	DEBIT	CREDIT	BALANCE	
					DEBIT	CREDIT

ACCOUNT _____ ACCOUNT NO. _____

DATE	DESCRIPTION	POST. REF.	DEBIT	CREDIT	BALANCE	
					DEBIT	CREDIT

ACCOUNT _____ ACCOUNT NO. _____

DATE	DESCRIPTION	POST. REF.	DEBIT	CREDIT	BALANCE	
					DEBIT	CREDIT

ACCOUNT _____ ACCOUNT NO. _____

DATE	DESCRIPTION	POST. REF.	DEBIT	CREDIT	BALANCE	
					DEBIT	CREDIT

Analyze: _____

_____

PROBLEM 9.2A or 9.2B

CASH PAYMENTS JOURNAL

PAGE _____

DATE	CK. NO.	DESCRIPTION	POST. REF.	ACCOUNTS PAYABLE DEBIT	OTHER ACCOUNTS DEBIT			PURCHASES DISCOUNT CREDIT	CASH CREDIT
					ACCOUNT NAME	POST. REF.	AMOUNT		

PROBLEM 9.2A or 9.2B (continued)

PETTY CASH ANALYSIS SHEET

PAGE ___

DATE	VOU. NO.	DESCRIPTION	RECEIPTS	PAYMENTS	DISTRIBUTION OF PAYMENTS				
					SUPPLIES DEBIT	DELIVERY EXPENSE DEBIT	MISC. EXPENSE DEBIT	OTHER ACCOUNTS DEBIT	
								ACCOUNT NAME	AMOUNT

PROBLEM 9.2A or 9.2B (continued)

GENERAL LEDGER

ACCOUNT _____ ACCOUNT NO. _____

DATE	DESCRIPTION	POST. REF.	DEBIT	CREDIT	BALANCE	
					DEBIT	CREDIT

ACCOUNT _____ ACCOUNT NO. _____

DATE	DESCRIPTION	POST. REF.	DEBIT	CREDIT	BALANCE	
					DEBIT	CREDIT

ACCOUNT _____ ACCOUNT NO. _____

DATE	DESCRIPTION	POST. REF.	DEBIT	CREDIT	BALANCE	
					DEBIT	CREDIT

ACCOUNT _____ ACCOUNT NO. _____

DATE	DESCRIPTION	POST. REF.	DEBIT	CREDIT	BALANCE	
					DEBIT	CREDIT

ACCOUNT _____ ACCOUNT NO. _____

DATE	DESCRIPTION	POST. REF.	DEBIT	CREDIT	BALANCE	
					DEBIT	CREDIT

PROBLEM 9.2A or 9.2B (continued)

GENERAL LEDGER

ACCOUNT _____ ACCOUNT NO. _____

DATE		DESCRIPTION	POST. REF.	DEBIT	CREDIT	BALANCE	
						DEBIT	CREDIT

ACCOUNT _____ ACCOUNT NO. _____

DATE		DESCRIPTION	POST. REF.	DEBIT	CREDIT	BALANCE	
						DEBIT	CREDIT

ACCOUNT _____ ACCOUNT NO. _____

DATE		DESCRIPTION	POST. REF.	DEBIT	CREDIT	BALANCE	
						DEBIT	CREDIT

ACCOUNT _____ ACCOUNT NO. _____

DATE		DESCRIPTION	POST. REF.	DEBIT	CREDIT	BALANCE	
						DEBIT	CREDIT

ACCOUNT _____ ACCOUNT NO. _____

DATE		DESCRIPTION	POST. REF.	DEBIT	CREDIT	BALANCE	
						DEBIT	CREDIT

PROBLEM 9.2A or 9.2B (continued)

GENERAL LEDGER

ACCOUNT _____ ACCOUNT NO. _____

DATE	DESCRIPTION	POST. REF.	DEBIT	CREDIT	BALANCE	
					DEBIT	CREDIT

ACCOUNT _____ ACCOUNT NO. _____

DATE	DESCRIPTION	POST. REF.	DEBIT	CREDIT	BALANCE	
					DEBIT	CREDIT

ACCOUNT _____ ACCOUNT NO. _____

DATE	DESCRIPTION	POST. REF.	DEBIT	CREDIT	BALANCE	
					DEBIT	CREDIT

ACCOUNT _____ ACCOUNT NO. _____

DATE	DESCRIPTION	POST. REF.	DEBIT	CREDIT	BALANCE	
					DEBIT	CREDIT

ACCOUNT _____ ACCOUNT NO. _____

DATE	DESCRIPTION	POST. REF.	DEBIT	CREDIT	BALANCE	
					DEBIT	CREDIT

Analyze: _____

_____

PROBLEM 9.3A or 9.3B

SALES JOURNAL

DATE	INVOICE NO.	CUSTOMER'S NAME	POST. REF.	ACCOUNTS RECEIVABLE DR./ SALES CR.	
					1
					2
					3
					4
					5
					6
					7
					8
					9
					10
					11

CASH RECEIPTS JOURNAL

DATE	DESCRIPTION	POST. REF.	ACCOUNTS RECEIVABLE CREDIT	SALES CREDIT	OTHER ACCOUNTS CREDIT			SALES DISCOUNT DEBIT	CASH DEBIT
					ACCOUNT NAME	POST. REF.	AMOUNT		

PROBLEM 9.3A or 9.3B (continued)

GENERAL JOURNAL

PAGE _____

	DATE	DESCRIPTION	POST. REF.	DEBIT	CREDIT	
1						1
2						2
3						3
4						4
5						5
6						6
7						7
8						8
9						9
10						10
11						11
12						12

GENERAL LEDGER (PARTIAL)

ACCOUNT _____ ACCOUNT NO. _____

DATE	DESCRIPTION	POST. REF.	DEBIT	CREDIT	BALANCE	
					DEBIT	CREDIT

ACCOUNT _____ ACCOUNT NO. _____

DATE	DESCRIPTION	POST. REF.	DEBIT	CREDIT	BALANCE	
					DEBIT	CREDIT

ACCOUNT _____ ACCOUNT NO. _____

DATE	DESCRIPTION	POST. REF.	DEBIT	CREDIT	BALANCE	
					DEBIT	CREDIT

PROBLEM 9.3A or 9.3B (continued)

GENERAL LEDGER (PARTIAL)

ACCOUNT _____ ACCOUNT NO. _____

DATE	DESCRIPTION	POST. REF.	DEBIT	CREDIT	BALANCE	
					DEBIT	CREDIT

ACCOUNT _____ ACCOUNT NO. _____

DATE	DESCRIPTION	POST. REF.	DEBIT	CREDIT	BALANCE	
					DEBIT	CREDIT

ACCOUNT _____ ACCOUNT NO. _____

DATE	DESCRIPTION	POST. REF.	DEBIT	CREDIT	BALANCE	
					DEBIT	CREDIT

Analyze: _____

PROBLEM 9.4A or 9.4B

PURCHASES JOURNAL

PAGE _____

DATE		PURCHASED FROM	INVOICE NUMBER	INVOICE DATE	TERMS	POST. REF.	PURCHASES DR./ ACCOUNTS PAYABLE CR.

GENERAL JOURNAL

PAGE _____

	DATE		DESCRIPTION	POST. REF.	DEBIT	CREDIT	
1							1
2							2
3							3
4							4
5							5
6							6
7							7
8							8
9							9
10							10
11							11
12							12
13							13
14							14
15							15
16							16
17							17
18							18
19							19
20							20
21							21
22							22
23							23

PROBLEM 9.4A or 9.4B (continued)

PAGE _____

CASH PAYMENTS JOURNAL

DATE	CK. NO.	DESCRIPTION	POST. REF.	ACCOUNTS PAYABLE DEBIT	OTHER ACCOUNTS DEBIT			PURCHASES DISCOUNT CREDIT	CASH CREDIT
					ACCOUNT NAME	POST. REF.	AMOUNT		

PROBLEM 9.4A or 9.4B (continued)

GENERAL LEDGER

ACCOUNT _____ ACCOUNT NO. _____

DATE	DESCRIPTION	POST. REF.	DEBIT	CREDIT	BALANCE	
					DEBIT	CREDIT

ACCOUNT _____ ACCOUNT NO. _____

DATE	DESCRIPTION	POST. REF.	DEBIT	CREDIT	BALANCE	
					DEBIT	CREDIT

ACCOUNT _____ ACCOUNT NO. _____

DATE	DESCRIPTION	POST. REF.	DEBIT	CREDIT	BALANCE	
					DEBIT	CREDIT

ACCOUNT _____ ACCOUNT NO. _____

DATE	DESCRIPTION	POST. REF.	DEBIT	CREDIT	BALANCE	
					DEBIT	CREDIT

PROBLEM 9.4A or 9.4B (continued)

GENERAL LEDGER

ACCOUNT _____ ACCOUNT NO. _____

DATE	DESCRIPTION	POST. REF.	DEBIT	CREDIT	BALANCE	
					DEBIT	CREDIT

ACCOUNT _____ ACCOUNT NO. _____

DATE	DESCRIPTION	POST. REF.	DEBIT	CREDIT	BALANCE	
					DEBIT	CREDIT

ACCOUNT _____ ACCOUNT NO. _____

DATE	DESCRIPTION	POST. REF.	DEBIT	CREDIT	BALANCE	
					DEBIT	CREDIT

ACCOUNT _____ ACCOUNT NO. _____

DATE	DESCRIPTION	POST. REF.	DEBIT	CREDIT	BALANCE	
					DEBIT	CREDIT

ACCOUNT _____ ACCOUNT NO. _____

DATE	DESCRIPTION	POST. REF.	DEBIT	CREDIT	BALANCE	
					DEBIT	CREDIT

ACCOUNT _____ ACCOUNT NO. _____

DATE	DESCRIPTION	POST. REF.	DEBIT	CREDIT	BALANCE	
					DEBIT	CREDIT

PROBLEM 9.4A or 9.4B (continued)

Analyze: _____

EXTRA FORM

PROBLEM 9.5A or 9.5B

_____
_____
_____

GENERAL JOURNAL

PAGE _____

	DATE	DESCRIPTION	POST. REF.	DEBIT	CREDIT	
1						1
2						2
3						3
4						4
5						5
6						6
7						7
8						8
9						9
10						10
11						11
12						12
13						13

Analyze: _____
_____

PROBLEM 9.6A or 9.6B

PROBLEM 9.6A or 9.6B (continued)

GENERAL JOURNAL   PAGE _____

	DATE		DESCRIPTION	POST. REF.	DEBIT	CREDIT	
1							1
2							2
3							3
4							4
5							5
6							6
7							7
8							8
9							9
10							10
11							11
12							12
13							13
14							14
15							15
16							16
17							17
18							18
19							19
20							20
21							21
22							22
23							23
24							24
25							25
26							26
27							27
28							28

Analyze: _____

_____

_____

_____

_____

_____

PROBLEM 9.7A or 9.7B

_____
_____

GENERAL JOURNAL

PAGE _____

	DATE	DESCRIPTION	POST. REF.	DEBIT	CREDIT	
1						1
2						2
3						3
4						4
5						5
6						6
7						7
8						8
9						9
10						10
11						11
12						12
13						13

Analyze: _____

_____

CHAPTER 9 CHALLENGE PROBLEM

SALES JOURNAL
PAGE _____

	DATE	SALES SLIP NO.	CUSTOMER'S NAME	POST. REF.	ACCOUNTS RECEIVABLE DEBIT	SALES TAX PAYABLE CREDIT	SALES CREDIT	
1								1
2								2
3								3
4								4
5								5
6								6
7								7
8								8
9								9
10								10
11								11
12								12
13								13
14								14
15								15
16								16

PURCHASES JOURNAL
PAGE _____

DATE	PURCHASED FROM	INVOICE NUMBER	INVOICE DATE	TERMS	POST. REF.	ACCOUNTS PAYABLE CREDIT	PURCHASES DEBIT	FREIGHT IN DEBIT

Name _____

CHAPTER 9 CHALLENGE PROBLEM (continued)

GENERAL JOURNAL   PAGE _____

	DATE		DESCRIPTION	POST. REF.	DEBIT	CREDIT	
1							1
2							2
3							3
4							4
5							5
6							6
7							7
8							8
9							9
10							10
11							11
12							12
13							13
14							14
15							15
16							16
17							17
18							18
19							19
20							20
21							21
22							22
23							23
24							24
25							25
26							26
27							27
28							28
29							29
30							30
31							31
32							32
33							33
34							34
35							35
36							36
37							37

CHAPTER 9 CHALLENGE PROBLEM (continued)

CASH RECEIPTS JOURNAL

DATE	DESCRIPTION	POST. REF.	ACCOUNTS RECEIVABLE CREDIT	SALES TAX PAYABLE CREDIT	SALES CREDIT	OTHER ACCOUNTS CREDIT			CASH DEBIT
						ACCOUNT NAME	POST. REF.	AMOUNT	

CHAPTER 9 CHALLENGE PROBLEM (continued)

CASH PAYMENTS JOURNAL

PAGE

DATE	CK. NO.	DESCRIPTION	POST. REF.	ACCOUNTS PAYABLE DEBIT	OTHER ACCOUNTS DEBIT			PURCHASES DISCOUNT CREDIT	CASH CREDIT
					ACCOUNT NAME	POST. REF.	AMOUNT		

Name _____

CHAPTER 9 CHALLENGE PROBLEM (continued)

GENERAL LEDGER

ACCOUNT _____ ACCOUNT NO. _____

DATE	DESCRIPTION	POST. REF.	DEBIT	CREDIT	BALANCE	
					DEBIT	CREDIT

ACCOUNT _____ ACCOUNT NO. _____

DATE	DESCRIPTION	POST. REF.	DEBIT	CREDIT	BALANCE	
					DEBIT	CREDIT

ACCOUNT _____ ACCOUNT NO. _____

DATE	DESCRIPTION	POST. REF.	DEBIT	CREDIT	BALANCE	
					DEBIT	CREDIT

ACCOUNT _____ ACCOUNT NO. _____

DATE	DESCRIPTION	POST. REF.	DEBIT	CREDIT	BALANCE	
					DEBIT	CREDIT

ACCOUNT _____ ACCOUNT NO. _____

DATE	DESCRIPTION	POST. REF.	DEBIT	CREDIT	BALANCE	
					DEBIT	CREDIT

CHAPTER 9 CHALLENGE PROBLEM (continued)

GENERAL LEDGER

ACCOUNT _____ ACCOUNT NO. _____

DATE	DESCRIPTION	POST. REF.	DEBIT	CREDIT	BALANCE	
					DEBIT	CREDIT

ACCOUNT _____ ACCOUNT NO. _____

DATE	DESCRIPTION	POST. REF.	DEBIT	CREDIT	BALANCE	
					DEBIT	CREDIT

ACCOUNT _____ ACCOUNT NO. _____

DATE	DESCRIPTION	POST. REF.	DEBIT	CREDIT	BALANCE	
					DEBIT	CREDIT

ACCOUNT _____ ACCOUNT NO. _____

DATE	DESCRIPTION	POST. REF.	DEBIT	CREDIT	BALANCE	
					DEBIT	CREDIT

ACCOUNT _____ ACCOUNT NO. _____

DATE	DESCRIPTION	POST. REF.	DEBIT	CREDIT	BALANCE	
					DEBIT	CREDIT

CHAPTER 9 CHALLENGE PROBLEM (continued)

GENERAL LEDGER

ACCOUNT _____ ACCOUNT NO. _____

DATE	DESCRIPTION	POST. REF.	DEBIT	CREDIT	BALANCE	
					DEBIT	CREDIT

ACCOUNT _____ ACCOUNT NO. _____

DATE	DESCRIPTION	POST. REF.	DEBIT	CREDIT	BALANCE	
					DEBIT	CREDIT

ACCOUNT _____ ACCOUNT NO. _____

DATE	DESCRIPTION	POST. REF.	DEBIT	CREDIT	BALANCE	
					DEBIT	CREDIT

ACCOUNT _____ ACCOUNT NO. _____

DATE	DESCRIPTION	POST. REF.	DEBIT	CREDIT	BALANCE	
					DEBIT	CREDIT

ACCOUNT _____ ACCOUNT NO. _____

DATE	DESCRIPTION	POST. REF.	DEBIT	CREDIT	BALANCE	
					DEBIT	CREDIT

CHAPTER 9 CHALLENGE PROBLEM (continued)

GENERAL LEDGER

ACCOUNT _____ ACCOUNT NO. _____

DATE	DESCRIPTION	POST. REF.	DEBIT	CREDIT	BALANCE	
					DEBIT	CREDIT

ACCOUNT _____ ACCOUNT NO. _____

DATE	DESCRIPTION	POST. REF.	DEBIT	CREDIT	BALANCE	
					DEBIT	CREDIT

ACCOUNT _____ ACCOUNT NO. _____

DATE	DESCRIPTION	POST. REF.	DEBIT	CREDIT	BALANCE	
					DEBIT	CREDIT

ACCOUNT _____ ACCOUNT NO. _____

DATE	DESCRIPTION	POST. REF.	DEBIT	CREDIT	BALANCE	
					DEBIT	CREDIT

ACCOUNT _____ ACCOUNT NO. _____

DATE	DESCRIPTION	POST. REF.	DEBIT	CREDIT	BALANCE	
					DEBIT	CREDIT

CHAPTER 9 CHALLENGE PROBLEM (continued)

GENERAL LEDGER

ACCOUNT _____ ACCOUNT NO. _____

DATE	DESCRIPTION	POST. REF.	DEBIT	CREDIT	BALANCE	
					DEBIT	CREDIT

ACCOUNT _____ ACCOUNT NO. _____

DATE	DESCRIPTION	POST. REF.	DEBIT	CREDIT	BALANCE	
					DEBIT	CREDIT

ACCOUNT _____ ACCOUNT NO. _____

DATE	DESCRIPTION	POST. REF.	DEBIT	CREDIT	BALANCE	
					DEBIT	CREDIT

ACCOUNT _____ ACCOUNT NO. _____

DATE	DESCRIPTION	POST. REF.	DEBIT	CREDIT	BALANCE	
					DEBIT	CREDIT

ACCOUNT _____ ACCOUNT NO. _____

DATE	DESCRIPTION	POST. REF.	DEBIT	CREDIT	BALANCE	
					DEBIT	CREDIT

CHAPTER 9 CHALLENGE PROBLEM (continued)

ACCOUNTS RECEIVABLE SUBSIDIARY LEDGER

NAME _____ TERMS _____

	DATE		DESCRIPTION	POST. REF.	DEBIT	CREDIT	BALANCE

NAME _____ TERMS _____

	DATE		DESCRIPTION	POST. REF.	DEBIT	CREDIT	BALANCE

NAME _____ TERMS _____

	DATE		DESCRIPTION	POST. REF.	DEBIT	CREDIT	BALANCE

NAME _____ TERMS _____

	DATE		DESCRIPTION	POST. REF.	DEBIT	CREDIT	BALANCE

CHAPTER 9 CHALLENGE PROBLEM (continued)

ACCOUNTS RECEIVABLE SUBSIDIARY LEDGER

NAME _____ TERMS _____

	DATE	DESCRIPTION	POST. REF.	DEBIT	CREDIT	BALANCE

NAME _____ TERMS _____

	DATE	DESCRIPTION	POST. REF.	DEBIT	CREDIT	BALANCE

NAME _____ TERMS _____

	DATE	DESCRIPTION	POST. REF.	DEBIT	CREDIT	BALANCE

NAME _____ TERMS _____

	DATE	DESCRIPTION	POST. REF.	DEBIT	CREDIT	BALANCE

NAME _____ TERMS _____

	DATE	DESCRIPTION	POST. REF.	DEBIT	CREDIT	BALANCE

CHAPTER 9 CHALLENGE PROBLEM (continued)

_____
_____

ACCOUNTS PAYABLE SUBSIDIARY LEDGER

NAME _____ TERMS _____

DATE	DESCRIPTION	POST. REF.	DEBIT	CREDIT	BALANCE

NAME _____ TERMS _____

DATE	DESCRIPTION	POST. REF.	DEBIT	CREDIT	BALANCE

NAME _____ TERMS _____

DATE	DESCRIPTION	POST. REF.	DEBIT	CREDIT	BALANCE

NAME _____ TERMS _____

DATE	DESCRIPTION	POST. REF.	DEBIT	CREDIT	BALANCE

CHAPTER 9 CHALLENGE PROBLEM (continued)

ACCOUNTS PAYABLE SUBSIDIARY LEDGER

NAME _____ TERMS _____

	DATE	DESCRIPTION	POST. REF.	DEBIT	CREDIT	BALANCE

NAME _____ TERMS _____

	DATE	DESCRIPTION	POST. REF.	DEBIT	CREDIT	BALANCE

NAME _____ TERMS _____

	DATE	DESCRIPTION	POST. REF.	DEBIT	CREDIT	BALANCE

Analyze: _____

_____

CHAPTER 9 CRITICAL THINKING PROBLEM

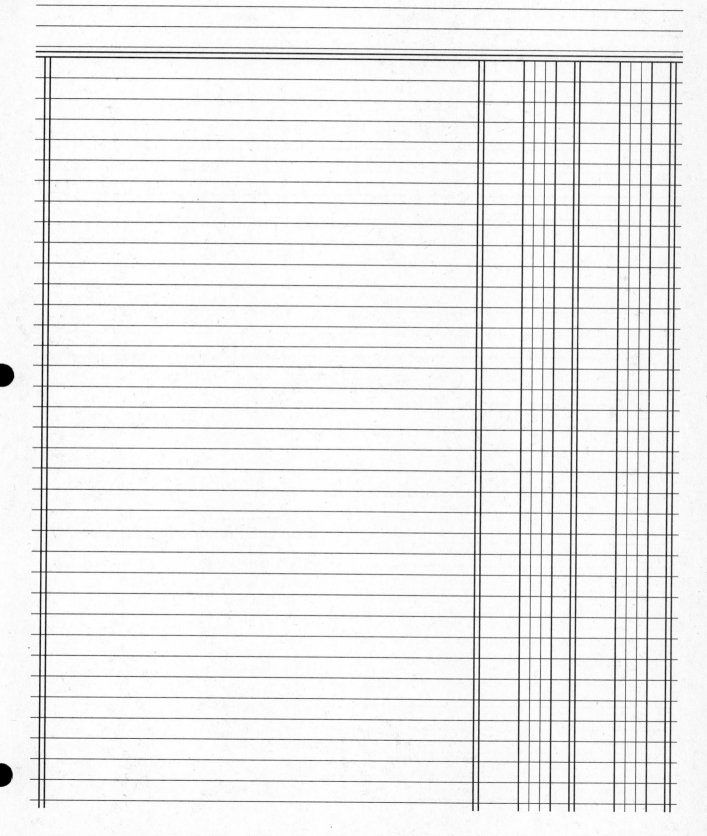

CHAPTER 9 CRITICAL THINKING PROBLEM (continued)

_____

_____

_____

_____

_____

_____

_____

_____

_____

_____

_____

_____

_____

_____

_____

_____

_____

_____

_____

_____

_____

_____

_____

_____

_____

_____

_____

Chapter 9 Practice Test Answer Key

Part A True-False		Part B Matching
1. F	12. F	1. k
2. T	13. T	2. j
3. T	14. F	3. l
4. T	15. T	4. e
5. F	16. T	5. b
6. T	17. F	6. i
7. F	18. T	7. c
8. T	19. F	8. a
9. F	20. T	9. h
10. T	21. T	10. f
11. F		11. g
		12. d

STUDY GUIDE

Understanding the Chapter

Objectives	**1.** Explain the major federal laws relating to employee earnings and withholding. **2.** Compute gross earnings of employees. **3.** Determine employee deductions for social security taxes. **4.** Determine employee deductions for Medicare taxes. **5.** Determine employee deductions for income taxes. **6.** Enter gross earnings, deductions, and net pay in the payroll register. **7.** Journalize payroll transactions in the general journal. **8.** Maintain an earnings record for each employee. **9.** Define the accounting terms new to this chapter.
Reading Assignment	Read Chapter 10 in the textbook. Complete the Section Self Review as you finish reading each section of the chapter, and the Comprehensive Self Review at the end of the chapter. Refer to the Chapter 10 Glossary or to the Glossary at the end of the book to find definitions for terms that are not familiar to you.

Activities

❏ **Thinking Critically** — Answer the *Thinking Critically* questions for Adobe Systems, Accounting on the Job, and Managerial Implications.

❏ **Internet Applications** — Complete the activity for Accounting on the Job.

❏ **Discussion Questions** — Answer each assigned review question in Chapter 10.

❏ **Exercises** — Complete each assigned exercise in Chapter 10. Use the forms provided in this SGWP. The objectives covered by an exercise are given after the exercise number. If you need help with an exercise, review the portion of the chapter related to the objective(s) covered.

❏ **Problems A/B** — Complete each assigned problem in Chapter 10. Use the forms provided in this SGWP. The objectives covered by a problem are given after the problem number. If you need help with a problem, review the portion of the chapter related to the objective(s) covered.

❏ **Challenge Problem** — Complete the challenge problem as assigned. Use the forms provided in this SGWP.

❏ **Critical Thinking Problem** — Complete the critical thinking problem as assigned. Use the forms provided in this SGWP.

❏ **Business Connections** — Complete the Business Connections activities as assigned to gain a deeper understanding of Chapter 10 concepts.

Practice Tests — Complete the Practice Tests, which cover the main points in your reading assignment. Compare your answers with those in the Practice Test Answer Key for Chapter 10 at the end of this chapter. If you have answered any questions incorrectly, review the related section of the text.

Part A True-False *For each of the following statements, circle T in the answer column if the statement is true or F if the statement is false.*

T   F   **1.** The Medicare tax is in addition to the social security tax (FICA).

T   F   **2.** Most employers determine the amount of income tax to be withheld from the employee's pay by using withholding tables.

T   F   **3.** Employees can choose whether they want to be covered by the social security laws.

T   F   **4.** The Fair Labor Standards Act fixes a minimum wage for supervisory employees paid a monthly salary.

T   F   **5.** Payroll taxes apply to salaries and wages paid employees and to amounts paid independent contractors.

T   F   **6.** A company hires P. J. Chandy, a public accountant, to prepare monthly financial statements. Chandy comes to the company's office, reviews source documents, and later returns the statements. Chandy would be classified as an employee.

T   F   **7.** An employee worked 45 hours during the week. Her regular hourly pay is $9 per hour. Her gross pay for the week is $427.50.

T   F   **8.** The payroll register provides all the information required to make a general journal entry to record the payroll.

T   F   **9.** The workers' compensation program is a federal program.

T   F   **10.** The state unemployment tax rate can be reduced by the rate charged by the federal government in the federal unemployment tax program.

T   F   **11.** The employer is required to contribute the same amount of federal unemployment tax as the amount withheld from the employee's earnings.

T   F   **12.** The employee's marital status, number of exemptions, earnings for the pay period, and length of pay period are all factors in determining the amount of social security tax to be withheld.

Part B Matching *For each numbered item, choose the matching term from the box and write the identifying letter in the answer column.*

_____ 1. Time worked in excess of 40 hours per week

_____ 2. Provides for funding of retirement and disability benefits.

_____ 3. The form that employees file in order to claim the number of allowances to which they are entitled.

_____ 4. Wages before deductions

_____ 5. Wages paid in a year above the base amount subject to a tax.

_____ 6. A columnar record that shows each employee's earnings, deductions, and net pay.

_____ 7. A record for each employee showing the person's earnings and deductions for the period, along with cumulative data.

_____ 8. Deductions to pay for medical benefits for retired persons.

_____ 9. A tax levied on the employer to provide benefits to employees who lose their jobs.

_____ 10. A government publication containing withholding tables for employee taxes.

---

a. Employee earnings record

b. Payroll register

c. Exempt wages

d. Workers' compensation insurance

e. Overtime

f. Circular E

g. Medicare premiums

h. Unemployment tax

i. Federal Insurance Contributions Act

j. Employee's Withholding Allowance Certificate Form W4

k. Gross pay

Demonstration Problem

Arrow Consulting Company pays its employees monthly. Payments made by the company on November 30, 2007, follow. Cumulative amounts paid to the persons named prior to November 30 are also given.

1. John Arrow, President, gross monthly salary of $16,500; gross earnings prior to November 30, $165,000.

2. Virginia Richey, Vice President, gross monthly salary of $13,500; gross earnings paid prior to November 30, $135,000.

3. Kathryn Price, independent accountant who audits the company's accounts and performs consulting services, $17,500; gross amounts paid prior to November 30, $35,000.

4. Carolyn Wells, Treasurer, gross monthly salary of $8,000; gross earnings prior to November 30, $80,000.

5. Payment to Hankins Research Services for monthly services of Robert Hankins, a tax and financial accounting consultant, $6,000; amount paid to Hankins Research Services prior to November 30, $24,000.

Instructions

1. Use an earnings ceiling of $90,000 and a tax rate of 6.2 percent for social security taxes and a tax rate of 1.45 percent on all earnings for medicare taxes. Prepare a schedule showing:

   a. Each employee's cumulative earnings prior to November 30.

   b. Each employee's gross earnings for November.

   c. The amounts to be withheld for each payroll tax from each employee's earnings; the employee's income tax withholdings are Arrow, $5,050; Richey, $3,250; Wells, $1,175.

   d. The net amount due each employee.

   e. The total gross earnings, the total of each payroll tax deduction, and the total net amount payable to employees.

2. Give the general journal entry to record the company's payroll on November 30. Use journal page 24. Omit description.

3. Give the general journal entry to record payments to employees on November 30.

SOLUTION

EARNINGS SCHEDULE

EMPLOYEE NAME	CUMULATIVE EARNINGS	MONTHLY PAY	SOCIAL SECURITY	MEDICARE	EMPLOYEE INCOME TAX WITHHOLDING	NET PAY
John Arrow	$165,000.00	$16,500.00	—	$239.25	$5,050.00	$11,210.75
Virginia Richey	135,000.00	13,500.00	—	195.75	3,250.00	10,054.25
Carolyn Wells	80,000.00	8,000.00	496.00	116.00	1,175.00	6,213.00
Totals	$380,000.00	$38,000.00	496.00	551.00	9,475.00	$27,478.00

Kathryn Price and Robert Hankins are not employees of Arrow Consulting Company.

GENERAL JOURNAL   PAGE ___24___

	DATE		DESCRIPTION	POST. REF.	DEBIT	CREDIT	
1	2007						1
2	Nov.	30	Salaries Expense		38 0 0 0 00		2
3			Social Security Tax Payable			4 9 6 00	3
4			Medicare Tax Payable			5 5 1 00	4
5			Employee Income Tax Payable			9 4 7 5 00	5
6			Salaries Payable			27 4 7 8 00	6
7							7
8		30	Salaries Payable		27 4 7 8 00		8
9			Cash			27 4 7 8 00	9
10							10

WORKING PAPERS

Name _____

EXERCISE 10.1

EMPLOYEE NO.	HOURLY RATE	HOURS WORKED	GROSS EARNINGS
_____	_____	_____	_____
_____	_____	_____	_____
_____	_____	_____	_____
_____	_____	_____	_____

EXERCISE 10.2

EMPLOYEE NO.	HOURLY RATE	HOURS WORKED	REGULAR EARNINGS	OVERTIME EARNINGS	GROSS EARNINGS
_____	_____	_____	_____	_____	_____
_____	_____	_____	_____	_____	_____
_____	_____	_____	_____	_____	_____
_____	_____	_____	_____	_____	_____

EXERCISE 10.3

EMPLOYEE NO.	DECEMBER SALARY	EARNINGS THROUGH NOVEMBER 30	SOC. SEC. TAXABLE EARNINGS	SOCIAL SECURITY TAX
_____	_____	_____	_____	_____
_____	_____	_____	_____	_____
_____	_____	_____	_____	_____
_____	_____	_____	_____	_____

EXERCISE 10.4

EMPLOYEE NO.	DECEMBER SALARY	EARNINGS THROUGH NOVEMBER 30	MEDICARE TAXABLE EARNINGS	MEDICARE TAX
_____	_____	_____	_____	_____
_____	_____	_____	_____	_____
_____	_____	_____	_____	_____
_____	_____	_____	_____	_____

EXERCISE 10.5

EMPLOYEE NO.	MARITAL STATUS	WITHHOLDING ALLOWANCES	WEEKLY SALARY	INCOME TAX WITHHOLDING
_____	_____	_____	_____	_____
_____	_____	_____	_____	_____
_____	_____	_____	_____	_____

EXERCISE 10.6

GENERAL JOURNAL   PAGE _____

	DATE		DESCRIPTION	POST. REF.	DEBIT	CREDIT	
1							1
2							2
3							3
4							4
5							5
6							6
7							7
8							8
9							9
10							10
11							11
12							12
13							13
14							14
15							15

EXERCISE 10.7

GENERAL JOURNAL   PAGE _____

	DATE		DESCRIPTION	POST. REF.	DEBIT	CREDIT	
1							1
2							2
3							3
4							4
5							5
6							6
7							7
8							8
9							9
10							10
11							11
12							12
13							13
14							14
15							15

PROBLEM 10.1A or 10.1B

EMPLOYEE NO.	HOURLY RATE	HOURS WORKED	REGULAR EARNINGS	OVERTIME EARNINGS	GROSS EARNINGS
_____	_____	_____	_____	_____	_____
_____	_____	_____	_____	_____	_____
_____	_____	_____	_____	_____	_____
_____	_____	_____	_____	_____	_____

Gross Pay _____

Social Security Tax _____

Medicare Tax _____

Income Tax Withholding _____

Health & Disability _____

United Way _____

U.S. Savings Bond _____

Net Pay _____

GENERAL JOURNAL   PAGE _____

	DATE	DESCRIPTION	POST. REF.	DEBIT	CREDIT	
1						1
2						2
3						3
4						4
5						5
6						6
7						7
8						8
9						9
10						10
11						11
12						12
13						13
14						14
15						15

Analyze: _____

_____

PROBLEM 10.2A or 10.2B

PAYROLL REGISTER   WEEK BEGINNING _____

NAME	NO. OF ALLOW.	MARITAL STATUS	CUMULATIVE EARNINGS	NO. OF HRS.	RATE	EARNINGS			CUMULATIVE EARNINGS
						REGULAR	OVERTIME PREMIUM	GROSS AMOUNT	

AND ENDING _____   PAID _____

TAXABLE WAGES		DEDUCTIONS				NET AMOUNT	CHECK NO.	DISTRIBUTION	
SOCIAL SECURITY	MEDICARE	FUTA	SOCIAL SECURITY	MEDICARE	INCOME TAX			THEATER WAGES	OFFICE WAGES

Name _____

GENERAL JOURNAL

PAGE _____

	DATE		DESCRIPTION	POST. REF.	DEBIT	CREDIT	
1							1
2							2
3							3
4							4
5							5
6							6
7							7
8							8
9							9
10							10
11							11
12							12
13							13
14							14
15							15
16							16
17							17
18							18
19							19
20							20
21							21
22							22
23							23
24							24
25							25
26							26
27							27
28							28
29							29
30							30
31							31
32							32
33							33
34							34

Analyze: _____

_____

PROBLEM 10.3A or 10.3B

PAYROLL REGISTER   WEEK BEGINNING

NAME	NO. OF ALLOW.	MARITAL STATUS	CUMULATIVE EARNINGS	NO. OF HRS.	RATE	EARNINGS			CUMULATIVE EARNINGS
						REGULAR	OVERTIME PREMIUM	GROSS AMOUNT	

AND ENDING   PAID

TAXABLE WAGES		DEDUCTIONS				NET AMOUNT	CHECK NO.	DISTRIBUTION	
SOCIAL SECURITY	MEDICARE	FUTA	SOCIAL SECURITY	MEDICARE	INCOME TAX			OFFICE WAGES	DELIVERY WAGES

PROBLEM 10.3A or 10.3B (continued)

GENERAL JOURNAL   PAGE _____

	DATE		DESCRIPTION	POST. REF.	DEBIT	CREDIT	
1							1
2							2
3							3
4							4
5							5
6							6
7							7
8							8
9							9
10							10
11							11
12							12
13							13
14							14
15							15
16							16
17							17
18							18
19							19
20							20
21							21
22							22
23							23
24							24
25							25
26							26
27							27
28							28
29							29
30							30
31							31
32							32
33							33
34							34

Analyze: _____

_____

PROBLEM 10.4A or 10.4B

EMPLOYEE NAME	CUMULATIVE EARNINGS	MONTHLY PAY	SOCIAL SECURITY	MEDICARE	EMPLOYEE INCOME TAX WITHHOLDING	NET PAY
Totals						

GENERAL JOURNAL

PAGE _____

	DATE	DESCRIPTION	POST. REF.	DEBIT	CREDIT	
1						1
2						2
3						3
4						4
5						5
6						6
7						7
8						8
9						9
10						10
11						11
12						12
13						13
14						14
15						15
16						16
17						17
18						18
19						19
20						20
21						21
22						22
23						23
24						24
25						25
26						26

Analyze: _____

_____

CHAPTER 10 CHALLENGE PROBLEM

EMPLOYEE NAME	CUMULATIVE EARNINGS	MONTHLY PAY	SOCIAL SECURITY	MEDICARE	EMPLOYEE INCOME TAX WITHHOLDING	NET AMOUNT

GENERAL JOURNAL

PAGE _____

	DATE	DESCRIPTION	POST. REF.	DEBIT	CREDIT	
1						1
2						2
3						3
4						4
5						5
6						6
7						7
8						8
9						9
10						10
11						11
12						12
13						13
14						14
15						15

Analyze: _____

_____

CHAPTER 10 CRITICAL THINKING PROBLEM

_____

_____

_____

_____

_____

_____

_____

_____

_____

_____

_____

_____

_____

_____

_____

_____

_____

_____

_____

_____

_____

_____

_____

_____

Chapter 10 Practice Test Answer Key

Part A True-False	Part B Matching
1. T	1. e
2. T	2. i
3. F	3. j
4. F	4. k
5. F	5. c
6. F	6. b
7. T	7. a
8. T	8. g
9. F	9. h
10. F	10. f
11. F	
12. F	

CHAPTER 11

Payroll Taxes, Deposits, and Reports

STUDY GUIDE

Understanding the Chapter

Objectives

1. Explain how and when payroll taxes are paid to the government. 2. Compute and record the employer's social security and Medicare taxes. 3. Record deposit of social security, Medicare, and employee income taxes. 4. Prepare an Employer's Quarterly Federal Tax Return, Form 941. 5. Prepare Wage and Tax Statement (Form W-2) and Annual Transmittal of Wage and Tax Statements (Form W-3). 6. Compute and record liability for federal and state unemployment taxes and record payment of the taxes. 7. Prepare an Employer's Federal Unemployment Tax Return, Form 940 or 940-EZ. 8. Compute and record workers' compensation insurance premiums. 9. Define the accounting terms new to this chapter.

Reading Assignment

Read Chapter 11 in the textbook. Complete the textbook Section Self Review as you finish reading each section of the chapter, and Comprehensive Self Review at the end of the chapter. Refer to the Chapter 11 Glossary or to the Glossary at the end of the book to find definitions for terms that are not familiar to you.

Activities

❏ **Thinking Critically**   Answer the *Thinking Critically* questions for IKEA, Computers in Accounting, and Managerial Implications.

❏ **Internet Application**   Complete the activity for Computers in Accounting.

❏ **Discussion Questions**   Answer each assigned discussion question in Chapter 11.

❏ **Exercises**   Complete each assigned exercise in Chapter 11. Use the forms provided in this SGWP. The objectives covered by an exercise are given after the exercise number. If you need help with an exercise, review the portion of the chapter related to the objective(s) covered.

❏ **Problems A/B**   Complete each assigned problem in Chapter I1. Use the forms provided in this SGWP. The objectives covered by a problem are given after the problem number. If you need help with a problem, review the portion of the chapter related to the objective(s) covered.

❏ **Challenge Problem**   Complete the challenge problem as assigned. Use the forms provided in this SGWP.

❏ **Critical Thinking Problem**   Complete the critical thinking problem as assigned. Use the forms provided in this SGWP.

❏ **Business Connections**   Complete the Business Connections activities as assigned to gain a deeper understanding of Chapter 11 concepts.

Practice Tests   Complete the Practice Tests, which cover the main points in your reading assignment. Compare your answers with those in the Practice Test Answer Key for Chapter 11 at the end of this chapter. If you have answered any questions incorrectly, review the related section of the text.

Part A True-False

For each of the following statements, circle T in the answer column if the statement is true or F if the statement is false.

T   F   1. A business firm pays income tax withholding at the same rate and on the same taxable wages as employees.

T   F   2. The employer's payroll taxes are usually recorded at the end of each payroll period, even though the cash will not be paid out until later.

T   F   3. Most states allow a credit against the SUTA for amounts paid to the federal government as FUTA.

T   F   4. The federal government grants a lower federal unemployment rate under an experience rating system to those employers who provide stable employment.

T   F   5. Under a typical state plan, the federal government actually receives 0.6 percent of the taxable wages because the employer is allowed credits for payments made to the state.

T   F   6. The federal unemployment tax for the year is based on an audit of the payroll for the year.

T   F   7. Premiums on workers' compensation insurance vary with the type of work performed by employees.

T   F   8. The premium on workers' compensation insurance is based on the federal unemployment tax.

T   F   9. The credit against the federal unemployment tax is the amount actually paid to the state under its unemployment compensation insurance program.

T   F   10. Employers with a small number of employees are frequently required to deposit the entire amount of estimated workers' compensation insurance premiums early in the year.

T   F   11. The base for the state unemployment tax may be greater than the base for federal unemployment tax.

T   F   12. Each employer subject to the Federal Unemployment Compensation Tax Act must file an annual return on Form 940 by January 15 of the following year.

T   F   13. The employee must attach a Form W-3 to his or her federal income tax return.

T   F   14. Payments of social security tax, Medicare tax, and employee income tax withheld for a year may be deposited without penalty in an authorized depository at any time up to January 31 of the following year.

T   F   15. Only the amount of each employee's earnings up to $7,000 each year is subject to Medicare tax.

T   F   16. Employees' individual earnings records provide much of the information needed to prepare the Employer's Quarterly Federal Tax Return, Form 941.

T   F   17. On each date of payment of an employee's wages, the employer must provide the employee with a statement, on Form W-2, of earnings and taxes withheld.

T   F   18. During the month immediately following the close of each calendar quarter, an employer is required to file a quarterly tax report and pay in or deposit any balance owed for social security and Medicare taxes and employees' income tax withheld.

Part B Matching *For each number item, choose the matching term from the box and write the identifying letter in the answer column.*

_____ 1. A tax borne equally by the employer and employee.

_____ 2. A tax paid solely by the employer.

_____ 3. An IRS publication containing tax rates and other information about payroll taxes.

_____ 4. Plan providing benefits to employees who are injured or become ill on the job.

_____ 5. A plan under which the SUTA is adjusted to reflect the unemployment experience of the employer.

_____ 6. A deposit "coupon" accompanying the employer's deposit of taxes in a commercial bank.

_____ 7. An annual report to the federal government summarizing the employer's unemployment compensation tax for the year.

_____ 8. A quarterly report to the federal government summarizing taxable wages and payroll taxes due for the quarter.

_____ 9. A yearly form sent to the U.S. government summarizing earnings and payroll taxes withheld for the year.

_____ 10. A statement of earnings and deductions for each employee.

| a. Workers' compensation |
| b. Form 8109 |
| c. Form 941 |
| d. Form 940 |
| e. Form W-3 |
| f. Form W-2 |
| g. Experience rating system |
| h. Publication 15, Circular E |
| i. Federal unemployment tax |
| j. Medicare tax |

Demonstration Problem

The payroll register of the Quick Copy Center showed employee earnings of $12,960 for the month ended January 31, 2007. Employee income tax withholding was $3,500. Tax rates are: social security, 6.2 percent, and Medicare, 1.45 percent.

Instructions

1. Compute the employees' social security and Medicare taxes.

2. Record the payroll for January in the general journal, page 4.

3. Compute the employer's payroll taxes for the period.

4. Prepare a general journal entry to record the employer's payroll taxes for the period.

5. Prepare a general journal entry to record the February 5 deposit of the social security, Medicare, and employee income taxes for the month.

SOLUTION

CALCULATION OF EMPLOYEE TAXES

Social security: 0.062 × $12,960	$803.52
Medicare: 0.0145 × $12,960	187.92
	$991.44

CALCULATION OF EMPLOYER TAXES

Social security: 0.062 × $12,960	$803.52
Medicare: 0.0145 × $12,960	187.92
	$991.44

SOLUTION (continued)

GENERAL JOURNAL

PAGE 3

	DATE		DESCRIPTION	POST. REF.	DEBIT	CREDIT	
1	2007						1
2	Jan.	31	Salaries Expense		1 2 9 6 0 00		2
3			Social Security Tax Payable			8 0 3 52	3
4			Medicare Tax Payable			1 8 7 92	4
5			Employee Income Tax Payable			3 5 0 0 00	5
6			Salaries Payable			8 4 6 8 56	6
7			Payroll for January				7
8							8
9		31	Payroll Tax Expense		9 9 1 44		9
10			Social Security Tax Payable			8 0 3 52	10
11			Medicare Tax Payable			1 8 7 92	11
12			Payroll for January				12
13							13
14	Feb.	5	Social Security Tax Payable		1 6 0 7 04		14
15			Medicare Tax Payable		3 7 5 84		15
16			Employee Income Tax Payable		3 5 0 0 00		16
17			Cash			5 4 8 2 88	17
18			Deposit of payroll taxes withholding				18
19							19
20							20
21							21
22							22
23							23
24							24
25							25
26							26
27							27
28							28
29							29
30							30
31							31
32							32
33							33
34							34
35							35
36							36
37							37
38							38

270 ■ Chapter 11

WORKING PAPERS

Name _____

EXERCISE 11.1

_____

_____

_____

_____

EXERCISE 11.2

GENERAL JOURNAL

PAGE _____

	DATE	DESCRIPTION	POST. REF.	DEBIT	CREDIT	
1						1
2						2
3						3
4						4
5						5
6						6
7						7

EXERCISE 11.3

TAX	BASE	RATE	AMOUNT
_____	_____	_____	_____
_____	_____	_____	_____
_____	_____	_____	_____
_____	_____	_____	_____
_____	_____	_____	_____

EXERCISE 11.4

GENERAL JOURNAL

PAGE _____

	DATE	DESCRIPTION	POST. REF.	DEBIT	CREDIT	
1						1
2						2
3						3
4						4
5						5
6						6
7						7

EXERCISE 11.5

_____

_____

_____

EXERCISE 11.6

GENERAL JOURNAL   PAGE _____

	DATE		DESCRIPTION	POST. REF.	DEBIT	CREDIT	
1							1
2							2
3							3
4							4
5							5
6							6
7							7

EXERCISE 11.7

_____

_____

_____

_____

EXERCISE 11.8

WORK CLASSIFICATION	ESTIMATED EARNINGS	RATE	ESTIMATED PREMIUM
_____	_____	_____	_____
_____	_____	_____	_____
_____	_____	_____	_____

PROBLEM 11.1A or 11.1B

TAX	BASE	RATE	AMOUNT
_____	_____	_____	_____
_____	_____	_____	_____
_____	_____	_____	_____
_____	_____	_____	_____
_____	_____	_____	_____

GENERAL JOURNAL

PAGE __28__

	DATE	DESCRIPTION	POST. REF.	DEBIT	CREDIT	
1						1
2						2
3						3
4						4
5						5
6						6
7						7
8						8
9						9
10						10
11						11
12						12

Analyze: _____

_____

PROBLEM 11.2A or 11.2B

GENERAL JOURNAL   PAGE _____

	DATE	DESCRIPTION	POST. REF.	DEBIT	CREDIT	
1						1
2						2
3						3
4						4
5						5
6						6
7						7
8						8
9						9
10						10
11						11
12						12
13						13
14						14
15						15
16						16
17						17
18						18
19						19
20						20
21						21
22						22
23						23
24						24
25						25
26						26
27						27
28						28
29						29
30						30
31						31
32						32
33						33

Analyze: _____

PROBLEM 11.3A or 11.3B

GENERAL JOURNAL   PAGE _____

	DATE	DESCRIPTION	POST. REF.	DEBIT	CREDIT	
1						1
2						2
3						3
4						4
5						5
6						6
7						7
8						8
9						9
10						10
11						11
12						12
13						13
14						14
15						15
16						16
17						17
18						18
19						19
20						20
21						21
22						22
23						23
24						24
25						25
26						26
27						27
28						28
29						29
30						30
31						31
32						32
33						33

Analyze: _____

_____

PROBLEM 11.3A or 11.3B (continued)

Form **941 for 2007:** **Employer's Quarterly Federal Tax Return**

(Rev. January 2005)

Department of the Treasury — Internal Revenue Service

9901

OMB No. 1545-0029

Employer identification number ☐☐ – ☐☐☐☐☐☐☐

Name (not your trade name) _____

Trade name (if any) _____

Address _____

Number   Street   Suite or room number

_____

City   State   ZIP code

☐ **1:** January, February, March

☐ **2:** April, May, June

☐ **3:** July, August, September

☐ **4:** October, November, December

Read the separate instructions before you fill out this form. Please type or print within the boxes.

1	Number of employees who received wages, tips, or other compensation for the pay period including: *Mar. 12* (Quarter 1), *June 12* (Quarter 2), *Sept. 12* (Quarter 3), *Dec. 12* (Quarter 4) **1**	
2	Wages, tips, and other compensation **2**	
3	Total income tax withheld from wages, tips, and other compensation **3**	
4	If no wages, tips, and other compensation are subject to social security or Medicare tax .	☐ Check and go to line 6.
5	Taxable social security and Medicare wages and tips:	

	Column 1		Column 2
5a Taxable social security wages		× .124 =	
5b Taxable social security tips		× .124 =	
5c Taxable Medicare wages & tips		× .029 =	

5d Total social security and Medicare taxes (*Column 2,* lines 5a + 5b + 5c = line 5d) . **5d**	
6	Total taxes before adjustments (lines 3 + 5d = line 6) **6**	
7	Tax adjustments (If your answer is a negative number, write it in brackets.):	
	7a Current quarter's fractions of cents	
	7b Current quarter's sick pay	
	7c Current quarter's adjustments for tips and group-term life insurance	
	7d Current year's income tax withholding (Attach Form 941c) . .	
	7e Prior quarters' social security and Medicare taxes (Attach Form 941c)	
	7f Special additions to federal income tax (reserved use)	
	7g Special additions to social security and Medicare (reserved use)	
	7h Total adjustments (Combine all amounts: lines 7a through 7g.) **7h**	
8	Total taxes after adjustments (Combine lines 6 and 7h.) **8**	
9	Advance earned income credit (EIC) payments made to employees **9**	
10	Total taxes after adjustment for advance EIC (lines 8 – 9 = line 10) **10**	
11	Total deposits for this quarter, including overpayment applied from a prior quarter . . **11**	
12	Balance due (lines 10 – 11 = line 12) Make checks payable to the *United States Treasury* . **12**	
13	Overpayment (If line 11 is more than line 10, write the difference here.) _____	Check one ☐ Apply to next return. ☐ Send a refund.

→

For Privacy Act and Paperwork Reduction Act Notice, see the back of the Payment Voucher.

Cat. No. 17001Z   Form **941**

PROBLEM 11.3A or 11.3B (continued)

9902

Name (not your trade name)	Employer identification number

If you are unsure about whether you are a monthly schedule depositor or a semiweekly schedule depositor, see *Pub. 15 (Circular E),* **section 11.**

14 ☐☐ Write the state abbreviation for the state where you made your deposits OR write "MU" if you made your deposits in *multiple* states.

15 Check one: ☐ **Line 10 is less than $2,500.** Go to Part 3.

☐ **You were a monthly schedule depositor for the entire quarter. Fill out your tax liability for each month.** Then go to Part 3.

Tax liability:	Month 1	☐ .
	Month 2	☐ .
	Month 3	☐ .
	Total	☐ .	Total must equal line 10.

☐ **You were a semiweekly schedule depositor for any part of this quarter.** Fill out *Schedule B (Form 941): Report of Tax Liability for Semiweekly Schedule Depositors,* and attach it to this form.

16 **If your business has closed and you do not have to file returns in the future** . . . . ☐ Check here, and

enter the final date you paid wages ☐ / / .

17 **If you are a seasonal employer and you do not have to file a return for every quarter of the year** . ☐ Check here.

Do you want to allow an employee, a paid tax preparer, or another person to discuss this return with the IRS? See the instructions for details.

☐ **Yes.** Designee's name ☐

Phone ( ) – Personal Identification Number (PIN) ☐☐☐☐☐

☐ **No.**

Under penalties of perjury, I declare that I have examined this return, including accompanying schedules and statements, and to the best of my knowledge and belief, it is true, correct, and complete.

X

Sign your name here ☐

Print name and title ☐

Date ☐ / / Phone ( ) –

Preparer's signature	
Firm's name	
Address	EIN
	ZIP code
Date / / Phone ( ) –	SSN/PTIN

☐ Check if you are self-employed.

Form **941**

PROBLEM 11.4A or 11.4B

_____

_____

_____

GENERAL JOURNAL   PAGE _____

	DATE		DESCRIPTION	POST. REF.	DEBIT	CREDIT	
1							1
2							2
3							3
4							4
5							5
6							6
7							7
8							8
9							9
10							10
11							11
12							12
13							13
14							14
15							15
16							16
17							17
18							18
19							19
20							20
21							21
22							22
23							23
24							24
25							25
26							26
27							27
28							28
29							29

Analyze: _____

PROBLEM 11.5A or 11.5B

GENERAL JOURNAL   PAGE _____

	DATE		DESCRIPTION	POST. REF.	DEBIT	CREDIT	
1							1
2							2
3							3
4							4
5							5
6							6
7							7
8							8
9							9
10							10
11							11
12							12
13							13
14							14
15							15
16							16
17							17
18							18
19							19
20							20
21							21
22							22
23							23
24							24
25							25
26							26
27							27
28							28
29							29
30							30
31							31
32							32
33							33
34							34

Analyze: _____
_____

PROBLEM 11.5A or 11.5B (continued)

Form **940-EZ**	**Employer's Annual Federal Unemployment (FUTA) Tax Return**	OMB No. 1545-1110

Department of the Treasury
Internal Revenue Service   (99)

▶ See the separate Instructions for Form 940-EZ for information on completing this form.

2007

T	
FF	
FD	
FP	
I	
T	

You must complete this section. ▶

Name (as distinguished from trade name)   Calendar year

Trade name, if any   Employer identification number (EIN)

Address (number and street)   City, state, and ZIP code

*Answer the questions under **Who May Use Form 940-EZ** on page 2. If you cannot use Form 940-EZ, you must use Form 940.*

A   Enter the amount of contributions paid to your state unemployment fund (see the separate instructions) . . ▶ $ _ _ _ _ _ _ _ _ _ _ _ _ _ _

B   (1) Enter the name of the state where you have to pay contributions . . . . ▶ _ _ _ _ _ _ _ _ _ _ _ _ _ _

   (2) Enter your state reporting number as shown on your state unemployment tax return ▶ _ _ _ _ _ _ _ _ _

If you will not have to file returns in the future, check here (see **Who Must File** in separate instructions) **and complete and sign the return.** ▶ ☐

If this is an **Amended Return, check here** (see **Amended Returns** in the separate instructions) . . . . ▶ ☐

Taxable Wages and FUTA Tax

1	Total payments (including payments shown on lines 2 and 3) during the calendar year for services of employees	**1**	
2	Exempt payments. (Explain all exempt payments, attaching additional sheets if necessary.) ▶ _	**2**	
3	Payments of more than $7,000 for services. Enter only amounts over the first $7,000 paid to each employee (**see the separate instructions**)	**3**	
4	Add lines 2 and 3	**4**	
5	**Total taxable wages** (subtract line 4 from line 1) . . . . ▶	**5**	
6	**FUTA tax.** Multiply the wages on line 5 by .008 and enter here. (**If the result is over $100, also complete Part II.**)	**6**	
7	Total FUTA tax deposited for the year, including any overpayment applied from a prior year	**7**	
8	**Balance due** (subtract line 7 from line 6). Pay to the "United States Treasury." . . . . ▶	**8**	
	If you owe more than $100, see **Depositing FUTA tax** in the separate instructions.		
9	**Overpayment** (subtract line 6 from line 7). Check if it is to be: ☐ **Applied to next return** or ☐ **Refunded** ▶	**9**	

Record of Quarterly Federal Unemployment Tax Liability (Do not include state liability.) Complete only if line 6 is over $100.

Quarter	First (Jan. 1 – Mar. 31)	Second (Apr. 1 – June 30)	Third (July 1 – Sept. 30)	Fourth (Oct. 1 – Dec. 31)	Total for year
Liability for quarter					

Third–Party Designee

Do you want to allow another person to discuss this return with the IRS (see the separate instructions)? ☐ **Yes.** Complete the following. ☐ **No**

Designee's name ▶   Phone no. ▶ ( )   Personal identification number (PIN) ▶ | | | | | |

Under penalties of perjury, I declare that I have examined this return, including accompanying schedules and statements, and, to the best of my knowledge and belief, it is true, correct, and complete, and that no part of any payment made to a state unemployment fund claimed as a credit was, or is to be, deducted from the payments to employees.

Signature ▶   Title (Owner, etc.) ▶   Date ▶

▼ **DETACH HERE** ▼   Cat. No. 10983G   Form **940-EZ**

Form **940-V(EZ)**	**Payment Voucher**	OMB No. 1545-1110

Department of the Treasury
Internal Revenue Service

Use this voucher only when making a payment with your return.

2007

Complete boxes 1, 2, and 3. Do not send cash, and do not staple your payment to this voucher. Make your check or money order payable to the "United States Treasury." Be sure to enter your employer identification number (EIN), "Form 940-EZ," and "2004" on your payment.

1 Enter your employer identification number (EIN).	2 **Enter the amount of your payment.** ▶	Dollars	Cents
	3 Enter your business name (individual name for sole proprietors).		
	Enter your address.		
	Enter your city, state, and ZIP code.		

PROBLEM 11.6A or 11.6B

WORK CLASSIFICATION	ESTIMATED EARNINGS	INSURANCE RATE	ESTIMATED PREMIUMS

WORK CLASSIFICATION	ACTUAL EARNINGS	INSURANCE RATE	ACTUAL PREMIUMS

PROBLEM 11.6A or 11.6B (continued)

GENERAL JOURNAL   PAGE _____

	DATE	DESCRIPTION	POST. REF.	DEBIT	CREDIT	
1						1
2						2
3						3
4						4
5						5
6						6
7						7
8						8
9						9
10						10
11						11
12						12
13						13
14						14
15						15
16						16
17						17
18						18
19						19

Analyze: _____

CHAPTER 11 CHALLENGE PROBLEM

1. _____

   _____

2. _____

   _____

3. _____

   _____

4. _____

   _____

5. _____

   _____

Analyze: _____

_____

CHAPTER 11 CRITICAL THINKING PROBLEM

1. _____

   _____

   _____

   _____

2. **YEARLY COST—CURRENT SYSTEM**

   _____

   _____

   _____

   _____

   _____

   _____

   _____

   _____

   _____

   _____

   _____

   _____

   _____

   _____

   _____

CHAPTER 11 CRITICAL THINKING PROBLEM (continued)

YEARLY COST—PROPOSED SYSTEM

_____

_____

_____

_____

_____

_____

_____

_____

_____

_____

_____

_____

_____

_____

3. _____

_____

_____

_____

Chapter 11 Practice Test Answer Key

Part A True-False		Part B Matching
1. F	10. T	1. j
2. T	11. T	2. i
3. F	12. F	3. h
4. F	13. F	4. a
5. F	14. F	5. g
6. F	15. F	6. b
7. T	16. T	7. d
8. F	17. F	8. c
9. F	18. T	9. e
		10. f

CHAPTER 12

Accruals, Deferrals, and the Worksheet

STUDY GUIDE

Understanding the Chapter

Objectives	**1.** Determine the adjustment for merchandise inventory and enter the adjustment on the worksheet. **2.** Compute adjustments for accrued and prepaid expense items and enter the adjustments on the worksheet. **3.** Compute adjustments for accrued and deferred income items and enter the adjustments on the worksheet. **4.** Complete a ten-column worksheet. **5.** Define the accounting terms new to this chapter.
Reading Assignment	Read Chapter 12 in the textbook. Complete the textbook Section Self Review as you finish reading each section of the chapter, and the Comprehensive Self Review at the end of the chapter. Refer to the Chapter 12 Glossary or to the Glossary at the end of the book to find definitions for terms that are not familiar to you.

Activities

❏ **Thinking Critically**	Answer the Part 4 *Thinking Critically* question for Johnson & Johnson. Answer the *Thinking Critically* questions for American Eagle Outfitters, Accounting on the Job, and Managerial Implications.
❏ **Internet Application**	Complete the activity for Accounting on the Job.
❏ **Discussion Questions**	Answer each assigned discussion question in Chapter 12.
❏ **Exercises**	Complete each assigned exercise in Chapter 12. Use the forms provided in this SGWP. The objectives covered by an exercise are given after the exercise number. If you need help with an exercise, review the portion of the chapter related to the objective(s) covered.
❏ **Problems A/B**	Complete each assigned problem in Chapter 12. Use the forms provided in this SGWP. The objectives covered by a problem are given after the problem number. If you need help with a problem, review the portion of the chapter related to the objective(s) covered.
❏ **Challenge Problem**	Complete the challenge problem as assigned. Use the forms provided in this SGWP.
❏ **Critical Thinking Problem**	Complete the critical thinking problem as assigned. Use the forms provided in this SGWP.
❏ **Business Connections**	Complete the Business Connections activities as assigned to gain a deeper understanding of Chapter 12 concepts.

Practice Tests

Complete the Practice Tests, which cover the main points in your reading assignment. Compare your answers with those in the Practice Test Answer Key for Chapter 12 at the end of this chapter. If you have answered any questions incorrectly, review the related section of the text.

Part A True-False *For each of the following statements, circle T in the answer column if the statement is true or F if the statement is false.*

T F **1.** It is not necessary to adjust the accounts when preparing monthly or quarterly statements.

T F **2.** A prepaid expense incorrectly charged to expense in an accounting period results in an understatement of net income in that period and an overstatement of net income in the following period.

T F **3.** In preparing financial statements, it is unnecessary to make adjustments for relatively small items because they are immaterial and will not affect the statements.

T F **4.** Accrued income has been earned but not recorded, while deferred income has been recorded but not earned.

T F **5.** The entry to record accrued interest on notes payable is a credit to **Interest Payable** and a debit to **Interest Expense.**

T F **6. Interest Receivable** is usually classified as a revenue account.

T F **7.** In most cases, **Prepaid Interest Expense** will be classified as a current liability on the balance sheet.

T F **8.** The **Interest Expense** account must be adjusted if an interest-bearing note payable is outstanding at the end of the fiscal period and interest has not been paid on that date.

T F **9.** Under the accrual basis of accounting, purchases are recorded when the title to the goods passes to the buyer.

T F **10.** In the "adjustments" column of the worksheet, the **Merchandise Inventory** is debited for the amount of ending inventory and credited for the amount of beginning inventory.

T F **11.** The **Unearned Subscriptions Income** account will appear in the Assets section of the balance sheet.

T F **12.** The trial balance figures for accumulated depreciation accounts do not contain the depreciation for the current period.

T F **13.** At the end of an accounting period, an adjustment is needed to record as an expense any part of the balance in an asset account that has been used up or has expired.

T F **14.** On the trial balance, the **Store Supplies** account shows a debit balance of $300. A physical count showed supplies on hand of $80. The adjusting entry includes a debit of $80 to the **Store Supplies Expense** account.

T F **15.** An adjustment for depreciation results in an entry debiting the **Depreciation Expense** account and crediting the **Accumulated Depreciation** account.

T F **16.** Office or store supplies that have been paid for in cash do not need any adjusting entries.

T F **17.** The net income for the business is entered as a debit entry in the Balance Sheet section and as a credit entry in the Income Statement section of the worksheet.

T F **18.** The accountant completes the worksheet and prepares the financial statements as soon as all adjustments have been entered on the worksheet.

T F **19.** The Adjusted Trial Balance column of the worksheet tests only the arithmetic accuracy of the worksheet to that point in the worksheet and statement preparation process.

T F **20.** After the amounts shown in the Adjusted Trial Balance section have been extended the difference between the total debits and total credits in the balance sheet section represents the net income or loss for the period.

T F **21.** Adjusting entries are recorded in the general journal after the worksheet and the financial statements are completed.

T F **22.** The beginning merchandise inventory does not appear in the Adjusted Trial Balance.

T F **23.** The **Drawing** account balance is extended to the Debit column in the Income Statement section.

T F **24.** The statement of owner's equity should be prepared before the income statement is prepared.

T F **25.** The financial statements are prepared directly from the worksheet.

Part B Exercise *In each of the following independent cases give the general journal entry to adjust the accounts for the year on December 31, 2007. Omit the descriptions.*

1. Store supplies costing $1,250 were purchased during the year and were charged to the **Store Supplies** account. At the end of the year, supplies costing $250 were on hand.

GENERAL JOURNAL   PAGE _____

	DATE	DESCRIPTION	POST. REF.	DEBIT	CREDIT	
1						1
2						2

2. On December 1, 2007 the company gave a $4,000 note payable to a supplier. The note bears interest at 6 percent.

GENERAL JOURNAL   PAGE _____

	DATE	DESCRIPTION	POST. REF.	DEBIT	CREDIT	
1						1
2						2

3. On November 1, 2004, the company received a four-month, 12 percent note for $1,500 from settlement of an overdue account. No interest has been recorded on the note.

GENERAL JOURNAL   PAGE _____

	DATE	DESCRIPTION	POST. REF.	DEBIT	CREDIT	
1						1
2						2

4. On October 1, 2007, the company purchased a one-year insurance policy for $1,520. The amount was charged to **Prepaid Insurance.**

GENERAL JOURNAL   PAGE _____

	DATE	DESCRIPTION	POST. REF.	DEBIT	CREDIT	
1						1
2						2

Demonstration Problem

The trial balance for Peggy's Imports on December 31, 2007, the end of its accounting period, is shown on the worksheet.

Instructions

1. Complete the worksheet for the year, using the following information:
   a-b. Ending merchandise inventory, $107,170.
   c. Uncollectible accounts expense, $750.
   d. Supplies on hand December 31, 2007, $680.
   e. Depreciation on store equipment, $8,030.
   f. Depreciation on office equipment, $2,950.
   g. Accrued sales salaries, $4,000; accrued office salaries, $750.
   h. Tax on accrued salaries: social security, $294.50; Medicare, $68.88.

2. Journalize the adjusting entries on page 15 of the general journal.

SOLUTION

Peggy's Imports

Worksheet

December 31, 2007

#	ACCOUNT NAME	TRIAL BALANCE DEBIT	TRIAL BALANCE CREDIT	ADJUSTMENTS DEBIT	ADJUSTMENTS CREDIT
1	Cash	9 8 1 0 00			
2	Accounts Receivable	32 3 4 0 00			
3	Allowance for Doubtful Accounts		5 0 6 0 00		(c) 7 5 0 00
4	Merchandise Inventory	116 7 8 0 00		(b)107 1 7 0 00	(a)116 7 8 0 00
5	Supplies	10 6 0 0 00			(d) 9 9 2 0 00
6	Store Equipment	84 0 0 0 00			
7	Accumulated Depreciation—Store Equip.		16 5 9 0 00		(e) 8 0 3 0 00
8	Office Equipment	25 7 0 0 00			
9	Accumulated Depreciation—Office Equip.		7 0 3 3 00		(f) 2 9 5 0 00
10	Accounts Payable		22 5 6 0 00		
11	Salaries Payable				(g) 4 7 5 0 00
12	Social Security Tax Payable				(h) 2 9 4 50
13	Medicare Tax Payable				(h) 6 8 88
14	Peggy Culey, Capital		230 7 6 4 00		
15	Peggy Culey, Drawing	26 0 0 0 00			
16	Income Summary			(a)116 7 8 0 00	(b)107 1 7 0 00
17	Sales		394 6 4 2 00		
18	Sales Returns and Allowances	8 1 5 5 00			
19	Purchases	197 5 3 4 00			
20	Purchase Returns and Allowances		1 2 0 0 00		
21	Purchase Discounts		6 0 0 00		
22	Freight In	12 2 6 0 00			
23	Sales Salaries Expense	94 5 8 0 00		(g) 4 0 0 0 00	
24	Rent Expense	31 0 0 0 00			
25	Advertising Expense	12 0 4 5 00			
26	Supplies Expense			(d) 9 9 2 0 00	
27	Depreciation Expense—Store Equipment			(e) 8 0 3 0 00	
28	Office Salaries Expense	17 6 4 5 00		(g) 7 5 0 00	
29	Payroll Taxes Expense			(h) 3 6 3 38	
30	Depreciation Expense—Office Equipment			(f) 2 9 5 0 00	
31	Uncollectible Accounts Expense			(c) 7 5 0 00	
32		678 4 4 9 00	678 4 4 9 00	250 7 1 3 38	250 7 1 3 38
33	Net Loss				
34					
35					

#	ADJUSTED TRIAL BALANCE DEBIT	ADJUSTED TRIAL BALANCE CREDIT	INCOME STATEMENT DEBIT	INCOME STATEMENT CREDIT	BALANCE SHEET DEBIT	BALANCE SHEET CREDIT
1	9 8 1 0 00				9 8 1 0 00	
2	32 3 4 0 00				32 3 4 0 00	
3		5 8 1 0 00				5 8 1 0 00
4	107 1 7 0 00				107 1 7 0 00	
5	6 8 0 00				6 8 0 00	
6	84 0 0 0 00				84 0 0 0 00	
7		24 6 2 0 00				24 6 2 0 00
8	25 7 0 0 00				25 7 0 0 00	
9		9 9 8 3 00				9 9 8 3 00
10		22 5 6 0 00				22 5 6 0 00
11		4 7 5 0 00				4 7 5 0 00
12		2 9 4 50				2 9 4 50
13		6 8 88				6 8 88
14		230 7 6 4 00				230 7 6 4 00
15	26 0 0 0 00				26 0 0 0 00	
16	116 7 8 0 00	107 1 7 0 00	116 7 8 0 00	107 1 7 0 00		
17		394 6 4 2 00		394 6 4 2 00		
18	8 1 5 5 00		8 1 5 5 00			
19	197 5 3 4 00		197 5 3 4 00			
20		1 2 0 0 00		1 2 0 0 00		
21		6 0 0 00		6 0 0 00		
22	12 2 6 0 00		12 2 6 0 00			
23	98 5 8 0 00		98 5 8 0 00			
24	31 0 0 0 00		31 0 0 0 00			
25	12 0 4 5 00		12 0 4 5 00			
26	9 9 2 0 00		9 9 2 0 00			
27	8 0 3 0 00		8 0 3 0 00			
28	18 3 9 5 00		18 3 9 5 00			
29	3 6 3 38		3 6 3 38			
30	2 9 5 0 00		2 9 5 0 00			
31	7 5 0 00		7 5 0 00			
32	802 4 6 2 38	802 4 6 2 38	516 7 6 2 38	503 6 1 2 00	285 7 0 0 00	298 8 5 0 38
33				13 1 5 0 38	13 1 5 0 38	
34			516 7 6 2 38	516 7 6 2 38	298 8 5 0 38	298 8 5 0 38
35						

SOLUTION (continued)

GENERAL JOURNAL

PAGE ___15___

	DATE		DESCRIPTION	POST. REF.	DEBIT	CREDIT	
1	2007						1
2			(a)				2
3	Dec.	31	Income Summary		116 7 8 0 00		3
4			Merchandise Inventory			116 7 8 0 00	4
5			Close beginning merchandise inventory				5
6			(b)				6
7		31	Merchandise Inventory		107 1 7 0 00		7
8			Income Summary			107 1 7 0 00	8
9			Record ending merchandise inventory				9
10			(c)				10
11		31	Uncollectible Accounts Expense		7 5 0 00		11
12			Allowance for Doubtful Accounts			7 5 0 00	12
13			Record estimated uncollectible accounts expense				13
14			(d)				14
15		31	Supplies Expense		9 9 2 0 00		15
16			Supplies			9 9 2 0 00	16
17			Record supplies used during year				17
18			(e)				18
19		31	Depreciation Expense—Store Equipment		8 0 3 0 00		19
20			Accumulated Depreciation—Store Equipment			8 0 3 0 00	20
21			Record depreciation on store equipment for year				21
22			(f)				22
23		31	Depreciation Expense—Office Equipment		2 9 5 0 00		23
24			Accumulated Depreciation—Office Equipment			2 9 5 0 00	24
25			Record depreciation on office equipment for year				25
26			(g)				26
27		31	Sales Salaries Expense		4 0 0 0 00		27
28			Office Salaries Expense		7 5 0 00		28
29			Salaries Payable			4 7 5 0 00	29
30			Record accrued salaries				30
31			(h)				31
32		31	Payroll Taxes Expense		3 6 3 38		32
33			Social Security Tax Payable			2 9 4 50	33
34			Medicare Tax Payable			6 8 88	34
35			Record accrued payroll taxes				35
36							36

WORKING PAPERS

Name _____

EXERCISE 12.1

GENERAL JOURNAL   PAGE _____

	DATE	DESCRIPTION	POST. REF.	DEBIT	CREDIT	
1						1
2						2
3						3
4						4
5						5
6						6
7						7

EXERCISE 12.2

_____

_____

_____

EXERCISE 12.3

GENERAL JOURNAL   PAGE _____

	DATE	DESCRIPTION	POST. REF.	DEBIT	CREDIT	
1						1
2						2
3						3
4						4
5						5
6						6
7						7
8						8
9						9
10						10
11						11
12						12
13						13
14						14
15						15
16						16
17						17
18						18

EXERCISE 12.4

GENERAL JOURNAL

PAGE _____

	DATE		DESCRIPTION	POST. REF.	DEBIT	CREDIT	
1							1
2							2
3							3
4							4
5							5
6							6
7							7
8							8
9							9
10							10
11							11
12							12
13							13

EXERCISE 12.5

GENERAL JOURNAL

PAGE _____

	DATE		DESCRIPTION	POST. REF.	DEBIT	CREDIT	
1							1
2							2
3							3
4							4
5							5
6							6
7							7
8							8

EXERCISE 12.6

GENERAL JOURNAL

PAGE _____

	DATE		DESCRIPTION	POST. REF.	DEBIT	CREDIT	
1							1
2							2
3							3
4							4

EXERCISE 12.7

GENERAL JOURNAL   PAGE _____

	DATE	DESCRIPTION	POST. REF.	DEBIT	CREDIT	
1						1
2						2
3						3
4						4
5						5
6						6
7						7
8						8
9						9
10						10
11						11
12						12
13						13

PROBLEM 12.1A or 12.1B

GENERAL JOURNAL   PAGE ___1___

	DATE		DESCRIPTION	POST. REF.	DEBIT	CREDIT	
1							1
2							2
3							3
4							4
5							5
6							6
7							7
8							8
9							9
10							10
11							11
12							12
13							13
14							14
15							15
16							16
17							17
18							18
19							19
20							20
21							21
22							22
23							23
24							24
25							25
26							26
27							27
28							28
29							29
30							30
31							31
32							32
33							33
34							34
35							35
36							36
37							37

PROBLEM 12.1A or 12.1B (continued)

GENERAL JOURNAL   PAGE _____2_____

	DATE		DESCRIPTION	POST. REF.	DEBIT	CREDIT	
1							1
2							2
3							3
4							4
5							5
6							6
7							7
8							8
9							9
10							10
11							11
12							12
13							13
14							14
15							15
16							16
17							17
18							18
19							19
20							20
21							21
22							22
23							23
24							24
25							25
26							26
27							27
28							28
29							29
30							30
31							31
32							32
33							33
34							34

Analyze: _____
_____

PROBLEM 12.2A or 12.2B

_____
_____

	ACCOUNT NAME	TRIAL BALANCE		ADJUSTMENTS	
		DEBIT	CREDIT	DEBIT	CREDIT
1					
2					
3					
4					
5					
6					
7					
8					
9					
10					
11					
12					
13					
14					
15					
16					
17					
18					
19					
20					
21					
22					
23					
24					
25					
26					
27					
28					
29					
30					
31					
32					

PROBLEM 12.2A or 12.2B (continued)

_____

_____

ADJUSTED TRIAL BALANCE		INCOME STATEMENT		BALANCE SHEET		
DEBIT	CREDIT	DEBIT	CREDIT	DEBIT	CREDIT	
						1
						2
						3
						4
						5
						6
						7
						8
						9
						10
						11
						12
						13
						14
						15
						16
						17
						18
						19
						20
						21
						22
						23
						24
						25
						26
						27
						28
						29
						30
						31
						32

Analyze: _____

_____

PROBLEM 12.3A or 12.3B

_____

_____

	ACCOUNT NAME	TRIAL BALANCE		ADJUSTMENTS	
		DEBIT	CREDIT	DEBIT	CREDIT
1					
2					
3					
4					
5					
6					
7					
8					
9					
10					
11					
12					
13					
14					
15					
16					
17					
18					
19					
20					
21					
22					
23					
24					
25					
26					
27					
28					
29					
30					
31					
32					
33					
34					

PROBLEM 12.3A or 12.3B (continued)

	ADJUSTED TRIAL BALANCE		INCOME STATEMENT		BALANCE SHEET		
	DEBIT	CREDIT	DEBIT	CREDIT	DEBIT	CREDIT	
							1
							2
							3
							4
							5
							6
							7
							8
							9
							10
							11
							12
							13
							14
							15
							16
							17
							18
							19
							20
							21
							22
							23
							24
							25
							26
							27
							28
							29
							30
							31
							32
							33
							34

PROBLEM 12.3A or 12.3B (continued)

	ACCOUNT NAME	TRIAL BALANCE		ADJUSTMENTS	
		DEBIT	CREDIT	DEBIT	CREDIT
1					
2					
3					
4					
5					
6					
7					
8					
9					
10					
11					
12					
13					
14					
15					
16					
17					
18					
19					
20					
21					
22					
23					
24					
25					
26					
27					
28					
29					
30					
31					
32					

PROBLEM 12.3A or 12.3B (continued)

_____
_____

	ADJUSTED TRIAL BALANCE		INCOME STATEMENT		BALANCE SHEET		
	DEBIT	CREDIT	DEBIT	CREDIT	DEBIT	CREDIT	
							1
							2
							3
							4
							5
							6
							7
							8
							9
							10
							11
							12
							13
							14
							15
							16
							17
							18
							19
							20
							21
							22
							23
							24
							25
							26
							27
							28
							29
							30
							31
							32

Analyze: _____
_____

PROBLEM 12.4A or 12.4B

_____

	ACCOUNT NAME	TRIAL BALANCE		ADJUSTMENTS	
		DEBIT	CREDIT	DEBIT	CREDIT
1					
2					
3					
4					
5					
6					
7					
8					
9					
10					
11					
12					
13					
14					
15					
16					
17					
18					
19					
20					
21					
22					
23					
24					
25					
26					
27					
28					
29					
30					
31					
32					
33					
34					

PROBLEM 12.4A or 12.4B (continued)

	ADJUSTED TRIAL BALANCE		INCOME STATEMENT		BALANCE SHEET		
	DEBIT	CREDIT	DEBIT	CREDIT	DEBIT	CREDIT	
							1
							2
							3
							4
							5
							6
							7
							8
							9
							10
							11
							12
							13
							14
							15
							16
							17
							18
							19
							20
							21
							22
							23
							24
							25
							26
							27
							28
							29
							30
							31
							32
							33
							34

PROBLEM 12.4A or 12.4B (continued)

	ACCOUNT NAME	TRIAL BALANCE		ADJUSTMENTS	
		DEBIT	CREDIT	DEBIT	CREDIT
1					
2					
3					
4					
5					
6					
7					
8					
9					
10					
11					
12					
13					
14					
15					
16					
17					
18					
19					
20					
21					
22					
23					
24					
25					
26					
27					
28					
29					
30					
31					
32					

PROBLEM 12.4A or 12.4B (continued)

_____

_____

	ADJUSTED TRIAL BALANCE		INCOME STATEMENT		BALANCE SHEET		
	DEBIT	CREDIT	DEBIT	CREDIT	DEBIT	CREDIT	
							1
							2
							3
							4
							5
							6
							7
							8
							9
							10
							11
							12
							13
							14
							15
							16
							17
							18
							19
							20
							21
							22
							23
							24
							25
							26
							27
							28
							29
							30
							31
							32

Analyze: _____

_____

Name _____

CHAPTER 12 CHALLENGE PROBLEM

	ACCOUNT NAME	TRIAL BALANCE		ADJUSTMENTS	
		DEBIT	CREDIT	DEBIT	CREDIT
1					
2					
3					
4					
5					
6					
7					
8					
9					
10					
11					
12					
13					
14					
15					
16					
17					
18					
19					
20					
21					
22					
23					
24					
25					
26					
27					
28					
29					
30					
31					
32					
33					

CHAPTER 12 CHALLENGE PROBLEM (continued)

	ADJUSTED TRIAL BALANCE		INCOME STATEMENT		BALANCE SHEET		
	DEBIT	CREDIT	DEBIT	CREDIT	DEBIT	CREDIT	
							1
							2
							3
							4
							5
							6
							7
							8
							9
							10
							11
							12
							13
							14
							15
							16
							17
							18
							19
							20
							21
							22
							23
							24
							25
							26
							27
							28
							29
							30
							31
							32
							33

CHAPTER 12 CHALLENGE PROBLEM (continued)

	ACCOUNT NAME	TRIAL BALANCE		ADJUSTMENTS	
		DEBIT	CREDIT	DEBIT	CREDIT
1					
2					
3					
4					
5					
6					
7					
8					
9					
10					
11					
12					
13					
14					
15					
16					
17					
18					
19					
20					
21					
22					
23					
24					
25					
26					
27					
28					
29					
30					
31					
32					

Name _____

CHAPTER 12 CHALLENGE PROBLEM (continued)

	ADJUSTED TRIAL BALANCE		INCOME STATEMENT		BALANCE SHEET		
	DEBIT	CREDIT	DEBIT	CREDIT	DEBIT	CREDIT	
							1
							2
							3
							4
							5
							6
							7
							8
							9
							10
							11
							12
							13
							14
							15
							16
							17
							18
							19
							20
							21
							22
							23
							24
							25
							26
							27
							28
							29
							30
							31
							32

CHAPTER 12 CHALLENGE PROBLEM (continued)

GENERAL JOURNAL   PAGE ___30___

	DATE	DESCRIPTION	POST. REF.	DEBIT	CREDIT	
1						1
2						2
3						3
4						4
5						5
6						6
7						7
8						8
9						9
10						10
11						11
12						12
13						13
14						14
15						15
16						16
17						17
18						18
19						19
20						20
21						21
22						22
23						23
24						24
25						25
26						26
27						27
28						28
29						29
30						30
31						31
32						32
33						33
34						34
35						35
36						36
37						37

CHAPTER 12 CHALLENGE PROBLEM (continued)

GENERAL JOURNAL

	DATE	DESCRIPTION	POST. REF.	DEBIT	CREDIT	
1						1
2						2
3						3
4						4
5						5
6						6
7						7
8						8
9						9
10						10
11						11
12						12
13						13
14						14
15						15
16						16
17						17
18						18
19						19
20						20
21						21
22						22
23						23
24						24
25						25
26						26
27						27
28						28
29						29
30						30
31						31
32						32
33						33
34						34
35						35
36						36
37						37

CHAPTER 12 CHALLENGE PROBLEM (continued)

a. Net Sales _____

_____

_____

b. Net Delivered
Cost of Purchases _____

_____

_____

_____

_____

_____

c. Cost of Goods Sold _____

_____

_____

_____

_____

d. Net Income _____

e. Capital _____

_____

_____

_____

_____

Analyze: _____

CHAPTER 12 CRITICAL THINKING PROBLEM

1. _____
_____
_____
_____

2. _____
_____
_____
_____
_____
_____
_____
_____
_____
_____
_____
_____
_____
_____
_____
_____
_____
_____
_____

Chapter 12 Practice Test Answer Key

Part A True-False

1.	F	14.	F
2.	T	15.	T
3.	F	16.	F
4.	T	17.	F
5.	T	18.	T
6.	F	19.	T
7.	F	20.	T
8.	T	21.	T
9.	T	22.	T
10.	T	23.	F
11.	F	24.	F
12.	T	25.	T
13.	T		

Part B Exercises

2007	(Adjustment 1)		
Dec. 31	Supplies Expense	1,000.00	
	Store Supplies		1,000.00
	(Adjustment 2)		
31	Interest Expense	20.00	
	Interest Payable		20.00
	(Adjustment 3)		
31	Interest Receivable	30.00	
	Interest Income		30.00
	(Adjustment 4)		
31	Insurance Expense	380.00	
	Prepaid Insurance		380.00

STUDY GUIDE

Understanding the Chapter

Objectives

1. Prepare a classified income statement from the worksheet. **2.** Prepare a statement of owner's equity from the worksheet. **3.** Prepare a classified balance sheet from the worksheet. **4.** Journalize and post the adjusting entries. **5.** Journalize and post the closing entries. **6.** Prepare a postclosing trial balance. **7.** Journalize and post reversing entries. **8.** Define the accounting terms new to this chapter.

Reading Assignment

Read Chapter 13 in the textbook. Complete the textbook Section Self Review as you finish reading each section of the chapter, and the Comprehensive Self Review at the end of the chapter. Refer to the Chapter 13 Glossary or to the Glossary at the end of the book to find definitions for terms that are not familiar to you.

Activities

❏ **Thinking Critically**

Answer the *Thinking Critically* questions for Safeway Inc., Computers in Accounting, and Managerial Implications.

❏ **Internet Applications**

Complete the activity for Computers in Accounting.

❏ **Discussion Questions**

Answer each assigned discussion question in Chapter 13.

❏ **Exercises**

Complete each assigned exercise in Chapter 13. Use the forms provided in this SGWP. The objectives covered by an exercise are given after the exercise number. If you need help with an exercise, review the portion of the chapter related to the objective(s) covered.

❏ **Problems A/B**

Complete each assigned problem in Chapter 13. Use the forms provided in this SGWP. The objectives covered by a problem are given after the problem number. If you need help with a problem review the portion of the chapter related to the objective(s) covered.

❏ **Challenge Problem**

Complete the challenge problem as assigned. Use the forms provided in this SGWP.

❏ **Critical Thinking Problem**

Complete the critical thinking problem as assigned. Use the forms provided in this SGWP.

❏ **Business Connections**

Complete the Business Connections activities as assigned to gain a deeper understanding of Chapter 13 concepts.

Practice Tests

Complete the Practice Tests, which cover the main points in your reading assignment. Compare your answers with those in the Practice Test Answer Key for Chapter 13 at the end of this chapter. If you have answered any questions incorrectly, review the related section of text.

Part A True-False

True-False For each of the following statements, circle T in the answer column if the statement is true or F if the statement is false.

T F **1.** Short-term notes receivable, cash, accounts receivable, merchandise inventory and prepaid expense items appear in the Current Assets section of the classified balance sheet.

T F **2.** The gross profit on sales shown on the classified income statement is the difference between the net sales and the operating expenses.

T F **3.** Current liabilities are debts that are due for payment within one year from the balance sheet date.

T F **4.** The Cost of Goods Sold section of the classified income statement includes information about the beginning and ending merchandise inventory and the purchases and net sales made during the year.

T F **5.** The net income or loss from operations shown on the classified income statement is the difference between gross profit on sales and total operating expenses.

T F **6.** The depreciation expense for the store equipment appears in the Plant and Equipment section of the classified balance sheet.

T F **7.** Adjustments are posted from the worksheet to the general ledger accounts.

T F **8.** The ending merchandise inventory is recorded in the accounting records by an adjusting entry.

T F **9. Income Summary** is credited for the total of the expenses and the beginning inventory.

T F **10.** Closing journal entries for December 31, 2007 should be reversed on January 1, 2008.

T F **11.** The drawing account is closed into the **Income Summary** account as one of the last closing entries.

T F **12.** After completing the worksheet and the financial statements, adjustments are entered in the general journal.

T F **13.** After all adjustments have been journalized and posted, the ledger account balances should be the same as the post-closing trial balance amounts on the worksheet.

T F **14.** The revenue and expense accounts are the only accounts carried forward from one year to the next.

T F **15.** The information needed to close the revenue and expense accounts is taken directly from the ledger accounts to ensure accuracy.

T F **16.** Asset and liability accounts are the only accounts carried forward from one year to the next.

T F **17.** The **Income Summary** account is closed at the end of the period.

T F **18.** It is desirable to prepare a postclosing trial balance before the adjusting and closing entries have been journalized and posted.

T F **19.** The postclosing trial balance shows essentially the same account balances that appear in the balance sheet.

| T | F | **20.** | In closing the **Income Summary** account, the net income or loss is closed into the owner's capital account. |

| T | F | **21.** | Reversing entries are not required, but are highly recommended in order to improve efficiency and reduce errors. |

| T | F | **22.** | The information found in the Statement of Owner's Equity may be shown in the balance sheet instead of on a separate statement. |

| T | F | **23.** | Some accounts adjusted in the Adjustment columns of the worksheet do not require a reversing entry. |

| T | F | **24.** | **Accrued Interest on Notes Payable** and **Depreciation Expense** are typical of accounts that do not require reversing entries. |

| T | F | **25.** | If an adjusting entry opens a new asset or liability account, the entry will probably be reversed. |

Demonstration Problem

A partial worksheet showing the end-of-year operating results for Super Sports for 2007 follows.

Instructions

1. Prepare a classified income statement. Super Sports does not classify its operating expenses as selling and administrative expenses.

2. Prepare a statement of owner's equity. No additional investments were made during the period.

3. Prepare a classified balance sheet as of December 31, 2007. All notes payable are due within one year.

4. Journalize the closing entries on page 45 of the general journal.

DEMONSTRATION PROBLEM (continued)

Super Sports

Worksheet (Partial)

Year Ended December 31, 2007

	ACCOUNT NAME	INCOME STATEMENT DEBIT	INCOME STATEMENT CREDIT	BALANCE SHEET DEBIT	BALANCE SHEET CREDIT
1	Cash			17 2 8 5 00	
2	Accounts Receivable			56 2 5 8 00	
3	Allowance for Doubtful Accounts				5 8 4 0 00
4	Merchandise Inventory			197 2 1 4 00	
5	Supplies			3 6 1 2 00	
6	Prepaid Insurance			37 0 0 0 00	
7	Equipment			83 2 9 0 00	
8	Accumulated Depreciation—Equipment				24 3 3 0 00
9	Notes Payable				47 5 0 0 00
10	Accounts Payable				42 8 6 0 00
11	Social Security Tax Payable				2 6 8 3 00
12	Medicare Tax Payable				8 4 5 00
13	Salaries Payable				6 5 3 0 00
14	Interest Payable				3 6 6 0 00
15	Nau Flores, Capital				260 7 3 0 00
16	Nau Flores, Drawing			50 0 0 0 00	
17	Income Summary	201 3 4 5 00	197 2 1 4 00		
18	Sales		610 6 9 0 00		
19	Sales Returns and Allowances	11 9 5 0 00			
20	Purchases	277 1 7 4 00			
21	Purchases Returns and Allowances		10 4 4 0 00		
22	Freight In	11 4 1 0 00			
23	Purchases Discounts		11 9 2 1 00		
24	Telephone Expense	3 1 7 1 00			
25	Salaries Expense	240 3 8 0 00			
26	Payroll Tax Expense	13 1 0 4 00			
27	Supplies Expense	5 9 6 0 00			
28	Insurance Expense	4 0 0 0 00			
29	Depreciation Expense—Equipment	7 4 2 0 00			
30	Uncollectible Accounts Expense	2 5 1 0 00			
31	Interest Expense	2 1 6 0 00			
32	Totals	780 5 8 4 00	830 2 6 5 00	444 6 5 9 00	394 9 7 8 00
33	Net Income	49 6 8 1 00			49 6 8 1 00
34		830 2 6 5 00	830 2 6 5 00	444 6 5 9 00	444 6 5 9 00
35					

SOLUTION

Super Sports

Income Statement

Year Ended December 31, 2007

Operating Revenue					
Sales					610 6 9 0 00
Less Sales Returns and Allowances					11 9 5 0 00
Net Sales					598 7 4 0 00
Cost of Goods Sold					
Merchandise Inventory, Jan. 1, 2007				201 3 4 5 00	
Purchases		277 1 7 4 00			
Freight In		11 4 1 0 00			
Delivered Cost of Purchases		288 5 8 4 00			
Less Purchase Returns and Allow.	10 4 4 0 00				
Purchase Discounts	11 9 2 1 00	22 3 6 1 00			
Net Delivered Cost of Purchases				266 2 2 3 00	
Total Merchandise Available for Sale				467 5 6 8 00	
Less Merchandise Inv., Dec. 31, 2007				197 2 1 4 00	
Cost of Goods Sold					270 3 5 4 00
Gross Profit on Sales					328 3 8 6 00
Operating Expenses					
Telephone Expense				3 1 7 1 00	
Salaries Expense				240 3 8 0 00	
Payroll Tax Expense				13 1 0 4 00	
Supplies Expense				5 9 6 0 00	
Insurance Expense				4 0 0 0 00	
Depreciation Expense—Equipment				7 4 2 0 00	
Uncollectible Accounts Expense				2 5 1 0 00	
Total Operating Expenses					276 5 4 5 00
Income from Operations					51 8 4 1 00
Other Expenses					
Interest Expense					2 1 6 0 00
Net Income for Year					49 6 8 1 00

SOLUTION (continued)

Super Sports

Statement of Owner's Equity

Year Ended December 31, 2007

Nau Flores, Capital, Jan. 1, 2007				260 7 3 0 00
Net Income for Year		49 6 8 1 00		
Less Withdrawals for the Year		50 0 0 0 00		
Increase in Capital				− 3 1 9 00
Nau Flores, Capital, Dec. 31, 2007				260 4 1 1 00

Super Sports

Balance Sheet

December 31, 2007

Assets				
Current Assets				
Cash				17 2 8 5 00
Accounts Receivable		56 2 5 8 00		
Less Allowance for Doubtful Accounts		5 8 4 0 00		50 4 1 8 00
Merchandise Inventory				197 2 1 4 00
Prepaid Expenses				
Supplies		3 6 1 2 00		
Prepaid Insurance		37 0 0 0 00		40 6 1 2 00
Total Current Assets				305 5 2 9 00
Plant and Equipment				
Equipment	83 2 9 0 00			
Less Accumulated Depreciation	24 3 3 0 00	58 9 6 0 00		
Total Plant and Equipment				58 9 6 0 00
Total Assets				364 4 8 9 00
Liabilities and Owner's Equity				
Current Liabilities				
Notes Payable		47 5 0 0 00		
Accounts Payable		42 8 6 0 00		
Interest Payable		3 6 6 0 00		
Social Security Tax Payable		2 6 8 3 00		
Medicare Tax Payable		8 4 5 00		
Salaries Payable		6 5 3 0 00		
Total Current Liabilities				104 0 7 8 00
Owner's Equity				
Nau Flores, Capital				260 4 1 1 00
Total Liabilities and Owner's Equity				364 4 8 9 00

SOLUTION (continued)

GENERAL JOURNAL PAGE 45

	DATE		DESCRIPTION	POST. REF.	DEBIT	CREDIT	
1			**Closing Entries**				1
2	2007						2
3	Dec.	31	Sales		610 6 9 0 00		3
4			Purchase Returns and Allowances		10 4 4 0 00		4
5			Purchases Discounts		11 9 2 1 00		5
6			Income Summary			633 0 5 1 00	6
7							7
8		31	Income Summary		579 2 3 9 00		8
9			Sales Returns and Allowances			11 9 5 0 00	9
10			Purchases			277 1 7 4 00	10
11			Freight In			11 4 1 0 00	11
12			Telephone Expense			3 1 7 1 00	12
13			Salaries Expense			240 3 8 0 00	13
14			Payroll Taxes Expense			13 1 0 4 00	14
15			Supplies Expense			5 9 6 0 00	15
16			Insurance Expense			4 0 0 0 00	16
17			Depreciation Expense—Equipment			7 4 2 0 00	17
18			Uncollectible Accounts Expense			2 5 1 0 00	18
19			Interest Expense			2 1 6 0 00	19
20							20
21		31	Income Summary		49 6 8 1 00		21
22			Nau Flores, Capital			49 6 8 1 00	22
23							23
24		31	Nau Flores, Capital		50 0 0 0 00		24
25			Nau Flores, Drawing			50 0 0 0 00	25
26							26
27							27
28							28
29							29
30							30
31							31
32							32
33							33
34							34
35							35
36							36

WORKING PAPERS

EXERCISE 13.1

1. Rent Expense _____

2. Depreciation Expense—
   Store Equipment _____

3. Sales _____

4. Interest Expense _____

5. Merchandise Inventory _____

6. Interest Income _____

7. Purchases _____

8. Sales Returns and Allowances _____

9. Utilities Expense _____

10. Purchase Returns
    and Allowances _____

EXERCISE 13.2

1. Rent Payable _____

2. Cash _____

3. Raja Julia, Capital _____

4. Merchandise Inventory _____

5. Accounts Payable _____

6. Store Supplies _____

7. Sales Tax Payable _____

8. Prepaid Insurance _____

9. Delivery Van _____

10. Accounts Receivable _____

EXERCISE 13.3

(continued)

EXERCISE 13.3 (continued)

EXERCISE 13.4

EXERCISE 13.5

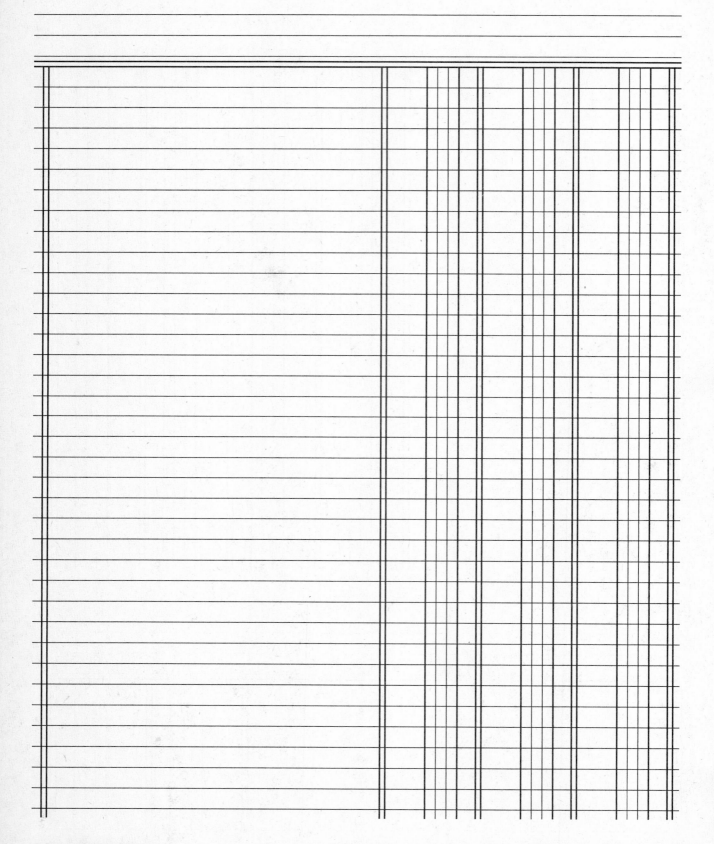

EXERCISE 13.6

GENERAL JOURNAL

PAGE _____

	DATE	DESCRIPTION	POST. REF.	DEBIT	CREDIT	
1						1
2						2
3						3
4						4
5						5
6						6
7						7
8						8
9						9
10						10
11						11
12						12
13						13
14						14
15						15
16						16
17						17
18						18
19						19
20						20
21						21
22						22
23						23
24						24
25						25
26						26
27						27
28						28
29						29
30						30
31						31
32						32
33						33
34						34
35						35
36						36
37						37

EXERCISE 13.7

GENERAL JOURNAL   PAGE ___1___

	DATE	DESCRIPTION	POST. REF.	DEBIT	CREDIT	
1						1
2						2
3						3
4						4
5						5
6						6
7						7
8						8
9						9
10						10
11						11
12						12
13						13
14						14
15						15
16						16
17						17
18						18
19						19
20						20
21						21
22						22
23						23
24						24
25						25
26						26
27						27
28						28
29						29
30						30
31						31
32						32
33						33
34						34
35						35
36						36
37						37

EXERCISE 13.8

ACCOUNT NAME	DEBIT	CREDIT

PROBLEM 13.1A or 13.1B

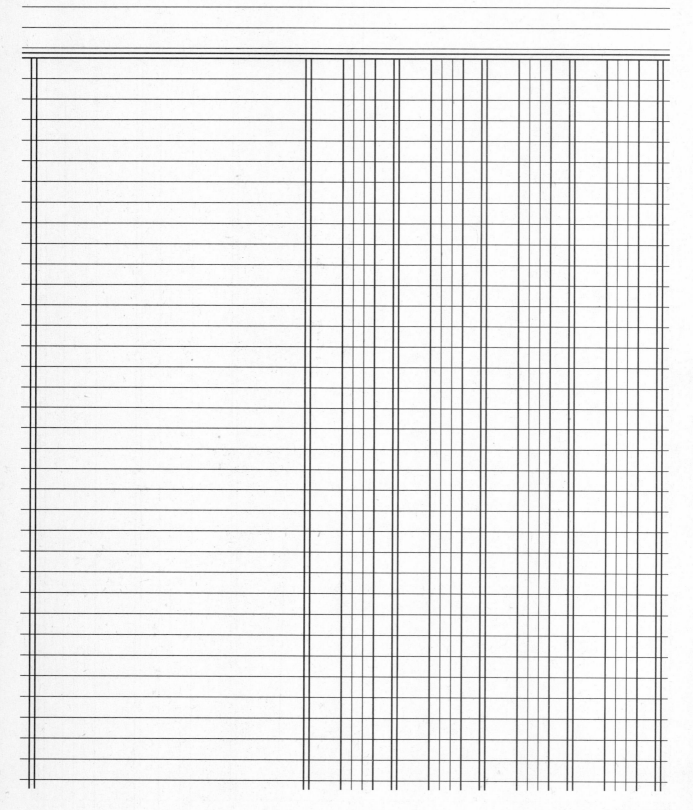

(continued)

PROBLEM 13.1A or 13.1B (continued)

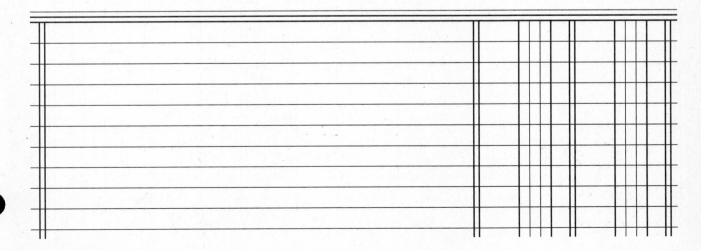

PROBLEM 13.1A or 13.1B (continued)

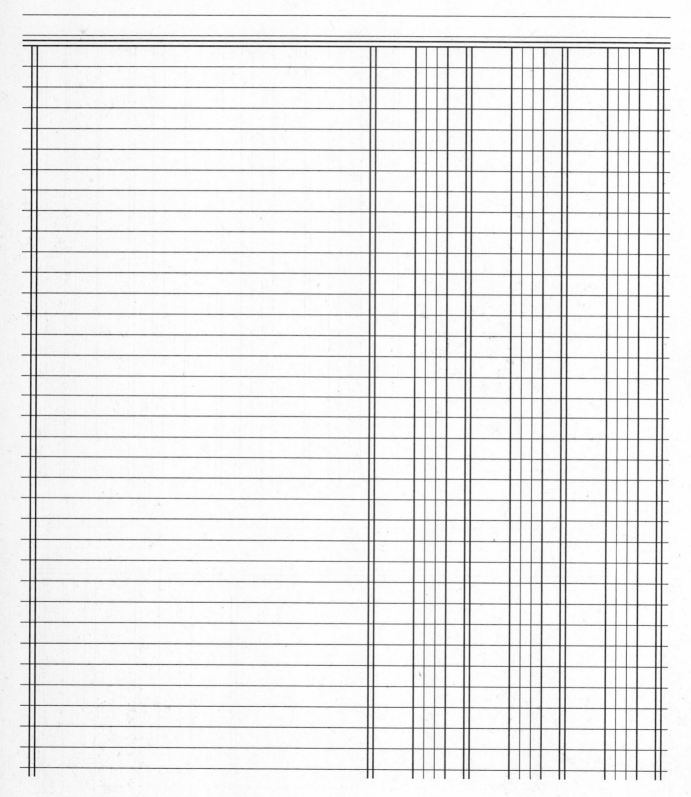

(continued)

PROBLEM 13.1A or 13.1B (continued)

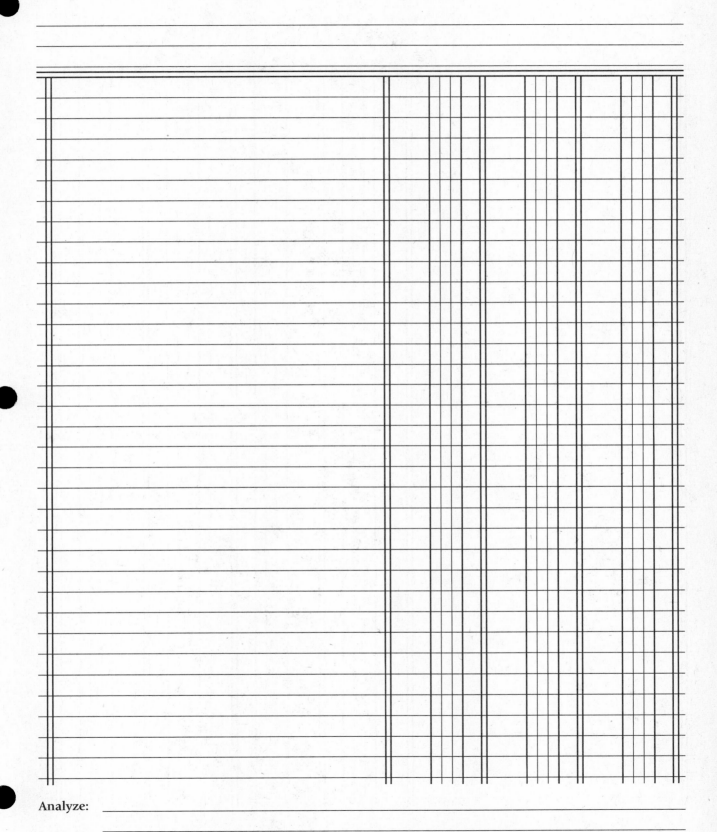

Analyze:

PROBLEM 13.2A or 13.2B

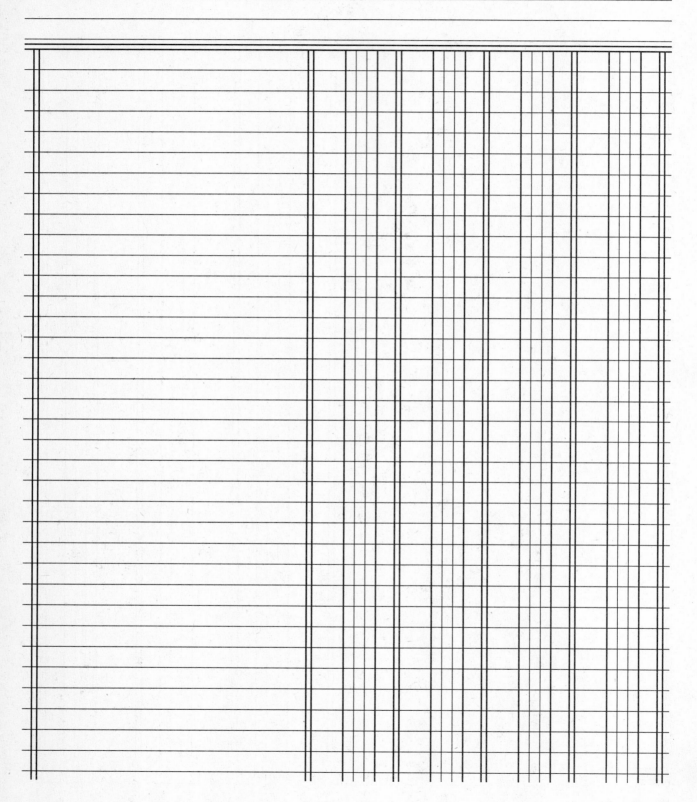

(continued)

PROBLEM 13.2A or 13.2B (continued)

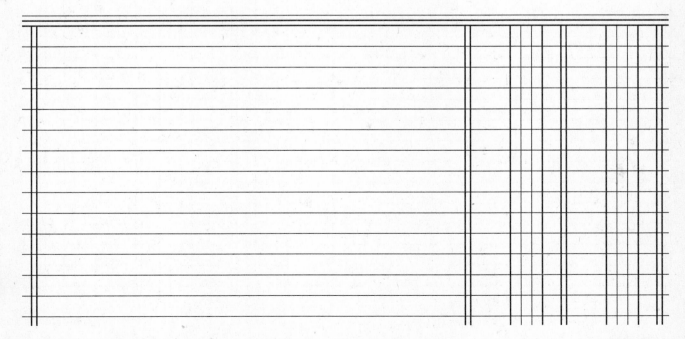

PROBLEM 13.2A or 13.2B (continued)

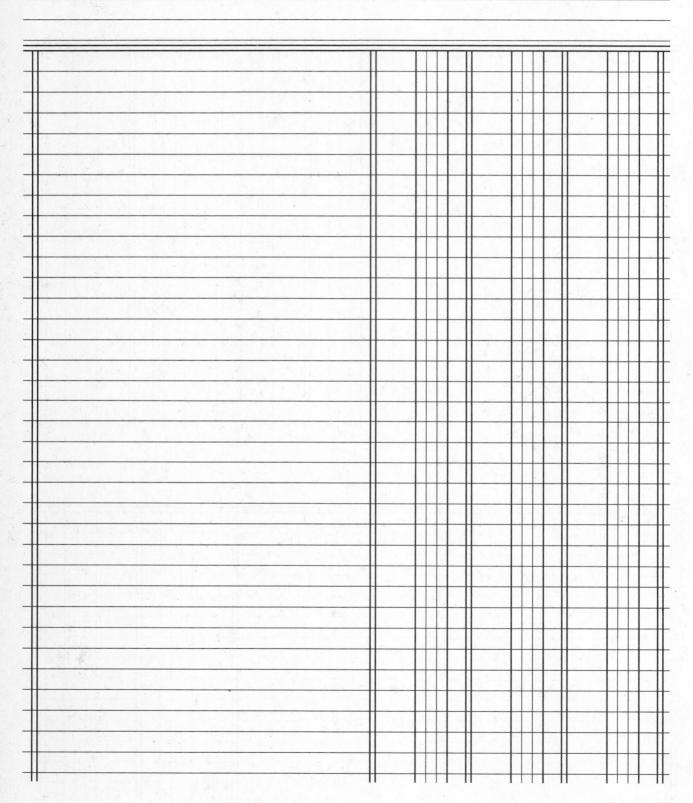

(continued)

PROBLEM 13.2A or 13.2B (continued)

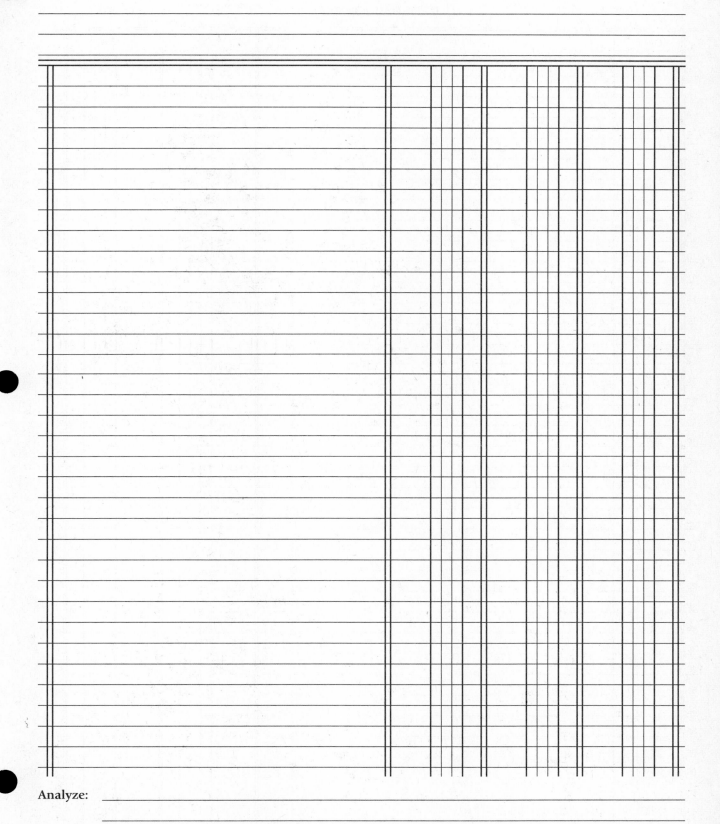

Analyze: _____

PROBLEM 13.3A or 13.3B

GENERAL JOURNAL

PAGE _____

	DATE		DESCRIPTION	POST. REF.	DEBIT	CREDIT	
1							1
2							2
3							3
4							4
5							5
6							6
7							7
8							8
9							9
10							10
11							11
12							12
13							13
14							14
15							15
16							16
17							17
18							18
19							19
20							20
21							21
22							22
23							23
24							24
25							25
26							26
27							27
28							28
29							29
30							30
31							31
32							32
33							33
34							34
35							35
36							36
37							37

Name _____

PROBLEM 13.3A or 13.3B (continued)

GENERAL JOURNAL PAGE _____

	DATE	DESCRIPTION	POST. REF.	DEBIT	CREDIT	
1						1
2						2
3						3
4						4
5						5
6						6
7						7
8						8
9						9
10						10
11						11
12						12
13						13
14						14
15						15
16						16
17						17
18						18
19						19
20						20
21						21
22						22
23						23
24						24
25						25
26						26
27						27
28						28
29						29
30						30
31						31
32						32
33						33
34						34
35						35
36						36
37						37

PROBLEM 13.3A or 13.3B (continued)

GENERAL JOURNAL   PAGE _____

	DATE		DESCRIPTION	POST. REF.	DEBIT	CREDIT	
1							1
2							2
3							3
4							4
5							5
6							6
7							7
8							8
9							9
10							10
11							11
12							12
13							13
14							14
15							15
16							16
17							17
18							18
19							19
20							20
21							21
22							22
23							23
24							24
25							25
26							26
27							27
28							28
29							29
30							30
31							31
32							32
33							33
34							34
35							35
36							36
37							37

PROBLEM 13.3A or 13.3B (continued)

GENERAL JOURNAL PAGE _____

	DATE		DESCRIPTION	POST. REF.	DEBIT	CREDIT	
1							1
2							2
3							3
4							4
5							5
6							6
7							7
8							8
9							9
10							10
11							11
12							12
13							13
14							14
15							15
16							16
17							17
18							18
19							19
20							20
21							21
22							22
23							23
24							24
25							25
26							26
27							27
28							28
29							29
30							30
31							31
32							32
33							33
34							34

Analyze: _____

_____

PROBLEM 13.4A or 13.4B

GENERAL JOURNAL   PAGE _____

	DATE		DESCRIPTION	POST. REF.	DEBIT	CREDIT	
1							1
2							2
3							3
4							4
5							5
6							6
7							7
8							8
9							9
10							10
11							11
12							12
13							13
14							14
15							15
16							16
17							17
18							18
19							19
20							20
21							21
22							22
23							23
24							24
25							25
26							26
27							27
28							28
29							29
30							30
31							31
32							32
33							33
34							34
35							35
36							36

PROBLEM 13.4A or 13.4B (continued)

GENERAL JOURNAL   PAGE _____

	DATE		DESCRIPTION	POST. REF.	DEBIT	CREDIT	
1							1
2							2
3							3
4							4
5							5
6							6
7							7
8							8
9							9
10							10
11							11
12							12
13							13
14							14
15							15
16							16

Analyze: _____

_____

EXTRA FORM

GENERAL JOURNAL   PAGE _____

	DATE		DESCRIPTION	POST. REF.	DEBIT	CREDIT	
1							1
2							2
3							3
4							4
5							5
6							6
7							7
8							8
9							9
10							10
11							11
12							12
13							13

CHAPTER 13 CHALLENGE PROBLEM

_____

_____

_____

	ACCOUNT NAME	TRIAL BALANCE DEBIT	TRIAL BALANCE CREDIT	ADJUSTMENTS DEBIT	ADJUSTMENTS CREDIT
1					
2					
3					
4					
5					
6					
7					
8					
9					
10					
11					
12					
13					
14					
15					
16					
17					
18					
19					
20					
21					
22					
23					
24					
25					
26					
27					
28					
29					
30					
31					
32					
33					
34					
35					
36					

CHAPTER 13 CHALLENGE PROBLEM (continued)

_____

_____

	ADJUSTED TRIAL BALANCE		INCOME STATEMENT		BALANCE SHEET		
	DEBIT	CREDIT	DEBIT	CREDIT	DEBIT	CREDIT	
							1
							2
							3
							4
							5
							6
							7
							8
							9
							10
							11
							12
							13
							14
							15
							16
							17
							18
							19
							20
							21
							22
							23
							24
							25
							26
							27
							28
							29
							30
							31
							32
							33
							34
							35
							36

CHAPTER 13 CHALLENGE PROBLEM (continued)

CHAPTER 13 CHALLENGE PROBLEM (continued)

EXTRA FORM

CHAPTER 13 CHALLENGE PROBLEM (continued)

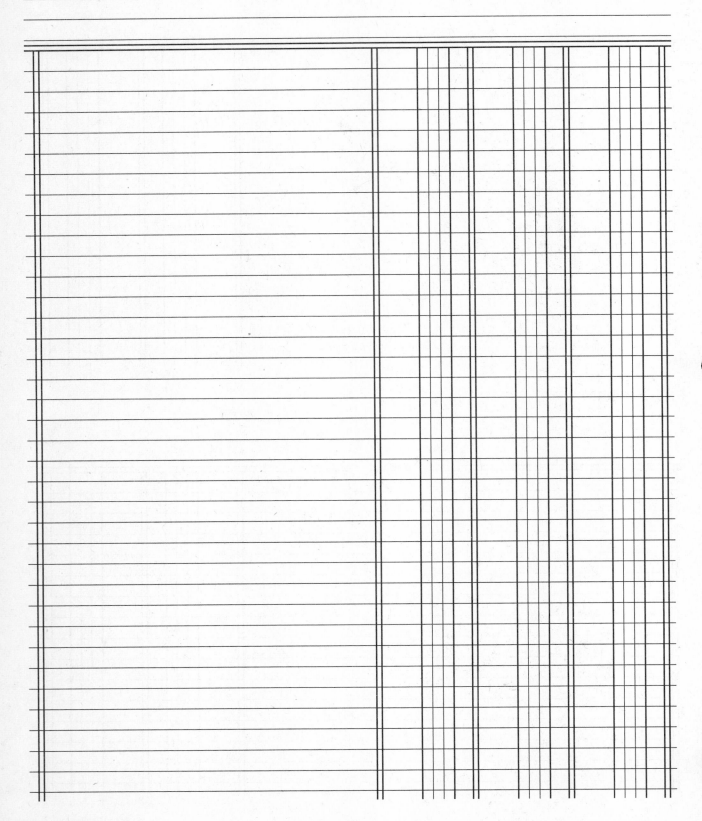

CHAPTER 13 CHALLENGE PROBLEM (continued)

GENERAL JOURNAL

PAGE _____

	DATE	DESCRIPTION	POST. REF.	DEBIT	CREDIT	
1						1
2						2
3						3
4						4
5						5
6						6
7						7
8						8
9						9
10						10
11						11
12						12
13						13
14						14
15						15
16						16
17						17
18						18
19						19
20						20
21						21
22						22
23						23
24						24
25						25
26						26
27						27
28						28
29						29
30						30
31						31
32						32
33						33
34						34
35						35
36						36
37						37

CHAPTER 13 CHALLENGE PROBLEM (continued)

GENERAL JOURNAL   PAGE _____

	DATE	DESCRIPTION	POST. REF.	DEBIT	CREDIT	
1						1
2						2
3						3
4						4
5						5
6						6
7						7
8						8
9						9
10						10
11						11
12						12
13						13
14						14
15						15
16						16
17						17
18						18
19						19
20						20
21						21
22						22
23						23
24						24
25						25
26						26
27						27
28						28
29						29
30						30
31						31
32						32
33						33
34						34
35						35
36						36
37						37

CHAPTER 13 CHALLENGE PROBLEM (continued)

GENERAL JOURNAL   PAGE _____

	DATE		DESCRIPTION	POST. REF.	DEBIT	CREDIT	
1							1
2							2
3							3
4							4
5							5
6							6
7							7
8							8
9							9
10							10
11							11
12							12
13							13
14							14
15							15
16							16
17							17
18							18
19							19
20							20
21							21
22							22
23							23
24							24
25							25
26							26
27							27
28							28
29							29
30							30
31							31
32							32
33							33
34							34
35							35
36							36
37							37

CHAPTER 13 CHALLENGE PROBLEM (continued)

GENERAL JOURNAL   PAGE _____

	DATE	DESCRIPTION	POST. REF.	DEBIT	CREDIT	
1						1
2						2
3						3
4						4
5						5
6						6
7						7
8						8
9						9
10						10
11						11
12						12
13						13
14						14
15						15
16						16
17						17
18						18
19						19
20						20
21						21
22						22
23						23
24						24
25						25
26						26
27						27
28						28
29						29
30						30
31						31
32						32
33						33
34						34

Analyze: _____

_____

CHAPTER 13 CRITICAL THINKING PROBLEM

1.

_____

_____

2. _____

_____

_____

_____

_____

_____

_____

CHAPTER 13 CRITICAL THINKING PROBLEM (continued)

3. _____

Chapter 13 Practice Test Answer Key

Part A True-False

1. T	6. F	11. F	16. F	21. T
2. F	7. F	12. T	17. T	22. T
3. T	8. T	13. F	18. F	23. T
4. F	9. F	14. F	19. T	24. F
5. T	10. F	15. F	20. T	25. T

MINI-PRACTICE SET 2

Merchandising Business Accounting Cycle

SALES JOURNAL

PAGE _____

	DATE	SALES SLIP NO.	CUSTOMER'S NAME	POST. REF.	ACCOUNTS RECEIVABLE DEBIT	SALES TAX PAYABLE CREDIT	SALES CREDIT	
1								1
2								2
3								3
4								4
5								5
6								6
7								7
8								8
9								9
10								10
11								11
12								12
13								13
14								14

PURCHASES JOURNAL

PAGE _____

DATE	PURCHASED FROM	INVOICE NUMBER	INVOICE DATE	TERMS	POST. REF.	PURCHASES DR./ ACCOUNTS PAYABLE CR.

PAGE _____

CASH RECEIPTS JOURNAL

DATE	DESCRIPTION	POST. REF.	ACCOUNTS RECEIVABLE CREDIT	SALES TAX PAYABLE CREDIT	SALES CREDIT	OTHER ACCOUNTS CREDIT			CASH DEBIT
						ACCOUNT NAME	POST. REF.	AMOUNT	

Name

CASH PAYMENTS JOURNAL

DATE	CK. NO.	DESCRIPTION	POST. REF.	ACCOUNTS PAYABLE DEBIT	OTHER ACCOUNTS DEBIT			PURCHASES DISCOUNT CREDIT	CASH CREDIT
					ACCOUNT NAME	POST. REF.	AMOUNT		

Name _____

GENERAL JOURNAL

PAGE _____

	DATE	DESCRIPTION	POST. REF.	DEBIT	CREDIT	
1						1
2						2
3						3
4						4
5						5
6						6
7						7
8						8
9						9
10						10
11						11
12						12
13						13
14						14
15						15
16						16
17						17
18						18
19						19
20						20
21						21
22						22
23						23
24						24
25						25
26						26
27						27
28						28
29						29
30						30
31						31
32						32
33						33
34						34
35						35
36						36
37						37
38						38

Name _____

GENERAL JOURNAL

PAGE _____

	DATE		DESCRIPTION	POST. REF.	DEBIT	CREDIT	
1							1
2							2
3							3
4							4
5							5
6							6
7							7
8							8
9							9
10							10
11							11
12							12
13							13
14							14
15							15
16							16
17							17
18							18
19							19
20							20
21							21
22							22
23							23
24							24
25							25
26							26
27							27
28							28
29							29
30							30
31							31
32							32
33							33
34							34
35							35
36							36
37							37
38							38

Name

GENERAL JOURNAL

PAGE _____

	DATE		DESCRIPTION	POST. REF.	DEBIT	CREDIT	
1							1
2							2
3							3
4							4
5							5
6							6
7							7
8							8
9							9
10							10
11							11
12							12
13							13
14							14
15							15
16							16
17							17
18							18
19							19
20							20
21							21
22							22
23							23
24							24
25							25
26							26
27							27
28							28
29							29
30							30
31							31
32							32
33							33
34							34
35							35
36							36
37							37
38							38

GENERAL LEDGER

ACCOUNT _____ ACCOUNT NO. _____

DATE	DESCRIPTION	POST. REF.	DEBIT	CREDIT	BALANCE	
					DEBIT	CREDIT

ACCOUNT _____ ACCOUNT NO. _____

DATE	DESCRIPTION	POST. REF.	DEBIT	CREDIT	BALANCE	
					DEBIT	CREDIT

ACCOUNT _____ ACCOUNT NO. _____

DATE	DESCRIPTION	POST. REF.	DEBIT	CREDIT	BALANCE	
					DEBIT	CREDIT

ACCOUNT _____ ACCOUNT NO. _____

DATE	DESCRIPTION	POST. REF.	DEBIT	CREDIT	BALANCE	
					DEBIT	CREDIT

Name _____

GENERAL LEDGER

ACCOUNT _____ ACCOUNT NO. _____

DATE	DESCRIPTION	POST. REF.	DEBIT	CREDIT	BALANCE	
					DEBIT	CREDIT

ACCOUNT _____ ACCOUNT NO. _____

DATE	DESCRIPTION	POST. REF.	DEBIT	CREDIT	BALANCE	
					DEBIT	CREDIT

ACCOUNT _____ ACCOUNT NO. _____

DATE	DESCRIPTION	POST. REF.	DEBIT	CREDIT	BALANCE	
					DEBIT	CREDIT

ACCOUNT _____ ACCOUNT NO. _____

DATE	DESCRIPTION	POST. REF.	DEBIT	CREDIT	BALANCE	
					DEBIT	CREDIT

ACCOUNT _____ ACCOUNT NO. _____

DATE	DESCRIPTION	POST. REF.	DEBIT	CREDIT	BALANCE	
					DEBIT	CREDIT

Name _____

GENERAL LEDGER

ACCOUNT _____ ACCOUNT NO. _____

DATE	DESCRIPTION	POST. REF.	DEBIT	CREDIT	BALANCE	
					DEBIT	CREDIT

ACCOUNT _____ ACCOUNT NO. _____

DATE	DESCRIPTION	POST. REF.	DEBIT	CREDIT	BALANCE	
					DEBIT	CREDIT

ACCOUNT _____ ACCOUNT NO. _____

DATE	DESCRIPTION	POST. REF.	DEBIT	CREDIT	BALANCE	
					DEBIT	CREDIT

ACCOUNT _____ ACCOUNT NO. _____

DATE	DESCRIPTION	POST. REF.	DEBIT	CREDIT	BALANCE	
					DEBIT	CREDIT

GENERAL LEDGER

ACCOUNT _____ ACCOUNT NO. _____

DATE		DESCRIPTION	POST. REF.	DEBIT	CREDIT	BALANCE	
						DEBIT	CREDIT

ACCOUNT _____ ACCOUNT NO. _____

DATE		DESCRIPTION	POST. REF.	DEBIT	CREDIT	BALANCE	
						DEBIT	CREDIT

ACCOUNT _____ ACCOUNT NO. _____

DATE		DESCRIPTION	POST. REF.	DEBIT	CREDIT	BALANCE	
						DEBIT	CREDIT

ACCOUNT _____ ACCOUNT NO. _____

DATE		DESCRIPTION	POST. REF.	DEBIT	CREDIT	BALANCE	
						DEBIT	CREDIT

ACCOUNT _____ ACCOUNT NO. _____

DATE		DESCRIPTION	POST. REF.	DEBIT	CREDIT	BALANCE	
						DEBIT	CREDIT

MINI-PRACTICE SET 2 (continued)

Name _____

GENERAL LEDGER

ACCOUNT _____ ACCOUNT NO. _____

DATE	DESCRIPTION	POST. REF.	DEBIT	CREDIT	BALANCE	
					DEBIT	CREDIT

ACCOUNT _____ ACCOUNT NO. _____

DATE	DESCRIPTION	POST. REF.	DEBIT	CREDIT	BALANCE	
					DEBIT	CREDIT

ACCOUNT _____ ACCOUNT NO. _____

DATE	DESCRIPTION	POST. REF.	DEBIT	CREDIT	BALANCE	
					DEBIT	CREDIT

ACCOUNT _____ ACCOUNT NO. _____

DATE	DESCRIPTION	POST. REF.	DEBIT	CREDIT	BALANCE	
					DEBIT	CREDIT

GENERAL LEDGER

ACCOUNT _____ ACCOUNT NO. _____

DATE	DESCRIPTION	POST. REF.	DEBIT	CREDIT	BALANCE	
					DEBIT	CREDIT

ACCOUNT _____ ACCOUNT NO. _____

DATE	DESCRIPTION	POST. REF.	DEBIT	CREDIT	BALANCE	
					DEBIT	CREDIT

ACCOUNT _____ ACCOUNT NO. _____

DATE	DESCRIPTION	POST. REF.	DEBIT	CREDIT	BALANCE	
					DEBIT	CREDIT

ACCOUNT _____ ACCOUNT NO. _____

DATE	DESCRIPTION	POST. REF.	DEBIT	CREDIT	BALANCE	
					DEBIT	CREDIT

ACCOUNT _____ ACCOUNT NO. _____

DATE	DESCRIPTION	POST. REF.	DEBIT	CREDIT	BALANCE	
					DEBIT	CREDIT

GENERAL LEDGER

ACCOUNT _____ ACCOUNT NO. _____

DATE		DESCRIPTION	POST. REF.	DEBIT	CREDIT	BALANCE	
						DEBIT	CREDIT

ACCOUNT _____ ACCOUNT NO. _____

DATE		DESCRIPTION	POST. REF.	DEBIT	CREDIT	BALANCE	
						DEBIT	CREDIT

ACCOUNT _____ ACCOUNT NO. _____

DATE		DESCRIPTION	POST. REF.	DEBIT	CREDIT	BALANCE	
						DEBIT	CREDIT

ACCOUNT _____ ACCOUNT NO. _____

DATE		DESCRIPTION	POST. REF.	DEBIT	CREDIT	BALANCE	
						DEBIT	CREDIT

ACCOUNT _____ ACCOUNT NO. _____

DATE		DESCRIPTION	POST. REF.	DEBIT	CREDIT	BALANCE	
						DEBIT	CREDIT

GENERAL LEDGER

ACCOUNT _____   ACCOUNT NO. _____

DATE	DESCRIPTION	POST. REF.	DEBIT	CREDIT	BALANCE	
					DEBIT	CREDIT

ACCOUNT _____   ACCOUNT NO. _____

DATE	DESCRIPTION	POST. REF.	DEBIT	CREDIT	BALANCE	
					DEBIT	CREDIT

ACCOUNT _____   ACCOUNT NO. _____

DATE	DESCRIPTION	POST. REF.	DEBIT	CREDIT	BALANCE	
					DEBIT	CREDIT

ACCOUNT _____   ACCOUNT NO. _____

DATE	DESCRIPTION	POST. REF.	DEBIT	CREDIT	BALANCE	
					DEBIT	CREDIT

ACCOUNT _____   ACCOUNT NO. _____

DATE	DESCRIPTION	POST. REF.	DEBIT	CREDIT	BALANCE	
					DEBIT	CREDIT

ACCOUNTS RECEIVABLE SUBSIDIARY LEDGER

NAME _____ TERMS _____

	DATE	DESCRIPTION	POST. REF.	DEBIT	CREDIT	BALANCE

NAME _____ TERMS _____

	DATE	DESCRIPTION	POST. REF.	DEBIT	CREDIT	BALANCE

NAME _____ TERMS _____

	DATE	DESCRIPTION	POST. REF.	DEBIT	CREDIT	BALANCE

NAME _____ TERMS _____

	DATE	DESCRIPTION	POST. REF.	DEBIT	CREDIT	BALANCE

NAME _____ TERMS _____

	DATE	DESCRIPTION	POST. REF.	DEBIT	CREDIT	BALANCE

MINI-PRACTICE SET 2 (continued)

Name _____

ACCOUNTS RECEIVABLE SUBSIDIARY LEDGER

NAME _____ TERMS _____

DATE	DESCRIPTION	POST. REF.	DEBIT	CREDIT	BALANCE

NAME _____ TERMS _____

DATE	DESCRIPTION	POST. REF.	DEBIT	CREDIT	BALANCE

ACCOUNTS PAYABLE SUBSIDIARY LEDGER

NAME _____ TERMS _____

DATE	DESCRIPTION	POST. REF.	DEBIT	CREDIT	BALANCE

NAME _____ TERMS _____

DATE	DESCRIPTION	POST. REF.	DEBIT	CREDIT	BALANCE

ACCOUNTS PAYABLE SUBSIDIARY LEDGER

NAME _____   TERMS _____

DATE		DESCRIPTION	POST. REF.	DEBIT	CREDIT	BALANCE

	ACCOUNT NAME	TRIAL BALANCE		ADJUSTMENTS	
		DEBIT	CREDIT	DEBIT	CREDIT
1					
2					
3					
4					
5					
6					
7					
8					
9					
10					
11					
12					
13					
14					
15					
16					
17					
18					
19					
20					
21					
22					
23					
24					
25					
26					
27					
28					
29					
30					
31					
32					
33					
34					
35					
36					

ADJUSTED TRIAL BALANCE		INCOME STATEMENT		BALANCE SHEET		
DEBIT	CREDIT	DEBIT	CREDIT	DEBIT	CREDIT	
						1
						2
						3
						4
						5
						6
						7
						8
						9
						10
						11
						12
						13
						14
						15
						16
						17
						18
						19
						20
						21
						22
						23
						24
						25
						26
						27
						28
						29
						30
						31
						32
						33
						34
						35
						36

Name _____

_____

	ACCOUNT NAME	TRIAL BALANCE		ADJUSTMENTS	
		DEBIT	CREDIT	DEBIT	CREDIT
1					
2					
3					
4					
5					
6					
7					
8					
9					
10					
11					
12					
13					
14					
15					
16					
17					
18					
19					
20					
21					
22					
23					
24					
25					
26					
27					
28					
29					
30					
31					
32					
33					
34					
35					
36					

	ADJUSTED TRIAL BALANCE		INCOME STATEMENT		BALANCE SHEET		
	DEBIT	CREDIT	DEBIT	CREDIT	DEBIT	CREDIT	
							1
							2
							3
							4
							5
							6
							7
							8
							9
							10
							11
							12
							13
							14
							15
							16
							17
							18
							19
							20
							21
							22
							23
							24
							25
							26
							27
							28
							29
							30
							31
							32
							33
							34
							35
							36

Name _____

Name

Name _____

_____

ACCOUNT NAME	DEBIT	CREDIT

EXTRA FORMS

	ACCOUNT NAME	TRIAL BALANCE		ADJUSTMENTS	
		DEBIT	CREDIT	DEBIT	CREDIT
1					
2					
3					
4					
5					
6					
7					
8					
9					
10					
11					
12					
13					
14					
15					
16					
17					
18					
19					
20					
21					
22					
23					
24					
25					
26					
27					
28					
29					
30					
31					
32					
33					
34					

Name _____

ADJUSTED TRIAL BALANCE		INCOME STATEMENT		BALANCE SHEET		
DEBIT	CREDIT	DEBIT	CREDIT	DEBIT	CREDIT	
						1
						2
						3
						4
						5
						6
						7
						8
						9
						10
						11
						12
						13
						14
						15
						16
						17
						18
						19
						20
						21
						22
						23
						24
						25
						26
						27
						28
						29
						30
						31
						32
						33
						34

Name _____

EXTRA FORM

GENERAL JOURNAL   PAGE _____

	DATE		DESCRIPTION	POST. REF.	DEBIT	CREDIT	
1							1
2							2
3							3
4							4
5							5
6							6
7							7
8							8
9							9
10							10
11							11
12							12
13							13
14							14
15							15
16							16
17							17
18							18
19							19
20							20
21							21
22							22
23							23
24							24
25							25
26							26
27							27
28							28
29							29
30							30
31							31
32							32
33							33
34							34
35							35
36							36
37							37

GENERAL JOURNAL

	DATE		DESCRIPTION	POST. REF.	DEBIT	CREDIT	
1							1
2							2
3							3
4							4
5							5
6							6
7							7
8							8
9							9
10							10
11							11
12							12
13							13
14							14
15							15
16							16
17							17
18							18
19							19
20							20
21							21
22							22
23							23
24							24
25							25
26							26
27							27
28							28
29							29
30							30
31							31
32							32
33							33
34							34
35							35
36							36
37							37

GENERAL JOURNAL

	DATE		DESCRIPTION	POST. REF.	DEBIT	CREDIT	
1							1
2							2
3							3
4							4
5							5
6							6
7							7
8							8
9							9
10							10
11							11
12							12
13							13
14							14
15							15
16							16
17							17
18							18
19							19
20							20
21							21
22							22
23							23
24							24
25							25
26							26
27							27
28							28
29							29
30							30
31							31
32							32
33							33
34							34
35							35
36							36
37							37

GENERAL LEDGER

ACCOUNT _____ ACCOUNT NO. _____

DATE	DESCRIPTION	POST. REF.	DEBIT	CREDIT	BALANCE DEBIT	CREDIT

ACCOUNT _____ ACCOUNT NO. _____

DATE	DESCRIPTION	POST. REF.	DEBIT	CREDIT	BALANCE DEBIT	CREDIT

ACCOUNT _____ ACCOUNT NO. _____

DATE	DESCRIPTION	POST. REF.	DEBIT	CREDIT	BALANCE DEBIT	CREDIT

ACCOUNT _____ ACCOUNT NO. _____

DATE	DESCRIPTION	POST. REF.	DEBIT	CREDIT	BALANCE DEBIT	CREDIT

ACCOUNT _____ ACCOUNT NO. _____

DATE	DESCRIPTION	POST. REF.	DEBIT	CREDIT	BALANCE DEBIT	CREDIT

GENERAL LEDGER

ACCOUNT _____ ACCOUNT NO. _____

DATE		DESCRIPTION	POST. REF.	DEBIT	CREDIT	BALANCE	
						DEBIT	CREDIT

ACCOUNT _____ ACCOUNT NO. _____

DATE		DESCRIPTION	POST. REF.	DEBIT	CREDIT	BALANCE	
						DEBIT	CREDIT

ACCOUNT _____ ACCOUNT NO. _____

DATE		DESCRIPTION	POST. REF.	DEBIT	CREDIT	BALANCE	
						DEBIT	CREDIT

ACCOUNT _____ ACCOUNT NO. _____

DATE		DESCRIPTION	POST. REF.	DEBIT	CREDIT	BALANCE	
						DEBIT	CREDIT

ACCOUNT _____ ACCOUNT NO. _____

DATE		DESCRIPTION	POST. REF.	DEBIT	CREDIT	BALANCE	
						DEBIT	CREDIT

STUDY GUIDE

Understanding the Chapter

Objectives	**1.** Understand the process used to develop generally accepted accounting principles. **2.** Identify the major accounting standards-setting bodies and their roles in the standards-setting process. **3.** Describe the users and uses of financial reports. **4.** Identify and explain the qualitative characteristics of accounting information. **5.** Describe and explain the basic assumptions about accounting reports. **6.** Explain and apply the basic principles of accounting. **7.** Describe and apply the modifying constraints on accounting principles. **8.** Define the accounting terms new to this chapter.
Reading Assignment	Read Chapter 14 in the textbook. Complete the textbook Section Self Review as you finish reading each section of the chapter, and the Comprehensive Self Review at the end of the chapter. Refer to the Chapter 14 Glossary or to the Glossary at the end of the book to find definitions for terms that are not familiar to you.

Activities

❑ **Thinking Critically**	Answer the *Thinking Critically* questions for The Goodyear Tire & Rubber Company, Accounting on the Job, and Managerial Implications.
❑ **Internet Application**	Complete the activity for Accounting on the Job.
❑ **Discussion Questions**	Answer each assigned discussion question in Chapter 14.
❑ **Exercises**	Complete each assigned exercise in Chapter 14. Use the forms provided in this SGWP. The objectives covered by an exercise are given after the exercise number. If you need help with an exercise, review the portion of the chapter related to the objective(s) covered.
❑ **Problems A/B**	Complete each assigned problem in Chapter 14. Use the forms provided in this SGWP. The objectives covered by a problem are given after the problem number. If you need help with a problem, review the portion of the chapter related to the objective(s) covered.
❑ **Challenge Problem**	Complete the challenge problem as assigned. Use the forms provided in this SGWP.
❑ **Critical Thinking Problem**	Complete the critical thinking problem as assigned. Use the forms provided in this SGWP.
❑ **Business Connections**	Complete the Business Connections activities as assigned to gain a deeper understanding of Chapter 14 concepts.

Practice Tests

Complete the Practice Tests, which cover the main points in your reading assignment. Compare your answers with those in the Practice Test Answer Key for Chapter 14 at the end of this chapter. If you have answered any questions incorrectly, review the related section of the text.

Part A True-False *For each of the following statements, circle T in the answer column if the statement is true or F if the statement is false.*

T   F   **1.** The "stable monetary unit" assumption complicates accounting records.

T   F   **2.** The SEC discourages disclosures outside the financial statements.

T   F   **3.** The Securities and Exchange Commission has little power to dictate accounting methods used by companies whose stocks are traded on the stock exchanges.

T   F   **4.** Revenue should not be recognized until cash is received.

T   F   **5.** Statement users have the right to assume that the figures in audited statements are objective and are based on verifiable evidence.

T   F   **6.** Because of the separate entity assumption, the personal activities of the owner of a sole proprietorship should be combined with his or her business activities in the accounting records.

T   F   **7.** The Financial Accounting Standards Board is a governmental organization.

T   F   **8.** The statements of the Financial Accounting Standards Board are binding on the members of the American Institute of Certified Public Accountants.

T   F   **9.** The Sarbanes-Oxley Act reaffirms the SEC's option to depend on a private sector organization in developing accounting principles and standards and the SEC has chosen the FASB as that organization.

T   F   **10.** Long-term assets are usually carried in the accounts at original cost, less depreciation, until used up or disposed of.

T   F   **11.** The Conceptual Framework assumes that readers of financial reports know little about accounting and financial reporting.

T   F   **12.** The traits of objectivity and verifiability reduce subjective decisions.

T   F   **13.** For convenience, accountants assume that the value of money is stable or that changes in its value are insignificant.

T   F   **14.** There is only one accepted method of accounting for each transaction.

T   F   **15.** The matching principle requires that all known costs be charged to the current period of operations.

T   F   **16.** Adjusting entries are necessary because of the matching principle.

T   F   **17.** In order for information to be reliable, it must be verifiable.

T   F   **18.** There is a conflict between the "going concern" concept and the historical cost principle.

T   F   **19.** An understatement of an expense account in one accounting period results in an understatement of profit in the succeeding period or periods.

T   F   **20.** The "constraints" serve to modify basic principles of accounting.

Part B Completion *In the answer column, supply the missing word or words needed to complete each of the following statements.*

_____ 1. The assumption that permits the cost of assets acquired to be included in the same account is the _____ assumption.

_____ 2. The _____ assumption implies that an enterprise's economic activities can be divided into time periods.

_____ 3. The _____ quality of financial statements permits the reports of different entities to be compared meaningfully with one another.

_____ 4. The _____ assumption permits carrying forward the un-depreciated cost of assets to be charged against future operations.

_____ 5. The idea that the same accounting principles should be followed each year is called the _____ characteristic.

_____ 6. The _____ constraint may make it possible for a transaction with small value to be exempt from GAAP.

_____ 7. Under the modifying convention of _____, assets are sometimes stated at a lower amount than they might be stated if other principles could be logically applied under GAAP.

_____ 8. The notes to the financial statements illustrate application of the principle of _____.

_____ 9. If the accounting records are kept on the accrual basis, income is recognized in the period in which it has been _____ and _____.

_____ 10. Matching revenues and expenses of specific fiscal periods is called the _____ basis of accounting.

_____ 11. The agency with statutory authority to establish accounting standards for publicly-held corporations is the _____.

_____ 12. Before the FASB was established, the _____ was recognized as the private sector source of GAAP.

_____ 13. _____ refers to the significance of an item in relation to other items in the financial statements.

_____ 14. The business enterprise is normally thought of by the accountant as a _____ entity.

_____ 15. The international body that was established to develop accounting rules that might be followed on a world-wide basis is the _____ _____.

Part C Exercise

Answer each of the following in the space provided. Make your answers complete but as brief as possible.

1. Explain the role of the FASB's conceptual framework of accounting.

_____

_____

_____

_____

_____

_____

2. Does the separate entity assumption conform to the legal obligations of a sole proprietor? Explain.

_____

_____

_____

_____

_____

_____

3. Explain why the accountant assumes continuity in the operation of the business?

_____

_____

_____

_____

_____

_____

4. Explain the tests that must be met for revenue to be recognized.

_____

_____

_____

_____

_____

_____

5. In its accounting, Ace Company has been following a FASB Standard issued three years ago. It discovers in November 2007 that the International Accounting Standards Board has issued a "Standard" with greatly different reporting requirements from those of the FASB. What must Ace Company do?

_____

_____

_____

_____

_____

_____

_____

Demonstration Problem

You are an independent CPA performing audits of financial statements. In your work you encounter the independent situations described in items 1–6. For each situation, indicate which accounting assumption, principle or constraint is most relevant. If the treatment described conforms to GAAP, explain why. If the treatment does not conform, explain which concept is violated and how the situation should be reported.

1. Mandolin Company has been sued in court by customers for defective merchandise. The company's attorney expects a liability of at least $5 million. In the statements, the lawsuits are not mentioned.

2. During 2007 Morris received and reported as income $2 million in deposits accompanying orders for products to be manufactured and delivered in 2008.

3. Bigtown Company's income statement shows only sales, cost of sales, total expenses and net profit.

4. Tomato Company occupies a building purchased 5 years ago. Because the value of the building has increased each year, no depreciation has been taken.

5. Modern BioLabs has constructed special-purpose equipment designed for research use. Because of its special use, this equipment has virtually no resale value to any other company. Therefore, Modern BioLabs charged the entire cost to build the equipment, $4,500,000 to expense in the year it was put into service.

6. Happy Days Holidays spends a large sum on sales promotions during this year. Management thinks the advertising will generate revenues for three years, so has charged to expense only one-third of the amount spent this year. The remainder will be charged off in equal amounts in the next two years.

SOLUTION

1. __Full disclosure. Assuming that this is a material amount, disclosure of the lawsuits should be given in the__
   footnotes to the financial statements. It probably is not reasonable to expect the company to reveal the attorney's
   attitude toward the case. However, disclosure of the amount of the suit, with some indication of the impact of a
   decision in favor of the plaintiffs should be made.

2. __Revenue recognition and matching. Revenue should be reported only if it has been realized (which it has)__
   and earned (which it has not). The revenue should be deferred and matched against costs to be incurred in
   the next year.

3. __Full disclosure. The disclosure of such few items does not provide the user with information needed. The__
   components of the net income are important to users who are trying to evaluate the business, and in this instance
   the disclosures should take the form of inclusion in the income statement. Even though it is appropriate to make a
   summary of income and costs in the income statement, without all the details, the procedure being followed is
   not satisfactory.

4. __Matching. Historical cost principle. The cost of the building should be depreciated over its useful life. This is also__
   part of the historical cost framework of accounting.

5. __Going concern, matching and historical cost concepts. The accounting concept framework assumes a going__
   concern. Therefore historical cost of an asset is entered in the accounts and depreciated over the useful life of
   the asset. There is no intent to sell the asset, but to use it in the business. There is no indication that the asset has
   lost its usefulness or even that its usefulness has decreased.

6. __Objectivity and verifiability. To defer a cost such as advertising, there must be verification that a future benefit has__
   been created and it must be possible to objectively measure the benefit. Neither of these factors appears to be
   present, so the costs should be charged to expense in the year incurred.

EXTRA FORM

WORKING PAPERS

EXERCISE 14.1

1. _____
_____
_____
_____

2. _____
_____
_____
_____

3. _____
_____
_____
_____
_____

EXERCISE 14.2

1. _____
_____
_____
_____
_____

2. _____
_____
_____
_____

3. _____
_____
_____
_____
_____

EXERCISE 14.3

1. _____
_____
_____
_____
_____

2. _____
_____
_____
_____
_____

3. _____
_____
_____
_____
_____

EXERCISE 14.4

1. _____
_____
_____
_____
_____
_____

2. _____
_____
_____
_____
_____

3. _____
_____
_____
_____
_____

EXERCISE 14.5

EXERCISE 14.6

EXTRA FORM

Name

PROBLEM 14.1A

1. _____
2. _____
3. _____
4. _____
5. _____
6. _____
7. _____
8. _____
9. _____

EXTRA FORM

_____
_____
_____
_____
_____
_____
_____
_____
_____
_____
_____
_____
_____
_____
_____
_____
_____
_____
_____
_____

PROBLEM 14.2A or 14.2B

Handled Properly?	Basic Concept	Proper Presentation
1. _____	_____	_____
	_____	_____
	_____	_____
	_____	_____
2. _____	_____	_____
	_____	_____
	_____	_____
	_____	_____
3. _____	_____	_____
	_____	_____
	_____	_____
	_____	_____
4. _____	_____	_____
	_____	_____
	_____	_____
	_____	_____
5. _____	_____	_____
	_____	_____
	_____	_____
	_____	_____
6. _____	_____	_____
	_____	_____
	_____	_____
	_____	_____

Analyze: _____

_____

PROBLEM 14.3A or 14.3B

PROBLEM 14.3A or 14.3B (continued)

COMPUTATIONS

Analyze: _____

PROBLEM 14.4A or 14.4B

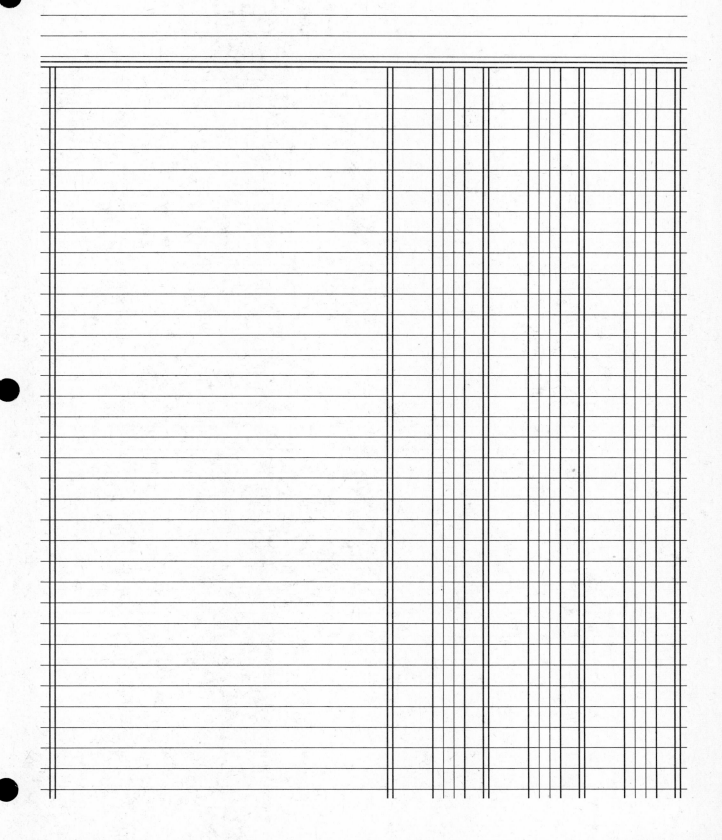

PROBLEM 14.4A or 14.4B (continued)

NOTES

_____
_____
_____
_____
_____
_____
_____
_____
_____
_____
_____
_____
_____
_____
_____
_____
_____
_____
_____
_____
_____
_____
_____
_____
_____
_____
_____
_____
_____
_____
_____

Analyze: _____
_____
_____

PROBLEM 14.5A or 14.5B

_____

_____

_____

_____

_____

_____

_____

_____

_____

_____

_____

_____

_____

_____

_____

_____

_____

_____

_____

_____

_____

_____

_____

_____

_____

_____

_____

_____

_____

_____

_____

_____

Analyze: _____

_____

CHAPTER 14 CHALLENGE PROBLEM

Analyze:

CHAPTER 14 CRITICAL THINKING PROBLEM

Chapter 14 Practice Test Answer Key

Part A True-False

1. F	8. T	15. F
2. F	9. T	16. T
3. F	10. T	17. T
4. F	11. F	18. F
5. T	12. T	19. T
6. F	13. T	20. T
7. F	14. F	

Part B Completion

1. stable monetary unit
2. periodicity of income
3. comparability
4. going concern
5. consistency
6. cost-benefit
7. conservatism
8. full disclosure
9. earned and realized
10. accrual
11. Securities and Exchange Commission
12. American Institute of CPAs (Accounting Principles Board)
13. materiality
14. separate
15. International Accounting Standards Board

Part C Exercise

1. The conceptual framework is designed to provide a sound basis for developing accounting standards and rules. It permits development of a coherent set of standards based on the same assumptions, basic principles and constraints.

2. No. The owner of a sole proprietorship is generally legally liable for the debts and other obligations of the business as well as for personal debts.

3. If continuity were not assumed, the accounting records would have to be kept on the assumption that the business is about to liquidate—presumably reflecting estimated value.

4. For revenue to be recognized, it must have been (1) realized (cash or other assets must have been received or debts liquidated) and (2) earned, which means that goods or services have been delivered and the costs related to the revenue have been incurred.

5. Assuming Ace is an American company, it must use the rules of the FASB.

CHAPTER 15 / Accounts Receivable and Uncollectible Accounts

STUDY GUIDE

Understanding the Chapter

Objectives	**1.** Record the estimated expense from uncollectible accounts receivable using the allowance method. **2.** Charge off uncollectible accounts using the allowance method. **3.** Record the collection of accounts previously written off using the allowance method. **4.** Record losses from uncollectible accounts using the direct charge-off method. **5.** Record the collection of accounts previously written off using the direct charge-off method. **6.** Recognize common internal controls for accounts receivable. **7.** Define the accounting terms new to this chapter.
Reading Assignment	Read Chapter 15 in the textbook. Complete the textbook Section Self Review as you finish reading each section of the chapter, and the Comprehensive Self Review at the end of the chapter. Refer to the Chapter 15 Glossary or to the Glossary at the end of the book to find definitions for terms that are not familiar to you.

Activities

❏ **Thinking Critically**	Answer the *Thinking Critically* questions for FedEx Corporation, Computers in Accounting, and Managerial Implications.
❏ **Internet Application**	Complete the activity for Computers in Accounting.
❏ **Discussion Questions**	Answer each assigned discussion question in Chapter 15.
❏ **Exercises**	Complete each assigned exercise in Chapter 15. Use the forms provided in this SGWP. The objectives covered by an exercise are given after the exercise number. If you need help with an exercise, review the portion of the chapter related to the objective(s) covered.
❏ **Problems A/B**	Complete each assigned problem in Chapter 15. Use the forms provided in this SGWP. The objectives covered by a problem are given after the problem number. If you need help with a problem, review the portion of the chapter related to the objective(s) covered.
❏ **Challenge Problem**	Complete the challenge problem as assigned. Use the forms provided in this SGWP.
❏ **Critical Thinking Problem**	Complete the critical thinking problem as assigned. Use the forms provided in this SGWP.
❏ **Business Connections**	Complete the Business Connections activities as assigned to gain a deeper understanding of Chapter 15 concepts.

Practice Tests

Complete the Practice Tests, which cover the main points in your reading assignment. Compare your answers with those in the Practice Test Answer Key for Chapter 15 at the end of this chapter. If you have answered any questions incorrectly, review the related section of the text.

Part A True-False

For each of the following statements, circle T in the answer column if the answer is true or F if the statement is false.

T F **1.** Under the allowance method, the entry to record estimated expenses from uncollectible accounts is a debit to **Uncollectible Accounts Expense** and a credit to **Accounts Receivable.**

T F **2.** The direct charge-off method of recording losses from uncollectible accounts is the preferred method.

T F **3.** The experience of other firms in the same line of business may be used in estimating losses from uncollectible accounts for a new firm.

T F **4.** **The Allowance for Doubtful Accounts** increases during the year as individual accounts receivable are deemed to be uncollectible and written off.

T F **5.** Basing the estimated uncollectible accounts on net credit sales is the method for estimating uncollectible accounts that emphasizes the valuation of assets.

T F **6.** Generally, as accounts receivable get older a lower percent of the receivables will be uncollectible.

T F **7.** On the balance sheet, the balance of Allowance for Doubtful Accounts is deducted from the Accounts Receivable account balance to arrive at the net value of the firm's receivables.

T F **8.** Uncollectible Accounts Expense should be deducted from the Sales account in the Revenue section of the income statement.

T F **9.** When a part of an account previously written off is collected, an entry should be made reversing the original write-off of the entire amount written off if the allowance method is being used.

T F **10.** When there is a partial collection of a balance previously written off, only the amount expected to be recoverable should be reversed in the creditor's accounting records.

T F **11.** The collection of an account previously written off is recorded in the general journal and the cash receipts journal.

T F **12.** Aging the accounts receivable will provide useful information for determining the loss from uncollectible accounts.

T F **13.** Providing for losses from uncollectible accounts before they occur permits the seller to match the estimated amount of uncollectible accounts against the sales revenue earned during the same accounting period.

T F **14.** Allowance for Doubtful Accounts is called a valuation account.

T F **15.** Losses resulting from uncollectible accounts should be considered when evaluating the operating efficiency of a firm's credit department.

T F **16.** Allowance for Doubtful Accounts is a liability account.

T F **17.** When losses from uncollectible accounts are recorded using the direct charge-off method, **Uncollectible Accounts Expense** is debited and **Accounts Receivable** and the customers' accounts are credited.

T F **18.** If the direct charge-off method is being used, if an account is charged off in 2007, but is recovered in 2008, the credit entry to reinstate the customer's account should be to **Uncollectible Accounts Expense.**

T F **19.** If the provision for estimated losses from uncollectible accounts is based on a percent of net sales, the balance of the allowance account is adjusted so that it equals the product of the percentage of net sales.

Part B Exercise I   *Determining the amount of uncollectible accounts expense using the allowance method.*

In each of the following cases, compute the amount of the adjusting entry to be debited to **Uncollectible Accounts Expense** and enter the amount in the space provided. Round all calculations to the nearest dollar.

The balance of the Accounts Receivable account on December 31 is $122,000. Total sales for the year were $1.2 million. Total sales returns and allowances were $32,000. Gross credit sales were $980,000, and returns of credit sales were $22,700.

_____   1. **Allowance for Doubtful Accounts** has a credit balance of $80. Losses from uncollectible accounts are estimated as six-tenths of one percent of net credit sales.

_____   2. **Allowance for Doubtful Accounts** has a debit balance of $60. Losses from uncollectible accounts are estimated to be six-tenths of 1 percent of net credit sales.

_____   3. **Allowance for Doubtful Accounts** has a credit balance of $80. It is estimated that 5 percent of **Accounts Receivable** are uncollectible.

_____   4. Allowance for Doubtful Accounts has a debit balance of $110. It is estimated that 5 percent of Accounts Receivable are uncollectible.

Part C Exercise II   *Prepare a schedule of accounts receivable by age, based on the information that follows. Use the form provided.*

At the end of its first year of operations, on December 31, 2007, Network Distributors had accounts receivable totaling $32,800. The accounts and amounts outstanding are shown below. Sales terms are 2/10, net 30 days.

Alfred Ameche
Invoice of 10/3 $2,500
Invoice of 12/04   2,500

Total $5,000

Dwayne Delvin
Invoice of 9/15 $4,500
Invoice of 10/25   2,500

Total $7,000

Graham Girroir
Invoice of 12/08 $6,000

Harold Hess
Invoice of 11/12 $4,800
Invoice of 11/19   2,000

Total $6,800

Adolph Uris
Invoice of 12/15 $8,000

Instructions: Prepare an aging schedule for the accounts receivable, using the form provided below.

ACCOUNT	BALANCE	CURRENT	PAST DUE—DAYS		
			1–30	31–60	OVER 60
Ameche, Alfred					
Delvin, Dwayne					
Girroir, Graham					
Hess, Harold					
Uris, Adolph					

Demonstration Problem

Manor Carts is a retailer of golf carts and other motorized sports vehicles. In 2007, its net credit sales were $28,260,000. The company's trial balance for December 31, contained the following account balances.

Accounts Receivable	$3,126,000
Allowance for Doubtful Accounts (credit)	2,600

In preparing the trial balance, the following additional accounts were identified as being uncollectible and should be charged off.

Philip Baker	$1,949
Douglas Elliott	2,308

Instructions

(Omit explanations in journal entries.)

1. Record the general journal entry to charge off the two accounts identified as being uncollectible.

2. Assume that the company uses the percentage of sales method to estimate uncollectible accounts expense. Historical data shows that approximately 0.35 percent of net credit sales prove uncollectible. Enter the necessary adjusting journal entry to record estimated uncollectible accounts expense.

3. Assume that the company bases its estimated uncollectible accounts on accounts receivable. The company estimates that approximately three percent of accounts receivable will be uncollectible. Prepare the general journal entry to adjust the accounts on that basis.

4. Assume that the company uses the aging of accounts receivable method to estimate uncollectible accounts. Using the following information, calculate the estimated uncollectible amount on December 31, 2007, and prepare the general journal entry to adjust the accounts.

Receivable Category	Estimated Loss Rate	Amount in Receivables
Current	0.5%	$2,315,000
1–30 days past due	3.5%	543,400
31–60 days past due	15.5%	194,370
Over 60 days past due	41.0%	68,973
		$3,121,743

5. Assume that on February 8, 2008, Philip Baker, whose account was charged off on December 31, 2007 (Instruction 1), sent a check for the entire amount of his account. Give the entries, in general journal form to account for this event.

SOLUTION

GENERAL JOURNAL   PAGE ___6___

	DATE		DESCRIPTION	POST. REF.	DEBIT	CREDIT	
1	2007						1
2	Dec.	31	Allowance for Doubtful Accounts		4 2 5 7 00		2
3			Accounts Receivable/Philip Baker			1 9 4 9 00	3
4			Accounts Receivable/Douglas Elliott			2 3 0 8 00	4
5							5
6		31	Uncollectible Accounts Expense		98 9 1 0 00		6
7			Allowance for Doubtful Accounts			98 9 1 0 00	7
8							8
9		31	Uncollectible Accounts Expense		95 3 0 9 00		9
10			Allowance for Doubtful Accounts			95 3 0 9 00	10
11							11
12		31	Uncollectible Accounts Expense		90 6 5 7 00		12
13			Allowance for Doubtful Accounts			90 6 5 7 00	13
14							14
15	2008						15
16	Feb.	8	Accounts Receivable/Philip Baker		1 9 4 9 00		16
17			Allowance for Doubtful Accounts			1 9 4 9 00	17
18							18
19		8	Cash		1 9 4 9 00		19
20			Accounts Receivable/Philip Baker			1 9 4 9 00	20
21							21
22							22
23							23
24							24

WORKING PAPERS

EXERCISE 15.1

_____
_____
_____
_____
_____

GENERAL JOURNAL

PAGE _____

	DATE		DESCRIPTION	POST. REF.	DEBIT	CREDIT	
1							1
2							2
3							3
4							4
5							5
6							6
7							7
8							8
9							9

EXERCISE 15.2

_____
_____
_____
_____

GENERAL JOURNAL

PAGE _____

	DATE		DESCRIPTION	POST. REF.	DEBIT	CREDIT	
1							1
2							2
3							3
4							4
5							5
6							6
7							7
8							8
9							9
10							10
11							11
12							12

EXERCISE 15.3

_____
_____
_____
_____
_____

GENERAL JOURNAL

PAGE _____

	DATE	DESCRIPTION	POST. REF.	DEBIT	CREDIT	
1						1
2						2
3						3
4						4
5						5
6						6
7						7
8						8

EXERCISE 15.4

GENERAL JOURNAL

PAGE _____

	DATE	DESCRIPTION	POST. REF.	DEBIT	CREDIT	
1						1
2						2
3						3
4						4
5						5
6						6
7						7
8						8

EXERCISE 15.5

GENERAL JOURNAL   PAGE _____

	DATE		DESCRIPTION	POST. REF.	DEBIT	CREDIT	
1							1
2							2
3							3
4							4
5							5
6							6
7							7
8							8
9							9
10							10
11							11

EXERCISE 15.6

GENERAL JOURNAL   PAGE _____

	DATE		DESCRIPTION	POST. REF.	DEBIT	CREDIT	
1							1
2							2
3							3
4							4
5							5
6							6
7							7
8							8
9							9
10							10

EXERCISE 15.7

GENERAL JOURNAL   PAGE _____

	DATE	DESCRIPTION	POST. REF.	DEBIT	CREDIT	
1						1
2						2
3						3
4						4
5						5
6						6
7						7
8						8
9						9
10						10
11						11
12						12
13						13
14						14
15						15

EXERCISE 15.8

GENERAL JOURNAL   PAGE _____

	DATE	DESCRIPTION	POST. REF.	DEBIT	CREDIT	
1						1
2						2
3						3
4						4
5						5
6						6
7						7
8						8
9						9
10						10
11						11
12						12
13						13
14						14
15						15

EXERCISE 15.8 (continued)

GENERAL JOURNAL

PAGE _____

	DATE	DESCRIPTION	POST. REF.	DEBIT	CREDIT	
1						1
2						2
3						3
4						4
5						5
6						6
7						7
8						8
9						9
10						10
11						11
12						12
13						13
14						14
15						15

EXTRA FORM

GENERAL JOURNAL

PAGE _____

	DATE	DESCRIPTION	POST. REF.	DEBIT	CREDIT	
1						1
2						2
3						3
4						4
5						5
6						6
7						7
8						8
9						9
10						10
11						11
12						12
13						13
14						14
15						15

PROBLEM 15.1A or 15.1B

_____
_____
_____

GENERAL JOURNAL

PAGE _____

	DATE		DESCRIPTION	POST. REF.	DEBIT	CREDIT	
1							1
2							2
3							3
4							4
5							5
6							6
7							7
8							8
9							9
10							10
11							11
12							12
13							13
14							14
15							15
16							16
17							17
18							18

Analyze: _____

PROBLEM 15.2A or 15.2B

ESTIMATE OF UNCOLLECTIBLE ACCOUNTS

_____

_____

_____

_____

_____

ADJUSTMENT FOR ESTIMATED UNCOLLECTIBLE ACCOUNTS

_____

_____

_____

GENERAL JOURNAL   PAGE _____

	DATE	DESCRIPTION	POST. REF.	DEBIT	CREDIT	
1						1
2						2
3						3
4						4
5						5
6						6
7						7
8						8
9						9
10						10
11						11
12						12
13						13
14						14
15						15
16						16
17						17

2						2
3						3
4						4
5						5
6						6
7						7

Analyze: _____

PROBLEM 15.3A or 15.3B

1. a. _____

b. _____

2. a. _____

b. _____

Analyze: _____

PROBLEM 15.4A or 15.4B

GENERAL JOURNAL

PAGE _____

	DATE		DESCRIPTION	POST. REF.	DEBIT	CREDIT	
1							1
2							2
3							3
4							4
5							5
6							6
7							7
8							8
9							9
10							10
11							11
12							12
13							13
14							14
15							15
16							16
17							17
18							18
19							19
20							20
21							21
22							22
23							23
24							24
25							25
26							26
27							27
28							28
29							29
30							30
31							31
32							32
33							33
34							34
35							35

Analyze: _____

_____

Name _____

CHAPTER 15 CHALLENGE PROBLEM

GENERAL JOURNAL

PAGE _____

	DATE	DESCRIPTION	POST. REF.	DEBIT	CREDIT
1					
2					
3					
4					
5					
6					
7					
8					
9					
10					
11					
12					
13					
14					
15					
16					
17					
18					
19					
20					
21					

ESTIMATE OF UNCOLLECTIBLE ACCOUNTS

Allowance for Doubtful Accounts

Accounts Receivable

CHAPTER 15 CHALLENGE PROBLEM (continued)

Analyze: _____

CHAPTER 15 CRITICAL THINKING PROBLEM

GENERAL JOURNAL

PAGE _____

	DATE		DESCRIPTION	POST. REF.	DEBIT	CREDIT	
1							1
2							2
3							3
4							4
5							5
6							6
7							7
8							8
9							9
10							10
11							11
12							12
13							13
14							14
15							15
16							16
17							17
18							18
19							19
20							20
21							21
22							22
23							23
24							24
25							25
26							26
27							27
28							28

ESTIMATED UNCOLLECTIBLE ACCOUNTS

_____

_____

_____

_____

CHAPTER 15 CRITICAL THINKING PROBLEM (continued)

GENERAL JOURNAL   PAGE _____

	DATE		DESCRIPTION	POST. REF.	DEBIT	CREDIT	
1							1
2							2
3							3
4							4
5							5
6							6
7							7
8							8
9							9
10							10
11							11

Allowance for Doubtful Accounts

ANALYSIS BY TERRITORY

EXTRA FORM

GENERAL JOURNAL

PAGE _____

	DATE		DESCRIPTION	POST. REF.	DEBIT	CREDIT	
1							1
2							2
3							3
4							4
5							5
6							6
7							7
8							8
9							9
10							10
11							11
12							12
13							13
14							14
15							15
16							16
17							17
18							18
19							19
20							20

GENERAL JOURNAL

PAGE _____

	DATE		DESCRIPTION	POST. REF.	DEBIT	CREDIT	
1							1
2							2
3							3
4							4
5							5
6							6
7							7
8							8
9							9
10							10
11							11
12							12

Chapter 15 Practice Test Answer Key

Part A True-False

1. F	18. F
2. F	19. F
3. T	
4. F	
5. F	
6. F	
7. T	
8. F	
9. F	
10. T	
11. T	
12. T	
13. T	
14. T	
15. T	
16. F	
17. T	

Part B Exercise I

1. $5,744
2. $5,744
3. $6,020
4. $6,210

Part C Exercise II

NETWORK DISTRIBUTORS
Schedule of Accounts Receivable by Age
December 31, 2007

ACCOUNT	BALANCE	CURRENT	PAST DUE—DAYS 1–30	31–60	OVER 60
Ameche, Alfred	$ 5,000	$ 2,500		$2,500	
Delvin, Dwayne	7,000			2,500	$4,500
Girroir, Graham	6,000	6,000			
Hess, Harold	6,800		$6,800		
Uris, Adolph	8,000	8,000			
Totals	$32,800	$16,500	$6,800	$5,000	$4,500

CHAPTER 16

Notes Payable and Notes Receivable

STUDY GUIDE

Understanding the Chapter

Objectives

1. Determine whether an instrument meets all the requirements of negotiability. **2.** Calculate the interest on a note. **3.** Determine the maturity date of a note. **4.** Record routine notes payable transactions. **5.** Record discounted notes payable transactions. **6.** Record routine notes receivable transactions. **7.** Compute the proceeds from a discounted note receivable and record transactions related to discounting of notes receivable. **8.** Understand how to use bank drafts and trade acceptances and how to record transactions related to those instruments. **9.** Define the accounting terms new to this chapter.

Reading Assignment

Read Chapter 16 in the textbook. Complete the textbook Section Self Review as you finish reading each section of the chapter, and the Comprehensive Self Review at the end of the chapter. Refer to the Chapter 16 Glossary or to the Glossary at the end of the book to find definitions for terms that are not familiar to you.

Activities

❑ **Thinking Critically**
Answer the *Thinking Critically* questions for KB Home, Accounting on the Job, and Managerial Implications.

❑ **Internet Application**
Complete the activity for Accounting on the Job.

❑ **Discussion Questions**
Answer each assigned discussion question in Chapter 16.

❑ **Exercises**
Complete each assigned exercise in Chapter 16. Use the forms provided in this SGWP. The objectives covered by an exercise are given after the exercise number. If you need help with an exercise, review the portion of the chapter related to the objective(s) covered.

❑ **Problems A/B**
Complete each assigned problem in Chapter 16. Use the forms provided in this SGWP. The objectives covered by a problem are given after the problem number. If you need help with a problem, review the portion of the chapter related to the objective(s) covered.

❑ **Challenge Problem**
Complete the challenge problem as assigned. Use the forms provided in this SGWP.

❑ **Critical Thinking Problem**
Complete the critical thinking problem as assigned. Use the forms provided in this SGWP.

❑ **Business Connections**
Complete the Business Connections activities as assigned to gain a deeper understanding of Chapter 16 concepts.

Practice Tests

Complete the Practice Tests, which cover the main points in your reading assignment. Compare your answers with those in the Practice Test Answer Key for Chapter 16 at the end of this chapter. If you have answered any questions incorrectly, review the related section of the text.

Part A True-False

For each of the following statements, circle T in the answer column if the statement is true, F if the statement is false.

1. To be negotiable, an instrument must:

T   F   **a.** Be payable only to a named person

T   F   **b.** Be signed by the maker or drawer

T   F   **c.** Be payable on demand or at a future time that is fixed or that can be determined

T   F   **d.** Contain an unconditional promise to pay a definite sum

T   F   **e.** Be written on a standard note form

T   F   **f.** Name or identify any drawee mentioned in the instrument

T   F   **2.** Interest = Principal × Rate × Time

T   F   **3.** In computing interest, a "bankers' year" of 365 days is normally used.

T   F   **4.** The maturity value of a note is the amount of principal less any interest that is payable on the due date of the note.

T   F   **5.** Banks deduct interest in advance when discounting a note payable.

T   F   **6.** Notes Payable may appear in the Current Assets section or in the Long-Term Assets section of the balance sheet.

T   F   **7.** The payment of a promissory note results in a debit to Cash and a credit to Notes Payable.

T   F   **8.** The methods used in computing maturity dates and interest on a note receivable are the same as those used for a note payable.

T   F   **9.** The discounting of a note receivable involves a debit to Cash.

T   F   **10.** Short-term notes receivable are listed in the Assets section on the balance sheet, just above Cash.

T   F   **11. The Notes Receivable—Discounted** account is a liability account.

T   F   **12.** A bank draft is a draft written by a bank on its own funds.

13. The Alamar Company receives a $2,000 note from a customer. The note is dated July 31, matures four months later, and bears interest at 6 percent.

T   F   **a.** The maturity date of the note is December 1.

T   F   **b.** The maturity value of the note is $2,120.

T   F   **c.** If the note is discounted on November 1 at a discount rate of 10 percent, the proceeds will be $2,013.08.

T   F   **d.** If the customer dishonors the note at maturity and the bank charges a protest fee of $25, the total amount to be charged to Alamar's account by the bank will be $2,025.

Part B Exercises *Complete each of the following in the spaces provided.*

1. Fill in the blanks in each case below.

	Date of Note	Face Amount	Length of Note	Maturity Date	Interest Rate	Total Interest	Maturity Value
a.	3/8/07	$4,000	3 months	_____	10%	$_____	$_____
b.	6/10/07	$2,400	60 days	_____	_____	$ 24.00	_____

2. The maturity value of a note receivable is $1,800. The holder of the note discounts it at the bank with 30 days left until its maturity date. The bank charges a discount rate of 10 percent. Compute the proceeds of the note.

_____

_____

_____

3. Give the general journal entry to record the following transactions. Omit the description.

Alonzo Jamison borrowed $9,000 from the Mid Cities Bank on April 10, 2007, signing a 60-day, 10 percent, interest-bearing note for that amount. On the maturity date, Jamison paid the note.

GENERAL JOURNAL   PAGE _____

	DATE	DESCRIPTION	POST. REF.	DEBIT	CREDIT	
1						1
2						2
3						3
4						4
5						5
6						6

Demonstration Problem

Compute each of the amounts called for in the situations described below. Show all your computations.

   1. Compute the maturity value of a $3,200 note payable. The note carries interest of 8 percent and is payable 60 days from February 27, 2007, the date of the note.

   2. What is the amount of a bank's discount on a 120-day note for $9,000, discounted at 7 percent?

   3. What is the maturity value of a $3,000, 6-month note receivable, bearing interest at 8 percent?

   4. On July 31, 2007, Mark discounted a $5,000 note payable at the bank. The discount rate was 10 percent. The term is three months. Give the journal entry to record the transaction.

   5. Claudia Cox is late paying her account of $2,000 at your business. Cox signs a note for that amount with interest at 8 percent. The note is due 60 days from July 31, the date of signing.
   a. Give the general journal entry to record this transaction. Omit descriptions.
   b. Give the general journal entry to record payment in full on the note's maturity date.
   c. Suppose, instead, that the note holder discounted Cox's note at the bank with 45 days remaining on the note. The bank charged a discount rate of 10 percent. Give the general journal to record discounting of this note receivable.

SOLUTION

1. Maturity Value = Principal + Interest

= $3,200 + ($3,200 × 0.08 × 60/360)

= $3,200 + $42.67

= $3,242.67

2. Discount = $9,000 × 0.07 × 120/360

= $210.00

3. Maturity Value = Principal + Interest

= $3,000 + ($3,000 × .08 × 6/12)

= $3,000 + $120

= $3,120

4. Discount = ($5,000 × .10 × 3/12)

= $125

Proceeds = $5,000 − $125

= $4,875

GENERAL JOURNAL

PAGE _____

	DATE		DESCRIPTION	POST. REF.	DEBIT	CREDIT	
1	2007						1
2	July	31	Cash		4 8 7 5 00		2
3			Interest Expense		1 2 5 00		3
4			Notes Payable			5 0 0 0 00	4
5							5

5. a. Notes Receivable = Amount of account balance = $2,000

b. Maturity Value = $2,000 + ($2,000 × 0.08 × 60/360)

= $2,000 + $26.67

= $2,026.67

c. Proceeds = Maturity Value − Discount

= $2,026.67 − ($2,026.67 × .10 × 45/360)

= $2,026.67 − $25.33

= $2,001.34

GENERAL JOURNAL

PAGE __12__

	DATE		DESCRIPTION	POST. REF.	DEBIT	CREDIT	
1	2007						1
2	a. July	31	Notes Receivable		2 0 0 0 00		2
3			Accounts Receivable/Claudia Cox			2 0 0 0 00	3
4							4
5	b. Sept.	29	Cash		2 0 2 6 67		5
6			Interest Income			2 6 67	6
7			Notes Receivable			2 0 0 0 00	7
8							8
9	c. Aug.	15	Cash		2 0 0 1 34		9
10			Notes Receivable Discounted			2 0 0 0 00	10
11			Interest Income			1 34	11

WORKING PAPERS

Name _____

EXERCISE 16.1

1. _____
2. _____
3. _____

EXERCISE 16.2

1. _____
_____
_____
_____

2. _____
_____
_____
_____

EXERCISE 16.3

1. _____
_____
_____
_____

2. _____
_____
_____
_____

EXERCISE 16.4

GENERAL JOURNAL   PAGE _____

	DATE	DESCRIPTION	POST. REF.	DEBIT	CREDIT	
1						1
2						2
3						3
4						4
5						5
6						6
7						7
8						8
9						9
10						10
11						11
12						12
13						13
14						14
15						15

EXERCISE 16.5

GENERAL JOURNAL   PAGE _____

	DATE		DESCRIPTION	POST. REF.	DEBIT	CREDIT	
1							1
2							2
3							3
4							4
5							5
6							6

EXERCISE 16.6

GENERAL JOURNAL   PAGE _____

	DATE		DESCRIPTION	POST. REF.	DEBIT	CREDIT	
1							1
2							2
3							3
4							4
5							5
6							6
7							7
8							8
9							9
10							10
11							11
12							12

EXERCISE 16.7

GENERAL JOURNAL   PAGE _____

	DATE		DESCRIPTION	POST. REF.	DEBIT	CREDIT	
1							1
2							2
3							3
4							4
5							5
6							6

EXERCISE 16.8

GENERAL JOURNAL   PAGE _____

	DATE	DESCRIPTION	POST. REF.	DEBIT	CREDIT	
1						1
2						2
3						3
4						4
5						5
6						6
7						7

EXTRA FORM

GENERAL JOURNAL   PAGE _____

	DATE	DESCRIPTION	POST. REF.	DEBIT	CREDIT	
1						1
2						2
3						3
4						4
5						5
6						6
7						7
8						8
9						9
10						10
11						11
12						12
13						13
14						14
15						15
16						16
17						17
18						18
19						19
20						20
21						21

PROBLEM 16.1A or 16.1B

1. _____

_____

_____

_____

2. _____

_____

3. _____

_____

Analyze: _____

_____

PROBLEM 16.2A or 16.2B

GENERAL JOURNAL

PAGE _____

	DATE	DESCRIPTION	POST. REF.	DEBIT	CREDIT	
1						1
2						2
3						3
4						4
5						5
6						6
7						7
8						8
9						9
10						10
11						11
12						12
13						13
14						14
15						15
16						16
17						17
18						18
19						19
20						20
21						21

Analyze: _____

_____

PROBLEM 16.3A or 16.3B

_____

_____

_____

_____

_____

_____

_____

_____

_____

Analyze: _____

_____

PROBLEM 16.4A or 16.4B

_____

_____

_____

_____

_____

_____

_____

_____

_____

_____

_____

_____

_____

_____

_____

_____

_____

_____

Analyze: _____

_____

PROBLEM 16.5A or 16.5B

GENERAL JOURNAL   PAGE _____

	DATE		DESCRIPTION	POST. REF.	DEBIT	CREDIT	
1							1
2							2
3							3
4							4
5							5
6							6
7							7
8							8
9							9
10							10
11							11
12							12
13							13
14							14
15							15
16							16
17							17
18							18
19							19
20							20

Analyze: _____

_____

CHAPTER 16 CHALLENGE PROBLEM

Omit descriptions   GENERAL JOURNAL   PAGE _____

	DATE	DESCRIPTION	POST. REF.	DEBIT	CREDIT	
1						1
2						2
3						3
4						4
5						5
6						6
7						7
8						8
9						9
10						10
11						11
12						12
13						13
14						14
15						15
16						16
17						17
18						18
19						19
20						20
21						21
22						22
23						23
24						24
25						25
26						26
27						27
28						28
29						29
30						30
31						31
32						32
33						33
34						34
35						35
36						36
37						37

CHAPTER 16 CHALLENGE PROBLEM (continued)

Omit descriptions   GENERAL JOURNAL   PAGE _____

	DATE	DESCRIPTION	POST. REF.	DEBIT	CREDIT	
1						1
2						2
3						3
4						4
5						5
6						6
7						7
8						8
9						9
10						10
11						11

Analyze: _____

_____

CHAPTER 16 CRITICAL THINKING PROBLEM

_____

_____

_____

_____

_____

_____

_____

_____

_____

_____

_____

_____

_____

_____

_____

_____

_____

_____

_____

Chapter 16 Practice Test Answer Key

Part A True-False

1. a.	F	**3.**	F	**10.**	F	
b.	T	**4.**	F	**11.**	F	
c.	T	**5.**	T	**12.**	F	
d.	T	**6.**	F	**13. a.**	T	
e.	F	**7.**	F	**b.**	F	
f.	T	**8.**	T	**c.**	F	
2.	T	**9.**	T	**d.**	F	

Part B Exercises

1. a. Maturity date,   6/8/07
   Total interest, $ 100
   Maturity value, $4,100
b. Maturity date,   8/9/07
   Interest rate   6%
   Maturity value $2,424

2. Discount = $1,800 × .10 × 30/360 = $15
   Proceeds = $1,800 − $15 = $1,785

3.

Apr. 10	Cash	9,000.00	
	Notes Payable—Bank		9,000.00
June 9	Notes Payable—Bank	9,000.00	
	Interest Expense	150.00	
	Cash		9,150.00

STUDY GUIDE

Understanding the Chapter

Objectives	**1.** Compute inventory cost by applying four commonly used costing methods. **2.** Compare the different methods of inventory costing. **3.** Compute inventory value under the lower of cost or market rule. **4.** Estimate inventory cost using the gross profit method. **5.** Estimate inventory cost using the retail method. **6.** Define the accounting terms new to this chapter.
Reading Assignment	Read Chapter 17 in the textbook. Complete the textbook Section Self Review as you finish reading each section of the chapter, and the Comprehensive Self Review at the end of the chapter. Refer to the Chapter 17 Glossary or to the Glossary at the end of the book to find definitions for terms that are not familiar to you.

Activities

❏ **Thinking Critically**	Answer the *Thinking Critically* questions for Circuit City Stores, Inc., Computers in Accounting, and Managerial Implications.
❏ **Internet Application**	Complete the activity for Computers in Accounting.
❏ **Discussion Questions**	Answer each assigned discussion question in Chapter 17.
❏ **Exercises**	Complete each assigned exercise in Chapter 17. Use the forms provided in this SGWP. The objectives covered by an exercise are given after the exercise number. If you need help with an exercise, review the portion of the chapter related to the objective(s) covered.
❏ **Problems A/B**	Complete each assigned problem in Chapter 17. Use the forms provided in this SGWP. The objectives covered by a problem are given after the problem number. If you need help with a problem, review the portion of the chapter related to the objective(s) covered.
❏ **Challenge Problem**	Complete the challenge problem as assigned. Use the forms provided in this SGWP.
❏ **Critical Thinking Problem**	Complete the critical thinking problem as assigned. Use the forms provided in this SGWP.
❏ **Business Connections**	Complete the Business Connections activities as assigned to gain a deeper understanding of Chapter 17 concepts.

Practice Tests

Complete the Practice Tests, which cover the main points in your reading assignment. Compare your answers with those in the Practice Test Answer Key for Chapter 17 at the end of this chapter. If you have answered any questions incorrectly, review the related section of the text.

Part A True-False

T   F   **1.** LIFO inventory costing parallels the actual flow of goods in most businesses.

T   F   **2.** The valuation of the ending inventory has a direct effect on the net income for a period.

T   F   **3.** As used in inventory valuation, market price is the price at which an item can be bought at the inventory date through the usual channels and in the usual quantities.

T   F   **4.** During a period of falling prices, the FIFO method of inventory valuation will result in a higher reported net income than the LIFO method.

T   F   **5.** The gross profit method of estimating inventory and the retail method utilize the same basic concept—the relation between sales price of inventory and its cost.

T   F   **6.** Applying the lower of cost or market rule on the basis of total cost and total market will generally result in a higher value than its application on the basis of individual items or groups of items.

T   F   **7.** The average cost method of inventory valuation will usually result in the lowest reported net income of the valuation methods that may be used.

T   F   **8.** A decline in the market value of inventory to less than its cost should be reflected in the financial statements of the period in which the decline occurs.

T   F   **9.** Under the perpetual inventory system, the cost of goods on hand at any given time can be determined.

T   F   **10.** Ending Merchandise Inventory appears on both the balance sheet and the income statement.

T   F   **11.** It is necessary to count the goods on hand to estimate the inventory cost under the retail method.

T   F   **12.** The most conservative method of applying the lower of cost or market rule is to apply it to inventory items on a group by group basis.

T   F   **13.** During a period of rising prices, the FIFO method will yield a lower ending inventory cost than the LIFO method.

Part B Matching

For each of the numbered items, choose the matching term from the box and write the identifying letter in the answer column.

_____	**1.** Reduction of an originally established selling price.
_____	**2.** The inventory valuation method that attempts to match the current cost of goods purchased with current sales.
_____	**3.** The difference between the cost and the original retail selling price of merchandise.
_____	**4.** The inventory valuation method in which the actual cost of each individual item is determined.
_____	**5.** An inventory valuation method that assumes the oldest items of inventory are sold first.
_____	**6.** Determining the sales value of the goods on hand and computing the approximate cost by applying the ratio of cost to the selling price during the accounting period.
_____	**7.** The cost of all like items available for sale during a period are averaged to determine a unit cost in valuing the ending inventory.

a.	Average cost
b.	First in, first out
c.	Last in, first out
d.	Markdown
e.	Markup
f.	Retail method
g.	Specific identification

Demonstration Problem

The Top Brands Bargain Store has three types of electronic weather systems in its electronics department. Group A, Group P and Group X. The following data relates to January 2007 inventory transactions for the three groups.

Inventory, January 1, 2007:

Group A	8 @ $100.00
Group P	16 @ $105.00
Group X	8 @ $200.00

Purchases

Date	Group	Units	Unit Cost	Total
Jan. 6	A	32	$110.00	$3,520.00
	P	20	120.00	2,400.00
	X	30	205.00	6,150.00
Jan. 16	A	24	115.00	2,760.00
	P	24	125.00	3,000.00
	X	20	210.00	4,200.00
Jan. 26	A	20	116.00	2,320.00
	P	20	130.00	2,600.00
	X	10	217.50	2,175.00

The company uses the LIFO method of determining cost of inventory.
Sales for the month were as follows:

Group A	74 units
Group P	40 units
Group X	44 units

1. What is the cost of goods sold during the month?
2. What is the cost of the ending inventory?

SOLUTION

1. **Cost of Goods Sold:**

Group A	20 units @ $116.00	=	$ 2,320.00
	24 units @ $115.00	=	2,760.00
	30 units @ $110.00	=	3,300.00
	Total, Group A		$ 8,380.00
Group P	20 units @ $130.00	=	$ 2,600.00
	20 units @ $125.00	=	2,500.00
	Total, Group P		$ 5,100.00
Group X	10 units @ $217.50	=	$ 2,175.00
	20 units @ $210.00	=	4,200.00
	14 units @ $205.00	=	2,870.00
	Total, Group X		$ 9,245.00
Total Cost of Goods Sold			**$ 22,725.00**

2. **Cost of Ending Inventory**

Group A	2 units @ $110.00	=	$ 220.00
	8 units @ $100.00	=	800.00
	Total, Group A	=	$ 1,020.00
Group P	4 units @ $125.00	=	$ 500.00
	20 units @ $120.00	=	2,400.00
	16 units @ $105.00	=	1,680.00
	Total, Group P		$ 4,580.00
Group X	16 units @ $205.00	=	$ 3,280.00
	8 units @ $200.00	=	1,600.00
	Total, Group X		$ 4,880.00
Total Ending Inventory			**$ 10,480.00**

WORKING PAPERS

EXERCISE 17.1

Description	Number of Units	Unit Cost	Total Cost
_____	_____	_____	_____
_____	_____	_____	_____
_____	_____	_____	_____
_____	_____	_____	_____
_____	_____	_____	_____
_____	_____	_____	_____
_____	_____	_____	_____

1. Average Cost Method

_____	_____	_____	_____
_____	_____	_____	_____
_____	_____	_____	_____
_____	_____	_____	_____

2. FIFO Method

_____	_____	_____	_____
_____	_____	_____	_____
_____	_____	_____	_____
_____	_____	_____	_____

3. LIFO Method

_____	_____	_____	_____
_____	_____	_____	_____
_____	_____	_____	_____
_____	_____	_____	_____

EXERCISE 17.2

_____

_____

_____

_____

_____

_____

_____

_____

_____

EXERCISE 17.3

Description	Quantity	Unit Cost	Market Value	Total Cost	Total Market

1. Item by Item

_____

_____

2. Total Cost or Total Market Value of Ending Inventory

_____

3. By Groups

_____

EXERCISE 17.4

_____

EXERCISE 17.5

ESTIMATED INVENTORY COST

	Cost	Retail

PROBLEM 17.1A or 17.1B

Description	Number of Units	Unit Cost	Total Cost
_____	_____	_____	_____
_____	_____	_____	_____
_____	_____	_____	_____
_____	_____	_____	_____
_____	_____	_____	_____
_____	_____	_____	_____
_____	_____	_____	_____
_____	_____	_____	_____

a. Average Cost Method

_____	_____	_____	_____
_____	_____	_____	_____
_____	_____	_____	_____
_____	_____	_____	_____
_____	_____	_____	_____

b. FIFO Method

_____	_____	_____	_____
_____	_____	_____	_____
_____	_____	_____	_____
_____	_____	_____	_____
_____	_____	_____	_____

c. LIFO Method

_____	_____	_____	_____
_____	_____	_____	_____
_____	_____	_____	_____
_____	_____	_____	_____
_____	_____	_____	_____

Analyze: _____

_____

PROBLEM 17.2A or 17.2B

1.

Description	Number of Units	Unit Cost	Total Cost
_____	_____	_____	_____
_____	_____	_____	_____
_____	_____	_____	_____
_____	_____	_____	_____
_____	_____	_____	_____
_____	_____	_____	_____
_____	_____	_____	_____

Description	Number of Units	Unit Cost	Total Cost	Inventory Valuation	Cost of Goods Sold
a. FIFO Method					
_____	_____	_____	_____	_____	_____
_____	_____	_____	_____	_____	_____
_____	_____	_____	_____	_____	_____
_____	_____	_____	_____	_____	_____
_____	_____	_____	_____	_____	_____
b. LIFO Method					
_____	_____	_____	_____	_____	_____
_____	_____	_____	_____	_____	_____
_____	_____	_____	_____	_____	_____
_____	_____	_____	_____	_____	_____
_____	_____	_____	_____	_____	_____
_____	_____	_____	_____	_____	_____
c. Average Cost Method					
_____	_____	_____	_____	_____	_____
_____	_____	_____	_____	_____	_____
_____	_____	_____	_____	_____	_____
_____	_____	_____	_____	_____	_____

2.

Method	Number of Units	Valuation Based On: Cost	Valuation Based On: Market	Valuation Basis	Lower of Cost or Market
a. FIFO	_____	_____	_____	_____	_____
b. LIFO	_____	_____	_____	_____	_____
c. Average Cost	_____	_____	_____	_____	_____

Analyze: _____

_____

PROBLEM 17.3A or 17.3B

Description	Quantity	Unit Cost	Market Value	Total Cost	Total Market	Lower of Cost or Market
_____	_____	_____	_____	_____	_____	_____
_____	_____	_____	_____	_____	_____	_____
_____	_____	_____	_____	_____	_____	_____
_____	_____	_____	_____	_____	_____	_____
_____	_____	_____	_____	_____	_____	_____
_____	_____	_____	_____	_____	_____	_____
_____	_____	_____	_____	_____	_____	_____
_____	_____	_____	_____	_____	_____	_____
_____	_____	_____	_____	_____	_____	_____
_____	_____	_____	_____	_____	_____	_____

Inventory Valuations

Lower of Cost or Market

_____

_____

_____

_____

_____

_____

_____

Analyze: _____

PROBLEM 17.4A or 17.4B

_____

_____

_____

_____

_____

_____

_____

_____

Analyze: _____

PROBLEM 17.5A or 17.5B

Estimated Inventory	Cost	Retail
_____	_____	_____
_____	_____	_____
_____	_____	_____
_____	_____	_____
_____	_____	_____
_____	_____	_____
_____	_____	_____
_____	_____	_____
_____	_____	_____
_____	_____	_____
_____	_____	_____

Analyze: _____
_____

PROBLEM 17.6A or 17.6B

_____
_____
_____
_____

Item	Cost
_____	_____
_____	_____
_____	_____
_____	_____
_____	_____
_____	_____
_____	_____
_____	_____
_____	_____
_____	_____
_____	_____

Analyze: _____
_____

CHAPTER 17 CHALLENGE PROBLEM

_____
_____
_____

Estimated Inventory	Cost	Retail

Analyze: _____

CHAPTER 17 CRITICAL THINKING PROBLEM

_____
_____
_____
_____
_____
_____
_____
_____
_____

Chapter 17 Practice Test Answer Key

Part A True-False

1. F	6. T	11. F
2. T	7. F	12. F
3. T	8. T	13. F
4. F	9. T	
5. T	10. T	

Part B Matching

1. **d** (markdown)
2. **c** (last in, first out)
3. **e** (markon)
4. **g** (specific identification)
5. **b** (First in, first out)
6. **f** (retail method)
7. **a** (average cost)

CHAPTER 18 Property, Plant, and Equipment

STUDY GUIDE

Understanding the Chapter

Objectives

1. Determine the amount to record as an asset's cost. 2. Compute and record depreciation of property, plant, and equipment by commonly used methods. 3. Apply the Modified Accelerated Cost Recovery System (MACRS) for federal income tax purposes. 4. Record sales of plant and equipment. 5. Record asset trade-ins using the financial accounting rules and income tax requirements. 6. Compute and record depletion of natural resources. 7. Recognize asset impairment and understand the general concepts of accounting for impairment. 8. Compute and record amortization and impairment of intangible assets. 9. Define the accounting terms new to this chapter.

Reading Assignment

Read Chapter 18 in the textbook. Complete the textbook Section Self Review as you finish reading each section of the chapter, and the Comprehensive Self Review at the end of the chapter. Refer to the Chapter 18 Glossary or to the Glossary at the end of the book to find definitions for terms that are not familiar to you.

Activities

❏ **Thinking Critically**

Answer the *Thinking Critically* questions for The Coca-Cola Company, Accounting on the Job, and Managerial Implications.

❏ **Internet Application**

Complete the activity for Accounting on the Job.

❏ **Discussion Questions**

Answer each assigned discussion question in Chapter 18.

❏ **Exercises**

Complete each assigned exercise in Chapter 18. Use the forms provided in this SGWP. The objectives covered by an exercise are given after the exercise number. If you need help with an exercise, review the portion of the chapter related to the objective(s) covered.

❏ **Problems A/B**

Complete each assigned problem in Chapter 18. Use the forms provided in this SGWP. The objectives covered by a problem are given after the problem number. If you need help with a problem, review the portion of the chapter related to the objective(s) covered.

❏ **Challenge Problem**

Complete the challenge problem as assigned. Use the forms provided in this SGWP.

❏ **Critical Thinking Problem**

Complete the critical thinking problem as assigned. Use the forms provided in this SGWP.

❏ **Business Connections**

Complete the Business Connections activities as assigned to gain a deeper understanding of Chapter 18 concepts.

Practice Tests

Complete the Practice Tests, which cover the main points in your reading assignment. Compare your answers with those in the Practice Test Answer Key for Chapter 18 at the end of this chapter. If you have answered any questions incorrectly, review the related section of the text.

T   F   **1.** The cost of paving a parking lot for a business is debited to the land account on which the lot is located.

T   F   **2.** At the end of an accounting period, current depreciation or depletion is debited to an expense account and credited to a contra-asset account.

T   F   **3. Prepaid Insurance** is included in plant and equipment.

T   F   **4.** A building under construction is an example of an intangible asset.

T   F   **5.** The cost of installing or modifying a new asset should be charged to expense.

T   F   **6.** If the declining-balance depreciation method is used, salvage is ignored until that time at which the accumulated depreciation equals estimated salvage. From that point forward, no further depreciation is recorded.

T   F   **7.** The sum-of-the-years'-digits method is an accelerated method of depreciation.

T   F   **8.** Salvage is ignored if the sum-of-years'-digits method of depreciation is used.

T   F   **9.** A business must use the same depreciation method for all its assets.

T   F   **10.** The decline in market value of an asset each period is generally a satisfactory measure of depreciation of the asset for that period.

T   F   **11.** Depreciation should be debited to expense and credited to the asset account.

T   F   **12.** Salvage value is ignored under the units-of-output method.

T   F   **13.** If the trade-in allowance for an old asset is greater than its book value, for financial accounting purposes a gain should be recognized on the trade-in.

T   F   **14.** Neither gain nor loss is recognized for income tax purposes on the exchange or trade-in of like assets.

T   F   **15.** Under GAAP, a loss on the trade-in of an old asset of like kind must be recognized.

T   F   **16.** The declining-balance method should be used in computing depletion on the cost of mineral deposits.

T   F   **17.** Under GAAP most R & D costs must be charged to expense when incurred.

T   F   **18.** Amortization of the costs of amortizable intangibles is charged to an expense account and credited directly to the asset account.

T   F   **19.** Costs of intangible assets having limited lives, such as patents and copyrights, should be amortized over the legal life of the intangible or its useful life, whichever is shorter.

T   F   **20.** Purchased intangibles with unlimited lives, such as goodwill, are not amortized, but are subject to an impairment test each year.

Part B Matching *For each numbered item, choose the matching term from the box and write the identifying letter in the answer column.*

_____ **1.** A means of computing annual depreciation by applying a constant percentage to the book value of an asset at the beginning of the year.

_____ **2.** A method of computing annual depreciation by dividing the depreciable cost of the asset by the expected units of production and multiplying that rate by the units produced during the year.

_____ **3.** The term used to describe the periodic transfer of capitalized costs of plant and equipment to expense.

_____ **4.** Assets such as patents, goodwill, trademarks and copyrights.

_____ **5.** The difference between the capitalized costs of an asset and the accumulated depreciation for the asset.

_____ **6.** A method of computing depreciation in which the same amount is recorded for each accounting period over the useful life of an asset.

_____ **7.** The term used to describe the periodic transfer of acquisition costs to expense when natural resources such as ores or oil are physically removed by production.

_____ **8.** The term used to describe the situation when an asset is determined to have a market value or value-in-use less than its book value.

_____ **9.** The transfer of cost of an intangible asset with a fixed life to expense.

_____ **10.** The value of a business in excess of its net identifiable assets.

a. Amortization

b. Book value

c. Declining balance method

d. Depletion

e. Depreciation

f. Goodwill

g. Impairment

h. Intangibles

i. Straight-line method

j. Unit-of-production methods

Part C Exercise

On January 1, 2007, a business acquired at a cost of $11,000 new office equipment with an estimated useful life of 8 years. Estimated salvage value at the end of that time is $1,000. Compute depreciation for 2007 and 2008 using the following methods. (Round all computations to nearest whole dollar.)

a. straight-line method.

b. the sum-of-years'-digits method.

c. double-declining-balance method.

Demonstration Problem

Agrilu Company was formed in January 2007 to operate a research laboratory.

1. In January it acquired a tract of land at a cost of $192,000. In connection with the purchase, Agrilu paid closing costs of $8,000. The company immediately began preparations for constructing the new laboratory. This included costs of $3,000 to demolish a shed located on the land, $2,000 to have the debris removed, $10,000 for leveling the building site, $4,000 for "clean-up of the property" required as condition of purchase, and $3,500 for drainage of low areas of land. The owners paid $17,000 for design and engineering of the building, $1,000 for legal fees associated with the building permit, and $800 for the city permit fee. Erecting a fence along the rear of the property cost $13,600. The building was completed in December, 2007. Determine the total cost of each asset involved. Show the details of cost of each.

SOLUTION

Land:

Purchase price	$192,000
Closing costs	8,000
Shed demolition	3,000
Debris removal	2,000
Property clean-up	4,000
Leveling site	10,000
Drainage	3,500
Land total	$222,500

Land Improvements:

Paving parking lot	$ 88,000
Erect fence	13,600
Improvements total	$101,600

Building:

Design and engineering	$ 17,000
Legal fees—permit	1,000
City permit fee	800
Construction contract	800,000
Building total	$818,800

2. Agrilu completed the building at the end of 2007 and placed in use on January 2, 2008. Its useful life is estimated as 30 years, with estimated net salvage value of $38,800. Three chemical research "vats," the items of equipment to be used, were installed and were put into operation on January 2, 2008. The four units are quite different in use and in physical characteristics.

   a. Vat one cost $240,000 and has an estimated life of five years, and estimated net salvage value of $24,000. Because of high operating cost as the unit is used, Agrilu decided to use the double-declining-balance method of depreciation on the asset.

   b. Vat two cost $150,000 nad has an estimated useful life of 10 years, with expected net salvage of $15,000. Because its operating costs and the hours of use are expected to be fairly constant, straight-line depreciation is used.

   c. Vat three cost $350,000 and is expected to have a salvage value of $30,000, with an expected useful life of 8 years. It is decided to apply the sum-of-years'-digits method to this asset.

   Compute depreciation on the building and each of these three vats for 2007 and 2008. (Round all amounts to nearest whole dollar.)

SOLUTION

<u>Building:</u>

2008 depreciation ($818,800 − $38,800) ÷ 30 years	=	$26,000
2009 depreciation ($818,800 − $38,800) ÷ 30 years	=	$26,000

<u>Vat 1:</u>

2008 depreciation ($240,000 × .40)	=	$96,000
2009 depreciation ($240,000 − $96,000) × .40	=	$57,600

<u>Vat 2:</u>

2008 depreciation ($150,000 − $15,000) × .10	=	$13,500
2009 depreciation ($150,000 − $15,000) × .10	=	$13,500

<u>Vat 3:</u>

2008 depreciation ($350,000 − $30,000) × 8/36	=	$71,111
2009 depreciation ($350,000 − $30,000) × 7/36	=	$62,222

3. On March 31, 2009, Agrilu realized that Vat 2 was inadequate and traded it on a new vat (Vat 4) with a fair value and list price of $250,000. Agrilu received a trade-in allowance of $65,000 for Vat 2 and paid the difference of $185,000 in cash.
   a. What amount of depreciation will be recorded on March 31 on Vat 2?
   b. Will gain or loss be recorded on the trade-in? If so, which? If so, how much?
   c. What amount will be recorded in the asset account for Vat 4?

SOLUTION

a. Depreciation for three months = [($150,000 − $15,000) × .10 × 3/12] = $3,375.

b. Losses, but not gains, are recognized. In this case the loss is $54,625:

Trade-in allowance received	$ 65,000
Less: book value of old asset (150,000 − $16,875)	133,125
= Loss on trade-in	$ 68,125

c. Vat 4 cost is deemed to be cash paid ($185,000) + trade-in allowance ($65,000) = $250,000. This is also the fair market value of the new asset.

WORKING PAPERS

Name _____

EXERCISE 18.1

	Land	Warehouse
_____	_____	_____
_____	_____	_____
_____	_____	_____
_____	_____	_____
_____	_____	_____

EXERCISE 18.2

_____		_____
_____		_____
_____		_____
_____		_____
_____		_____

EXERCISE 18.3

GENERAL JOURNAL
PAGE _____

	DATE	DESCRIPTION	POST. REF.	DEBIT	CREDIT	
1						1
2						2
3						3
4						4
5						5
6						6
7						7

EXTRA FORM

GENERAL JOURNAL
PAGE _____

	DATE	DESCRIPTION	POST. REF.	DEBIT	CREDIT	
1						1
2						2
3						3
4						4
5						5
6						6
7						7

EXERCISE 18.4

STRAIGHT-LINE METHOD

Year	Acquisition Cost	Salvage Value	Useful Life	Depreciation	Accumulated Depreciation
_____	_____	_____	_____	_____	_____
_____	_____	_____	_____	_____	_____

DOUBLE-DECLINING-BALANCE METHOD

Year	Beginning Book Value	Rate	Depreciation	Accumulated Depreciation
_____	_____	_____	_____	_____
_____	_____	_____	_____	_____

SUM-OF-THE-YEARS'-DIGITS METHOD

Year	Fraction	Cost Less Salvage	Depreciation	Accumulated Depreciation
_____	_____	_____	_____	_____
_____	_____	_____	_____	_____

EXERCISE 18.5

_____ _____ _____

_____

_____

_____

_____

_____

_____

_____

_____

_____

_____

_____

_____

_____

_____

EXERCISE 18.6

_____
_____
_____
_____
_____
_____
_____
_____

EXERCISE 18.7

GENERAL JOURNAL

PAGE _____

	DATE		DESCRIPTION	POST. REF.	DEBIT	CREDIT	
1							1
2							2
3							3
4							4
5							5
6							6
7							7
8							8
9							9
10							10
11							11
12							12
13							13

EXERCISE 18.8

_____
_____
_____
_____
_____
_____
_____
_____

GENERAL JOURNAL

PAGE _____

	DATE	DESCRIPTION	POST. REF.	DEBIT	CREDIT	
1						1
2						2
3						3
4						4
5						5
6						6
7						7
8						8
9						9
10						10
11						11
12						12
13						13

EXERCISE 18.9

1. _____

2. _____

_____

_____

_____

_____

_____

_____

_____

_____

_____

EXERCISE 18.10

_____

_____

_____

_____

_____

_____

EXERCISE 18.11

a. _____
_____
_____
_____

b. _____
_____
_____
_____

EXERCISE 18.12

1. _____
_____
_____
_____
_____
_____
_____

2. _____
_____
_____
_____
_____
_____
_____

PROBLEM 18.1A or 18.1B

1. _____ _____
   _____ _____
   _____ _____
   _____ _____
   _____ _____

2. _____ _____
   _____ _____
   _____ _____
   _____ _____
   _____ _____
   _____ _____
   _____ _____
   _____ _____
   _____ _____
   _____ _____
   _____ _____
   _____ _____

3. _____ _____
   _____ _____
   _____ _____
   _____ _____
   _____ _____
   _____ _____

Analyze: _____ _____
   _____ _____
   _____ _____

PROBLEM 18.2A or 18.2B

STRAIGHT-LINE METHOD

Year	Acquisition Cost	Salvage Value	Useful Life	Annual Depreciation	Accumulated Depreciation
____	____	____	____	____	____
____	____	____	____	____	____
____	____	____	____	____	____

SUM-OF-THE-YEARS'-DIGITS METHOD

Year	Fraction	Cost Less Salvage	Annual Depreciation	Accumulated Depreciation
____	____	____	____	____
____	____	____	____	____
____	____	____	____	____

DOUBLE-DECLINING-BALANCE METHOD

Year	Beginning Book Value	Rate	Annual Depreciation	Accumulated Depreciation
____	____	____	____	____
____	____	____	____	____
____	____	____	____	____

Analyze: _____
_____

PROBLEM 18.3A or 18.3B

STRAIGHT-LINE METHOD

Year	Acquisition Cost	Salvage Value	Useful Life	Annual Depreciation	Accumulated Depreciation
____	____	____	____	____	____
____	____	____	____	____	____
____	____	____	____	____	____

UNITS-OF-PRODUCTION METHOD

Year	Acquisition Cost	Salvage Value	Total Expected Units of Production	Actual Units of Production	Cost per Unit	Annual Depreciation	Accumulated Depreciation
____	____	____	____	____	____	____	____
____	____	____	____	____	____	____	____
____	____	____	____	____	____	____	____

Analyze: _____
_____

PROBLEM 18.4A or 18.4B

1. _____

   _____

   _____

   _____

   _____

2. _____

   _____

   _____

   _____

   _____

   _____

3. _____

   _____

   _____

   _____

   _____

4. _____

   _____

   _____

   _____

   _____

Analyze: _____

   _____

   _____

   _____

   _____

PROBLEM 18.5A or 18.5B

GENERAL JOURNAL   PAGE _____

	DATE	DESCRIPTION	POST. REF.	DEBIT	CREDIT	
1						1
2						2
3						3
4						4
5						5
6						6
7						7
8						8
9						9
10						10
11						11
12						12
13						13
14						14
15						15
16						16
17						17
18						18
19						19
20						20
21						21
22						22
23						23
24						24
25						25
26						26
27						27
28						28
29						29
30						30
31						31
32						32
33						33
34						34
35						35
36						36

Analyze: _____

PROBLEM 18.6A or 18.6B

GENERAL JOURNAL   PAGE _____

	DATE		DESCRIPTION	POST. REF.	DEBIT	CREDIT	
1							1
2							2
3							3
4							4
5							5
6							6
7							7
8							8
9							9
10							10
11							11
12							12
13							13
14							14
15							15
16							16
17							17
18							18
19							19
20							20
21							21
22							22
23							23
24							24
25							25
26							26
27							27
28							28
29							29
30							30
31							31
32							32
33							33
34							34
35							35
36							36
37							37

PROBLEM 18.6A or 18.6B (continued)

GENERAL JOURNAL   PAGE _____

	DATE	DESCRIPTION	POST. REF.	DEBIT	CREDIT	
1						1
2						2
3						3
4						4
5						5
6						6
7						7
8						8
9						9
10						10
11						11
12						12
13						13
14						14
15						15
16						16
17						17
18						18
19						19
20						20
21						21
22						22
23						23
24						24
25						25
26						26
27						27
28						28
29						29
30						30
31						31
32						32
33						33
34						34
35						35
36						36

Analyze: _____

PROBLEM 18.7A or 18.7B

1. _____
_____
_____
_____
_____
_____

2. a. _____
_____
_____

   b. _____
_____
_____

   c. _____
_____
_____
_____
_____
_____
_____
_____
_____
_____

   d. _____
_____
_____

Analyze: _____
_____
_____
_____
_____

PROBLEM 18.8A or 18.8B

1. _____

_____

_____

_____

_____

_____

_____

_____

2. _____

_____

_____

3. _____

_____

_____

4. _____

_____

_____

_____

_____

Analyze: _____

_____

_____

_____

_____

_____

_____

PROBLEM 18.9A or 18.9B

GENERAL JOURNAL   PAGE _____

	DATE	DESCRIPTION	POST. REF.	DEBIT	CREDIT	
1						1
2						2
3						3
4						4
5						5
6						6
7						7
8						8
9						9
10						10
11						11
12						12
13						13
14						14
15						15
16						16
17						17
18						18
19						19
20						20
21						21
22						22
23						23
24						24
25						25
26						26
27						27
28						28
29						29
30						30
31						31
32						32
33						33
34						34
35						35
36						36
37						37

PROBLEM 18.9A or 18.9B (continued)

GENERAL JOURNAL   PAGE _____

	DATE	DESCRIPTION	POST. REF.	DEBIT	CREDIT	
1						1
2						2
3						3
4						4
5						5
6						6
7						7
8						8
9						9
10						10
11						11
12						12
13						13
14						14
15						15
16						16
17						17
18						18
19						19
20						20
21						21
22						22
23						23
24						24
25						25
26						26
27						27
28						28
29						29
30						30
31						31
32						32
33						33
34						34
35						35
36						36
37						37

CHAPTER 18 CHALLENGE PROBLEM

GENERAL JOURNAL   PAGE _____

	DATE		DESCRIPTION	POST. REF.	DEBIT	CREDIT	
1							1
2							2
3							3
4							4
5							5
6							6
7							7
8							8
9							9
10							10
11							11
12							12
13							13
14							14
15							15
16							16
17							17
18							18
19							19
20							20
21							21
22							22
23							23
24							24
25							25
26							26
27							27
28							28
29							29
30							30
31							31
32							32
33							33

Analyze: _____

CHAPTER 18 CRITICAL THINKING PROBLEM

1. _____

_____

_____

_____

_____

_____

_____

2. _____

_____

_____

_____

_____

_____

_____

3. _____

_____

_____

_____

_____

_____

_____

4. _____

_____

_____

_____

_____

_____

_____

Chapter 18 Practice Test Answer Key

Part A True-False			Part B Matching	
1. F	8. F	15. T	1. c	6. i
2. T	9. F	16. F	2. j	7. d
3. F	10. F	17. T	3. e	8. g
4. F	11. F	18. T	4. h	9. a
5. F	12. F	19. T	5. b	10. f
6. T	13. F	20. T		
7. T	14. T			

Part C Exercise

1. Depreciation for 2007 = ($11,000 − $1,000) ÷ 8 years = $1,250
   Depreciation for 2008 = ($11,000 − $1,000) ÷ 8 years = $1,250
2. Depreciation for 2007 = ($11,000 − $1,000) × 8/36 = $2,222
   Depreciation for 2008 = ($11,000 − $1,000) × 7/36 = $1,944
3. Depreciation for 2007 = $11,000 × .25 = $2,750
   Depreciation for 2008 = ($11,000 − $2,750) × .25 = $2,063

STUDY GUIDE

Understanding the Chapter

Objectives

1. Explain the major advantages and disadvantages of a partnership. **2.** State the important provisions that should be included in every partnership agreement. **3.** Account for the formation of a partnership. **4.** Compute and record the division of net income or net loss between partners in accordance with the partnership agreement. **5.** Prepare a statement of partners' equities. **6.** Account for the revaluation of assets and liabilities prior to the dissolution of a partnership. **7.** Account for the sale of a partnership interest. **8.** Account for the investment of a new partner in an existing partnership. **9.** Account for the withdrawal of a partner from a partnership. **10.** Define the accounting terms new to this chapter.

Reading Assignment

Read Chapter 19 in the textbook. Complete the textbook Section Self Review as you finish reading each section of the chapter, and the Comprehensive Self Review at the end of the chapter. Refer to the Chapter 19 Glossary or to the Glossary at the end of the book to find definitions for terms that are not familiar to you.

Activities

❏ **Thinking Critically**

Answer the *Thinking Critically* questions for Healthcare Venture Professionals, L.L.C., Computers in Accounting, and Managerial Implications.

❏ **Internet Application**

Complete the activity for Computers in Accounting.

❏ **Discussion Questions**

Answer each assigned discussion question in Chapter 19.

❏ **Exercises**

Complete each assigned exercise in Chapter 19. Use the forms provided in this SGWP. The objectives covered by an exercise are given after the exercise number. If you need help with an exercise, review the portion of the chapter related to the objective(s) covered.

❏ **Problems A/B**

Complete each assigned problem in Chapter 19. Use the forms provided in this SGWP. The objectives covered by a problem are given after the problem number. If you need help with a problem, review the portion of the chapter related to the objective(s) covered.

❏ **Challenge Problem**

Complete the challenge problem as assigned. Use the forms provided in this SGWP.

❏ **Critical Thinking Problem**

Complete the critical thinking problem as assigned. Use the forms provided in this SGWP.

❏ **Business Connections**

Complete the Business Connections activities as assigned to gain a deeper understanding of Chapter 19 concepts.

Practice Tests

Complete the Practice Tests, which cover the main points in your reading assignment. Compare your answers with those in the Practice Test Answer Key for Chapter 19 at the end of this chapter. If you have answered any questions incorrectly, review the related section of the text.

Part A True-False *For each of the following statements, circle T in the answer column if the statement is true or F if the statement is false.*

T F **1.** A major advantage of the partnership form of business entity is that it does not pay federal income taxes.

T F **2.** Unless the partnership agreement states otherwise, partners share profits and losses equally among the partners.

T F **3.** General partners have personal liability for all debts of the partnership.

T F **4.** Limited partners do not, generally, have a voice in operating decisions.

T F **5.** Unless otherwise stated in the partnership agreement, a partnership has a life of 28 years.

T F **6.** A legal partnership may exist without a written partnership agreement.

T F **7.** Unless the partnership agreement provides otherwise, profits and losses are shared in proportion to average balances in their capital accounts during the year.

T F **8.** When the assets and liabilities of an existing sole proprietorship are transferred to a partnership, they are recorded on the partnership books at their fair market values.

T F **9.** Salary allowances to partners are deducted in arriving at net income for financial accounting purposes; however they are not deductible in determining net income for federal income tax purposes.

T F **10.** If fixed assets are transferred from an existing sole proprietorship to a partnership, the accumulated balance of the **Allowance for Depreciation** account should be brought forward to the partnership books.

T F **11.** Each partner should have a drawing account and a capital account.

T F **12.** Salary allowances to partners are considered in dividing net income or loss, even though the partnership may have a loss for the period.

T F **13.** A salary may be allowed to one partner, even though other partners do not receive salary allowances.

T F **14.** Salaries allowed a partner must be deducted in arriving at the partnership's net profit or loss for the year.

T F **15.** The partnership's accounting records should reflect the sales price of an existing partnership interest to a new partner.

T F **16.** If a new partner purchases an interest from an old partner, no cash comes into the partnership, and the only entry necessary is one to record the transfer between the capital accounts.

T F **17.** A gain or loss on revaluation of assets should be allocated to the partners in accordance with ratio of the balance of the partners' capital accounts.

T F **18.** If a new partner's investment is greater than the corresponding partnership equity, it may be said that a bonus has been allowed the original partners.

Part B Matching *For each numbered item, choose the matching term from the box and write the identifying letter in the answer column.*

_____ 1. The rule that one partner's actions can bind all other partners.

_____ 2. The adjustment of asset and liability accounts to reflect current value.

_____ 3. The situation in which all assets are sold and cash is distributed to partners.

_____ 4. The situation in which a business continues even though an owner dies or transfers ownership to someone else.

_____ 5. The value placed on the partnership interest of a partner who dies.

_____ 6. A legal contract between the partners creating the partnership.

_____ 7. A factor that may be used in dividing profits and losses.

_____ 8. A characteristic of partnerships under which a partner is responsible for all debts of the partnership.

_____ 9. The account that is debited for salary payments to a partner.

_____ 10. A partner who has general liability for losses and debts of a partnership without being limited to that partner's investment in the partnership.

_____ 11. The amount that may be credited to the old partners' accounts when the amount invested by a new partner is greater than that partner's share of total equity.

a. Bonus

b. Business continuity

c. Dissolution value

d. General partner

e. Liquidation

f. Mutual agency

g. Partner's Drawing

h. Partnership agreement

i. Revaluation

j. Salary allowance

k. Unlimited liability

Part C Completion *In the answer column, supply the missing word or words needed to complete each of the following statements.*

_____ 1. The _____ is a written contract between the partners containing the major provisions of their agreement.

_____ 2. _____ partners have liability for debts of the partnership only to the extent of their investments.

_____ 3. Articles of Partnership are commonly referred to as the _____.

_____ 4. A partnership is said to lack _____ because the partnership is terminated if a partner dies or is incapacitated.

_____ 5. The _____ (partnership, partners) must pay federal income tax on a partnership's profits.

_____ 6. Assets transferred to a partnership by a sole proprietor in return for a partnership interest should be recorded in the partnership's records at their _____.

_____ 7. A partnership _____ occurs when the partnership is completely terminated and the business ceases to exist.

_____ 8. Payments of salaries to a partner should be charged to the _____ account.

_____ 9. At the end of the period each partner's drawing account is closed into the _____ account.

_____ 10. If an incoming partner invests less than the book value of his or her interest, the _____ partner(s) can be said to have received a bonus.

Demonstration Problem

For several years, Sam Davis has operated the Davis Hardware Store (there are actually three stores) as a sole proprietor. Near the end of 2007, he agreed to form a partnership with Ken Ingram to operate the stores under the name Davis-Ingram Stores, effective January 1, 2008. Pertinent terms of the partnership agreement follow:

1. Davis-Ingram Stores is to withdraw all cash from his business on December 31, 2007. He is to transfer to the partnership the accounts receivable, merchandise inventory, furniture and equipment, and all liabilities of the sole proprietorship in return for a partnership interest of 60 percent of the partnership capital. Davis Hardware Store assets are to be appraised and transferred to the partnership at the appraised values.

   Balances in the relevant accounts of Davis' sole proprietorship at the close of business on December 31, 2007, were:

Accounts Receivable	$126,800 Dr.
Allowance for Doubtful Accounts	8,400 Cr.
Merchandise Inventory	213,000 Dr.
Furniture and Equipment	138,000 Dr.
Allowance for Depreciation of	
Furniture and Equipment	10,000 Cr.
Accounts Payable	70,000 Cr.

2. The two parties agreed there are $2,000 of additional unrecorded accounts payable and unrecorded accrued expenses of $1,500. They also agreed that $4,000 of the accounts receivable were definitely uncollectible and should not be transferred to the partnership and that the balance for **Allowance for Doubtful Accounts** should be $6,000. The appraised values of the other assets were: Merchandise Inventory, $198,000, and Furniture and Equipment, $108,000.

3. In return for a 40 percent interest in partnership capital, Ingram is to invest cash in an amount equal to two-thirds of Davis' net investment.

4. Each partner is to be allowed a salary, payable on the 15th day of each month. Davis' salary is to be $8,000 per month and Ingram's is to be $6,000 per month.

5. The partners are to be allowed interest of 10 percent of their beginning Capital balances.

6. The balance of profit or loss after salary and interest allowance is to be divided equally between the two partners.

7. Revenues for 2008 were $2,060,000, expenses were $528,000, and cost of goods sold was $1,292,000. Payments for salary allowances were charged to the Drawing accounts.

Instructions

1. Record the general journal entries for the following transactions. Omit descriptions.

   a. Receipt by the partnership of assets and liabilities from Davis on January 1, 2008.

   b. Investment of cash by Ingram on January 1, 2008.

   c. Summary of cash withdrawals for salaries for the two partners during the year (date entry as December 31, 2008.)

2. Prepare a schedule showing the division of net income to the partners as it would appear on the income statement for 2008.

3. Prepare journal entries to record the following factors related to distribution of net income or loss for the year:

   a. Entry to record salary allowances

   b. Entry to record interest allowances

   c. Entry to close balance of **Income Summary** account

SOLUTION

1.

GENERAL JOURNAL

PAGE ___1___

	DATE		DESCRIPTION	POST. REF.	DEBIT	CREDIT	
1	**2008**		a.				1
2	**Jan.**	**1**	**Accounts Receivable**		126 8 0 0 00		2
3			**Merchandise Inventory**		198 0 0 0 00		3
4			**Furniture and Equipment**		108 0 0 0 00		4
5			**Allowance for Doubtful Accounts**			6 0 0 0 00	5
6			**Accounts Payable**			72 0 0 0 00	6
7			**Accrued Expenses**			1 5 0 0 00	7
8			**Sam Davis, Capital**			353 3 0 0 00	8
9							9
10			b.				10
11		**1**	**Cash**		235 5 3 4 00		11
12			**Ken Ingram, Capital**			235 5 3 4 00	12
13							13
14			c.				14
15	**Dec.**	**31**	**Sam Davis, Drawing**		96 0 0 0 00		15
16			**Ken Ingram, Drawing**		72 0 0 0 00		16
17			**Cash**			168 0 0 0 00	17
18							18
19							19
20							20
21							21
22							22
23							23
24							24
25							25
26							26
27							27
28							28
29							29
30							30
31							31
32							32
33							33
34							34
35							35
36							36
37							37

SOLUTION (continued)

2.

Davis-Ingram Stores

Income Statement (Partial)

Year Ended December 31, 2008

	Davis	Ingram	
Net Income for Year			240 0 0 0 00
Salary Allowance	96 0 0 0 00	72 0 0 0 00	168 0 0 0 00
Interest Allowance	35 3 3 0 00	23 5 5 3 00	58 8 8 3 00
Remainder in 50:50 Ratio	6 5 5 8 50	6 5 5 8 50	13 1 1 7 00
	137 8 8 8 50	102 1 1 1 50	240 0 0 0 00

3.

GENERAL JOURNAL PAGE _____

	DATE		DESCRIPTION	POST. REF.	DEBIT	CREDIT	
1	2008		a.				1
2	Dec.	31	Income Summary		168 0 0 0 00		2
3			Sam Davis, Capital			96 0 0 0 00	3
4			Ken Ingram, Capital			72 0 0 0 00	4
5							5
6			b.				6
7		31	Income Summary		58 8 8 3 00		7
8			Sam Davis, Capital			35 3 3 0 00	8
9			Ken Ingram, Capital			23 5 5 3 00	9
10							10
11			c.				11
12		31	Income Summary		13 1 1 7 00		12
13			Sam Davis, Capital			6 5 5 8 50	13
14			Ken Ingram, Capital			6 5 5 8 50	14
15							15
16							16
17							17

WORKING PAPERS

EXERCISE 19.1

GENERAL JOURNAL

PAGE _____

	DATE	DESCRIPTION	POST. REF.	DEBIT	CREDIT	
1						1
2						2
3						3
4						4

EXERCISE 19.2

GENERAL JOURNAL

PAGE _____

	DATE	DESCRIPTION	POST. REF.	DEBIT	CREDIT	
1						1
2						2
3						3
4						4
5						5
6						6
7						7
8						8
9						9

EXERCISE 19.3

EXERCISE 19.4

_____

_____

EXERCISE 19.5

GENERAL JOURNAL   PAGE _____

	DATE	DESCRIPTION	POST. REF.	DEBIT	CREDIT	
1						1
2						2
3						3
4						4
5						5

EXERCISE 19.6

GENERAL JOURNAL   PAGE _____

	DATE	DESCRIPTION	POST. REF.	DEBIT	CREDIT	
1						1
2						2
3						3
4						4
5						5
6						6
7						7
8						8
9						9
10						10
11						11

EXERCISE 19.7

_____

_____

_____

_____

_____

_____

_____

EXERCISE 19.8

_____
_____
_____
_____
_____
_____
_____
_____

EXERCISE 19.9

_____
_____
_____
_____
_____
_____
_____
_____
_____

EXERCISE 19.10

_____
_____
_____
_____
_____

GENERAL JOURNAL   PAGE _____

	DATE		DESCRIPTION	POST. REF.	DEBIT	CREDIT	
1							1
2							2
3							3
4							4
5							5
6							6
7							7
8							8
9							9

EXERCISE 19.10 (continued)

_____
_____
_____

EXERCISE 19.11

GENERAL JOURNAL   PAGE _____

	DATE	DESCRIPTION	POST. REF.	DEBIT	CREDIT	
1						1
2						2
3						3
4						4
5						5
6						6
7						7
8						8
9						9
10						10

_____
_____
_____

EXERCISE 19.12

_____
_____
_____
_____
_____
_____
_____
_____
_____
_____

PROBLEM 19.1A or 19.1B

Debit – Credit = Capitol

08'

GENERAL JOURNAL

PAGE _____

	DATE	DESCRIPTION	POST. REF.	DEBIT	CREDIT	
1	1/1	Merchandise Inventory		48,900		1
2		Acct. Rec.		14,900		2
3		Fur & Equip		11,300		3
4		CASH		3,750		4
5		Allow for Doubtful Accts			1,400	5
6		A/P			3,000	6
7		B/O Grady Capitol			74,450	7
8		CASH		74,450		8
9		C.loche, Capital			74,450	9
10						10
11						11
12						12
13						13
14						14

CASH			78,200
Accts Recv.	14,900		
Less Allow for Doubtful Accts	1,400		13,500
Merch Inventory			48,900
Fur & Equip			11,300
Total Assets			151,900
Liabilities + owners Equity			
A/P			
Total Liabilities			3,000
B/O Grady, Capitol	74,450		
C.loche, Capital	74,450		
Total Liabilities + O.E			148,900
			151,900

Analyze: 10,200 Net Asset Decreased

PROBLEM 19.2A or 19.2B

GENERAL JOURNAL

PAGE _____

	DATE	DESCRIPTION	POST. REF.	DEBIT	CREDIT	
1		CASH		10 000		1
2		A/R		29 000		2
3		Merch Inv.		173 000		3
4		Furn & Equip		35 800		4
5		A/P			22 000	5
6		Allow for D. Accts			2 200	6
7		T. Isom, Capital			223 600	7
8		CASH		178 880		8
9		A Carl Capital			178 880	9
10						10
11						11
12						12
13						13
14						14

Balance Sheet
_____

Cash				188 880
A/R		29 000		
Less Allow for Doubtful Accts		2 200		26 800
Merch Inventory				173 000
Furn & Equip				35 800
Total Assets				424 480
Liabilities				
A/P				22 000
T. Isom Capital				223 600
A Carl Capital				178 880
				424 480

Analyze: _____

PROBLEM 19.3A or 19.3B

GENERAL JOURNAL

PAGE _____

	DATE	DESCRIPTION	POST. REF.	DEBIT	CREDIT	
1	12/31	Income Summary		70000		1
2		S.G. Cap			42000	2
3		D.L Cap			28000	3
4						4
5	31	S.G Cap (Drawing)		36000		5
6		D.L Cap (Drawing)		45600		6
7		S.G. Drawing			36000	7
8		D.L Drawing			45600	8
9						9
10	31	S.G Cap		12000		10
11		J.L Cap		8000		11
12		Income Summary			20000	12
13						13
14		S.G Cap		36000		14
15		D.L Cap		45600		15
16		S.G Drawing			36000	16
17		D.L Drawing			45600	17

Analyze: Gadd +80000
83,000 / +42,000
92000   56,000

PROBLEM 19.4A or 19.4B

Pg. 689

• GENERAL JOURNAL •   PAGE _____

	DATE	DESCRIPTION	POST. REF.	DEBIT	CREDIT	
1	12/2/07	Tray Miller Capital		40 000		1
2		CASH			40 000	2
3	31	Income Summary		80 000		3
4		S.K. & TM Capital			44 000	4
5		T.M. Capital			36 000	5
6	31	Income Summary		38 000		6
7		SK Cap			17 000	7
8		TM CAP			21 000	8
9						9
10	31	Income Summary		144 000		10
11		SK Cap			10 400	11
12		TM Cap			15 600	12
13	31	SK Cap		44 000		13
14		SK Drawing			44 000	14
15		TM Cap		36 000		15
16		TM Drawing			36 000	16
17						17
18						18
19						19
20						20
21						21
22						22
23						23
24						24
25						25
26						26
27						27
28						28
29						29
30						30
31						31
32						32
33						33
34						34
35						35
36						36
37						37

subtract from (handwritten annotation pointing to line 10)

Austin Antiques
Income Statement

(Partie)

	S.K	T.M	
Net Income for a year			144,000
Distribution of Net Income			
Salary Allowance	44,000	36,000	80,000
Interest Allowance	17,000	21,000	38,000
Remainder 40/60	10,400	15,600	26,000
	71,400	72,600	144,000

Austin Antiques
Statement of Partners Equities

	S.K	T.M	Total
Capital Balances 1-1-07	170,000	210,000	380,000
Net Income	71,400	72,600	144,000
	241,400	282,600	524,000
Less:			
Permanent Withdrawals During Year		40,000	40,000
Normal Withdrawals During Year	44,000	36,000	80,000
Capital Balance Dec 31	197,400	206,600	404,000

Analyze: _____

PROBLEM 19.5A or 19.5B

GENERAL JOURNAL

PAGE _____

	DATE	DESCRIPTION	POST. REF.	DEBIT	CREDIT	
1						1
2						2
3						3
4						4
5						5
6						6
7						7
8						8
9						9
10						10
11						11
12						12
13						13
14						14
15						15
16						16
17						17
18						18
19						19
20						20
21						21
22						22
23						23
24						24
25						25
26						26
27						27
28						28
29						29
30						30
31						31
32						32
33						33
34						34
35						35
36						36
37						37

PROBLEM 19.5A or 19.5B (continued)

GENERAL JOURNAL   PAGE _____

	DATE	DESCRIPTION	POST. REF.	DEBIT	CREDIT	
1						1
2						2
3						3
4						4
5						5
6						6
7						7
8						8
9						9
10						10
11						11
12						12
13						13
14						14
15						15
16						16
17						17
18						18
19						19
20						20
21						21
22						22
23						23
24						24
25						25
26						26
27						27
28						28
29						29
30						30
31						31
32						32
33						33
34						34
35						35
36						36

Analyze: _____

PROBLEM 19.6A or 19.6B

GENERAL JOURNAL PAGE _____

	DATE	DESCRIPTION	POST. REF.	DEBIT	CREDIT	
1						1
2						2
3						3
4						4
5						5
6						6
7						7
8						8
9						9
10						10
11						11
12						12
13						13
14						14
15						15
16						16
17						17
18						18
19						19
20						20
21						21
22						22
23						23
24						24
25						25
26						26
27						27
28						28
29						29
30						30
31						31
32						32
33						33
34						34

Analyze: _____

_____

Name _____

CHAPTER 19 CHALLENGE PROBLEM

(1)

GENERAL JOURNAL

PAGE _____

	DATE		DESCRIPTION	POST. REF.	DEBIT	CREDIT	
1							1
2							2
3							3
4							4
5							5
6							6
7							7
8							8
9							9
10							10
11							11
12							12
13							13
14							14
15							15
16							16
17							17
18							18
19							19
20							20
21							21
22							22
23							23
24							24
25							25
26							26
27							27
28							28
29							29
30							30
31							31
32							32
33							33
34							34
35							35
36							36
37							37

CHAPTER 19 CHALLENGE PROBLEM (continued)

(2)

GENERAL JOURNAL

PAGE _____

	DATE	DESCRIPTION	POST. REF.	DEBIT	CREDIT	
1						1
2						2
3						3
4						4
5						5
6						6
7						7
8						8
9						9
10						10

(3)

GENERAL LEDGER (PARTIAL)

ACCOUNT _____ ACCOUNT NO. _____

DATE	DESCRIPTION	POST. REF.	DEBIT	CREDIT	BALANCE	
					DEBIT	CREDIT

ACCOUNT _____ ACCOUNT NO. _____

DATE	DESCRIPTION	POST. REF.	DEBIT	CREDIT	BALANCE	
					DEBIT	CREDIT

CHAPTER 19 CHALLENGE PROBLEM (continued)

(4)

(5)

(6)

GENERAL JOURNAL

PAGE _____

	DATE		DESCRIPTION	POST. REF.	DEBIT	CREDIT	
1							1
2							2
3							3
4							4
5							5
6							6
7							7
8							8
9							9
10							10

Analyze: _____

CHAPTER 19 CRITICAL THINKING PROBLEM

_____
_____
_____
_____
_____
_____
_____
_____
_____
_____
_____
_____
_____
_____
_____
_____
_____
_____
_____
_____
_____
_____
_____

Chapter 19 Practice Test Answer Key

Part A True-False

1. T	7. F	13. T
2. T	8. T	14. F
3. T	9. F	15. F
4. T	10. F	16. T
5. F	11. T	17. F
6. T	12. T	18. T

Part B Matching

1. f	7. j
2. i	8. k
3. e	9. g
4. b	10. d
5. c	11. a
6. h	

Part C Completion

1. partnership agreement	6. market values
2. limited	7. liquidation
3. partnership agreement	8. partners' drawing
4. continuity	9. capital
5. partners	10. incoming

Corporations: Formation and Capital Stock Transactions

STUDY GUIDE

Understanding the Chapter

Objectives

1. Explain the characteristics of a corporation. **2.** Describe special "hybrid" organizations that have some characteristics of partnerships and some characteristics of corporations. **3.** Describe the different types of stock. **4.** Compute the number of shares of common stock to be issued on the conversion of convertible preferred stock. **5.** Compute dividends payable on stock. **6.** Record the issuance of capital stock at par value. **7.** Prepare a balance sheet for a corporation. **8.** Record organization costs. **9.** Record stock issued at a premium and stock with no par value. **10.** Record transactions for stock subscriptions. **11.** Describe the capital stock records for a corporation. **12.** Define the accounting terms new to this chapter.

Reading Assignment

Read Chapter 20 in the textbook. Complete the textbook Section Self Review as you finish reading each section of the chapter, and the Comprehensive Self Review at the end of the chapter. Refer to the Chapter 20 Glossary or to the Glossary at the end of the book to find definitions for terms that are not familiar to you.

Activities

❏ **Thinking Critically**

Answer the *Thinking Critically* questions for Sara Lee Corporation, Accounting on the Job, and Managerial Implications.

❏ **Internet Application**

Complete the activity for Accounting on the Job.

❏ **Discussion Questions**

Answer each assigned discussion question in Chapter 20.

❏ **Exercises**

Complete each assigned exercise in Chapter 20. Use the forms provided in this SGWP. The objectives covered by an exercise are given after the exercise number. If you need help with an exercise, review the portion of the chapter related to the objective(s) covered.

❏ **Problems A/B**

Complete each assigned problem in Chapter 20. Use the forms provided in this SGWP. The objectives covered by a problem are given after the problem number. If you need help with a problem, review the portion of the chapter related to the objective(s) covered.

❏ **Challenge Problem**

Complete the challenge problem as assigned. Use the forms provided in this SGWP.

❏ **Critical Thinking Problem**

Complete the critical thinking problem as assigned. Use the forms provided in this SGWP.

❏ **Business Connections**

Complete the Business Connections activities as assigned to gain a deeper understanding of Chapter 20 concepts.

Practice Tests

Complete the Practice Tests, which cover the main points in your reading assignment. Compare your answers with those in the Practice Test Answer Key for Chapter 20 at the end of this chapter. If you have answered any questions incorrectly, review the related section of the text.

Part A True-False *For each of the following statements, circle T in the answer column if the answer is true or F if the answer is false.*

T   F   **1.** A shareholder generally has the right to sell the shares he or she owns without prior approval of the corporation.

T   F   **2.** It is necessary to obtain a charter from the United States government before a corporation can commence business.

T   F   **3.** A corporation is a legal entity, separate and apart from its owners.

T   F   **4.** Owners of stock of a corporation are usually personally liable for the corporation's debts.

T   F   **5.** Stockholders are empowered to act for the corporation in most circumstances.

T   F   **6.** Most preferred stock does not have a par value.

T   F   **7.** Usually a corporation must pay federal income taxes on its net income.

T   F   **8.** If dividends on participating preferred stock are not paid in one year, they must be paid in the following year before any dividends can be paid on common stock.

T   F   **9.** If only one class of stock is issued by a corporation, it is referred to as *normal* stock.

T   F   **10.** A corporate charter specifies the classes and number of shares of stock authorized.

T   F   **11.** The preemptive right gives the stockholders the right to receive dividends when declared by the directors.

T   F   **12.** The conversion ratio establishes the number of shares of common stock into which a share of convertible preferred stock can be converted.

T   F   **13.** Callable preferred stock may be reacquired by the corporation from the stockholders at the option of the corporation, provided pre-established conditions are met.

T   F   **14.** Organization costs are now usually charged to expense when incurred.

T   F   **15.** If common stock has a par value, the Common Stock account should be debited for the par value of all common stock issued.

T   F   **16.** The stock certificate is usually issued as soon as the stock subscription is recorded.

T   F   **17.** Preferred stock must have the same par value as the corporation's common stock.

T   F   **18.** Convertible preferred stock must have the same par value as nonconvertible preferred stock.

T   F   **19.** Convertible preferred stock is redeemable for cash by the owner.

Part B Completion *In the answer column, supply the missing word or words needed to complete each of the following statements.*

_____ **1.** The figure shown in the corporate charter to establish a face value for each share of stock is known as _____.

_____ **2.** Stock that may have prior claims on profits or on assets in case of liquidation is known as _____ stock.

_____ **3.** An amount known as _____ may be set by the board of directors to be credited to the Capital Stock account for each share.

_____ **4.** A state government issues a _____, which establishes or creates a corporation.

_____ **5.** If preferred stock is _____, dividends stated must be paid to preferred stockholders for the current year and all prior years before any dividend can be paid on common stock.

_____ **6.** The amount above par value or stated value at which stock is issued is the _____.

_____ **7.** The transfer of stock between shareholders is recorded in the _____ journal.

_____ **8.** The paper that serves as evidence of ownership of stock is the _____.

_____ **9.** The _____ contains a record of all meetings of stockholders and directors.

_____ **10.** A record of the number of shares owned by each shareholder is kept in the _____.

_____ **11.** A corporation that is generally taxed as a partnership is a(an) _____ corporation.

Demonstration Problem

Just after its formation on January 1, 2007, the ledger accounts of the Turner Athletics Corporation showed the following balances.

Accrued Expenses	$ 12,000	Merchandise Inventory	34,750
Accounts Payable	40,000	Notes Payable—Short-Term	22,000
Accounts Receivable	36,000	Paid-in Capital in Excess of Par—Common	34,300
Allowance for Doubtful Accounts	7,000	Paid-in Capital in Excess of Par—Preferred	10,750
Building	200,000	Preferred Stock (8%, $25 Par)	50,000
Cash	37,500	Preferred Stock Subscribed	20,000
Common Stock ($50 Par)	200,000	Subscriptions Receivable—Common	8,800
Common Stock Subscribed	8,000	Subscriptions Receivable—Preferred	20,000
Furniture and Fixtures	67,000		

The corporation is authorized to issue 100,000 shares of $20 par common stock and 20,000 shares of 8 percent, $25 par noncumulative and nonparticipating preferred stock.

Instructions

Answer the questions that follow.

1. How many shares of common stock are outstanding?

2. How many shares of common stock are subscribed?

3. How many shares of preferred stock are outstanding?

4. How many shares of preferred stock are subscribed?

5. At what average price has common stock been subscribed or issued?

6. Assume that no dividends are paid in the first year of the corporation's existence. What are the rights of the preferred stockholders?

7. Assuming that all paid-in capital in excess of par on common stock was applicable to the shares of common stock that have been subscribed but not yet issued, what is the subscription price per share of the common stock subscribed?

8. Assuming that the board of directors declared no dividends in 2007, what amount would have to be paid to preferred stockholders in 2008 before any dividend could be paid to common stockholders?

9. Prepare a classified balance sheet for Turner Athletics Corporation just after its formation on July 1, 2007.

SOLUTION

1. $200,000 ÷ $20 = 10,000 shares of common stock

2. $ 8,000 ÷ $20 =   400 shares

3. $ 50,000 ÷ $25 = 2,000 shares

4. $ 20,000 ÷ $25 =   800 shares

5.	
Common Stock	$200,000
Common Stock Subscribed	8,000
Paid-in Capital in Excess of Par—Common	34,300
Total	$242,300

$242,300 ÷ 14,000 shares = $23.298 per share

6. None. The preferred stock is noncumulative.

7. ($8,000 + $34,300 = $42,300) ÷ 400 = $105.75 per share

8. $2.00 dividend per share must be paid to preferred stockholders ($25 × 0.08)

SOLUTION (continued)

Turner Athletics Corporation
Balance Sheet
July 1, 2007

Assets			
Current Assets			
Cash			37 5 0 0 00
Accounts Receivable	36 0 0 0 00		
Less Allowance for Doubtful Accounts	7 0 0 0 00		29 0 0 0 00
Subscriptions Receivable—Common			8 8 0 0 00
Subscriptions Receivable—Preferred			20 0 0 0 00
Merchandise Inventory			34 7 5 0 00
Total Current Assets			130 0 5 0 00
Property, Plant, and Equipment			
Building	200 0 0 0 00		
Furniture and Fixtures	67 0 0 0 00		
Total Property, Plant, and Equipment			267 0 0 0 00
Total Assets			397 0 5 0 00
Liabilities and Stockholders' Equity			
Current Liabilities			
Accrued Expenses	12 0 0 0 00		
Accounts Payable	40 0 0 0 00		
Notes Payable—Short-Term	22 0 0 0 00		
Total Liabilities			74 0 0 0 00
Stockholders' Equity			
Preferred Stock (8%, $25 par, 20,000 sh auth., 2,000 sh iss. and out.)	50 0 0 0 00		
Preferred Stock Subscribed (800 shares)	20 0 0 0 00		
Paid-in Capital in Excess of Par—Preferred	10 7 5 0 00	80 7 5 0 00	
Common Stock ($20 par, 100,000 shares authorized, 10,000 sh. iss. and out.)	200 0 0 0 00		
Common Stock Subscribed (400 shares)	8 0 0 0 00		
Paid-in Capital in Excess of Par—Common	34 3 0 0 00	242 3 0 0 00	
Total Stockholders' Equity			323 0 5 0 00
Total Liabilities and Stockholders' Equity			397 0 5 0 00

WORKING PAPERS

Name _____

EXERCISE 20.1

_____

_____

_____

_____

EXERCISE 20.2

1. _____

_____

_____

_____

_____

_____

_____

_____

_____

_____

_____

2. _____

_____

_____

_____

_____

_____

_____

_____

_____

_____

_____

_____

_____

_____

_____

_____

_____

_____

EXERCISE 20.3

1. _____
_____
_____
_____
_____
_____
_____
_____
_____
_____

2. _____
_____
_____
_____
_____
_____
_____
_____
_____
_____
_____

EXERCISE 20.4

_____
_____

EXERCISE 20.5

_____
_____
_____

EXERCISE 20.6

_____
_____
_____

EXERCISE 20.7

GENERAL JOURNAL

PAGE _____

	DATE		DESCRIPTION	POST. REF.	DEBIT	CREDIT	
1							1
2							2
3							3
4							4
5							5
6							6
7							7
8							8

EXERCISE 20.8

GENERAL JOURNAL

PAGE _____

	DATE		DESCRIPTION	POST. REF.	DEBIT	CREDIT	
1							1
2							2
3							3
4							4
5							5
6							6
7							7
8							8

EXERCISE 20.9

GENERAL JOURNAL

PAGE _____

	DATE		DESCRIPTION	POST. REF.	DEBIT	CREDIT	
1							1
2							2
3							3
4							4
5							5
6							6
7							7
8							8
9							9
10							10

EXERCISE 20.10

GENERAL JOURNAL

PAGE _____

	DATE	DESCRIPTION	POST. REF.	DEBIT	CREDIT	
1						1
2						2
3						3
4						4
5						5
6						6
7						7
8						8
9						9
10						10
11						11
12						12
13						13
14						14
15						15
16						16
17						17
18						18
19						19
20						20
21						21
22						22
23						23
24						24
25						25
26						26
27						27
28						28
29						29
30						30
31						31
32						32
33						33
34						34
35						35
36						36
37						37

500 × 30 × .10 =

Par value shares
× $ amount per value × % Preff. stock / % Normal shares

PROBLEM 20.1A or 20.1B

	Year	Total Dividends	Preferred Stock Total	Per Share	Common Stock Total	Per Share
CASE A	2005	1,000	1,000	$2.00	Ø	Ø
CASE A	2006	1500	1500	$3.00	Ø	Ø
CASE A	2007	26,500	1500	$3.00	$25,000	$2.50
CASE B	2005	1,000	1,000	$2.00	Ø	Ø
CASE B	2006	1,500	1,500	$3.00	Ø	Ø
CASE B	2007	2,000	2,000	$4.00	$24,500	$2.45
20.1B CASE A 8000×60×.5 $8000	2005	16,000	16,000	$7.00	Ø	Ø
CASE A	2006	24,000	$24,000	3.00	Ø	Ø
CASE A	2007	120,000	24,000	3.00	96,000	9.60
CASE B	2005	16,000	16,000	2.00	Ø	Ø
CASE B	2006	24,000	8000 18,000 24,000	3.00	Ø	Ø
CASE B	2007	120,000	8000+24000 32,000		88,000	8.80

Analyze: _____
_____

PROBLEM 20.2A or 20.2B

PART I

① 75000 × .09 = 6750

05 6750
06 6750
07 :   Payout 12000

② 12,000 ÷ 1500 = 8.00 per share

③ Ø

④ Ø

⑤ 8250

① 600,000 × .06 = 48,000
② 48,000 ÷ 6000 = 7.00
③ Ø
④ Ø
⑤ 102,000

20.2B

48000 ÷ 3
144,00
144,000

PROBLEM 20.2A or 20.2B (continued)

PART II

① 2800 × 0.09 = 6750
② 45,450 ÷ 11,800 =
③   1.80

144,000   48000 × 3 years
1. 24,00   20.2B   144,000 ÷ 600
46,000   240000 − 144,000 = 96,00
3.0

Analyze: _____

PROBLEM 20.3A or 20.3B

GENERAL JOURNAL

PAGE ___1___

	DATE	DESCRIPTION	POST. REF.	DEBIT	CREDIT	
1						1
2						2
3						3
4						4
5						5
6						6
7						7
8						8
9						9
10						10
11						11
12						12
13						13
14						14
15						15
16						16
17						17
18						18
19						19
20						20
21						21
22						22

Analyze: _____

PROBLEM 20.4A or 20.4B

(1)

GENERAL JOURNAL

PAGE _____

DATE	DESCRIPTION	POST. REF.	DEBIT	CREDIT	
Jan 2 07					1
	CASH		23600	23600	2
	Accounts Receivable		177400		3
	Allowance for Doubtful Accts			4800	4
	Merchandise Inv.		330000		5
	A/P			186000	6
	Accrued Exp			9600	7
	Com Stock 22,040 x 15			330600	8
			5000		9
2	CASH			5000	10
	Preferred Stock				11
	Issued 500 shares @ 10ᵃ				12
	CASH		30000		13
	Common Stock Issued 2000			30000	14
	CASH		10000		15
	Preferred Stock			10000	16

504 ■ Chapter 20

Copyright © 2007 The McGraw-Hill Companies, Inc. All rights reserved.

PROBLEM 20.4A or 20.4B (continued)

(2)

20.4 A	Current Assets		
	CASH		68 600
	Accounts Receivable	177 400	
	Less Allowance for doubtful Accounts	4 800	172 600
	Merchandise Inv		330 000
	Total Current Assets		571 200
	Current Liabilities		
	A/P		186 000
	Stockholders Equity		
	Preferred Stock	5 000	
	Common Stock	30 000	

Analyze: _____

PROBLEM 20.5A or 20.5B

GENERAL JOURNAL   PAGE _____

	DATE		DESCRIPTION	POST. REF.	DEBIT	CREDIT	
1							1
2							2
3							3
4							4
5							5
6							6
7							7
8							8
9							9
10							10
11							11
12							12
13							13
14							14
15							15
16							16
17							17
18							18
19							19
20							20
21							21
22							22
23							23
24							24
25							25
26							26
27							27
28							28
29							29
30							30
31							31
32							32
33							33
34							34
35							35
36							36
37							37

PROBLEM 20.5A or 20.5B (continued)

GENERAL JOURNAL

PAGE _____

	DATE	DESCRIPTION	POST. REF.	DEBIT	CREDIT	
1						1
2						2
3						3
4						4
5						5
6						6
7						7
8						8
9						9
10						10
11						11
12						12
13						13
14						14
15						15
16						16
17						17
18						18
19						19
20						20
21						21
22						22

GENERAL LEDGER

ACCOUNT _____ ACCOUNT NO. _____

DATE	DESCRIPTION	POST. REF.	DEBIT	CREDIT	BALANCE	
					DEBIT	CREDIT

PROBLEM 20.5A or 20.5B (continued)

GENERAL LEDGER

ACCOUNT _____ ACCOUNT NO. _____

DATE	DESCRIPTION	POST. REF.	DEBIT	CREDIT	BALANCE	
					DEBIT	CREDIT

ACCOUNT _____ ACCOUNT NO. _____

DATE	DESCRIPTION	POST. REF.	DEBIT	CREDIT	BALANCE	
					DEBIT	CREDIT

ACCOUNT _____ ACCOUNT NO. _____

DATE	DESCRIPTION	POST. REF.	DEBIT	CREDIT	BALANCE	
					DEBIT	CREDIT

ACCOUNT _____ ACCOUNT NO. _____

DATE	DESCRIPTION	POST. REF.	DEBIT	CREDIT	BALANCE	
					DEBIT	CREDIT

ACCOUNT _____ ACCOUNT NO. _____

DATE	DESCRIPTION	POST. REF.	DEBIT	CREDIT	BALANCE	
					DEBIT	CREDIT

PROBLEM 20.5A or 20.5B (continued)

GENERAL LEDGER

ACCOUNT _____ ACCOUNT NO. _____

DATE	DESCRIPTION	POST. REF.	DEBIT	CREDIT	BALANCE	
					DEBIT	CREDIT

ACCOUNT _____ ACCOUNT NO. _____

DATE	DESCRIPTION	POST. REF.	DEBIT	CREDIT	BALANCE	
					DEBIT	CREDIT

ACCOUNT _____ ACCOUNT NO. _____

DATE	DESCRIPTION	POST. REF.	DEBIT	CREDIT	BALANCE	
					DEBIT	CREDIT

Analyze: _____

CHAPTER 20 CHALLENGE PROBLEM

1. _____

CHAPTER 20 CHALLENGE PROBLEM (continued)

2. _____

Analyze: _____

CHAPTER 20 CRITICAL THINKING PROBLEM

_____
_____
_____
_____
_____
_____
_____
_____
_____
_____
_____
_____
_____
_____
_____
_____
_____
_____
_____
_____
_____
_____

Chapter 20 Practice Test Answer Key

Part A True-False		**Part B Completion**
1. T	**11.** F	**1.** par value
2. F	**12.** T	**2.** preferred stock
3. T	**13.** T	**3.** stated value
4. F	**14.** T	**4.** charter
5. F	**15.** F	**5.** cumulative
6. F	**16.** F	**6.** premium
7. T	**17.** F	**7.** capital stock transfer journal
8. F	**18.** F	**8.** stock certificate
9. F	**19.** F	**9.** minute book
10. T		**10.** capital stock ledger
		11. Subchapter S (or "S")

Corporate Earnings and Capital Transactions

STUDY GUIDE

Understanding the Chapter

Objectives

1. Estimate the federal corporate income tax and prepare related journal entries. **2.** Complete a worksheet for a corporation. **3.** Record corporate adjusting and closing entries. **4.** Prepare an income statement for a corporation. **5.** Record the declaration and payment of cash dividends. **6.** Record the declaration and issuance of stock dividends. **7.** Record stock splits. **8.** Record appropriations of retained earnings. **9.** Record a corporation's receipt of donated assets. **10.** Record treasury stock transactions. **11.** Prepare financial statements for a corporation. **12.** Define the accounting terms new to this chapter.

Reading Assignment

Read Chapter 21 in the textbook. Complete the textbook Section Self Review as you finish reading each section of the chapter, and the Comprehensive Self Review at the end of the chapter. Refer to the Chapter 21 Glossary or to the Glossary at the end of the book to find definitions for terms that are not familiar to you.

Activities

❏ **Thinking Critically**

Answer the *Thinking Critically* questions for McDonald's Corporation, Computers in Accounting, and Managerial Implications.

❏ **Internet Application**

Complete the activity for Computers in Accounting

❏ **Discussion Questions**

Answer each assigned discussion question in Chapter 21.

❏ **Exercises**

Complete each assigned exercise in Chapter 21. Use the forms provided in this SGWP. The objectives covered by an exercise are given after the exercise number. If you need help with an exercise, review the portion of the chapter related to the objective(s) covered.

❏ **Problems A/B**

Complete each assigned problem in Chapter 21. Use the forms provided in this SGWP. The objectives covered by a problem are given after the problem number. If you need help with a problem, review the portion of the chapter related to the objective(s) covered.

❏ **Challenge Problem**

Complete the challenge problem as assigned. Use the forms provided in this SGWP.

❏ **Critical Thinking Problem**

Complete the critical thinking problem as assigned. Use the forms provided in this SGWP.

❏ **Business Connections**

Complete the Business Connections activities as assigned to gain a deeper understanding of Chapter 21 concepts.

Practice Tests

Complete the Practice Tests, which cover the main points in your reading assignment. Compare your answers with those in the Practice Test Answer Key for Chapter 21 at the end of this chapter. If you have answered any questions incorrectly, review the related section of the text.

Part A True-False

For each of the following statements, circle T in the answer column if the statement is true or F if the statement is false.

T   F   **1.** A stock dividend increases the Paid-in Capital of the corporation.

T   F   **2.** The entry to record a stock dividend is made on the declaration date.

T   F   **3.** The **Treasury Stock** account is debited for the par value of treasury stock purchased.

T   F   **4.** Extraordinary gains and losses are commonly shown "net of tax."

T   F   **5.** Corporate income taxes may be shown as operating expenses or as a final deduction to arrive at "net income after taxes."

T   F   **6.** When a stock split is declared, the **Retained Earnings** account is debited for the estimated market value of the stock to be issued.

T   F   **7.** The statement of retained earnings shows all changes in the corporate capital during the year.

T   F   **8.** Treasury stock should be shown as an asset on the balance sheet.

T   F   **9.** Property received as a gift should be recorded at its fair market value and credited to an account such as **Donated Capital.**

T   F   **10.** When a stock dividend is declared, the **Retained Earnings** account is debited for the par value of the stock to be issued.

T   F   **11.** Appropriated retained earnings represents cash set aside for specific purposes.

T   F   **12.** Appropriations of retained earnings may reflect contractual requirements or may be purely discretionary.

T   F   **13.** The issuance of a stock dividend decreases the total stockholders' equity of the corporation.

T   F   **14.** Cash dividends are credited to the **Retained Earnings** account.

T   F   **15.** Extraordinary gains and losses should be classified as Other Income or Other Deductions in the income statement.

Part B Matching

For each numbered item, choose the matching term from the box and write the identifying letter in the answer column.

_____   **1.** An example of an appropriation of retained earnings for a specific project.

_____   **2.** The issuance of new shares to shareholders with a debit to **Retained Earnings,** a credit to **Paid-in Capital** and **Stock Dividends Distributable.**

_____   **3.** The section of a balance sheet that contains paid-in capital and retained earnings.

_____   **4.** The term used to describe the accumulated net income of a corporation.

_____   **5.** Stock that has been issued and reacquired.

_____   **6.** The account credited when a gift of property is received by a corporation.

_____   **7.** An analysis of the equity accounts of a corporation.

a. Retained Earnings
b. Donated Capital
c. Retained Earnings Appropriated for Plant Expansion
d. Statement of stockholders' equity
e. Stock dividend
f. Stockholders' equity
g. Treasury Stock

Part C Exercises

1. Prior to a 10 percent stock dividend, the total stockholders' equity of the Spring Corporation consists of $500,000 of common stock (5,000 shares of $100 par value, issued and outstanding) plus retained earnings of $250,000. Assets are $950,000 and liabilities, $200,000. The estimated market value of the stock to be issued is $160 per share. Compute the book value per share before and after the dividend is declared.

2. The Paducah Corporation has 1,000 shares of $50 par value, 10 percent, cumulative, nonparticipating preferred stock authorized and issued. On December 15, 2007, the directors declare a dividend on preferred stock payable on January 12, 2008, to stockholders of record on December 31, 2007. The dividend is the regular dividend for the current year and the dividends in arrears. (No dividend was paid in 2006.) Record the general journal entry for the dividend declaration.

GENERAL JOURNAL

PAGE _____

	DATE	DESCRIPTION	POST. REF.	DEBIT	CREDIT	
1						1
2						2
3						3
4						4
5						5

Demonstration Problem

The stockholders' equity section of the balance sheets of the County Landscaping Corporation on December 31, 2007, and December 31, 2008, plus other selected account balances, follows (some information is omitted). During 2008 the following transactions, other than net income or loss after taxes, affected stockholders' equity.

1. A stock dividend was declared on common stock and issued in March. No other common stock was issued during the year.

2. A cash dividend of $5 a share was declared and paid on common stock in December 2008.

3. Preferred treasury stock was purchased at par value in January.

4. Additional preferred stock was issued for cash in April 2008.

5. The yearly cash dividend of $4 per share was declared and paid on preferred stock outstanding as of December 2008.

Partial Balance Sheets

Stockholders' Equity	2008	2007
Paid-in Capital		
Preferred Stock (8%, $50 par, 20,000 shares authorized)	$ 110,000	$ 85,000
Paid-in Capital in Excess of Par—Preferred	2,000	–0–
Common Stock ($25 par value, 200,000 shares authorized)	1,200,000	1,160,000
Paid-In Capital in Excess of Par—Common	80,000	–0–
Total Paid-in Capital	$1,392,000	$1,245,000
Retained Earnings		
Appropriated for Plant Expansion	200,000	200,000
Appropriated for Treasury Stock	80,000	–0–
Unappropriated	1,020,000	555,000
Total Retained Earnings	1,300,000	755,000
	$2,692,000	$2,000,000
Less Treasury Stock, Preferred	80,000	–0–
Total Stockholders' Equity	$2,612,000	$2,000,000

Instructions

Answer these questions.

1. How many shares of preferred stock were outstanding on December 31, 2008?
2. How many shares of common stock were issued as a stock dividend during 2008?
3. What was the market value per share of common stock at the time the stock dividend was declared?
4. How many shares of preferred stock were purchased as treasury stock?
5. How many shares of preferred stock were issued for cash during 2008?
6. What was the sales price per share of the preferred stock issued during the year?
7. What was the total cash dividend on preferred stock during the year?
8. What was the total cash dividend on common stock?
9. What was the corporation's net income or loss after taxes during 2008?

SOLUTION

1. $110,000 ÷ $50 = 2,200 shares issued; 2,200 shares issued − 1,600 shares treasury stock ($80,000 ÷ $50) = 600 shares outstanding

2. $1,200,000 − $1,160,000 = $40,000; $40,000 ÷ $25 = 1,600 shares

3. $40,000 par value + $80,000 paid-in capital = $120,000; $120,000 ÷ 1,600 shares = $75 per share

4. $80,000 ÷ $50 = 1,600 shares of treasury stock purchased

5. $110,000 − $85,000 = $25,000; $25,000 ÷ $50 = 500 shares

6. $110,000 − $85,000 = $25,000; $25,000 ÷ $50 per share = 500 shares; $25,000 + $2,000 paid-in capital = $27,000; $27,000 ÷ 500 shares = $54 per share

7. 2,200 shares preferred stock − 1,600 shares treasury stock = 600 shares for dividends; 600 × $4 = $2,400 in dividends

8. $1,200,000 ÷ $25 = 48,000 shares of common stock; 48,000 × $5 = $240,000 in dividends

9.

Increase in retained earnings, unappropriated	$465,000
Stock dividend	120,000
Cash dividend, common stock	240,000
Cash dividend, preferred stock	2,400
Increase in appropriation for treasury stock	80,000
Income for year	$907,400

WORKING PAPERS

Name _____

EXERCISE 21.1

_____
_____
_____
_____
_____
_____
_____

EXERCISE 21.2

GENERAL JOURNAL
PAGE _____

	DATE	DESCRIPTION	POST. REF.	DEBIT	CREDIT	
1						1
2						2
3						3
4						4
5						5
6						6

EXERCISE 21.3

a. _____
_____

b. _____
_____

c. _____
_____

EXERCISE 21.4

GENERAL JOURNAL
PAGE _____

	DATE	DESCRIPTION	POST. REF.	DEBIT	CREDIT	
1						1
2						2
3						3
4						4
5						5
6						6

EXERCISE 21.5

GENERAL JOURNAL   PAGE _____

	DATE	DESCRIPTION	POST. REF.	DEBIT	CREDIT	
1						1
2						2
3						3
4						4
5						5
6						6
7						7
8						8

EXERCISE 21.6

GENERAL JOURNAL   PAGE _____

	DATE	DESCRIPTION	POST. REF.	DEBIT	CREDIT	
1						1
2						2
3						3
4						4
5						5
6						6
7						7
8						8
9						9

EXERCISE 21.7

GENERAL JOURNAL   PAGE _____

	DATE	DESCRIPTION	POST. REF.	DEBIT	CREDIT	
1						1
2						2
3						3
4						4
5						5

EXERCISE 21.8

GENERAL JOURNAL   PAGE _____

	DATE	DESCRIPTION	POST. REF.	DEBIT	CREDIT	
1						1
2						2
3						3
4						4

EXERCISE 21.9

GENERAL JOURNAL   PAGE _____

	DATE		DESCRIPTION	POST. REF.	DEBIT	CREDIT	
1							1
2							2
3							3
4							4
5							5
6							6

EXERCISE 21.10

GENERAL JOURNAL   PAGE _____

	DATE		DESCRIPTION	POST. REF.	DEBIT	CREDIT	
1							1
2							2
3							3
4							4
5							5

EXERCISE 21.11

GENERAL JOURNAL   PAGE _____

	DATE		DESCRIPTION	POST. REF.	DEBIT	CREDIT	
1							1
2							2
3							3
4							4
5							5

EXERCISE 21.12

PROBLEM 21.1A or 21.1B

GENERAL JOURNAL   PAGE _____

	DATE	DESCRIPTION	POST. REF.	DEBIT	CREDIT	
1						1
2						2
3						3
4						4
5						5
6						6
7						7
8						8
9						9
10						10
11						11
12						12
13						13
14						14
15						15
16						16
17						17
18						18
19						19
20						20
21						21
22						22
23						23
24						24
25						25
26						26
27						27
28						28
29						29
30						30
31						31
32						32
33						33
34						34
35						35
36						36
37						37
38						38

PROBLEM 21.1A or 21.1B (continued)

GENERAL JOURNAL   PAGE _____

	DATE	DESCRIPTION	POST. REF.	DEBIT	CREDIT	
1						1
2						2
3						3
4						4
5						5
6						6
7						7
8						8
9						9
10						10
11						11
12						12
13						13
14						14
15						15
16						16
17						17
18						18
19						19
20						20
21						21
22						22
23						23
24						24
25						25
26						26
27						27
28						28
29						29
30						30
31						31
32						32
33						33
34						34

Analyze: _____

_____

PROBLEM 21.2A or 21.2B

_____

	ACCOUNT NAME	TRIAL BALANCE DEBIT	TRIAL BALANCE CREDIT	ADJUSTMENTS DEBIT	ADJUSTMENTS CREDIT
1	CASH	17720			
2	Accounts Receivable	54800			
3	Allowance for Doubtful		260		
4	Merch Inv	74920			
5	Land	38000			
6	Buildings	88000			
7	Accum Depreciation - Buildings		8000		
8	Equipment	78000			
9	Accounts Payable		13600		
10	Dividends Payable - Pref.		24650		
11	Accured Exp. Payable		2400		
12	Income Tax Payable				
13	Preferred Stock 7%		80000		
14	Paid-in Capital Excess Value		6000		
15	Common Stock		60000		
16	Retained earnings		89170		
17	Sales (Net)		424580		
18	Purchases	220000			
19	Selling Expense Control	86310			
20					
21					
22					
23	General Expense Control	40000			
24					
25					
26					
27	Income Tax Expense	9200			
28	Income Summary				
29	Totals	707060	707060		
30					
31					
32					
33					
34					
35					

PROBLEM 21.2A or 21.2B (continued)

	INCOME STATEMENT		BALANCE SHEET		
	DEBIT	CREDIT	DEBIT	CREDIT	
					1
					2
					3
					4
					5
					6
					7
					8
					9
					10
					11
					12
					13
					14
					15
					16
					17
					18
					19
					20
					21
					22
					23
					24
					25
					26
					27
					28
					29
					30
					31
					32
					33
					34
					35

PROBLEM 21.2A or 21.2B (continued)

(continued)

PROBLEM 21.2A or 21.2B (continued)

PROBLEM 21.2A or 21.2B (continued)

GENERAL JOURNAL   PAGE _____

	DATE		DESCRIPTION	POST. REF.	DEBIT	CREDIT	
1							1
2							2
3							3
4							4
5							5
6							6
7							7
8							8
9							9
10							10
11							11
12							12
13							13
14							14
15							15
16							16
17							17
18							18
19							19
20							20
21							21
22							22
23							23
24							24
25							25
26							26
27							27
28							28
29							29
30							30
31							31
32							32
33							33
34							34
35							35
36							36
37							37

PROBLEM 21.2A or 21.2B (continued)

GENERAL JOURNAL   PAGE _____

	DATE		DESCRIPTION	POST. REF.	DEBIT	CREDIT	
1							1
2							2
3							3
4							4
5							5
6							6
7							7
8							8
9							9
10							10
11							11
12							12
13							13
14							14
15							15
16							16
17							17
18							18
19							19
20							20
21							21
22							22
23							23
24							24
25							25
26							26
27							27
28							28
29							29
30							30
31							31
32							32
33							33
34							34

Analyze: _____

_____

PROBLEM 21.3A or 21.3B

GENERAL JOURNAL   PAGE _____

	DATE		DESCRIPTION	POST. REF.	DEBIT	CREDIT	
1							1
2							2
3							3
4							4
5							5
6							6
7							7
8							8
9							9
10							10
11							11
12							12
13							13
14							14
15							15
16							16
17							17
18							18
19							19
20							20
21							21
22							22
23							23
24							24
25							25
26							26
27							27
28							28
29							29
30							30
31							31
32							32
33							33
34							34
35							35
36							36
37							37

PROBLEM 21.3A or 21.3B (continued)

GENERAL LEDGER

ACCOUNT _____ ACCOUNT NO. _____ **381** _____

DATE	DESCRIPTION	POST. REF.	DEBIT	CREDIT	BALANCE	
					DEBIT	CREDIT

Analyze: _____

PROBLEM 21.4A or 21.4B

GENERAL JOURNAL   PAGE _____

	DATE		DESCRIPTION	POST. REF.	DEBIT	CREDIT	
1							1
2							2
3							3
4							4
5							5
6							6
7							7
8							8
9							9
10							10
11							11
12							12
13							13
14							14
15							15
16							16
17							17
18							18
19							19
20							20
21							21
22							22
23							23
24							24
25							25
26							26
27							27
28							28
29							29
30							30
31							31
32							32
33							33
34							34
35							35
36							36
37							37

PROBLEM 21.4A or 21.4B (continued)

GENERAL JOURNAL

PAGE _____

	DATE	DESCRIPTION	POST. REF.	DEBIT	CREDIT	
1						1
2						2
3						3
4						4
5						5
6						6
7						7
8						8
9						9
10						10
11						11
12						12
13						13
14						14
15						15
16						16
17						17
18						18
19						19
20						20
21						21
22						22

GENERAL LEDGER

ACCOUNT __14% Preferred Stock, $10 Par__ ACCOUNT NO. ____301____

DATE	DESCRIPTION	POST. REF.	DEBIT	CREDIT	BALANCE	
					DEBIT	CREDIT

ACCOUNT __Paid-in Capital in Excess of Par Value—Preferred__ ACCOUNT NO. ____305____

DATE	DESCRIPTION	POST. REF.	DEBIT	CREDIT	BALANCE	
					DEBIT	CREDIT

PROBLEM 21.4A or 21.4B (continued)

GENERAL LEDGER

ACCOUNT __Common Stock, No-Par, Stated Value, $50_____ ACCOUNT NO. ___311___

DATE	DESCRIPTION	POST. REF.	DEBIT	CREDIT	BALANCE DEBIT	BALANCE CREDIT

ACCOUNT __Paid-in Capital in Excess of Stated Value—Common_____ ACCOUNT NO. ___315___

DATE	DESCRIPTION	POST. REF.	DEBIT	CREDIT	BALANCE DEBIT	BALANCE CREDIT

ACCOUNT __Donated Capital_____ ACCOUNT NO. ___371___

DATE	DESCRIPTION	POST. REF.	DEBIT	CREDIT	BALANCE DEBIT	BALANCE CREDIT

ACCOUNT __Treasury Stock—Preferred_____ ACCOUNT NO. ___372___

DATE	DESCRIPTION	POST. REF.	DEBIT	CREDIT	BALANCE DEBIT	BALANCE CREDIT

ACCOUNT __Retained Earnings_____ ACCOUNT NO. ___381___

DATE	DESCRIPTION	POST. REF.	DEBIT	CREDIT	BALANCE DEBIT	BALANCE CREDIT

PROBLEM 21.4A or 21.4B (continued)

GENERAL LEDGER

ACCOUNT __Retained Earnings Appropriated for Treasury Stock__   ACCOUNT NO. ___382___

DATE	DESCRIPTION	POST. REF.	DEBIT	CREDIT	BALANCE DEBIT	BALANCE CREDIT

Analyze: _____

CHAPTER 21 CHALLENGE PROBLEM

Analyze:

CHAPTER 21 CRITICAL THINKING PROBLEM

_____
_____
_____
_____
_____
_____
_____
_____
_____
_____
_____
_____
_____
_____
_____
_____
_____

Chapter 21 Practice Test Answer Key

Part A True-False		Part B Matching
1. T	9. T	1. c
2. T	10. F	2. e
3. F	11. F	3. f
4. T	12. T	4. a
5. T	13. F	5. g
6. F	14. F	6. b
7. F	15. F	7. d
8. F		

Part C Exercises

1. Book value **before** stock dividend:
   Stockholders' equity, $750,000 ÷ 5,000 shares = $150,000 per share

   Book value **after** stock dividend:
   Stockholders' equity, $750,000 ÷ 5,500 shares = $136.36 per share.

2. Entry to record dividend declaration:

   2007
   Dec. 15 Retained Earnings   10,000.00
           Preferred Stock Dividend Payable   10,000.00
           To record dividends payable on
           cumulative preferred stock for 2006
           and 2007. Payable on January 12, 2008
           to holders of record on December 31, 2007.

STUDY GUIDE

Understanding the Chapter

Objectives

1. Name and define the various types of bonds. **2.** Explain the advantages and disadvantages of using bonds as a method of financing. **3.** Record the issuance of bonds. **4.** Record the payment of interest on bonds. **5.** Record the accrual of interest on bonds. **6.** Compute and record the periodic amortization of a bond premium. **7.** Compute and record the periodic amortization of a bond discount. **8.** Record the transactions of a bond sinking fund investment. **9.** Record an increase or decrease in retained earnings appropriated for bond retirement. **10.** Record retirement of bonds payable. **11.** Define the accounting terms new to this chapter.

Reading Assignment

Read Chapter 22 in the textbook. Complete the textbook Section Self Review as you finish reading each section of the chapter, and the Comprehensive Self Review at the end of the chapter. Refer to the Chapter 22 Glossary or to the Glossary at the end of the book to find definitions for terms that are not familiar to you.

Activities

❑ **Thinking Critically**

Answer the *Thinking Critically* questions for 3M, Accounting on the Job, and Managerial Implications.

❑ **Internet Application**

Complete the activity for Accounting on the Job.

❑ **Discussion Questions**

Answer each assigned discussion question in Chapter 22.

❑ **Exercises**

Complete each assigned exercise in Chapter 22. Use the forms provided in this SGWP. The objectives covered by an exercise are given after the exercise number. If you need help with an exercise, review the portion of the chapter related to the objective(s) covered.

❑ **Problems A/B**

Complete each assigned problem in Chapter 22. Use the forms provided in this SGWP. The objectives covered by a problem are given after the problem number. If you need help with a problem, review the portion of the chapter related to the objective(s) covered.

❑ **Challenge Problem**

Complete the challenge problem as assigned. Use the forms provided in this SGWP.

❑ **Critical Thinking Problem**

Complete the critical thinking problem as assigned. Use the forms provided in this SGWP.

❑ **Business Connections**

Complete the Business Connections activities as assigned to gain a deeper understanding of Chapter 22 concepts.

Practice Tests

Complete the Practice Tests, which cover the main points in your reading assignment. Compare your answers with those in the Practice Test Answer Key for Chapter 22 at the end of this chapter. If you have answered any questions incorrectly, review the related section of the text.

Part A True-False

T   F   **1.** The issuance of bonds payable is a method for raising cash.

T   F   **2.** Interest paid on bonds payable is deductible for federal income tax purposes.

T   F   **3.** In case of liquidation of a corporation, the claims of stockholders take priority over the claims of bondholders.

T   F   **4.** The interest on coupon bonds is usually paid by check made payable to the bondholder.

T   F   **5.** The interest on registered bonds is paid when the bondholders detach the interest coupons from the bonds and submit them for payment.

T   F   **6.** Bonds cannot be issued at a price greater than their par value.

T   F   **7.** A premium on bonds payable is amortized over the remaining life of the bond.

T   F   **8.** The **Discount on Bonds Payable** is shown on the balance sheet as a current liability.

T   F   **9.** Amortization of bond discount increases the bond interest expense.

T   F   **10.** Bond issue costs may be offset against the premium or added to the discount.

T   F   **11.** When bonds are sold between interest payment dates, the purchaser pays the seller for any interest accrued on the bonds.

T   F   **12.** The **Premium on Bonds Payable** account has a debit balance and should be shown on the income statement as an expense.

T   F   **13.** At the end of the year, an adjusting entry is made to record amortization of discount or premium since the last interest payment.

T   F   **14.** A bond sinking fund is not another name for retained earnings appropriated for bond retirement.

T   F   **15.** The bond sinking fund represents assets put aside to be used to retire outstanding bonds.

Part B Matching

_____ **1.** The amount by which the par value of bonds exceeds their issue price

_____ **2.** The amount by which the issue price of bonds exceeds par

_____ **3.** Cash or other assets set aside for the retirement of bonds

_____ **4.** Bonds whose ownership may be transferred by delivery

_____ **5.** Bonds issued on the general credit of the corporation

_____ **6.** Bonds whose ownership is recorded on the books of the corporation

_____ **7.** A contract covering the issuance of bonds

_____ **8.** Bonds secured by the pledge of stocks or bonds of other corporations

_____ **9.** Bonds issued upon pledge of property

_____ **10.** Loans for an extended period, secured by notes given as part of the purchase price of land, building, or equipment

_____ **11.** A method of financing for an intermediate period of more than one year, and usually less than five years

a. Debenture bonds
b. Registered bonds
c. Secured bonds
d. Bond indenture
e. Premium
f. Bond sinking fund
g. Discount
h. Long-term notes
i. Collateral trust bonds
j. Unregistered bonds
k. Mortgage loans

Demonstration Problem

On December 31, 2007, the equity accounts of BPH Corporation contained these balances:

Common Stock ($2 par value, 500,000 shares authorized)

100,000 shares issued and outstanding	$200,000
Retained Earnings	400,000

For the year 2007, the corporation had net income before income taxes of $325,000, income taxes of $81,250, and net income after taxes of $243,750. The corporation's tax rate is 40 percent.

Construction of a new plant at a cost of $700,000 is planned. The corporation's president estimates that the new plant will generate additional net income of approximately $200,000 before interest and taxes. The financial vice-president is less optimistic and forecasts an increase in net income of about $150,000 before interest and taxes.

Management is considering two possibilities for financing the project:

1. Issuance of 140,000 additional shares of common stock for $5 per share.

2. Issuance of $700,000 face amount, 10-year, 10 percent bonds payable, secured by a mortgage lien on the plant.

Instructions

1. Assuming that profits from existing operations will remain the same and that the president's estimate of net income from the new plant is correct, prepare a table with two columns to show the cumulative effect of each financing plan for the items listed below.

   a. Total net income before interest and taxes

   b. Total bond interest

   c. Total income tax

   d. Total income after taxes

   e. Present income after taxes

   f. Increase (decrease) in total income after bond interest and taxes

   g. Present earnings per share of common stock (compute earnings per share by dividing net income after taxes by the shares of common stock outstanding)

   h. Estimated earnings per share of common stock under the proposed plans

   i. Ratio of net income, after income taxes for 2007 to total stockholders' equity on December 31, 2007 (divide net income by total stockholders' equity on December 31, 2007)

   j. Ratio of net income after income taxes to total stockholders' equity if the plant is constructed

2. Prepare a similar table assuming the financial vice-president's estimate of earnings is correct.

SOLUTION

		STOCK	BONDS
1. a. $325,000 + $200,000		$525,000	$525,000
b. $700,000 × 0.10		–0–	70,000
		$525,000	$455,000
c. Stock $81,250 + (0.40 tax rate × $200,000)		161,250	
Bonds $200,000 − $70,000 = $130,000 (increase in income before tax)			
$81,250 + (0.40 × $130,000)			133,250
d.		$363,750	$321,750
e.		243,750	243,750
f.		$120,000	$ 78,000
g. $243,750 ÷ 100,000 shares		$ 2.44	
h. $363,750 ÷ 240,000 shares; $321,750 ÷ 100,000 shares		$ 1.52	$ 3.22
i. $243,750 ÷ $600,000		40.63%	
j. $363,750 ÷ $1,300,000 ($600,000 + $700,000)		27.98%	
$321,750 ÷ $600,000			53.6%

		STOCK	BONDS
2. a. $325,000 + $150,000		$475,000	$475,000
b. $700,000 × 0.10			70,000
		$475,000	$405,000
c. Stock $81,250 + (0.40 × $150,000)		141,250	
Bonds $150,000 − $70,000 = $80,000 (increase in income before tax)			
$81,250 + (0.40 × $80,000)			113,250
d.		$333,750	$291,750
e.		243,750	243,750
f.		$ 90,000	$ 48,000
g. $243,750 ÷ 100,000 shares		$ 2.44	
h. $333,750 ÷ 240,000; $291,750 ÷ 100,000 shares		$ 1.39	$ 2.92
i. $243,750 ÷ $600,000		40.63%	
j. $333,750 ÷ $1,300,000 ($600,000 + $700,000)		25.67%	
$291,750 ÷ $600,000			48.6%

WORKING PAPERS

Name _____

EXERCISE 22.1

GENERAL JOURNAL   PAGE _____

	DATE	DESCRIPTION	POST. REF.	DEBIT	CREDIT	
1						1
2						2
3						3
4						4
5						5

EXERCISE 22.2

GENERAL JOURNAL   PAGE _____

	DATE	DESCRIPTION	POST. REF.	DEBIT	CREDIT	
1						1
2						2
3						3
4						4
5						5

EXERCISE 22.3

GENERAL JOURNAL   PAGE _____

	DATE	DESCRIPTION	POST. REF.	DEBIT	CREDIT	
1						1
2						2
3						3
4						4
5						5

EXERCISE 22.4

GENERAL JOURNAL   PAGE _____

	DATE	DESCRIPTION	POST. REF.	DEBIT	CREDIT	
1						1
2						2
3						3
4						4
5						5
6						6

EXERCISE 22.5

GENERAL JOURNAL

PAGE _____

	DATE	DESCRIPTION	POST. REF.	DEBIT	CREDIT	
1						1
2						2
3						3
4						4
5						5
6						6

EXERCISE 22.6

GENERAL JOURNAL

PAGE _____

	DATE	DESCRIPTION	POST. REF.	DEBIT	CREDIT	
1						1
2						2
3						3
4						4
5						5
6						6
7						7

EXERCISE 22.7

GENERAL JOURNAL

PAGE _____

	DATE	DESCRIPTION	POST. REF.	DEBIT	CREDIT	
1						1
2						2
3						3
4						4
5						5
6						6
7						7
8						8
9						9
10						10
11						11
12						12
13						13

EXERCISE 22.8

GENERAL JOURNAL

PAGE _____

	DATE		DESCRIPTION	POST. REF.	DEBIT	CREDIT	
1							1
2							2
3							3
4							4
5							5

EXERCISE 22.9

GENERAL JOURNAL

PAGE _____

	DATE		DESCRIPTION	POST. REF.	DEBIT	CREDIT	
1							1
2							2
3							3
4							4
5							5
6							6
7							7
8							8
9							9
10							10
11							11
12							12
13							13

EXTRA FORM

GENERAL JOURNAL

PAGE _____

	DATE		DESCRIPTION	POST. REF.	DEBIT	CREDIT	
1							1
2							2
3							3
4							4
5							5
6							6
7							7
8							8

500,000 x .09 = 45,000 yr
22,500 6mo
3750. month

PROBLEM 22.1A or 22.1B

GENERAL JOURNAL

PAGE _____

	DATE	DESCRIPTION	POST. REF.	DEBIT	CREDIT	
1	Apr 1	Cash		500 000		1
2		Bond Payable			500 000	2
3	Oct 1	Bond Int Exp		22 500		3
4		CASh			22 500	4
5	Dec 31	Bond Int Exp		11 250		5
6		Bond Int. Payable			11 250	6
7	31	Income Summary		33 750		7
8		Bond Int Exp			33 750	8
9						9
10						10
11		2008 Reverse Entry				11
12						12
13	Jan 1	Bond Int Payable		11 250		13
14		Bond Int Exp.			11 250	14
15	Apr 1	Bond Int Exp		22 500		15
16		CASh			22 500	16
17	Oct 1	Bond Int Payable		22 500		17
18		CASh			22 500	18
19	31	CASh		100 000		19
20		Bond Payable			100 000	20
21	Dec 31	Bond Int Exp.		11 250		21
22		Bond Int Exp		2 250		22
23		Bond Int Payable			13 500	23
24						24
25		Income Summary		47 250		25
26		Bond Int Exp.			47 250	26
27						27
28						28
29						29
30						30
31						31
32						32
33						33
34						34
35						35
36						36
37						37

PROBLEM 22.1A or 22.1B (continued)

GENERAL JOURNAL

	DATE	DESCRIPTION	POST. REF.	DEBIT	CREDIT	
1						1
2						2
3						3
4						4
5						5
6						6
7						7
8						8
9						9
10						10
11						11
12						12
13						13
14						14
15						15
16						16
17						17
18						18
19						19
20						20
21						21
22						22
23						23
24						24
25						25
26						26
27						27
28						28
29						29
30						30
31						31
32						32
33						33
34						34

Analyze: _____

600,000 ⟩ 506,000
101.2

800,000
× .09
45,000 y
22,500 6
3,750 M

6000/10/12 = $50

Name _____

PROBLEM 22.2A or 22.2B

GENERAL JOURNAL

PAGE _____

	DATE		DESCRIPTION	POST. REF.	DEBIT	CREDIT	
1	Apr 1		CASH		506 000		1
2			Prem on Bonds Payable			6000	2
3			Bonds Payable			500 000	3
4	Oct 1		BIE		22500		4
5			CASH			22 500	5
6			Premium Bond Payable		300		6
7			Bond dstl. Exp			300	7
8	Dec 31		BIE		11 250		8
9			BIE Payable			11 250	9
10			Premium on Bond Payable		150		10
11			BIE			150	11
12			Income Summary		33 300		12
13			BIE			33 300	13
14							14
15			2008 Reverse Entry				15
16			BI Payable		11 250		16
17			BIE			11 250	17
18			BIE		150		18
19			Prem on Report			150	19
20							20
21							21
22							22
23							23
24							24
25							25
26							26
27							27
28							28
29							29
30							30
31							31
32							32
33							33
34							34
35							35
36							36
37							37

PROBLEM 22.2A or 22.2B (continued)

_____
_____
_____

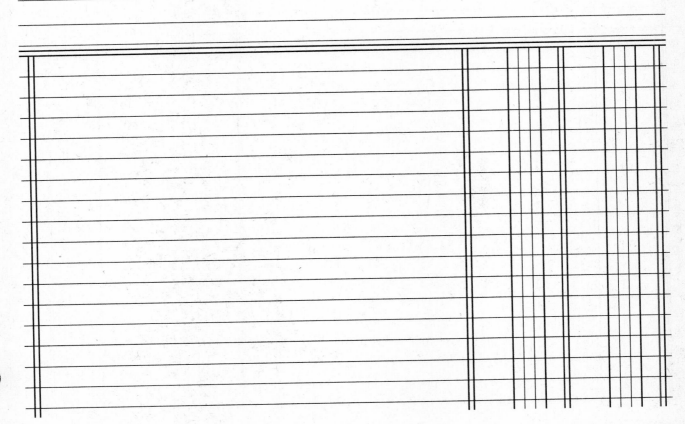

Analyze: _____
_____
_____

EXTRA FORM

_____
_____

PROBLEM 22.3A or 22.3B

GENERAL JOURNAL

	DATE	DESCRIPTION	POST. REF.	DEBIT	CREDIT	
1						1
2						2
3						3
4						4
5						5
6						6
7						7
8						8
9						9
10						10
11						11
12						12
13						13
14						14
15						15
16						16
17						17
18						18
19						19
20						20
21						21
22						22
23						23
24						24
25						25
26						26
27						27
28						28
29						29
30						30
31						31
32						32
33						33
34						34
35						35
36						36
37						37

PROBLEM 22.3A or 22.3B (continued)

_____

_____

Analyze: _____

_____

PROBLEM 22.4A or 22.4B

GENERAL JOURNAL

PAGE _____

	DATE	DESCRIPTION	POST. REF.	DEBIT	CREDIT	
1						1
2						2
3						3
4						4
5						5
6						6
7						7
8						8
9						9
10						10
11						11
12						12
13						13
14						14
15						15
16						16
17						17
18						18
19						19
20						20
21						21
22						22
23						23
24						24

Chapter 22 ■ *549*

PROBLEM 22.4A or 22.4B (continued)

_____

_____

Analyze: _____

_____

PROBLEM 22.5A or 22.5B

GENERAL JOURNAL   PAGE _____

	DATE		DESCRIPTION	POST. REF.	DEBIT	CREDIT	
1							1
2							2
3							3
4							4
5							5
6							6
7							7
8							8
9							9
10							10
11							11
12							12
13							13
14							14
15							15

Analyze: _____

_____

CHAPTER 22 CHALLENGE PROBLEM

	Issuing Common Stock	Issuing Bonds Payable
1. President's estimate of net income		
before interest and taxes =		
a. Net income before interest and taxes		
b. Total bond interest		
Taxable income		
c. Total income tax		
d. Total income after tax		
e. Present income after tax		
f. Increase in net income		
g. Present EPS		
h. Proposed EPS		
2. Financial VP's estimate of net income before		
interest and taxes =		
a. Net income before interest and taxes		
b. Total bond interest		
Taxable income		
c. Total income tax		
d. Total income after tax		
e. Present income after tax		
f. Increase in net income		
g. Present EPS		
h. Proposed EPS		

3. _____

_____

_____

_____

_____

_____

_____

Analyze: _____

_____

CHAPTER 22 CRITICAL THINKING PROBLEM

1. _____

_____

_____

_____

_____

_____

_____

_____

2. _____

_____

_____

_____

_____

_____

_____

_____

_____

Chapter 22 Practice Test Answer Key

Part A True-False	Part B Matching
1. T	1. g
2. T	2. e
3. F	3. f
4. F	4. j
5. F	5. a
6. F	6. b
7. T	7. d
8. F	8. i
9. T	9. c
10. T	10. k
11. T	11. h
12. F	
13. T	
14. T	
15. T	

Corporation Accounting Cycle

The Joshua Company

GENERAL JOURNAL PAGE ____1____

	DATE	DESCRIPTION	POST. REF.	DEBIT	CREDIT	
1						
2						2
3						3
4						4
5						5
6						6
7						7
8						8
9						9
10						10
11						11
12						12
13						13
14						14
15						15
16						16
17						17
18						18
19						19
20						20
21						21
22						22
23						23
24						24
25						25
26						26
27						27
28						28
29						29
30						30
31						31
32						32
33						33
34						34
35						35

Name _____

GENERAL JOURNAL

PAGE __2__

	DATE		DESCRIPTION	POST. REF.	DEBIT	CREDIT	
1							1
2							2
3							3
4							4
5							5
6							6
7							7
8							8
9							9
10							10
11							11
12							12
13							13
14							14
15							15
16							16
17							17
18							18
19							19
20							20
21							21
22							22
23							23
24							24
25							25
26							26
27							27
28							28
29							29
30							30
31							31
32							32
33							33
34							34
35							35
36							36
37							37
38							38
39							39

GENERAL JOURNAL

	DATE	DESCRIPTION	POST. REF.	DEBIT	CREDIT	
1						1
2						2
3						3
4						4
5						5
6						6
7						7
8						8
9						9
10						10
11						11
12						12
13						13
14						14
15						15
16						16
17						17
18						18
19						19
20						20
21						21
22						22
23						23
24						24
25						25
26						26
27						27
28						28
29						29
30						30
31						31
32						32
33						33
34						34
35						35
36						36
37						37
38						38
39						39

GENERAL JOURNAL   PAGE ____4____

	DATE		DESCRIPTION	POST. REF.	DEBIT	CREDIT	
1							1
2							2
3							3
4							4
5							5
6							6
7							7
8							8
9							9
10							10
11							11
12							12
13							13
14							14
15							15
16							16
17							17
18							18
19							19
20							20
21							21
22							22
23							23
24							24
25							25
26							26
27							27
28							28
29							29
30							30
31							31
32							32
33							33
34							34
35							35
36							36
37							37

Name _____

GENERAL JOURNAL

PAGE ___5___

	DATE		DESCRIPTION	POST. REF.	DEBIT	CREDIT	
1							1
2							2
3							3
4							4
5							5
6							6
7							7
8							8
9							9
10							10
11							11
12							12
13							13
14							14
15							15
16							16
17							17
18							18
19							19
20							20
21							21
22							22
23							23
24							24
25							25
26							26
27							27
28							28
29							29
30							30
31							31
32							32
33							33
34							34
35							35
36							36
37							37

Name _____

GENERAL LEDGER

ACCOUNT __Cash__   ACCOUNT NO. ____101____

DATE	DESCRIPTION	POST. REF.	DEBIT	CREDIT	BALANCE	
					DEBIT	CREDIT

ACCOUNT __Accounts Receivable__   ACCOUNT NO. ____103____

DATE	DESCRIPTION	POST. REF.	DEBIT	CREDIT	BALANCE	
					DEBIT	CREDIT

ACCOUNT __Allowance for Doubtful Accounts__   ACCOUNT NO. ____104____

DATE	DESCRIPTION	POST. REF.	DEBIT	CREDIT	BALANCE	
					DEBIT	CREDIT

GENERAL LEDGER

ACCOUNT __Subscriptions Receivable—Common Stock__   ACCOUNT NO. ___105___

DATE	DESCRIPTION	POST. REF.	DEBIT	CREDIT	BALANCE DEBIT	CREDIT

ACCOUNT __Interest Receivable__   ACCOUNT NO. ___121___

DATE	DESCRIPTION	POST. REF.	DEBIT	CREDIT	BALANCE DEBIT	CREDIT

ACCOUNT __Merchandise Inventory__   ACCOUNT NO. ___131___

DATE	DESCRIPTION	POST. REF.	DEBIT	CREDIT	BALANCE DEBIT	CREDIT

ACCOUNT __Land__   ACCOUNT NO. ___141___

DATE	DESCRIPTION	POST. REF.	DEBIT	CREDIT	BALANCE DEBIT	CREDIT

ACCOUNT __Buildings__   ACCOUNT NO. ___151___

DATE	DESCRIPTION	POST. REF.	DEBIT	CREDIT	BALANCE DEBIT	CREDIT

Name _____

GENERAL LEDGER

ACCOUNT __Accumulated Depreciation—Buildings__   ACCOUNT NO. __152__

DATE	DESCRIPTION	POST. REF.	DEBIT	CREDIT	BALANCE DEBIT	BALANCE CREDIT

ACCOUNT __Furniture and Equipment__   ACCOUNT NO. __161__

DATE	DESCRIPTION	POST. REF.	DEBIT	CREDIT	BALANCE DEBIT	BALANCE CREDIT

ACCOUNT __Accumulated Depreciation—Furniture and Equipment__   ACCOUNT NO. __162__

DATE	DESCRIPTION	POST. REF.	DEBIT	CREDIT	BALANCE DEBIT	BALANCE CREDIT

ACCOUNT __Organization Costs__   ACCOUNT NO. __181__

DATE	DESCRIPTION	POST. REF.	DEBIT	CREDIT	BALANCE DEBIT	BALANCE CREDIT

ACCOUNT __Accounts Payable__   ACCOUNT NO. __202__

DATE	DESCRIPTION	POST. REF.	DEBIT	CREDIT	BALANCE DEBIT	BALANCE CREDIT

MINI-PRACTICE SET 3 (continued)

Name _____

GENERAL LEDGER

ACCOUNT __Interest Payable__   ACCOUNT NO. __203__

DATE	DESCRIPTION	POST. REF.	DEBIT	CREDIT	BALANCE DEBIT	BALANCE CREDIT

ACCOUNT __Estimated Income Taxes Payable__   ACCOUNT NO. __205__

DATE	DESCRIPTION	POST. REF.	DEBIT	CREDIT	BALANCE DEBIT	BALANCE CREDIT

ACCOUNT __Dividends Payable—Preferred Stock__   ACCOUNT NO. __206__

DATE	DESCRIPTION	POST. REF.	DEBIT	CREDIT	BALANCE DEBIT	BALANCE CREDIT

ACCOUNT __Dividends Payable—Common Stock__   ACCOUNT NO. __207__

DATE	DESCRIPTION	POST. REF.	DEBIT	CREDIT	BALANCE DEBIT	BALANCE CREDIT

ACCOUNT __10-Year, 10% Bonds Payable__   ACCOUNT NO. __211__

DATE	DESCRIPTION	POST. REF.	DEBIT	CREDIT	BALANCE DEBIT	BALANCE CREDIT

Name _____

GENERAL LEDGER

ACCOUNT __**Premium on Bonds Payable**_____ ACCOUNT NO. ____**212**____

DATE	DESCRIPTION	POST. REF.	DEBIT	CREDIT	BALANCE DEBIT	CREDIT

ACCOUNT __**8% Preferred Stock ($100 par, 10,000 shares authorized)**_____ ACCOUNT NO. ____**301**____

DATE	DESCRIPTION	POST. REF.	DEBIT	CREDIT	BALANCE DEBIT	CREDIT

ACCOUNT __**Paid-in Capital in Excess of Par—Preferred Stock**_____ ACCOUNT NO. ____**302**____

DATE	DESCRIPTION	POST. REF.	DEBIT	CREDIT	BALANCE DEBIT	CREDIT

ACCOUNT __**Common Stock ($10 par, 100,000 shares authorized)**_____ ACCOUNT NO. ____**303**____

DATE	DESCRIPTION	POST. REF.	DEBIT	CREDIT	BALANCE DEBIT	CREDIT

ACCOUNT __**Paid-in Capital in Excess of Par—Common Stock**_____ ACCOUNT NO. ____**304**____

DATE	DESCRIPTION	POST. REF.	DEBIT	CREDIT	BALANCE DEBIT	CREDIT

Name _____

GENERAL LEDGER

ACCOUNT __Common Stock Subscribed__   ACCOUNT NO. __305__

DATE	DESCRIPTION	POST. REF.	DEBIT	CREDIT	BALANCE DEBIT	BALANCE CREDIT

ACCOUNT __Common Stock Dividend Distributable__   ACCOUNT NO. __306__

DATE	DESCRIPTION	POST. REF.	DEBIT	CREDIT	BALANCE DEBIT	BALANCE CREDIT

ACCOUNT __Retained Earnings Appropriated__   ACCOUNT NO. __311__

DATE	DESCRIPTION	POST. REF.	DEBIT	CREDIT	BALANCE DEBIT	BALANCE CREDIT

ACCOUNT __Retained Earnings Unappropriated__   ACCOUNT NO. __312__

DATE	DESCRIPTION	POST. REF.	DEBIT	CREDIT	BALANCE DEBIT	BALANCE CREDIT

ACCOUNT __Treasury Stock—Preferred__   ACCOUNT NO. __343__

DATE	DESCRIPTION	POST. REF.	DEBIT	CREDIT	BALANCE DEBIT	BALANCE CREDIT

Name _____

GENERAL LEDGER

ACCOUNT __Income Summary_____ ACCOUNT NO. ___399___

DATE	DESCRIPTION	POST. REF.	DEBIT	CREDIT	BALANCE DEBIT	CREDIT

ACCOUNT __Sales_____ ACCOUNT NO. ___401___

DATE	DESCRIPTION	POST. REF.	DEBIT	CREDIT	BALANCE DEBIT	CREDIT

ACCOUNT __Purchases_____ ACCOUNT NO. ___501___

DATE	DESCRIPTION	POST. REF.	DEBIT	CREDIT	BALANCE DEBIT	CREDIT

ACCOUNT __Operating Expenses_____ ACCOUNT NO. ___601___

DATE	DESCRIPTION	POST. REF.	DEBIT	CREDIT	BALANCE DEBIT	CREDIT

Name _____

GENERAL LEDGER

ACCOUNT __Interest Income__   ACCOUNT NO. ____701

DATE	DESCRIPTION	POST. REF.	DEBIT	CREDIT	BALANCE DEBIT	CREDIT

ACCOUNT __Gain on Early Retirement of Bonds Payable__   ACCOUNT NO. ____711

DATE	DESCRIPTION	POST. REF.	DEBIT	CREDIT	BALANCE DEBIT	CREDIT

ACCOUNT __Interest Expense__   ACCOUNT NO. ____751

DATE	DESCRIPTION	POST. REF.	DEBIT	CREDIT	BALANCE DEBIT	CREDIT

ACCOUNT __Amortization of Organization Costs__   ACCOUNT NO. ____753

DATE	DESCRIPTION	POST. REF.	DEBIT	CREDIT	BALANCE DEBIT	CREDIT

ACCOUNT __Income Tax Expense__   ACCOUNT NO. ____801

DATE	DESCRIPTION	POST. REF.	DEBIT	CREDIT	BALANCE DEBIT	CREDIT

Name _____

	ACCOUNT NAME	TRIAL BALANCE		ADJUSTMENTS	
		DEBIT	CREDIT	DEBIT	CREDIT
1	Cash				
2	Accounts Receivable				
3	Allowance for Doubtful Accounts				
4	Subscriptions Receivable—Common Stock				
5	Merchandise Inventory				
6	Land				
7	Buildings				
8	Accumulated Depreciation—Buildings				
9	Furniture and Equipment				
10	Accum. Depreciation—Furn. and Equip.				
11	Organization Costs				
12	Accounts Payable				
13	Interest Payable				
14	Estimated Income Taxes Payable				
15	Dividends Payable—Preferred Stock				
16	Dividends Payable—Common Stock				
17	10-Year, 10% Bonds Payable				
18	Premium on Bonds Payable				
19	8% Preferred Stock				
20	Paid-in Cap. in Excess of Par—Pref. Stock				
21	Common Stock				
22	Paid-in Cap. in Excess of Par—Com. Stock				
23	Common Stock Subscribed				
24	Common Stock Dividends Distributable				
25	Retained Earnings Appropriated				
26	Retained Earnings Unappropriated				
27	Treasury Stock—Preferred				
28	Income Summary				
29	Sales				
30	Purchases				
31	Operating Expenses				
32					
33					
34	Totals Carried Forward				
35					

ADJUSTED TRIAL BALANCE		INCOME STATEMENT		BALANCE SHEET		
DEBIT	CREDIT	DEBIT	CREDIT	DEBIT	CREDIT	
						1
						2
						3
						4
						5
						6
						7
						8
						9
						10
						11
						12
						13
						14
						15
						16
						17
						18
						19
						20
						21
						22
						23
						24
						25
						26
						27
						28
						29
						30
						31
						32
						33
						34
						35

Name _____

	ACCOUNT NAME	TRIAL BALANCE		ADJUSTMENTS	
		DEBIT	CREDIT	DEBIT	CREDIT
1	Totals Brought Forward				
2	Gain on Early Retirement of Bonds Payable				
3	Interest Expense				
4	Amortization of Organization Costs				
5	Income Tax Expense				
6	Totals				
7	Net Income After Tax				
8					
9					
10					
11					
12					
13					
14					
15					
16					
17					
18					
19					
20					
21					
22					
23					
24					
25					
26					
27					
28					
29					
30					
31					
32					

ADJUSTED TRIAL BALANCE		INCOME STATEMENT		BALANCE SHEET		
DEBIT	CREDIT	DEBIT	CREDIT	DEBIT	CREDIT	
						1
						2
						3
						4
						5
						6
						7
						8
						9
						10
						11
						12
						13
						14
						15
						16
						17
						18
						19
						20
						21
						22
						23
						24
						25
						26
						27
						28
						29
						30
						31
						32

Name _____

Summary Income Statement

Name _____

Statement of Retained Earnings

Name _____

Balance Sheet

(continued)

Balance Sheet (continued)

Analyze: _____

Name _____

CHAPTER 23

Statement Analysis: Comparative Statements

STUDY GUIDE

Understanding the Chapter

Objectives

1. Use vertical analysis techniques to analyze a comparative income statement and balance sheet. 2. Use horizontal analysis techniques to analyze a comparative income statement and balance sheet. 3. Use trend analysis to evaluate financial statements. 4. Interpret the results of the statement analysis by comparison with industry averages. 5. Define the accounting terms new to this chapter.

Reading Assignment

Read Chapter 23 in the textbook. Complete the textbook Section Self Review as you finish reading each section of the chapter, and the Comprehensive Self Review at the end of the chapter. Refer to the Chapter 23 Glossary or to the Glossary at the end of the book to find definitions for terms that are not familiar to you.

Activities

❏ **Thinking Critically**
Answer the *Thinking Critically* questions for Dole, Computers in Accounting, and Managerial Implications.

❏ **Internet Application**
Complete the activity for Computers in Accounting.

❏ **Discussion Questions**
Answer each assigned discussion question in Chapter 23.

❏ **Exercises**
Complete each assigned exercise in Chapter 23. Use the forms provided in this SGWP. The objectives covered by an exercise are given after the exercise number. If you need help with an exercise, review the portion of the chapter related to the objective(s) covered.

❏ **Problems A/B**
Complete each assigned problem in Chapter 23. Use the forms provided in this SGWP. The objectives covered by a problem are given after the problem number. If you need help with a problem, review the portion of the chapter related to the objective(s) covered.

❏ **Challenge Problem**
Complete the challenge problem as assigned. Use the forms provided in this SGWP.

❏ **Critical Thinking Problem**
Complete the critical thinking problem as assigned. Use the forms provided in this SGWP.

❏ **Business Connections**
Complete the Business Connections activities as assigned to gain a deeper understanding of Chapter 23 concepts.

Practice Tests

Complete the Practice Tests, which cover the main points in your reading assignment. Compare your answers with those in the Practice Test Answer Key for Chapter 23 at the end of this chapter. If you have answered any questions incorrectly, review the related section of the text.

Part A True-False *For each of the following statements, circle T if the statement is true or F if the statement is false.*

T   F   **1.** In horizontal analysis, the items on each line of the statements for two periods are compared to determine the change in dollar amounts and percentages.

T   F   **2.** The net sales figure of a business is normally used as the base, or 100%, for vertical analysis comparisons on the income statement.

T   F   **3.** In statement analysis, a small percentage change in a large dollar amount may be more important than a large percentage change in a small dollar amount.

T   F   **4.** In preparing comparative statements, the accountant normally lists the later period to the left and the earlier period to the right.

T   F   **5.** In vertical analysis, the percentages may be added and subtracted.

T   F   **6.** Common-size statements are statements of companies that sold approximately the same product.

T   F   **7.** In general, a period of two years is adequate for comparing figures such as net sales.

T   F   **8.** In vertical analysis of the balance sheet, each liability item is usually expressed as a percent of total liabilities.

T   F   **9.** Vertical analysis of the balance sheet expresses each item as a percentage of total liabilities.

T   F   **10.** The gross sales figure of a business is normally used as the base, or 100 percent, for vertical comparisons on the income statement.

T   F   **11.** The earlier period is considered to be the base period in the horizontal analysis of statements.

T   F   **12.** The interpretation phase of statement analysis is composed primarily of computing percentages and ratios.

T   F   **13.** One shortcoming of vertical statement analysis is that percentages cannot be compared with those of similar companies in the same industry.

T   F   **14.** The analyst is interested in both the amount of change and the percent of change in an item from year to year.

T   F   **15.** Computers are of minor help in performing analyses of financial statements.

Part B Completion

In the answer column, supply the missing word or words needed to complete the following statements.

_____ **1.** To compute the percent of office salaries to net sales, it would be necessary to divide _____ _____ by _____ _____.

_____ **2.** If _____ _____ statements are prepared, each item on the income statement is expressed as a percent of net sales rather than in dollar amounts.

_____ **3.** Comparing an item on a financial statement with the same item in one or more past years is called _____ analysis.

_____ **4.** Comparison of dollar amounts or percentages over several periods is called _____ analysis.

_____ **5.** In vertical analysis of a statement, each item on the balance sheet is expressed as a percent of _____ _____.

Demonstration Problem

A condensed income statement for Way Down Corporation, for the years 2008 and 2007, follows. This report has been condensed and simplified from the corporation's annual Form 10K for 2008, filed with the U.S. Securities and Exchange Commission. Amounts given are in millions of dollars.

Instructions

1. Prepare a combined horizontal and vertical analysis of the comparative income statement of Way Down Corporation.

2. Analyze the data on the Way Down Corporation. What conclusions might be drawn from the following increases or decreases?

  a. Sales
  b. Cost of goods sold
  c. Inventory
  d. General administrative expense
  e. Interest expense
  f. Net income after income taxes

SOLUTION

1.

Way Down Corporation

Comparative Income Statement

Years Ended December 31, 2008 and 2007

	AMOUNTS 2008	AMOUNTS 2007	PERCENT OF NET SALES 2008	PERCENT OF NET SALES 2007	INCREASE OR (DECREASE) AMOUNT	INCREASE OR (DECREASE) PERCENT
Gross Sales	1 388 872	1 395 000	101.3	101.1	(6 128)	(0.5)
Sales Returns and Allowances	17 520	15 700	1.3	1.1	1 820	11.6
Net Sales	1 371 120	1 379 300	100.0	100.0	(8 180)	(0.6)
Cost of Goods Sold						
Beginning Inventory, January 1	275 561	273 500	20.1	19.8	2 061	0.8
Merchandise Purchases	545 000	519 981	39.7	37.7	25 019	4.8
Total Goods Available for Sale	820 561	793 481	59.8	57.5	27 080	3.4
Less Ending Inventory, December 31	318 542	275 561	23.2	20.0	42 981	15.5
Cost of Goods Sold	502 019	517 920	36.6	37.5	(15 901)	(3.0)
Gross Profit on Sales	869 101	861 380	63.4	62.5	7 721	0.9
Operating Expenses						
Selling Expenses	296 423	325 526	21.6	23.6	(29 103)	(8.9)
General Administrative Expenses	265 014	220 005	19.3	16.0	45 009	20.5
Total Operating Expenses	561 437	545 531	40.9	39.6	15 906	2.9
Net Income from Operations	307 664	316 072	22.5	22.9	(8 408)	(2.7)
Interest Expense	5 200	9 200	0.4	0.7	(4 000)	(43.5)
Net Income Before Income Taxes	302 464	306 872	22.1	22.2	(4 408)	(1.5)
Income Tax Expense	45 370	46 060	3.3	3.3	(690)	(1.5)
Net Income After Income Taxes	257 094	260 812	18.8	18.9	(3 718)	(1.5)

SOLUTION (continued)

2.   Several items on the comparative income statement of Way Down Corporation merit additional investigation.

a.   Sales decreased slightly. Although the amount was small in both dollar amount and percentage, a decrease in sales is generally unfavorable.

b.   At the same time as sales decreased, cost of goods sold decreased by a higher percentage. This decrease is a good indication, resulting in an increase in gross profit percentage from 62.5 percent in 2007 to 63.4 percent in 2008.

c.   Note that even though sales decreased, the merchandise inventory increased. During 2007 the inventory increased by 0.8 percent, and during 2008, it increased by 15.5 percent. This increase needs to be investigated.

d.   The large percentage increase in general administrative expenses should be carefully investigated. At the same time, selling expenses decreased during 2008. It is possible that some selling expenses were improperly classified as general administrative expenses. However, there was an increase of 2.9 percent in total operating expenses.

e.   Interest expense decreased by 43.5 percent during the year, but the dollar amount was not large. This amount could probably be explained easily.

f.   Overall, there was a decrease in net income after income taxes. This decrease is the result of the increase in expenses.

WORKING PAPERS

EXERCISE 23.1

	2008		2007	

EXERCISE 23.2

	2008		2007	

EXERCISE 23.3

	2008	2007	Change	Percent

EXTRA FORM

EXERCISE 23.4

	2008	2007	Difference	Percent

EXERCISE 23.5

EXERCISE 23.6

PROBLEM 23.1A or 23.1B

Comparative Income Statement

1.

	AMOUNTS 2008	AMOUNTS 2007	PERCENT OF NET SALES 2008	PERCENT OF NET SALES 2007	INCREASE OR (DECREASE) AMOUNT	PERCENT
Revenue						
Sales	667800	598950	102%	102%	68850	11.5%
Less S.R.A.	12500	11650	2%	2%	850	7.3%
Net Sales	655300	587300	100%	100%	68000	12%
Cost of Goods Sold						
Merchandise Inv (Jan 1)	82500	79045	13%	14%	3455	4.4%
Net Purch	315510	260000	48%	44%	65510	8.4%
Total Merch. Avail. for Sale	398010	339045	61%	58%	58965	17%
Less Merch Inv (Dec 31)	85000	82500	13%	14%	2500	3%
Cost of Goods Sold	313010	256645	48%	44%	56465	22%
Gross Profit on Sales	342290	330755	52%	56%	11535	3%
Operating Expenses						
Selling Expenses						
Sales Sal Exp	84900	78000				
Payroll Tax Exp - Selling	8490	7800				
Other Selling Exp.	25800	15200				
Total Selling Exp	119190	101000				

PROBLEM 23.1A or 23.1B (continued)

Comparative Income Statement (continued)

	AMOUNTS		PERCENT OF NET SALES		INCREASE OR (DECREASE)	
	2008	2007	2008	2007	AMOUNT	PERCENT
General & Admin Exp						
Officers Salaries Exp	135000	105000				
Payroll Tax Exp-Admin.	12600	10600				
Depreciation Exp	6250	6260				
Other General & Admin Exp	9450	7000				
Total General & Admin Exp	155100	130750				
Total operating Exp	274390	231750				
Net Income Before Income Tax	167900	9 9005				
Income Tax Exp	111975	71912				
Net Income after Income Tax	55925	77093				

PROBLEM 23.1A or 23.1B (continued)

Comparative Balance Sheet

	AMOUNTS		PERCENT OF TOTAL ASSETS		INCREASE OR (DECREASE)	
	2008	2007	2008	2007	AMOUNT	PERCENT

PROBLEM 23.1A or 23.1B (continued)

Comparative Balance Sheet (continued)

	AMOUNTS		PERCENT OF TOTAL ASSETS		INCREASE OR (DECREASE)	
	2008	2007	2008	2007	AMOUNT	PERCENT

2.

Analyze:

PROBLEM 23.2A or 23.2B

1.

Comparative Income Statement

		AMOUNTS		PERCENT OF NET SALES		INCREASE OR (DECREASE)	
		2008	2007	2008	2007	AMOUNT	PERCENT

PROBLEM 23.2A or 23.2B (continued)

Comparative Income Statement (continued)

	AMOUNTS		PERCENT OF NET SALES		INCREASE OR (DECREASE)	
	2008	2007	2008	2007	AMOUNT	PERCENT

PROBLEM 23.2A or 23.2B (continued)

Comparative Balance Sheet

	AMOUNTS		PERCENT OF TOTAL ASSETS		INCREASE OR (DECREASE)	
	2008	2007	2008	2007	AMOUNT	PERCENT

PROBLEM 23.2A or 23.2B (continued)

Comparative Balance Sheet (continued)

	AMOUNTS		PERCENT OF TOTAL ASSETS		INCREASE OR (DECREASE)	
	2008	2007	2008	2007	AMOUNT	PERCENT

EXTRA FORM

Comparative Balance Sheet (continued)

		AMOUNTS		PERCENT OF TOTAL ASSETS		INCREASE OR (DECREASE)	
		2008	2007	2008	2007	AMOUNT	PERCENT

PROBLEM 23.2A or 23.2B (continued)

2. _____

_____

_____

_____

_____

_____

_____

_____

_____

_____

Analyze: _____

_____

_____

EXTRA FORM

CHAPTER 23 CHALLENGE PROBLEM

1.

Comparative Balance Sheet

		AMOUNTS		PERCENT OF TOTAL ASSETS		INCREASE OR (DECREASE)	
		2008	2007	2008	2007	AMOUNT	PERCENT

CHAPTER 23 CHALLENGE PROBLEM (continued)

Comparative Balance Sheet (continued)

		AMOUNTS		PERCENT OF TOTAL ASSETS		INCREASE OR (DECREASE)	
		2008	2007	2008	2007	AMOUNT	PERCENT

CHAPTER 23 CHALLENGE PROBLEM (continued)

2.

Comparative Income Statement

		AMOUNTS		PERCENT OF NET SALES		INCREASE OR (DECREASE)	
		2008	2007	2008	2007	AMOUNT	PERCENT

3.

Analyze: _____

CHAPTER 23 CRITICAL THINKING PROBLEM

EXTRA FORM

Chapter 23 Practice Test Answer Key

Part A True-False

1. T
2. T
3. T
4. T
5. T
6. F
7. F
8. F
9. F
10. F
11. T
12. F
13. F
14. T
15. F

Part B Completion

1. office salaries by net sales
2. common-size
3. horizontal
4. trend
5. total assets or total liabilities and stockholders' equity

STUDY GUIDE

Understanding the Chapter

Objectives

1. Compute and interpret financial ratios that measure profitability, operating results, and efficiency. **2.** Compute and interpret financial ratios that measure financial strength. **3.** Compute and interpret financial ratios that measure liquidity. **4.** Recognize certain shortcomings in financial statement analysis. **5.** Define the accounting terms new to this chapter.

Reading Assignment

Read Chapter 24 in the textbook. Complete the textbook Section Self Reviews as you finish reading each section of the chapter, and the Comprehensive Self Review at the end of the chapter. Refer to the Chapter 24 Glossary or to the Glossary at the end of the book to find definitions for terms that are not familiar to you.

Activities

❑ **Thinking Critically**

Answer the *Thinking Critically* questions for The Walt Disney Company, Accounting on the Job, and Managerial Implications.

❑ **Internet Application**

Complete the activity for Accounting on the Job.

❑ **Discussion Questions**

Answer each assigned discussion question in Chapter 24.

❑ **Exercises**

Complete each assigned exercise in Chapter 24. Use the forms provided in this SGWP. The objectives covered by an exercise are given after the exercise number. If you need help with an exercise, review the portion of the chapter related to the objective(s) covered.

❑ **Problems A/B**

Complete each assigned problem in Chapter 24. Use the forms provided in this SGWP. The objectives covered by a problem are given after the problem number. If you need help with a problem, review the portion of the chapter related to the objective(s) covered.

❑ **Challenge Problem**

Complete the challenge problem as assigned. Use the forms provided in this SGWP.

❑ **Critical Thinking Problem**

Complete the critical thinking problem as assigned. Use the forms provided in this SGWP.

❑ **Business Connections**

Complete the Business Connections activities as assigned to gain a deeper understanding of Chapter 24 concepts.

Practice Tests

Complete the Practice Tests, which cover the main points in your reading assignment. Compare your answers with those in the Practice Test Answer Key for Chapter 24 at the end of this chapter. If you have answered any questions incorrectly, review the related section of the text.

Part A True-False *For each of the following statements, circle T if the statement is true or F if the statement is false.*

T   F   **1.** The rate of return on total assets is affected by the source of financing used to acquire assets.

T   F   **2.** The rate of return on assets varies in proportion to changes in the rate of return on sales.

T   F   **3.** In computing the rate of return on total assets, net income before interest and taxes should be used.

T   F   **4.** The ratio of stockholders' equity to liabilities and the ratio of stockholders' equity to total equities are not related.

T   F   **5.** Having an accounts receivable collection period that exceeds 30 days will have no effect on your cash flow planning for the business.

T   F   **6.** The average collection period of accounts receivable should be compared with the firm's credit payment policy for customers.

T   F   **7.** The aging of accounts receivable usually has no short term relationship to the firm's ability to pay short term debt.

T   F   **8.** The rate of return on net sales will increase if operating expenses decrease while sales remain constant.

T   F   **9.** Current ratio and acid-test ratio are the same ratio.

T   F   **10.** The rate of return on net sales will increase if operating expenses decrease while sales remain constant.

T   F   **11.** In general, the lower the rate of inventory turnover, the better.

T   F   **12.** Cash, receivables, and equipment are included in quick assets.

T   F   **13.** The inventory turnover is computed by dividing net sales by the cost of goods sold.

T   F   **14.** In general, ratios between items on financial statements are more meaningful than absolute amounts.

T   F   **15.** A lender will be more interested in net income than in the acid-test ratio.

Part B Matching *For each of the transactions below, decide the effect (or effects) the transaction would have on the corporation's financial statements or ratios. In the space provided, enter the letter or letters corresponding to all effects that apply. If there is no appropriate response among the effects listed, write "none."*

Transaction	Effect
_____ **1.** Issued long-term notes payable for cash	**a.** Increases working capital
	b. Reduces working capital
_____ **2.** Declared and paid an ordinary cash dividend	**c.** Increases the current ratio
	d. Decreases the current ratio
_____ **3.** Omitted the payment of a dividend	**e.** Increases the dollar amount of the total capital stock
_____ **4.** Declared a cash dividend due in one month	**f.** Decreases the dollar amount of the total capital stock
_____ **5.** Issued new common stock shares on a 4 for 1 stock split	**g.** Increases total retained earnings
	h. Decreases total retained earnings
_____ **6.** Purchased a new office desk for cash	**i.** Reduces the book value of each share of common stock
	j. Reduces the book value of each common shareholder's interest

Demonstration Problem

The comparative financial statements that follow are for the Buy-it-Now Corporation. Calculate the missing amounts in the comparative income statement and balance sheet. (Note: since this is a demonstration problem, the missing amounts are those shown in *italics* in the solution. Look at the solution and decide how you would calculate these amounts.)

Using the comparative financial statements, calculate the following ratios for 2008 and 2007.

1. Rate of return on net sales
2. Asset turnover
3. Ratio of stockholders' equity to total equities
4. Ratio of stockholders' equity to total liabilities
5. Current ratio
6. Acid-test ratio

SOLUTION

Buy-it-Now Corporation

Comparative Balance Sheet

Years Ended December 31, 2008 and 2007

	AMOUNTS		INCREASE OR (DECREASE)	
	2008	2007	AMOUNT	PERCENT
Assets				
Current Assets				
Cash	27 5 0 0	16 6 0 0	10 9 0 0	65.7
Accounts Receivable	77 0 0 0	59 0 0 0	18 0 0 0	30.5
Merchandise Inventory	66 0 0 0	48 0 0 0	18 0 0 0	37.5
Total Current Assets	170 5 0 0	123 6 0 0	46 9 0 0	37.9
Property, Plant, and Equipment				
Land, Buildings, Equipment	117 4 0 0	77 4 0 0	40 0 0 0	51.7
Less: Accumulated Depreciation	27 6 0 0	20 5 0 0	7 1 0 0	34.6
Net Book Value—Property, Plant, and				
Equipment	89 8 0 0	56 9 0 0	32 9 0 0	57.8
Total Assets	*260 3 0 0*	*180 5 0 0*	79 8 0 0	44.2
Liabilities and Stockholders' Equity				
Current Liabilities				
Accounts Payable	68 2 5 0	49 6 0 0	18 6 5 0	37.6
Accrued Expenses	14 0 0 0	10 0 0 0	4 0 0 0	40.0
Total Current Liabilities	82 2 5 0	59 6 0 0	22 6 5 0	38.0
Stockholders' Equity				
Common Stock ($50 Par Value)	50 0 0 0	50 0 0 0	– 0 –	0.0
Retained Earnings	128 0 5 0	70 9 0 0	57 1 5 0	80.6
Total Stockholders' Equity	*178 0 5 0*	*120 9 0 0*	57 1 5 0	47.3
Total Liabilities and Stockholders' Equity	*260 3 0 0*	*180 5 0 0*	79 8 0 0	44.2

SOLUTION (continued)

Buy-it-Now Corporation

Comparative Income Statement

December 31, 2008 and 2007

	AMOUNTS		INCREASE OR (DECREASE)	
	2008	2007	AMOUNT	PERCENT
Net Sales	917000	852000	65000	7.6
Cost of Merchandise Sold	495000	398000	97000	24.4
Gross Profit on Sales	422000	454000	(32000)	(7.0)
Operating Expenses				
Selling Expenses	152500	141600	10900	7.7
General Expenses	82000	94000	(12000)	(12.8)
Total Operating Expenses	234500	235600	(1100)	(0.5)
Net Income Before Income Tax	187500	218400	(30900)	(14.1)
Income Tax Expense	56375	68426	(12051)	(17.6)
Net Income After Income Tax	131125	149974	(18849)	(12.6)

		2008		2007	
1.	$\dfrac{\text{Net income after taxes}}{\text{Net sales}}$	$= \dfrac{\$131,125}{\$917,000}$	$= 14.3\%$	$\dfrac{\$149,974}{\$852,000}$	$= 17.6\%$
2.	$\dfrac{\text{Net sales}}{\text{Total assets}}$	$= \dfrac{\$917,000}{\$260,300}$	$= 3.5 \text{ to } 1$	$\dfrac{\$852,000}{\$180,500}$	$= 4.7 \text{ to } 1$
3.	$\dfrac{\text{Stockholders' equity}}{\text{Total equities}}$	$= \dfrac{\$178,050}{\$260,300}$	$= 0.68 \text{ to } 1$	$\dfrac{\$120,900}{\$180,500}$	$= 0.67 \text{ to } 1$
4.	$\dfrac{\text{Stockholders' equity}}{\text{Total liabilities}}$	$= \dfrac{\$178,050}{\$82,250}$	$= 2.2 \text{ to } 1$	$\dfrac{\$120,900}{\$59,600}$	$= 2.0 \text{ to } 1$
5.	$\dfrac{\text{Current assets}}{\text{Current liabilities}}$	$= \dfrac{\$170,500}{\$82,250}$	$= 2.1 \text{ to } 1$	$\dfrac{\$123,600}{\$59,600}$	$= 2.1 \text{ to } 1$
6.	$\dfrac{\text{Cash + receivables + marketable securities}}{\text{Current liabilities}}$	$= \dfrac{\$27,500 + \$77,000}{\$82,250}$	$= 1.3 \text{ to } 1$	$\dfrac{\$16,600 + \$59,000}{\$59,600}$	$= 1.3 \text{ to } 1$

WORKING PAPERS

EXERCISE 24.1

	2008	2007

EXERCISE 24.2

	2008	2007

EXERCISE 24.3

	2008	2007

EXERCISE 24.4

	2008	2007

EXERCISE 24.5

	2008	2007

EXERCISE 24.6

	2008	2007

EXERCISE 24.7   2008   2007

_____

_____

EXERCISE 24.8   2008   2007

_____

EXERCISE 24.9   2008   2007

_____

_____

EXERCISE 24.10   2008   2007

_____

_____

EXERCISE 24.11   2008   2007

_____

_____

EXERCISE 24.12   2008   2007

_____

_____

EXERCISE 24.13   2008

_____

PROBLEM 24.1A or 24.1B

PART I

2007

2008

1.
2.
3.
4.
5.
6.
7.
8.
9.
10.
11.

PROBLEM 24.1A or 24.1B (continued)

PART II

Analyze:

PROBLEM 24.2A or 24.2B

2007

2008

1.

2.

3.

4.

5.

6.

7.

8.

9.

10.

11.

Analyze:

PROBLEM 24.3A or 24.3B

1.a.

b.

c.

d.

e.

f.

g.

h.

PROBLEM 24.3A or 24.3B (continued)

2. _____

3. _____

4. _____

Analyze: _____

CHAPTER 24 CHALLENGE PROBLEM

CHAPTER 24 CHALLENGE PROBLEM (continued)

_____

Analyze: _____

_____

CHAPTER 24 CRITICAL THINKING PROBLEM

	Quality Construction	On-Time Construction

1. Current Ratio _____

_____

_____

_____

2. Acid-Test Ratio _____

_____

_____

_____

3. Inventory Turnover _____

_____

_____

_____

4. Accounts Receivable Turnover _____

_____

_____

_____

_____

_____

_____

_____

_____

_____

Chapter 24 Practice Test Answer Key

Part A True-False		**Part B Matching**
1. F	9. F	1. a, c
2. F	10. T	2. b, d, h
3. T	11. F	3. i, j
4. F	12. F	4. b, d, h
5. F	13. F	5. i
6. T	14. T	6. b, d
7. F	15. F	
8. F		

STUDY GUIDE

Understanding the Chapter

Objectives	**1.** Distinguish between operating, investing, and financing activities. **2.** Compute cash flows from operating activities. **3.** Compute cash flows from investing activities. **4.** Compute cash flows from financing activities. **5.** Prepare a statement of cash flows. **6.** Define the accounting terms new to this chapter.
Reading Assignment	Read Chapter 25 in the textbook. Complete the textbook Section Self Reviews as you finish reading each section of the chapter, and the Comprehensive Self Review at the end of the chapter. Refer to the Chapter 25 Glossary or to the Glossary at the end of the book to find definitions for terms that are not familiar to you.

Activities

❏ **Thinking Critically**	Answer the *Thinking Critically* questions for Eastman Kodak Company, Computers in Accounting, and Managerial Implications.
❏ **Internet Application**	Complete the activity for Computers in Accounting.
❏ **Discussion Questions**	Answer each assigned discussion question in Chapter 25.
❏ **Exercises**	Complete each assigned exercise in Chapter 25. Use the forms provided in this SGWP. The objectives covered by an exercise are given after the exercise number. If you need help with an exercise, review the portion of the chapter related to the objective(s) covered.
❏ **Problems A/B**	Complete each assigned problem in Chapter 25. Use the forms provided in this SGWP. The objectives covered by a problem are given after the problem number. If you need help with a problem, review the portion of the chapter related to the objective(s) covered.
❏ **Challenge Problem**	Complete the challenge problem as assigned. Use the forms provided in this SGWP.
❏ **Critical Thinking Problem**	Complete the critical thinking problem as assigned. Use the forms provided in this SGWP.
❏ **Business Connections**	Complete the Business Connections activities as assigned to gain a deeper understanding of Chapter 25 concepts.

Practice Tests

Complete the Practice Tests, which cover the main points in your reading assignment. Compare your answers with those in the Practice Test Answer Key for Chapter 25 at the end of this chapter. If you have answered any questions incorrectly, review the related section of the text.

Part A True-False *For each of the following statements, circle T if the statement is true or F if the statement is false.*

T   F   **1.** A six month CD is an example of a cash equivalent.

T   F   **2.** The statement of cash flows provides an important link between the balance sheet and the income statement.

T   F   **3.** The statement of cash flows is designed to provide information about a corporation's cash position.

T   F   **4.** Interest expense is a cash outflow from an investing activity.

T   F   **5.** The sale of bonds is a financing activity.

T   F   **6.** The statement of cash flows reconciles the beginning and ending balances of cash and cash equivalents.

T   F   **7.** Repayment of a long-term note payable represents an investing activity.

T   F   **8.** The purchase of merchandise inventory for resale is an operating activity.

T   F   **9.** The issue of a mortgage payable for a building is a financing activity.

T   F   **10.** The issue of $100,000 of common stock for land with a fair market value of $100,000 represents an investing activity.

T   F   **11.** Short-term borrowing is classified as a financing activity for purposes of preparing the statement of cash flows.

T   F   **12.** A corporation issued $500,000 of bonds payable, receiving in exchange a building with that value. The transaction would be included in the footnotes of the statement of cash flows.

T   F   **13.** The indirect method of preparing the statement of cash flows is easier to prepare than the direct method.

T   F   **14.** The cash received from the sale of equipment represents a cash flow from operating activities.

T   F   **15.** The amortization of premium on bonds payable is added to net income in arriving at the cash flows from operations.

T   F   **16.** The FASB has expressed a preference for the direct method of preparing the statement of cash flows.

T   F   **17.** Depreciation expense is added to the net income figure in arriving at cash flow from operating activities.

Part B Matching *For each numbered item, choose the matching term from the box and write the identifying letter in the answer column.*

_____   **1.** Purchased office furniture for cash

_____   **2.** Reacquired common stock as treasury stock

_____   **3.** Paid cash on accounts payable

_____   **4.** Purchased land by issuing common stock

_____   **5.** Paid cash dividend on preferred stock

_____   **6.** Declared but did not pay a cash dividend

_____   **7.** Sold land held as a long-term investment

_____   **8.** Paid a cash dividend

_____   **9.** Paid interest on a five-year note payable

_____   **10.** Borrowed $59,000 by issuing a 90-day note payable

a.	Operating
b.	Investing
c.	Financing
d.	Not on statement of cash flows

Demonstration Problem

Broad Street Market, Inc. was formed and began business on December 31, 2006, when Roma Brandon transferred merchandise inventory with a value of $50,000, cash of $30,000, accounts receivable of $20,000, and accounts payable of $20,000 to the corporation in exchange for common stock with a recorded par value of $25 a share.

Information from the company's statement of cash flows for 2007 follows.

Instructions

Based on the data given, prepare the December 31, 2007, balance sheet for the corporation.

Cash Flows from Operating Activities		
Net Income		$ 100,000
Adjustments:		
Depreciation of building	$ 7,500	
Depreciation of equipment	5,000	
Increase in accounts receivable	(33,000)	
Increase in inventory	(10,000)	
Increase in prepaid insurance	(1,300)	
Increase in accounts payable	12,000	
Increase in income tax payable	4,000	
Total Adjustments		(15,800)
Net cash provided by operating activities		$ 84,200
Cash Flows from Investing Activities		
Purchase of land	$(20,000)	
Purchase of building*	(10,000)	
Purchase of equipment	(25,000)	
Net cash used in investing activities		(55,000)
Cash Flows from Financing Activities		
Issuance of common stock at $25	$ 75,000	
Borrowing at bank by issuance of note payable	20,000	
Payment on principal of bank note	(5,000)	
Net cash provided by financing activities		$ 90,000
Net Increase in Cash and Cash Equivalents		$ 119,200
Cash balance, January 1, 2007		30,000
Cash balance, December 31, 2007		$149,200

*A building was acquired at a cost of $75,000. Cash of $10,000 was paid, and a mortgage payable of $65,000 was given for the balance.

SOLUTION

Broad Street Market, Inc.

Balance Sheet

December 31, 2007

Assets					
Current Assets					
Cash			149 2 0 0 00		
Accounts Receivable			53 0 0 0 00		
Merchandise Inventory			60 0 0 0 00		
Prepaid Insurance			1 3 0 0 00		
Total Current Assets				263 5 0 0 00	
Property, Plant, and Equipment					
Land			20 0 0 0 00		
Building	75 0 0 0 00				
Less Accumulated Depreciation—Building	7 5 0 0 00		67 5 0 0 00		
Equipment	25 0 0 0 00				
Less Accumulated Depreciation—Equipment	5 0 0 0 00		20 0 0 0 00		
Total Property, Plant, and Equipment				107 5 0 0 00	
Total Assets				371 0 0 0 00	
Liabilities and Stockholders' Equity					
Current Liabilities					
Accounts Payable			32 0 0 0 00		
Notes Payable			15 0 0 0 00		
Income Tax Payable			4 0 0 0 00		
Total Current Liabilities			51 0 0 0 00		
Long-Term Liabilities					
Mortgage Payable			65 0 0 0 00		
Total Liabilities				116 0 0 0 00	
Stockholders' Equity					
Common Stock ($25 par, 6,200 shares authorized)			155 0 0 0 00		
Retained Earnings			100 0 0 0 00		
Total Stockholders' Equity				255 0 0 0 00	
Total Liabilities and Stockholders' Equity				371 0 0 0 00	

WORKING PAPERS

EXERCISE 25.1

1. _____
_____
_____
_____

2. _____
_____
_____
_____

EXERCISE 25.2

EXERCISE 25.3

EXERCISE 25.4

EXERCISE 25.5

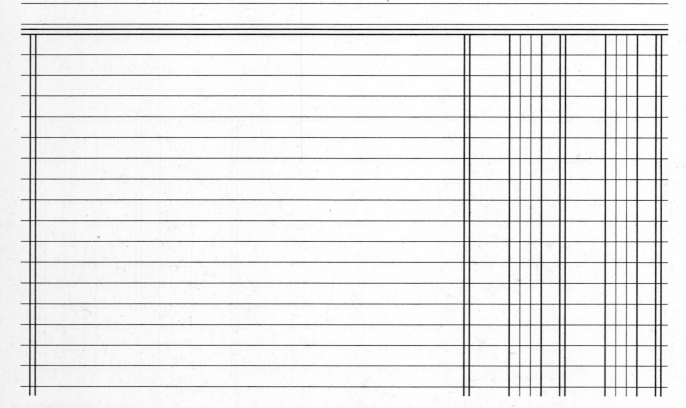

EXERCISE 25.6

_____
_____
_____
_____
_____

EXERCISE 25.7

_____
_____
_____
_____
_____

EXERCISE 25.8

_____
_____
_____
_____
_____

EXERCISE 25.9

_____
_____
_____
_____
_____

PROBLEM 25.1A or 25.1B

_____

Analyze: _____

PROBLEM 25.2A or 25.2B

_____

_____

Analyze: _____

_____

PROBLEM 25.3A or 25.3B

Analyze: _____

PROBLEM 25.4A or 25.4B

_____

_____

Analyze: _____

CHAPTER 25 CHALLENGE PROBLEM

Analyze:

CHAPTER 25 CRITICAL THINKING PROBLEM

_____

_____

_____

_____

_____

_____

_____

_____

_____

_____

_____

_____

_____

_____

_____

_____

_____

_____

_____

_____

_____

_____

_____

_____

_____

_____

_____

_____

_____

_____

_____

_____

_____

EXTRA FORM

Chapter 25 Practice Test Answer Key

Part A True-False

1. F	7. T	13. T
2. T	8. T	14. F
3. T	*9. F	15. F
4. F	10. F	16. T
5. T	11. T	17. T
6. T	12. T	

Part B Matching

1. b	6. d
2. c	7. b
3. a	8. c
4. d	9. a
5. c	10. c

*Financing & Investing Activity
Not Affecting Cash Flow

MINI-PRACTICE SET 4

Financial Analysis and Decision Making

Surf City Merchandise, Inc.

Introduction

Surf City Merchandise, Inc. sells a variety of consumer products. Its comparative income statement and balance sheet for the years 2008 and 2007 are presented on the following pages.

Instructions

1. Prepare a horizontal and a vertical analysis of the statements. Round all dollar calculations to the nearest whole dollar. Percentage calculations should be rounded to one decimal place (e.g., 11.2%). Remember that some vertical addition of percentages may not equal 100 percent due to rounding.

2. Calculate the following ratios for each year.

   a. The rate of return on net sales.

   b. The rate of return on common stockholders' equity. Preferred dividends are $5,000 for both years. (Remember that dividend requirements on preferred stock must be deducted from net income after taxes to obtain income available to common stockholders.)

   c. The earnings per share of common stock, assuming that the preferred stock is nonparticipating, noncumulative, and has no liquidation value. The number of outstanding shares of common stock remained constant at 100,000 throughout all of 2007 and 2008.

   d. The price-earnings ratio on common stock. The market values were $8.00 in 2008 and $6.00 in 2007.

   e. The rate of return on total assets.

   f. The ratio of stockholders' equity to total liabilities.

   g. The current ratio.

   h. The acid-test ratio.

   i. The merchandise inventory turnover. Inventory was $75,900 at January 1, 2007.

   j. The accounts receivable turnover. Credit sales were $2,000,000 for 2008 and $1,500,000 for 2007. The beginning accounts receivable balance for 2007 was $158,500.

Analyze: Assume that the firm declared and distributed a 5% common stock dividend in 2008. What is the effect on earnings per share in 2008? Assume that market value is equal to par value and all other information is the same.

Name _____

Surf City Merchandise, Inc.
Comparative Income Statement
Years Ended December 31, 2008 and 2007

	2008	2007
Revenue:		
Sales	2,309,450	1,975,500
Less: Sales Returns and Allowances	29,450	25,000
Net Sales	2,280,000	1,950,500
Cost of Goods Sold:		
Merchandise Inventory, January 1	72,500	75,900
Purchases	968,900	825,400
Freight In	9,900	7,500
Less: Purchases Discounts	10,000	8,254
Purchases Returns and Allowances	8,250	5,000
Total Merchandise Available for Sale	1,033,050	895,546
Less Merchandise Inventory, December 31	76,800	72,500
Cost of Goods Sold	956,250	823,046
Gross Profit on Sales	1,323,750	1,127,454
Operating Expenses:		
Selling Expenses		
Advertising	22,600	21,000
Sales Salaries	195,000	175,000
Payroll Taxes Sales	19,500	17,500
Supplies Expense	11,845	9,650
Miscellaneous Selling Expenses	9,575	7,995
Insurance Expense	7,700	7,500
Total Selling Expenses	266,220	238,645
Administrative Expenses		
Officers' Salaries	385,000	350,000
Office Employees	137,500	125,000
Payroll Taxes—Office Employees	52,250	47,500
Office Supplies	13,250	10,000
Insurance Expense—Administrative	7,800	7,500
Uncollectible Accounts Expense	9,000	8,000
Legal and Accounting	18,500	15,000
Depreciation Expense—Building	15,000	15,000
Depreciation Expense—Furniture	12,000	10,000
Utilities Expense	18,000	16,750
Total Administrative Expenses	668,300	604,750
Total Operating Expenses	934,520	843,395
Other Income:		
Interest and Dividends	4,675	4,500
Total Other Income	4,675	4,500
Other Expenses:		
Bond Interest Expense	6,930	6,930
Interest Expense	6,320	6,070
Total Other Expenses	13,250	13,000
Net Other Expenses	8,575	8,500
Net Income Before Taxes	380,655	275,559
Income Tax Expense	133,229	96,446
Net Income After Taxes	247,426	179,113

Surf City Merchandise, Inc.
Comparative Balance Sheet
December 31, 2008 and 2007

	2008	2007
Assets		
Current Assets		
Cash	138,813.00	106,732.00
Accounts Receivable	193,900.00	162,500.00
Merchandise Inventory	76,800.00	72,500.00
Prepaid Insurance	400.00	200.00
Supplies	975.00	1,000.00
Total Current Assets	410,888.00	342,932.00
Property, Plant, and Equipment		
Land	105,000.00	25,000.00
Building	300,000.00	300,000.00
Less: Accumulated Depreciation—Building	(45,000.00)	(30,000.00)
Furniture	60,000.00	50,000.00
Less: Accumulated Depreciation—Furniture	(22,000.00)	(10,000.00)
Total Property, Plant, and Equipment	398,000.00	335,000.00
Other Assets		
Marketable Securities (Long-Term)	40,000.00	40,000.00
Total Assets	848,888.00	717,932.00
Liabilities and Stockholders' Equity		
Current Liabilities		
Accounts Payable	69,900.00	64,000.00
Notes Payable	5,000.00	60,000.00
Bond Interest Payable	500.00	500.00
Income Taxes Payable	19,000.00	15,000.00
Sales Salaries Payable	25,000.00	14,000.00
Other Payables	5,200.00	7,500.00
Total Current Liabilities	124,600.00	161,000.00
Long-Term Liabilities		
10% Bonds Payable, due January 1, 2017	70,000.00	70,000.00
Premium on Bonds Payable	630.00	700.00
Total Long-Term Liabilities	70,630.00	70,700.00
Total Liabilities	195,230.00	231,700.00
Stockholders' Equity		
5% Preferred Stock, $100 par, 1,000 shares authorized/outstanding	100,000.00	100,000.00
Common Stock, $1 par, 500,000 shares authorized,		
100,000 shares outstanding	100,000.00	100,000.00
Paid-in Capital in Excess of Par—Common Stock	25,000.00	25,000.00
Total Paid-in Capital	225,000.00	225,000.00
Retained Earnings		
Retained Earnings—Unappropriated	403,658.00	236,232.00
Retained Earnings—Appropriated	25,000.00	25,000.00
Total Retained Earnings	428,658.00	261,232.00
Total Stockholders' Equity	653,658.00	486,232.00
Total Liabilities and Stockholders' Equity	848,888.00	717,932.00

Name _____

Comparative Balance Sheet

	AMOUNTS		PERCENT OF TOTAL ASSETS		INCREASE OR (DECREASE)	
	2008	2007	2008	2007	AMOUNT	PERCENT

Name

Comparative Balance Sheet (continued)

	AMOUNTS		PERCENT OF TOTAL ASSETS		INCREASE OR (DECREASE)	
	2008	2007	2008	2007	AMOUNT	PERCENT

Name _____

Comparative Balance Sheet (continued)

	AMOUNTS		PERCENT OF TOTAL ASSETS		INCREASE OR (DECREASE)	
	2008	2007	2008	2007	AMOUNT	PERCENT

Comparative Balance Sheet

	AMOUNTS		PERCENT OF TOTAL ASSETS		INCREASE OR (DECREASE)	
	2008	2007	2008	2007	AMOUNT	PERCENT

Name

Comparative Income Statement

		AMOUNTS		PERCENT OF NET SALES		INCREASE OR (DECREASE)	
		2008	2007	2008	2007	AMOUNT	PERCENT

Name

Comparative Income Statement (continued)

	AMOUNTS		PERCENT OF NET SALES		INCREASE OR (DECREASE)	
	2008	2007	2008	2007	AMOUNT	PERCENT

EXTRA FORM

Comparative Income Statement

		AMOUNTS		PERCENT OF NET SALES		INCREASE OR (DECREASE)	
		2008	2007	2008	2007	AMOUNT	PERCENT

Name _____

2007

2008

RATIO

a.

b.

c.

d.

e.

f.

g.

h.

i.

j.

Name _____

COMPUTATIONS

_____
_____
_____
_____
_____
_____
_____
_____
_____
_____
_____
_____
_____
_____
_____
_____
_____
_____
_____
_____
_____
_____

Analyze: _____
_____
_____
_____
_____
_____
_____
_____
_____
_____

CHAPTER 26

Internal Control and the Voucher System

STUDY GUIDE

Understanding the Chapter

Objectives

1. Explain the general principles of internal control. 2. Explain how the voucher system facilitates internal control. 3. Prepare vouchers. 4. Record vouchers in a voucher register. 5. Record payment of approved vouchers. 6. Record transactions that require special treatment in a voucher system. 7. Define the accounting terms new to this chapter.

Reading Assignment

Read Chapter 26 in the textbook. Complete the textbook Section Self Reviews as you finish reading each section of the chapter, and the Comprehensive Self Review at the end of the chapter. Refer to the Chapter 26 Glossary or to the Glossary at the end of the book to find definitions for terms that are not familiar to you.

Activities

❏ **Thinking Critically**
Answer the *Thinking Critically* questions for Amgen Inc., Dell Computer Corporation, Accounting on the Job, and Managerial Implications.

❏ **Internet Application**
Complete the activity for Accounting on the Job.

❏ **Discussion Questions**
Answer each assigned discussion question in Chapter 26.

❏ **Exercises**
Complete each assigned exercise in Chapter 26. Use the forms provided in this SGWP. The objectives covered by an exercise are given after the exercise number. If you need help with an exercise, review the portion of the chapter related to the objective(s) covered.

❏ **Problems A/B**
Complete each assigned problem in Chapter 26. Use the forms provided in this SGWP. The objectives covered by a problem are given after the problem number. If you need help with a problem, review the portion of the chapter related to the objective(s) covered.

❏ **Challenge Problem**
Complete the challenge problem as assigned. Use the forms provided in this SGWP.

❏ **Critical Thinking Problem**
Complete the critical thinking problem as assigned. Use the forms provided in this SGWP.

❏ **Business Connections**
Complete the Business Connections activities as assigned to gain a deeper understanding of Chapter 26 concepts.

Practice Tests

Complete the Practice Tests, which cover the main points in your reading assignment. Compare your answers with those in the Practice Test Answer Key for Chapter 26 at the end of this chapter. If you have answered any questions incorrectly, review the related section of the text.

Part A True-False

T F **1.** The use of the voucher system makes it unnecessary to maintain an accounts payable ledger.

T F **2.** For good internal control, the person approving vouchers should be responsible for preparing and mailing checks.

T F **3.** The rotation of duty assignments without advance notice makes internal control more effective.

T F **4.** It is necessary to prepare a voucher to authorize payment of a note payable.

T F **5.** The smaller the number of persons involved, the stronger the system of internal controls.

T F **6.** Internal control is strengthened by having bills for merchandise paid out of cash receipts.

T F **7.** The extensions and the total of an invoice should be verified after the voucher has been approved but before the check is written.

T F **8.** Adjustments, allowances, and similar corrections for invoices already vouchered may be made using the voucher system without requiring general journal entries.

T F **9.** Unpaid vouchers are generally filed according to the date on which they were prepared.

T F **10.** When an invoice for the purchase of merchandise is recorded at the gross amount, a discount lost is recorded when the check is written.

T F **11.** The voucher register replaces the purchases journal.

T F **12.** Recording purchase invoices at their net amounts after discounts promotes good internal control over the taking of discounts because discounts not taken will stand out for investigation.

Part B Exercise *The Brandon Company uses the following journals to record transactions: general journal (GJ), sales journal (SJ), cash receipts journal (CRJ), voucher register (VR), and check register (CR). For each of the following transactions, indicate the journal in which the transaction would be recorded and the account(s) to be debited and credited. Use the abbreviations given to identify the journals.*

1. Prepared a voucher for $1,000 for merchandise purchased on credit. Terms are 2/10, n/30. Invoices are recorded at gross amount.

   Journal _____   Account Dr. _____   Account Cr. _____

   _____   _____

2. Paid the voucher described in Transaction 1. Payment was made within the discount period.

   Journal _____   Account Dr. _____   Account Cr. _____

   _____   _____

3. Prepared a voucher and paid a $750 note payable and $35 in interest.

   Journal _____   Account Dr. _____   Account Cr. _____

   _____   _____

4. Cancelled old Voucher 10-8 for $800. Issued two new vouchers for $400 each. One of the new vouchers will be paid now; the other will be paid two weeks later.

   Journal _____   Account Dr. _____   Account Cr. _____

   _____   _____

Demonstration Problem

On June 6, 2007, the Retail Shop purchased merchandise from the Import Company and received Invoice 606 for $1000. Terms were 2/10, n/30.

Instructions

1. Record the entry for the purchase from the Import Company in the general journal, page 19. Assume the following conditions:
   a. Retail Shop recorded the purchases at the total invoice price (gross).
   b. Retail Shop recorded the purchases at the net invoice price.

2. Assume the Retail Shop paid the Import Company Invoice 606 on June 16, 2007, and took the cash discount. Record the entry for the payment to the Import Company in the general journal, assuming the following conditions:
   a. Retail Shop recorded the purchases at the total invoice price (gross).
   b. Retail Shop recorded the purchases at the net invoice price.

3. Assume that the Retail Shop paid the Import Company for Invoice 606 on July 7, 2007, and was not able to take the cash discount. Record the entry for payment to Import Company in the general journal, assuming the following conditions:
   a. Retail Shop recorded the purchases at the total invoice price (gross).
   b. Retail Shop recorded the purchases at the net invoice price.

SOLUTION

	DATE		DESCRIPTION	POST. REF.	DEBIT	CREDIT	
1	2007		1.a.				1
2	June	6	Purchases		1 0 0 0 00		2
3			Accounts Payable/Import Company			1 0 0 0 00	3
4			Purchased merchandise, Invoice 606				4
5							5
6			1.b.				6
7	June	6	Purchases		9 8 0 00		7
8			Accounts Payable/Import Company			9 8 0 00	8
9			Purchased merchandise, Invoice 606,				9
10			net of discount				10
11							11
12			2.a.				12
13	June	16	Accounts Payable/Import Company		1 0 0 0 00		13
14			Purchases Discounts			2 0 00	14
15			Cash			9 8 0 00	15
16			Paid Invoice 606 within discount period				16
17							17
18			2.b.				18
19	June	16	Accounts Payable/Import Company		9 8 0 00		19
20			Cash			9 8 0 00	20
21			Paid Invoice 606 within discount period				21
22							22
23			3.a.				23
24	July	7	Accounts Payable/Import Company		1 0 0 0 00		24
25			Cash			1 0 0 0 00	25
26			Paid Invoice 606 after discount period				26
27							27
28			3.b.				28
29	July	7	Accounts Payable/Import Company		9 8 0 00		29
30			Discounts Lost		2 0 00		30
31			Cash			1 0 0 0 00	31
32			Paid Invoice 606 after discount period				32
33							33
34							34
35							35
36							36
37							37

Name _____

EXERCISE 26.1

GENERAL JOURNAL

PAGE _____

	DATE	DESCRIPTION	POST. REF.	DEBIT	CREDIT	
1						1
2						2
3						3
4						4
5						5
6						6
7						7
8						8
9						9
10						10
11						11
12						12
13						13
14						14
15						15
16						16
17						17
18						18

EXERCISE 26.2

GENERAL JOURNAL

PAGE _____

	DATE	DESCRIPTION	POST. REF.	DEBIT	CREDIT	
1						1
2						2
3						3
4						4
5						5
6						6
7						7
8						8
9						9
10						10
11						11
12						12
13						13

EXERCISE 26.3

GENERAL JOURNAL   PAGE _____

	DATE	DESCRIPTION	POST. REF.	DEBIT	CREDIT	
1						1
2						2
3						3
4						4
5						5
6						6
7						7
8						8
9						9
10						10
11						11
12						12
13						13
14						14
15						15

EXTRA FORM

GENERAL JOURNAL   PAGE _____

	DATE	DESCRIPTION	POST. REF.	DEBIT	CREDIT	
1						1
2						2
3						3
4						4
5						5
6						6
7						7
8						8
9						9
10						10
11						11
12						12
13						13
14						14
15						15

PROBLEM 26.1A or 26.1B

VOUCHER REGISTER

	DATE	VOU. NO.	PAYABLE TO	PAID		ACCOUNTS PAYABLE CREDIT	SOCIAL SECURITY TAX PAYABLE CREDIT	MEDICARE TAX PAYABLE CREDIT
				DATE	CK. NO.			
1								
2								
3								
4								
5								
6								
7								
8								
9								
10								
11								
12								
13								
14								

CHECK REGISTER

PAGE _____

DATE	CK. NO.	PAYABLE TO	VOUCHER NUMBER	ACCOUNTS PAYABLE DEBIT	PURCHASES DISCOUNTS CREDIT	CASH CREDIT

PROBLEM 26.1A or 26.1B (continued)

PAGE _____

EMPLOYEE INCOME TAX PAYABLE CREDIT	PURCHASES DEBIT	FREIGHT IN DEBIT	STORE SUPPLIES DEBIT	OTHER ACCOUNTS				
				ACCOUNT NAME	POST. REF.	DEBIT	CREDIT	
								1
								2
								3
								4
								5
								6
								7
								8
								9
								10
								11
								12
								13
								14

EXTRA FORM

CHECK REGISTER

PAGE _____

DATE	CK. NO.	PAYABLE TO	VOUCHER NUMBER	ACCOUNTS PAYABLE DEBIT	PURCHASES DISCOUNTS CREDIT	CASH CREDIT

Analyze: _____

PROBLEM 26.2A or 26.2B

VOUCHER REGISTER

	DATE	VOU. NO.	PAYABLE TO	PAID DATE	CK. NO.	ACCOUNTS PAYABLE CREDIT	SOCIAL SECURITY TAX PAYABLE CREDIT	MEDICARE TAX PAYABLE CREDIT
1								
2								
3								
4								
5								
6								
7								
8								
9								
10								
11								
12								
13								
14								
15								
16								
17								
18								
19								
20								
21								
22								
23								
24								
25								
26								
27								
28								
29								
30								
31								
32								
33								
34								
35								
36								

PROBLEM 26.2A or 26.2B (continued)

PAGE _____

EMPLOYEE INCOME TAX PAYABLE CREDIT	PURCHASES DEBIT	FREIGHT IN DEBIT	STORE SUPPLIES DEBIT	OTHER ACCOUNTS			
				ACCOUNT NAME	POST. REF.	DEBIT	CREDIT
								1
								2
								3
								4
								5
								6
								7
								8
								9
								10
								11
								12
								13
								14
								15
								16
								17
								18
								19
								20
								21
								22
								23
								24
								25
								26
								27
								28
								29
								30
								31
								32
								33
								34
								35
								36

PROBLEM 26.2A or 26.2B (continued)

CHECK REGISTER   PAGE _____

DATE	CK. NO.	PAYABLE TO	VOUCHER NUMBER	ACCOUNTS PAYABLE DEBIT	PURCHASES DISCOUNTS CREDIT	CASH CREDIT

VOUCHER NO.	PAYABLE TO	AMOUNT

Analyze: _____

_____

CHAPTER 26 CHALLENGE PROBLEM

Cost of Goods Sold Schedule

Schedule of Vouchers Payable

VOUCHER NO.	PAYABLE TO	AMOUNT

Analyze: _____

_____

CHAPTER 26 CRITICAL THINKING PROBLEM

_____
_____
_____
_____
_____
_____
_____
_____
_____
_____
_____
_____
_____
_____
_____
_____
_____
_____
_____
_____
_____
_____
_____
_____
_____

Chapter 26 Practice Test Answer Key

Part A True-False

1. T	7. F
2. F	8. T
3. F	9. F
4. T	10. F
5. F	11. T
6. F	12. T

Part B Exercise

		Debit	Credit
1.	VR	Purchases	Accounts Payable
2.	CR	Accounts Payable	Cash
			Purchases Discounts
3.	VR	Notes Payable	Accounts Payable
		Interest Expense	
	CR	Accounts Payable	Cash
4.	VR	Accounts Payable	Accounts Payable
			Accounts Payable

CHAPTER 27

Departmentalized Profit and Cost Centers

STUDY GUIDE

Understanding the Chapter

Objectives	**1.** Explain profit centers and cost centers. **2.** Prepare the Gross Profit section of a departmental income statement. **3.** Explain and identify direct and indirect departmental expenses. **4.** Choose the basis for allocation of indirect expenses and compute the amounts to be allocated to each department. **5.** Prepare a departmental income statement showing the contribution margin and operating income for each department. **6.** Use a departmental income statement in making decisions such as whether a department should be closed. **7.** Define the accounting terms new to this chapter.
Reading Assignment	Read Chapter 27 in the textbook. Complete the textbook Section Self Reviews as you finish reading each section of the chapter, and the Comprehensive Self Review at the end of the chapter. Refer to the Chapter 27 Glossary or to the Glossary at the end of the book to find definitions for terms that are not familiar to you.

Activities

❏ **Thinking Critically**	Answer the *Thinking Critically* questions for Mattel, Inc., Computers in Accounting and Managerial Implications.
❏ **Internet Application**	Complete the activity for Computers in Accounting.
❏ **Discussion Questions**	Answer each assigned discussion question in Chapter 27.
❏ **Exercises**	Complete each assigned exercise in Chapter 27. Use the forms provided in this SGWP. The objectives covered by an exercise are given after the exercise number. If you need help with an exercise, review the portion of the chapter related to the objective(s) covered.
❏ **Problems A/B**	Complete each assigned problem in Chapter 27. Use the forms provided in this SGWP. The objectives covered by a problem are given after the problem number. If you need help with a problem, review the portion of the chapter related to the objective(s) covered.
❏ **Challenge Problem**	Complete the challenge problem as assigned. Use the forms provided in this SGWP.
❏ **Critical Thinking Problem**	Complete the critical thinking problem as assigned. Use the forms provided in this SGWP.
❏ **Business Connections**	Complete the Business Connections activities as assigned to gain a deeper understanding of Chapter 27 concepts.

Practice Tests

Complete the Practice Tests, which cover the main points in your reading assignment. Compare your answers with those in the Practice Test Answer Key for Chapter 27 at the end of this chapter. If you have answered any questions incorrectly, review the related section of the text.

Part A True-False

For each of the following statements, circle T in the answer column if the statement is true, or F if the statement is false.

T   F   **1.** Responsibility accounting is designed to help management evaluate the performance of each segment of business.

T   F   **2.** In a departmental accounting system, sales returns and allowances should be debited to the departmental sales account.

T   F   **3.** Sales discounts need not be departmentalized if they are treated as other expense.

T   F   **4.** Direct expenses are costs related to a specific department.

T   F   **5.** Cost centers are also called profit centers.

T   F   **6.** A separate column should be provided in the voucher register for purchases of each sales department.

T   F   **7.** Semi-direct expenses cannot be allocated to a sales department on any logical basis.

T   F   **8.** If a business is profitable, it is not important to know how much each department contributed to the overall profit.

T   F   **9.** Profit centers are usually business segments that sell to customers outside the business.

T   F   **10.** Purchases returns and allowances are not normally departmentalized in the accounts.

T   F   **11.** If a department has a negative contribution margin, the business would probably be more profitable if the department were eliminated.

T   F   **12.** Eliminating a department should eliminate all direct expenses of that department.

T   F   **13.** The contribution margin is the difference between gross profit and nonoperating expenses.

T   F   **14.** Beginning and ending inventories are allocated to the departments on the basis of net sales in each.

T   F   **15.** The net income of a department should receive more attention than its contribution margin in reaching managerial decisions.

T   F   **16.** Indirect expenses are allocated to the departments at the time the expense transactions are journalized.

T   F   **17.** Nonoperating income, such as interest income, should be allocated to departments on the basis of net sales.

T   F   **18.** Utilities expense should be allocated to departments on the basis of gross sales in each department.

T   F   **19.** Gross profit and contribution margin have the same meaning.

T   F   **20.** Payroll taxes applicable to sales salaries may be treated as an indirect expense, or as a direct expense if they are recorded by department.

Part B Matching
For each numbered item, choose the matching term from the box and write the identifying letter in the answer column.

_____ 1. Expenses that can be assigned to a specific department.

_____ 2. Expenses incurred for the benefit of several departments that cannot be assigned directly to any one particular department.

_____ 3. The procedure for dividing indirect expenses among several departments.

_____ 4. The difference between gross profit and direct expense.

_____ 5. Expenses that are closely related to the activities in each department but cannot be allocated to any specific department.

a. Contribution margin
b. Direct expenses
c. Indirect expenses
d. Semi-direct expenses
e. Allocation

Demonstration Problem

The Book Store is a retail store selling books, software, and supplies. The store has three departments: books, software, and supplies. Condensed information about the store's revenues and expenses for each department for the year ended December 31, 2007, follows. Indirect expenses have been allocated on bases similar to those discussed in the textbook chapter. The store had interest income of $300 for the year.

Instructions

1. Prepare a departmental income statement showing the contribution margin and the net profit for each department.

2. Based solely on accounting information, would you recommend closing any of the departments? Why or why not?

	Books	Software	Supplies
Allocated indirect expenses	$ 18,000	$12,000	$10,000
Beginning merchandise inventory	19,000	23,000	23,000
Direct expenses	20,000	10,000	17,000
Ending merchandise inventory	17,000	15,000	9,200
Purchases	86,000	41,000	31,500
Purchases returns and allowances	800	200	300
Sales	200,600	96,500	61,500
Sales returns and allowances	2,600	600	500

SOLUTION

	BOOKS	SOFTWARE	SUPPLIES	TOTAL
Sales	2 0 0 6 0 0	9 6 5 0 0	6 1 5 0 0	3 5 8 6 0 0
Less Sales Returns and Allowances	2 6 0 0	6 0 0	5 0 0	3 7 0 0
Net Sales	1 9 8 0 0 0	9 5 9 0 0	6 1 0 0 0	3 5 4 9 0 0
Cost of Goods Sold				
Merchandise Inventory, January 1	1 9 0 0 0	2 3 0 0 0	2 3 0 0 0	6 5 0 0 0
Purchases	8 6 0 0 0	4 1 0 0 0	3 1 5 0 0	1 5 8 5 0 0
Less Purchases Returns and Allowances	8 0 0	2 0 0	3 0 0	1 3 0 0
Net Purchases	8 5 2 0 0	4 0 8 0 0	3 1 2 0 0	1 5 7 2 0 0
Cost of Goods Available for Sale	1 0 4 2 0 0	6 3 8 0 0	5 4 2 0 0	2 2 2 2 0 0
Less Merchandise Inventory, December 31	1 7 0 0 0	1 5 0 0 0	9 2 0 0	4 1 2 0 0
Cost of Goods Sold	8 7 2 0 0	4 8 8 0 0	4 5 0 0 0	1 8 1 0 0 0
Gross Profit	1 1 0 8 0 0	4 7 1 0 0	1 6 0 0 0	1 7 3 9 0 0
Direct Expenses	2 0 0 0 0	1 0 0 0 0	1 7 0 0 0	4 7 0 0 0
Contribution Margin	9 0 8 0 0	3 7 1 0 0	(1 0 0 0)	1 2 6 9 0 0
Indirect Expenses	1 8 0 0 0	1 2 0 0 0	1 0 0 0 0	4 0 0 0 0
Net Income (Loss) from Operations	7 2 8 0 0	2 5 1 0 0	(1 1 0 0 0)	8 6 9 0 0
Other Income				
Interest Income				3 0 0
Net Income for Year				8 7 2 0 0

Based solely on the accounting information, the Supplies Department should be closed. The contribution margin is a loss of $1,000 and the department net loss is $11,000. The department is not generating enough revenue to pay all of its direct expenses. Generally, when this situation presents itself, the management of the firm would suggest closing that department.

WORKING PAPERS

EXERCISE 27.1

DEPARTMENT	BASIS: BOOK VALUE OF INVENTORY AND EQUIPMENT	PERCENT	TOTAL INSURANCE EXPENSE	ALLOCATION
_____	_____	_____	_____	_____
_____	_____	_____	_____	_____
_____	_____	_____	_____	_____
_____	_____	_____	_____	_____
_____	_____	_____	_____	_____

EXERCISE 27.2

DEPARTMENT	BASIS: TOTAL SALES	PERCENT	TOTAL OFFICE EXPENSE	ALLOCATION
_____	_____	_____	_____	_____
_____	_____	_____	_____	_____
_____	_____	_____	_____	_____
_____	_____	_____	_____	_____
_____	_____	_____	_____	_____

EXERCISE 27.3

DEPARTMENT	CREDIT SALES	SALES RETURNS AND ALLOWANCES	BASIS: NET CREDIT SALES	PERCENT	ALLOCATION
_____	_____	_____	_____	_____	_____
_____	_____	_____	_____	_____	_____
_____	_____	_____	_____	_____	_____
_____	_____	_____	_____	_____	_____
_____	_____	_____	_____	_____	_____

EXERCISE 27.4

EXTRA FORM

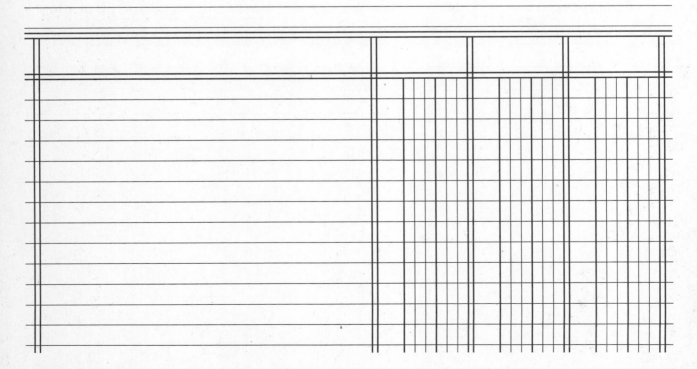

EXERCISE 27.5

_____

EXERCISE 27.6

_____

EXERCISE 27.7

_____

PROBLEM 27.1A or 27.1B

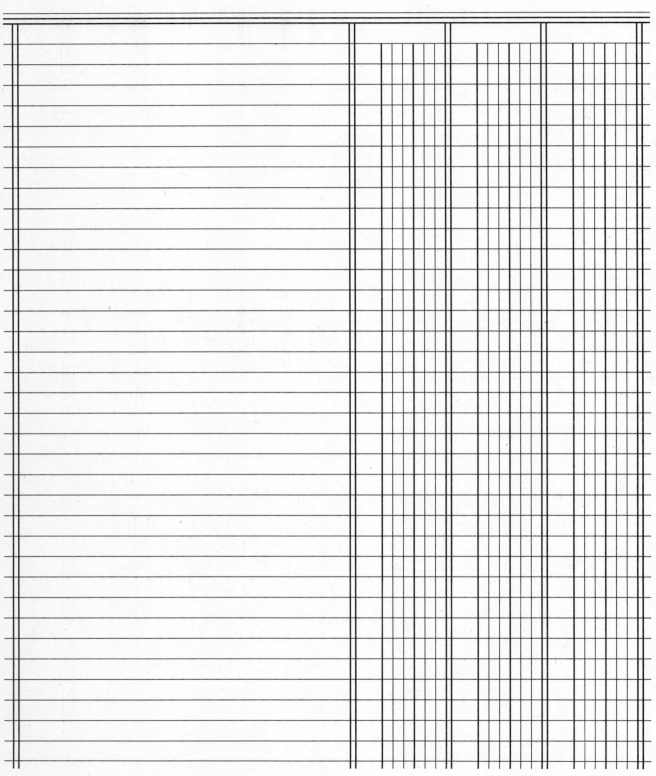

(continued)

PROBLEM 27.1A or 27.1B (continued)

ALLOCATION OF INDIRECT EXPENSES

Insurance Expense

1. _____

_____

_____

Rent Expense

2. _____

_____

_____

Utilities Expense

_____

_____

PROBLEM 27.1A or 27.1B (continued)

ALLOCATION OF INDIRECT EXPENSES (continued)

Office Salaries Expense

3. _____
_____
_____

Other Office Expenses

_____
_____
_____

Depreciation Expense—Office Equipment

_____
_____
_____

Uncollectible Accounts Expense

4. _____
_____
_____

Depreciation Expense—Furniture and Fixtures

5. _____
_____
_____

Analyze: _____
_____

PROBLEM 27.2A or 27.2B

1. _____

<u>Income Statement</u>

PROBLEM 27.2A or 27.2B (continued)

2.

3.

Analyze:

CHAPTER 27 CHALLENGE PROBLEM

_____

_____

_____

_____

_____

_____

_____

_____

_____

_____

_____

_____

_____

_____

_____

_____

_____

_____

_____

_____

_____

_____

_____

_____

_____

_____

_____

_____

_____

Analyze: _____

_____

CHAPTER 27 CRITICAL THINKING PROBLEM

_____

_____

_____

_____

_____

_____

_____

_____

_____

_____

_____

_____

_____

_____

_____

_____

_____

_____

_____

_____

_____

_____

_____

_____

_____

Chapter 27 Practice Test Answer Key

Part A True-False

1. T	6. T	11. T	16. F
2. F	7. F	12. T	17. F
3. T	8. F	13. F	18. F
4. T	9. T	14. F	19. F
5. F	10. F	15. F	20. T

Part B Matching

1. b
2. c
3. e
4. a
5. d

STUDY GUIDE

Understanding the Chapter

Objectives

1. Prepare a statement of cost of goods manufactured. 2. Explain the basic components of manufacturing cost. 3. Prepare an income statement for a manufacturing business. 4. Prepare a balance sheet for a manufacturing business. 5. Prepare a worksheet for a manufacturing business. 6. Record the end-of-period adjusting entries for a manufacturing business. 7. Record closing entries for a manufacturing business. 8. Record reversing entries for a manufacturing business. 9. Define the accounting terms new to this chapter.

Reading Assignment

Read Chapter 28 in the textbook. Complete the textbook Section Self Reviews as you finish reading each section of the chapter, and the Comprehensive Self Review at the end of the chapter. Refer to the Chapter 28 Glossary or to the Glossary at the end of the book to find definitions for terms that are not familiar to you.

Activities

❏ **Thinking Critically**   Answer the *Thinking Critically* questions for Goodrich Corporation, Accounting on the Job, and Managerial Implications.

❏ **Internet Application**   Complete the activity for Accounting on the Job.

❏ **Discussion Questions**   Answer each assigned discussion question in Chapter 28.

❏ **Exercises**   Complete each assigned exercise in Chapter 28. Use the forms provided in this SGWP. The objectives covered by an exercise are given after the exercise number. If you need help with an exercise, review the portion of the chapter related to the objective(s) covered.

❏ **Problems A/B**   Complete each assigned problem in Chapter 28. Use the forms provided in this SGWP. The objectives covered by a problem are given after the problem number. If you need help with a problem, review the portion of the chapter related to the objective(s) covered.

❏ **Challenge Problem**   Complete the challenge problem as assigned. Use the forms provided in this SGWP.

❏ **Critical Thinking Problem**   Complete the critical thinking problem as assigned. Use the forms provided in this SGWP.

❏ **Business Connections**   Complete the Business Connections activities as assigned to gain a deeper understanding of Chapter 28 concepts.

Practice Tests

Complete the Practice Tests, which cover the main points in your reading assignment. Compare your answers with those in the Practice Test Answer Key for Chapter 28 at the end of this chapter. If you have answered any questions incorrectly, review the related section of the text.

Part A True-False *For each of the following statements, circle T in the answer column if the answer is true or F if the answer is false.*

T   F   **1.** The cost of goods manufactured is the total of the direct labor, direct materials, and overhead costs involved in the manufacturing process during the period.

T   F   **2.** Small items, such as glue and nails, that become part of the finished product may be treated either as direct materials or as indirect materials, depending on company policy and cumulative cost of items.

T   F   **3.** The cost of indirect materials used is shown in the Raw Materials section of the statement of cost of goods manufactured.

T   F   **4.** The wages of a worker who saws and forms legs for tables in a furniture factory would be classified as direct labor.

T   F   **5.** In a manufacturing company, it is necessary to take a physical inventory of the finished goods.

T   F   **6.** In the Cost of Goods Manufactured section of the worksheet, the excess of the total of the Debit column over the total of the Credit column represents the cost of goods manufactured.

T   F   **7.** The entry to set up the ending work in process inventory is part of the adjustments process.

T   F   **8.** The ending inventory of finished goods is entered in the Credit column of the Cost of Goods Manufactured section of the worksheet.

T   F   **9.** On the worksheet of a manufacturing business, the amount of the ending work in process inventory is entered in the Debit column of the Balance Sheet section.

T   F   **10.** Payroll taxes on factory wages should be classified as an administrative expense in the income statement.

Part B Completion *In the answer column, supply the missing word or words needed to complete each of the following statements.*

_____   **1.** All raw materials used, direct labor costs incurred, and manufacturing costs incurred during the period make up the total _____.

_____   **2.** All materials that become part of the manufactured product are known as _____.

_____   **3.** The cost of indirect materials used appears in the _____ section of the statement of cost of goods manufactured.

_____   **4.** The partially completed product at year-end is called _____.

_____   **5.** In the worksheet, the cost of goods manufactured is entered in the _____ column of the Cost of Goods Manufactured section and in the _____ column of the Income Statement section.

_____   **6.** The statement on which the beginning and ending inventories of work in process appear is the _____.

_____   **7.** The adjusted balances of the manufacturing cost accounts are extended from the Adjusted Trial Balance section to the _____ section of a manufacturing company's worksheet.

_____   **8.** The postclosing trial balance contains the balances of the _____, _____, and _____ accounts.

Demonstration Problem

The Augusta Corporation makes golf clubs. Information about the company's operations follows.

Instructions

1. Prepare a statement of cost of goods manufactured for the year ended December 31, 2007.

	January 1, 2007	December 31, 2007
Finished Goods Inventory	$550,000	$ 475,000
Raw Materials Inventory	296,000	245,000
Work in Process Inventory	112,000	92,500
Direct Labor		895,000
Freight In		25,500
Indirect Labor		350,000
Indirect Materials and Supplies		56,350
Insurance—Factory		18,500
Depreciation—Factory Building and Equipment		75,000
Materials Purchases		1,800,000
Payroll Taxes—Factory		195,000
Utilities—Factory		65,000
Property Taxes—Factory		45,000
Materials Purchases Returns and Allowances		6,900
Repairs and Maintenance—Factory		39,500
Patent Amortization		1,500
Waste Removal—Factory		20,000

SOLUTION

The Augusta Corporation

Statement of Cost of Goods Manufactured

Year Ended December 31, 2007

Raw Materials				
Raw Materials Inventory, January 1, 2007			296 0 0 0 00	
Materials Purchases	1,800 0 0 0 00			
Freight In	25 5 0 0 00			
Delivered Cost of Material Purchases	1,825 5 0 0 00			
Less Materials Purchases Returns and Allowances	6 9 0 0 00			
Net Material Purchases			1,818 6 0 0 00	
Total Materials Available for Use			2,114 6 0 0 00	
Less Raw Materials Inventory, December 31, 2005			245 0 0 0 00	
Raw Materials Used				1,869 6 0 0 00
Direct Labor				895 0 0 0 00
Manufacturing Overhead				
Indirect Materials and Supplies		56 3 5 0 00		
Indirect Labor		350 0 0 0 00		
Payroll Taxes—Factory		195 0 0 0 00		
Utilities—Factory		65 0 0 0 00		
Repairs and Maintenance—Factory		39 5 0 0 00		
Depreciation—Factory Building and Equipment		75 0 0 0 00		
Insurance—Factory		18 5 0 0 00		
Property Taxes—Factory		45 0 0 0 00		
Patent Amortization		1 5 0 0 00		
Waste Removal—Factory		20 0 0 0 00		
Total Manufacturing Overhead				865 8 5 0 00
Total Manufacturing Costs				3,630 4 5 0 00
Add Work in Process Inventory, January 1, 2007				112 0 0 0 00
				3,742 4 5 0 00
Less Work in Process Inventory, December 31, 2007				92 5 0 0 00
Cost of Goods Manufactured				3,649 9 5 0 00

WORKING PAPERS

EXERCISE 28.1

_____

_____

EXERCISE 28.2

GENERAL JOURNAL

PAGE _____

	DATE	DESCRIPTION	POST. REF.	DEBIT	CREDIT	
1						1
2						2
3						3
4						4
5						5
6						6
7						7
8						8
9						9
10						10
11						11
12						12
13						13
14						14
15						15
16						16
17						17
18						18
19						19
20						20

EXERCISE 28.3

EXERCISE 28.4

EXERCISE 28.5

EXERCISE 28.6

EXERCISE 28.7

_____
_____
_____
_____
_____
_____
_____

EXERCISE 28.8

_____
_____
_____
_____
_____
_____
_____

EXERCISE 28.9

_____
_____
_____
_____
_____
_____
_____

EXERCISE 28.10

GENERAL JOURNAL   PAGE _____

	DATE	DESCRIPTION	POST. REF.	DEBIT	CREDIT	
1						1
2						2
3						3
4						4
5						5
6						6
7						7
8						8
9						9
10						10
11						11
12						12
13						13
14						14
15						15
16						16
17						17
18						18
19						19
20						20
21						21
22						22
23						23
24						24
25						25
26						26
27						27
28						28
29						29
30						30
31						31
32						32
33						33
34						34
35						35
36						36
37						37

EXERCISE 28.10 (continued)

GENERAL JOURNAL   PAGE _____

	DATE	DESCRIPTION	POST. REF.	DEBIT	CREDIT	
1						1
2						2
3						3
4						4
5						5
6						6
7						7
8						8
9						9
10						10
11						11
12						12
13						13
14						14
15						15
16						16
17						17
18						18
19						19
20						20
21						21
22						22
23						23
24						24
25						25
26						26
27						27
28						28
29						29
30						30
31						31
32						32
33						33
34						34
35						35
36						36
37						37

PROBLEM 28.1A or 28.1B

Statement of Cost of Goods Manufactured

PROBLEM 28.1A or 28.1B (continued)

_____

_____

Income Statement

_____

Analyze: _____

PROBLEM 28.2A or 28.2B

_____

	ACCOUNT NAME	TRIAL BALANCE		ADJUSTMENTS	
		DEBIT	CREDIT	DEBIT	CREDIT
1					
2					
3					
4					
5					
6					
7					
8					
9					
10					
11					
12					
13					
14					
15					
16					
17					
18					
19					
20					
21					
22					
23					
24					
25					
26					
27					
28					
29					
30					
31					
32					
33					
34					

PROBLEM 28.2A or 28.2B (continued)

ADJUSTED TRIAL BALANCE		COST OF GOODS MANUFACTURED		INCOME STATEMENT		BALANCE SHEET		
DEBIT	CREDIT	DEBIT	CREDIT	DEBIT	CREDIT	DEBIT	CREDIT	
								1
								2
								3
								4
								5
								6
								7
								8
								9
								10
								11
								12
								13
								14
								15
								16
								17
								18
								19
								20
								21
								22
								23
								24
								25
								26
								27
								28
								29
								30
								31
								32
								33
								34

PROBLEM 28.2A or 28.2B (continued)

	ACCOUNT NAME	TRIAL BALANCE		ADJUSTMENTS	
		DEBIT	CREDIT	DEBIT	CREDIT
1					
2					
3					
4					
5					
6					
7					
8					
9					
10					
11					
12					
13					
14					
15					
16					
17					
18					
19					
20					
21					
22					
23					
24					
25					
26					
27					
28					
29					
30					
31					
32					

PROBLEM 28.2A or 28.2B (continued)

ADJUSTED TRIAL BALANCE		COST OF GOODS MANUFACTURED		INCOME STATEMENT		BALANCE SHEET		
DEBIT	CREDIT	DEBIT	CREDIT	DEBIT	CREDIT	DEBIT	CREDIT	
								1
								2
								3
								4
								5
								6
								7
								8
								9
								10
								11
								12
								13
								14
								15
								16
								17
								18
								19
								20
								21
								22
								23
								24
								25
								26
								27
								28
								29
								30
								31
								32

PROBLEM 28.2A or 28.2B (continued)

Statement of Cost of Goods Manufactured

PROBLEM 28.2A or 28.2B (continued)

Income Statement

PROBLEM 28.2A or 28.2B (continued)

Statement of Retained Earnings

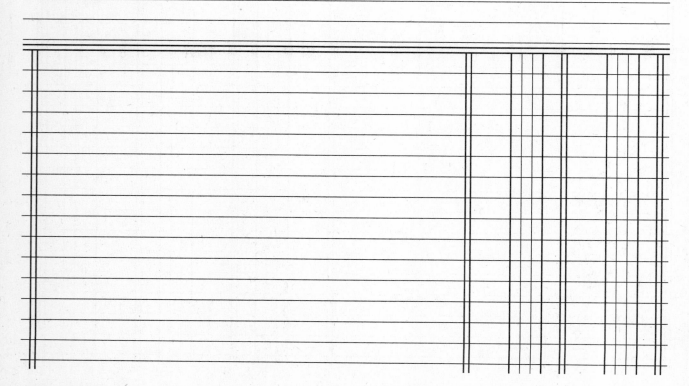

EXTRA FORM

PROBLEM 28.2A or 28.2B (continued)

Balance Sheet

PROBLEM 28.2A or 28.2B (continued)

GENERAL JOURNAL   PAGE _____

	DATE		DESCRIPTION	POST. REF.	DEBIT	CREDIT	
1							1
2							2
3							3
4							4
5							5
6							6
7							7
8							8
9							9
10							10
11							11
12							12
13							13
14							14
15							15
16							16
17							17
18							18
19							19
20							20
21							21
22							22
23							23
24							24
25							25
26							26
27							27
28							28
29							29
30							30
31							31
32							32
33							33
34							34
35							35
36							36
37							37

PROBLEM 28.2A or 28.2B (continued)

GENERAL JOURNAL   PAGE _____

	DATE	DESCRIPTION	POST. REF.	DEBIT	CREDIT	
1						1
2						2
3						3
4						4
5						5
6						6
7						7
8						8
9						9
10						10
11						11
12						12
13						13
14						14
15						15
16						16
17						17
18						18
19						19
20						20
21						21
22						22
23						23
24						24
25						25
26						26
27						27
28						28
29						29
30						30
31						31
32						32
33						33
34						34
35						35
36						36
37						37

PROBLEM 28.2A or 28.2B (continued)

GENERAL JOURNAL   PAGE _____

	DATE	DESCRIPTION	POST. REF.	DEBIT	CREDIT	
1						1
2						2
3						3
4						4
5						5
6						6
7						7
8						8
9						9
10						10
11						11
12						12
13						13
14						14
15						15
16						16
17						17
18						18
19						19
20						20
21						21
22						22
23						23
24						24
25						25
26						26
27						27
28						28
29						29
30						30
31						31
32						32
33						33
34						34
35						35
36						36
37						37

PROBLEM 28.2A or 28.2B (continued)

GENERAL JOURNAL   PAGE _____

	DATE	DESCRIPTION	POST. REF.	DEBIT	CREDIT	
1						1
2						2
3						3
4						4
5						5
6						6
7						7
8						8
9						9
10						10
11						11
12						12
13						13
14						14
15						15
16						16
17						17
18						18
19						19
20						20
21						21
22						22
23						23
24						24
25						25
26						26
27						27
28						28
29						29
30						30
31						31
32						32
33						33
34						34

Analyze: _____

CHAPTER 28 CHALLENGE PROBLEM

Statement of Cost of Goods Manufactured

Income Statement

CHAPTER 28 CHALLENGE PROBLEM (continued)

NOTES

_____

_____

_____

_____

_____

_____

_____

_____

_____

_____

_____

_____

_____

_____

_____

_____

_____

_____

_____

_____

_____

_____

_____

_____

_____

_____

_____

_____

_____

Analyze: _____

_____

CHAPTER 28 CRITICAL THINKING PROBLEM

Chapter 28 Practice Test Answer Key

Part A True-False

1. F	6. T
2. T	7. T
3. F	8. F
4. T	9. T
5. T	10. F

Part B Completion

1. manufacturing costs
2. direct materials
3. manufacturing overhead
4. work in process
5. credit; debit
6. statement of cost of goods manufactured
7. cost of goods manufactured
8. asset; liability; stockholders' equity

Job Order Cost Accounting

STUDY GUIDE

Understanding the Chapter

Objectives	**1.** Explain how a job order cost accounting system operates. **2.** Journalize the purchase and issuance of direct and indirect materials. **3.** Maintain perpetual inventory records. **4.** Record labor costs incurred and charge labor into production. **5.** Compute overhead rates and apply overhead to jobs. **6.** Compute overapplied or underapplied overhead and report it in the financial statements. **7.** Maintain job order cost sheets. **8.** Record the cost of jobs completed and the cost of goods sold under a perpetual inventory system. **9.** Define the accounting terms new to this chapter.
Reading Assignment	Read Chapter 29 in the textbook. Complete the textbook Section Self Reviews as you finish reading each section of the chapter, and the Comprehensive Self Review at the end of the chapter. Refer to the Chapter 29 Glossary or to the Glossary at the end of the book to find definitions for terms that are not familiar to you.

Activities

❑ **Thinking Critically**	Answer the *Thinking Critically* questions for Avery Dennison Corporation, Computers in Accounting, and Managerial Implications.
❑ **Internet Application**	Complete the activity for Computers in Accounting.
❑ **Discussion Questions**	Answer each assigned discussion question in Chapter 29.
❑ **Exercises**	Complete each assigned exercise in Chapter 29. Use the forms provided in this SGWP. The objectives covered by an exercise are given after the exercise number. If you need help with an exercise, review the portion of the chapter related to the objective(s) covered.
❑ **Problems A/B**	Complete each assigned problem in Chapter 29. Use the forms provided in this SGWP. The objectives covered by a problem are given after the problem number. If you need help with a problem, review the portion of the chapter related to the objective(s) covered.
❑ **Challenge Problem**	Complete the challenge problem as assigned. Use the forms provided in this SGWP.
❑ **Critical Thinking Problem**	Complete the critical thinking problem as assigned. Use the forms provided in this SGWP.
❑ **Business Connections**	Complete the Business Connections activities as assigned to gain a deeper understanding of Chapter 29 concepts.

Practice Tests

Complete the Practice Tests, which cover the main points in your reading assignment. Compare your answers with those in the Practice Test Answer Key for Chapter 29 at the end of this chapter. If you have answered any questions incorrectly, review the related section of the text.

For each of the following statements, circle T in the answer column if the statement is true or F if the statement is false.

T   F   **1.** The job order cost system is often used by businesses that produce what each customer wants on special order.

T   F   **2.** Applied overhead is usually posted each day to the job order cost sheets.

T   F   **3.** Perpetual inventory accounts for raw materials, work in process, and finished goods are commonly used in a job order system.

T   F   **4.** Underapplied or overapplied overhead may be closed into the **Cost of Goods Sold** account at the end of the year.

T   F   **5.** Purchases of raw materials are debited to the **Work in Process Inventory** account.

T   F   **6.** Idle time is generally treated as manufacturing overhead.

T   F   **7.** In a job order cost system, the individual job order cost sheets form a subsidiary ledger for the **Work in Process Inventory** account.

T   F   **8.** Under the job order system, unit costs of production are determined for all orders simultaneously.

T   F   **9.** A widely used method of applying manufacturing overhead to individual jobs is based on a percentage of indirect labor costs.

T   F   **10.** A just-in-time ordering system reduces the need for inventory storage space.

T   F   **11.** Charging manufacturing overhead to jobs on the basis of a predetermined rate usually results in overapplied or underapplied overhead.

T   F   **12.** The materials requisition provides the information needed to enter receipt of raw materials on the raw materials ledger cards.

T   F   **13.** The posting of labor costs to the individual job order cost sheets is made from the payroll register at the end of the week.

T   F   **14.** Under a job order cost system, the selling price of goods sold will be entered on the finished goods ledger sheet for the products sold.

Part B Completion   *In the answer column, supply the missing word or words needed to complete each of the following statements.*

_____ **1.** The three major inventories of a manufacturing business are generally maintained on a(n) _____ basis.

_____ **2.** Depreciation of factory equipment, indirect labor, and indirect materials are examples of _____.

_____ **3.** When more overhead costs are incurred than are applied to individual jobs, overhead is said to be _____.

_____ **4.** The _____ shows the costs incurred for materials, labor, and overhead on a job.

_____ **5.** If idle time is caused by a breakdown of factory equipment, the related cost will probably be charged to _____.

_____ **6.** Materials are issued by the storeroom clerk only on presentation of a(n) _____ signed by an authorized person.

_____ **7.** The receipt of materials from a supplier is reported by preparing a(n) _____.

_____ **8.** Under the _____ method of inventory pricing, the quantities issued are priced from the oldest inventory items available in the order they were received.

Demonstration Problem

The cost data that follows is for Alex Leather Products, Inc., a maker of shoes and boots. This data covers the month of December 2007.

a. Materials purchases, $75,000.

b. Materials issued to production, $60,200; direct materials, $59,000; indirect materials, $1,200.

c. Payroll: direct labor, $24,000; indirect labor, $5,200; social security tax deducted, $1,810; medicare tax deducted, $423; income tax deducted, $2,600. (Medicare and social security amounts rounded to the nearest dollar.)

d. Manufacturing overhead of $11,500 was incurred in addition to indirect materials and indirect labor. (Credit **Accounts Payable.**)

e. Manufacturing overhead is applied to production at a predetermined rate of 75 percent of direct labor costs.

f. Jobs costing $82,000 were completed and transferred to finished goods.

g. Finished goods costing $73,000 were sold and billed to customers at $96,000.

Instructions

1. Prepare general journal entries to record each item of cost data given (the general journal is on page 697). Use the account names given in the textbook chapter. Omit explanations.

2. Compute the amount of overapplied or underapplied overhead for the month.

3. Prepare a partial income statement for the month of December, adjusted for any overapplied or underapplied overhead.

SOLUTION

OVERHEAD COMPUTATIONS

Manufacturing Overhead (Debit Balance)		
Indirect Materials	$ 1,200	
Indirect Labor	5,200	
Other Overhead Costs	11,500	
Total Charged to Manufacturing Overhead		$17,900
Manufacturing Overhead Applied (Credit Balance)		18,000
Overapplied Overhead in December (Net Credit Balance)		$ 100

Alex Leather Products, Inc.

Partial Income Statement

Month Ended December 31, 2007

Sales		96 0 0 0 00
Cost of Goods Sold (per ledger account)	73 0 0 0 00	
Less Overapplied Manufacturing Overhead	1 0 0 00	
Cost of Goods Sold (adjusted to actual)		72 9 0 0 00
Gross Profit on Sales		23 1 0 0 00

SOLUTION (continued)

GENERAL JOURNAL   PAGE _____

	DATE		DESCRIPTION	POST. REF.	DEBIT	CREDIT	
1	2007						1
2	Dec.	31	Raw Materials Inventory		75 0 0 0 00		2
3			Accounts Payable			75 0 0 0 00	3
4							4
5		31	Work in Process Inventory (Direct Materials)		59 0 0 0 00		5
6			Manufacturing Overhead (Indirect Materials)		1 2 0 0 00		6
7			Raw Materials Inventory			60 2 0 0 00	7
8							8
9		31	Work in Process Inventory (Direct Labor)		24 0 0 0 00		9
10			Manufacturing Overhead (Indirect Labor)		5 2 0 0 00		10
11			Social Security Tax Payable			1 8 1 0 00	11
12			Medicare Tax Payable			4 2 3 00	12
13			Employee Income Tax Payable			2 6 0 0 00	13
14			Salaries and Wages Payable			24 3 6 7 00	14
15							15
16		31	Manufacturing Overhead		11 5 0 0 00		16
17			Accounts Payable			11 5 0 0 00	17
18							18
19		31	Work in Process Inventory		18 0 0 0 00		19
20			Manufacturing Overhead Applied			18 0 0 0 00	20
21							21
22		31	Finished Goods Inventory		82 0 0 0 00		22
23			Work in Process Inventory			82 0 0 0 00	23
24							24
25		31	Cost of Goods Sold		73 0 0 0 00		25
26			Finished Goods Inventory			73 0 0 0 00	26
27							27
28		31	Accounts Receivable		96 0 0 0 00		28
29			Sales			96 0 0 0 00	29
30							30
31							31
32							32
33							33
34							34
35							35
36							36
37							37

WORKING PAPERS

Name _____

EXERCISE 29.1

GENERAL JOURNAL   PAGE _____

	DATE	DESCRIPTION	POST. REF.	DEBIT	CREDIT	
1						1
2						2
3						3
4						4
5						5

EXERCISE 29.2

GENERAL JOURNAL   PAGE _____

	DATE	DESCRIPTION	POST. REF.	DEBIT	CREDIT	
1						1
2						2
3						3
4						4
5						5

EXERCISE 29.3

GENERAL JOURNAL   PAGE _____

	DATE	DESCRIPTION	POST. REF.	DEBIT	CREDIT	
1						1
2						2
3						3
4						4
5						5

EXERCISE 29.4

GENERAL JOURNAL   PAGE _____

	DATE	DESCRIPTION	POST. REF.	DEBIT	CREDIT	
1						1
2						2
3						3
4						4
5						5

EXERCISE 29.5

GENERAL JOURNAL   PAGE _____

	DATE	DESCRIPTION	POST. REF.	DEBIT	CREDIT	
1						1
2						2
3						3
4						4
5						5
6						6
7						7
8						8
9						9

EXERCISE 29.6

_____
_____
_____
_____
_____

EXERCISE 29.7

_____
_____
_____
_____
_____

GENERAL JOURNAL   PAGE _____

	DATE	DESCRIPTION	POST. REF.	DEBIT	CREDIT	
1						1
2						2
3						3
4						4
5						5

EXERCISE 29.8

_____
_____
_____
_____
_____
_____
_____
_____

EXERCISE 29.9

_____
_____
_____
_____
_____
_____
_____

EXERCISE 29.10

GENERAL JOURNAL   PAGE _____

	DATE		DESCRIPTION	POST. REF.	DEBIT	CREDIT	
1							1
2							2
3							3
4							4
5							5
6							6
7							7
8							8
9							9
10							10
11							11
12							12
13							13
14							14
15							15
16							16
17							17
18							18

PROBLEM 29.1A or 29.1B

GENERAL JOURNAL   PAGE _____

	DATE		DESCRIPTION	POST. REF.	DEBIT	CREDIT	
1							1
2							2
3							3
4							4
5							5
6							6
7							7
8							8
9							9
10							10
11							11
12							12
13							13
14							14
15							15
16							16
17							17
18							18
19							19
20							20
21							21
22							22
23							23
24							24
25							25
26							26
27							27
28							28
29							29
30							30
31							31
32							32
33							33
34							34
35							35
36							36
37							37
38							38

PROBLEM 29.1A or 29.1B (continued)

Manufacturing Overhead Computations

Partial Income Statement

Analyze:

PROBLEM 29.2A or 29.2B

JOB ORDER COST SHEET

For Stock _____   Job No. _____ Date _____

Customer's Name _____   Started _____

Address _____   Completed _____

Item _____   Quantity _____
                                                 (ordered)   (completed)

| MATERIAL | | LABOR | | OVERHEAD APPLIED | | | SUMMARY | |
Date	Amount	Date	Amount	Date	Rate	Amount	Item	Amount
							Materials	
							Labor	
							Overhead	
							Total	
							Unit Cost	
							Comments:	
Totals								

JOB ORDER COST SHEET

For Stock _____   Job No. _____ Date _____

Customer's Name _____   Started _____

Address _____   Completed _____

Item _____   Quantity _____
                                                 (ordered)   (completed)

| MATERIAL | | LABOR | | OVERHEAD APPLIED | | | SUMMARY | |
Date	Amount	Date	Amount	Date	Rate	Amount	Item	Amount
							Materials	
							Labor	
							Overhead	
							Total	
							Unit Cost	
							Comments:	
Totals								

JOB ORDER COST SHEET

For Stock _____   Job No. _____ Date _____

Customer's Name _____   Started _____

Address _____   Completed _____

Item _____   Quantity _____
                                                 (ordered)   (completed)

| MATERIAL | | LABOR | | OVERHEAD APPLIED | | | SUMMARY | |
Date	Amount	Date	Amount	Date	Rate	Amount	Item	Amount
							Materials	
							Labor	
							Overhead	
							Total	
							Unit Cost	
							Comments:	
Totals								

PROBLEM 29.2A or 29.2B (continued)

GENERAL JOURNAL

PAGE _____

	DATE		DESCRIPTION	POST. REF.	DEBIT	CREDIT	
1							1
2							2
3							3
4							4
5							5
6							6
7							7
8							8
9							9
10							10

OVERHEAD COMPUTATIONS

Analyze: _____

_____

CHAPTER 29 CHALLENGE PROBLEM

	Job DE31	Job JA01	Job JA02
Materials _____	_____	_____	_____
Labor _____	_____	_____	_____
Overhead (1) _____	_____	_____	_____
Total Costs _____	_____	_____	_____
_____	_____	_____	_____

Cost of Goods Sold

_____

_____

_____

_____

_____

_____

Notes:

_____

_____

_____

_____

_____

_____

_____

_____

_____

_____

_____

_____

_____

_____

_____

_____

_____

_____

Analyze: _____

_____

CHAPTER 29 CRITICAL THINKING PROBLEM

a. _____
_____
_____

b. _____
_____
_____

c. _____
_____
_____

d. _____
_____
_____

e. _____
_____
_____

f. _____
_____
_____
_____
_____

Chapter 29 Practice Test Answer Key

Part A True-False		Part B Completion
1. T	8. F	1. perpetual
2. F	9. F	2. manufacturing overhead
3. T	10. T	3. underapplied
4. T	11. T	4. job order cost sheet
5. F	12. F	5. manufacturing overhead
6. T	13. F	6. materials requisition
7. T	14. F	7. receiving report
		8. FIFO

Condensed Income Statement

CHAPTER 30 Process Cost Accounting

STUDY GUIDE

Understanding the Chapter

Objectives

1. Compute equivalent units of production with no beginning work in process inventory. 2. Prepare a cost of production report with no beginning work in process inventory. 3. Compute the unit cost of manufacturing under the process cost accounting system. 4. Record costs incurred and the flow of costs as products move through the manufacturing process and are sold. 5. Compute equivalent production and prepare a cost of production report with a beginning work in process inventory. 6. Define the accounting terms new to this chapter.

Reading Assignment

Read Chapter 30 in the textbook. Complete the textbook Section Self Reviews as you finish reading each section of the chapter, and the Comprehensive Self Review at the end of the chapter. Refer to the Chapter 30 Glossary or to the Glossary at the end of the book to find definitions for terms that are not familiar to you.

Activities

❏ **Thinking Critically**

Answer the *Thinking Critically* questions for Conoco Phillips, Accounting on the Job, and Managerial Implications.

❏ **Internet Application**

Complete the activity for Accounting on the Job.

❏ **Discussion Questions**

Answer each assigned discussion question in Chapter 30.

❏ **Exercises**

Complete each assigned exercise in Chapter 30. Use the forms provided in this SGWP. The objectives covered by an exercise are given after the exercise number. If you need help with an exercise, review the portion of the chapter related to the objective(s) covered.

❏ **Problems A/B**

Complete each assigned problem in Chapter 30. Use the forms provided in this SGWP. The objectives covered by a problem are given after the problem number. If you need help with a problem, review the portion of the chapter related to the objective(s) covered.

❏ **Challenge Problem**

Complete the challenge problem as assigned. Use the forms provided in this SGWP.

❏ **Critical Thinking Problem**

Complete the critical thinking problem as assigned. Use the forms provided in this SGWP.

❏ **Business Connections**

Complete these Business Connections activities as assigned to gain a deeper understanding of Chapter 30 concepts.

Practice Tests

Complete the Practice Tests, which cover the main points in your reading assignment. Compare your answers with those in the Practice Test Answer Key for Chapter 30 at the end of this chapter. If you have answered any questions incorrectly, review the related section of the text.

Part A True-False

For each of the following statements, circle T in the answer column if the statement is true or F if the statement is false.

T F   1. Separate cost records are kept for the various producing and service departments.

T F   2. The balance of the **Raw Materials Inventory** account at the end of any accounting period should reflect the cost of raw materials, supplies on hand, and work in process at that time.

T F   3. In a process cost system, the cost of service departments are allocated to the producing departments and charged to the work in process inventory accounts.

T F   4. Raw materials are always added at the start of production.

T F   5. In a process cost system, production costs are recorded on job order cost sheets.

T F   6. The Quantity Schedule section of a cost of production report shows the total quantities to be accounted for and explains what happened to them.

T F   7. A single **Raw Materials Inventory** account can be used for both direct materials and manufacturing supplies.

T F   8. The equivalent units for materials in a department are always the same as the equivalent units for labor in that department.

T F   9. A process cost system may be viewed as an average cost system.

T F   10. A physical inventory should be taken at least once a year to check the accuracy of the perpetual inventory figures.

T F   11. A department had no beginning work in process. During the month, 200 units were started into production and 150 were completed. On the other 50 units, 50 percent of the labor had been performed. The equivalent unit production for labor is 180 units for the month.

T F   12. If the figures from a physical inventory do not agree with the figures in the perpetual inventory records, then the records must be adjusted.

T F   13. The beginning work in process inventory of one accounting period is the same as the ending work in process of the prior period.

T F   14. The ending work in process inventory of one department becomes the beginning work in process inventory of the next department in the manufacturing process.

T F   15. The entry to record the sale of finished goods is a debit to **Accounts Receivable** and a credit to **Work in Process Inventory** for the selling price.

Part B Completion
In the answer column, supply the missing word or words needed to complete each of the following statements.

_____ 1. _____ is a control account with a supporting subsidiary ledger showing the detail of overhead items.

_____ 2. In a(n) _____ system, the total cost of a unit of production is found by adding the unit costs in each department through which the product passes as it is being manufactured.

_____ 3. In a(n) _____ department, work is performed directly on the product.

_____ 4. The maintenance department is an example of a(n) _____ department that assists in production but does not perform work on the actual product.

_____ 5. A(n) _____ system is normally used in situations where different products are manufactured and are started in batches or by jobs.

_____ 6. The _____ technique is used to express the amount of work accomplished in terms of equivalent whole units.

_____ 7. The _____ report shows the costs incurred in a department, the unit cost of each element of manufacturing costs, and the cost accounted for in the department.

_____ 8. The number of units to be accounted for and the number actually accounted for are shown in the _____ section of the cost of production report.

Part C Exercises
Compute the following units.

_____ 1. The assembly department of a manufacturing business had no beginning inventory. During March, 1,000 units of product were started. All materials are added at the beginning of the manufacturing process. During the month, 800 units were transferred to the next department and 200 units were still in work in process. Compute the equivalent units of materials for March.

_____ 2. A producing department had no beginning inventory. During the month, 5,000 units of product were begun in the department, of which 4,000 units were transferred to the next department and 1,000 units were in process at the end of the month. The 1,000 units were 30 percent complete as to labor. Compute the equivalent units for labor for the month.

_____ 3. The beginning inventory in a department was 1,000 units, which were 25 percent complete as to overhead. During May, 4,500 units were placed in process, 5,000 units were transferred to the next department, and 500 units were in the ending work in process inventory. The ending inventory was 40 percent complete as to overhead. Compute the equivalent units of overhead for May.

Demonstration Problem

Soccer Products, Inc. began business in August 2007. The company manufactures soccer balls. The product is started in the cutting and assembly department and is completed in the stitching and printing department. Data for the month of August follows.

Instructions

1. Prepare equivalent production computations for the cutting and assembly department.

2. Prepare a cost of production report for the cutting and assembly department.

	Cutting and Assembly Department
Costs	
Materials	$53,400
Labor	21,280
Manufacturing Overhead	15,000
Total Costs	$89,680
Quantities	
Started in production	12,000 units
Transferred out to next department	10,000
Work in Process—ending	2,000
Stage of Completion—Ending Work in Process	
Materials	100%
Labor	80%
Manufacturing Overhead	80%

SOLUTION

1.

Soccer Products, Inc.

Equivalent Production Computations

Month Ended August 31, 2007

Cutting and Assembly Department	
Materials: Units Transferred Out	10 0 0 0 00
Work in Process—Ending: 2,000 units × 100%	2 0 0 0 00
Equivalent Production for Materials	12 0 0 0 00
Labor and Manufacturing Overhead	
Units Transferred Out	10 0 0 0 00
Work in Process—Ending: 2,000 units × 80%	1 6 0 0 00
Equivalent Production for Labor and Overhead	11 6 0 0 00

SOLUTION (continued)

2.

Soccer Products, Inc.

Cost of Production Report—August 31, 2007

Cutting and Assembly Department

QUANTITY SCHEDULE	UNITS		
Quantity to Be Accounted For:			
Started in Production	12 0 0 0 00		
Total to Be Accounted For	12 0 0 0 00		
Quantity Accounted For:			
Transferred to next department	10 0 0 0 00		
Work In Process—Ending	2 0 0 0 00		
Total Accounted For	12 0 0 0 00		

COST SCHEDULE	TOTAL COST	E.P. UNITS	UNIT COST
Costs to Be Accounted For:			
Costs in Current Department			
Materials	53 4 0 0 00	÷ 12 0 0 0 =	4 45
Labor	21 2 8 0 00	÷ 11 6 0 0 =	1 83
Manufacturing Overhead	15 0 0 0 00	÷ 11 6 0 0 =	1 29
Cumulative Cost Total	89 6 8 0 00		7 57

STUDY GUIDE

EXERCISE 30.1

_____
_____
_____
_____
_____
_____

EXERCISE 30.2

_____
_____
_____
_____
_____
_____
_____

EXERCISE 30.3

_____
_____
_____
_____
_____
_____

EXERCISE 30.4

_____
_____
_____
_____
_____
_____
_____

EXERCISE 30.5

_____
_____
_____
_____
_____
_____
_____
_____
_____
_____
_____
_____
_____
_____

EXERCISE 30.6

_____
_____
_____
_____
_____
_____
_____
_____
_____
_____
_____
_____
_____
_____
_____
_____
_____
_____
_____

EXERCISE 30.7

GENERAL JOURNAL   PAGE _____

	DATE	DESCRIPTION	POST. REF.	DEBIT	CREDIT	
1						1
2						2
3						3
4						4
5						5
6						6
7						7
8						8
9						9
10						10
11						11
12						12
13						13
14						14
15						15
16						16

EXERCISE 30.8

GENERAL JOURNAL   PAGE _____

	DATE	DESCRIPTION	POST. REF.	DEBIT	CREDIT	
1						1
2						2
3						3
4						4
5						5
6						6
7						7

EXERCISE 30.9

GENERAL JOURNAL   PAGE _____

	DATE	DESCRIPTION	POST. REF.	DEBIT	CREDIT	
1						1
2						2
3						3
4						4
5						5
6						6
7						7

PROBLEM 30.1A or 30.1B

Equivalent Production Computations

Analyze: _____

PROBLEM 30.2A or 30.2B

GENERAL JOURNAL   PAGE _____

	DATE		DESCRIPTION	POST. REF.	DEBIT	CREDIT	
1							1
2							2
3							3
4							4
5							5
6							6
7							7
8							8
9							9
10							10
11							11
12							12
13							13
14							14
15							15
16							16
17							17
18							18
19							19
20							20
21							21
22							22
23							23
24							24
25							25
26							26
27							27
28							28
29							29
30							30
31							31
32							32
33							33
34							34
35							35
36							36
37							37

Name _____

PROBLEM 30.2A or 30.2B (continued)

Equivalent Production Computations

PROBLEM 30.2A or 30.2B (continued)

Cost of Production Report—Fabricating Department

QUANTITY SCHEDULE	UNITS		

COST SCHEDULE	TOTAL COST	E.P. UNITS	UNIT COST

PROBLEM 30.2A or 30.2B (continued)

<u>Cost of Production Report—Assembly Department</u>

QUANTITY SCHEDULE		UNITS		

COST SCHEDULE	TOTAL COST	E.P. UNITS	UNIT COST

Analyze: _____

PROBLEM 30.3A or 30.3B

Equivalent Production Computations

PROBLEM 30.3A or 30.3B (continued)

Cost of Production Report

QUANTITY SCHEDULE		UNITS
COST SCHEDULE	TOTAL COST	UNIT COST

Analyze: _____

CHAPTER 30 CHALLENGE PROBLEM

Equivalent Production Computations

CHAPTER 30 CHALLENGE PROBLEM (continued)

Cost of Production Report

QUANTITY SCHEDULE			UNITS	

COST SCHEDULE	TOTAL COST	UNIT COST

(continued)

CHAPTER 30 CHALLENGE PROBLEM (continued)

Cost of Production Report (continued)

Analyze: _____

EXTRA FORM

QUANTITY SCHEDULE		UNITS			
COST SCHEDULE	TOTAL COST	E.P. UNITS	UNIT COST		

EXTRA FORM

QUANTITY SCHEDULE	UNITS		

COST SCHEDULE	TOTAL COST	E.P. UNITS	UNIT COST

CHAPTER 30 CRITICAL THINKING PROBLEM

Raw Materials Inventory		Work in Process Mixing Department		Work in Process Cooking Department		Work in Process Cooling and Packaging Department	

Labor Costs	

Manufacturing Overhead		Finished Goods Inventory		Cost of Goods Sold	

Chapter 30 Practice Test Answer Key

Part A True-False

1. T
2. F
3. T
4. F
5. F
6. T
7. T
8. F
9. T
10. T
11. F
12. T
13. T
14. F
15. F

Part B Completion

1. Manufacturing Overhead (Control)
2. process cost
3. producing (or production)
4. service
5. job order cost
6. equivalent production
7. cost of production
8. quantity schedule

Part C Exercises

1. Transferred to next department
   (800 × 100%)   =   800
   Ending inventory of work in process
   (220 × 100%)   =   200
   Total equivalent units—materials   =   1,000

2. Transferred to next department
   (4,000 × 100%)   =   4,000
   Ending inventory of work in process
   (1,000 × 30%)   =   300
   Total equivalent units—labor   =   4,300

3. Transferred to next department
   (5,000 × 100%)   =   4,000
   Ending inventory of work in process
   (500 × 40%)   =   200
   Total equivalent units—overhead   =   5,200

CHAPTER 31 / Controlling Manufacturing Costs: Standard Costs

STUDY GUIDE

Understanding the Chapter

Objectives

1. Explain how fixed, variable, and semivariable costs change as the level of manufacturing activity changes. 2. Use the high-low point method to determine the fixed and variable components of a semivariable cost. 3. Prepare a fixed budget for manufacturing costs. 4. Develop a flexible budget for manufacturing costs. 5. Develop standard costs per unit of product. 6. Compute the standard costs of products manufactured during the period and determine cost variances between actual costs and standard costs. 7. Compute the amounts and analyze the nature of variances from standard for raw materials, labor, and manufacturing overhead. 8. Define the accounting terms new to this chapter.

Reading Assignment

Read Chapter 31 in the textbook. Complete the textbook Section Self Reviews as you finish reading each section of the chapter, and the Comprehensive Self Review at the end of the chapter. Refer to the Chapter 31 Glossary or to the Glossary at the end of the book to find definitions for terms that are not familiar to you.

Activities

❑ **Thinking Critically**   Answer the *Thinking Critically* questions for Harley-Davidson, Computers in Accounting, and Managerial Implications.

❑ **Internet Application**   Complete the activity for Computers in Accounting.

❑ **Discussion Questions**   Answer each assigned discussion question in Chapter 31.

❑ **Exercises**   Complete each assigned exercise in Chapter 31. Use the forms provided in this SGWP. The objectives covered by an exercise are given after the exercise number. If you need help with an exercise, review the portion of the chapter related to the objective(s) covered.

❑ **Problems A/B**   Complete each assigned problem in Chapter 31. Use the forms provided in this SGWP. The objectives covered by a problem are given after the problem number. If you need help with a problem, review the portion of the chapter related to the objective(s) covered.

❑ **Challenge Problem**   Complete the challenge problem as assigned. Use the forms provided in this SGWP.

❑ **Critical Thinking**   Complete the critical thinking problem as assigned. Use the forms provided in this SGWP.

❑ **Business Connections**   Complete the Business Connections activities as assigned to gain a deeper understanding of chapter concepts.

Practice Tests

Complete the Practice Tests, which cover the main points in your reading assignment. Compare your answers with those in the Practice Test Answer Key for Chapter 31 at the end of this chapter. If you have answered any questions incorrectly, review the related section of the text.

Part A True-False *For each of the following statements, circle T in the answer column if the statement is true or F if the statement is false.*

T   F   **1.** To properly budget manufacturing costs, those costs must be separated into their fixed and variable components.

T   F   **2.** The variable costs per unit change in direct proportion to changes in the volume of activity.

T   F   **3.** A fixed budget for manufacturing costs is ideal for controlling such costs.

T   F   **4.** Direct materials is a good example of a cost that generally is classified as a semivariable cost.

T   F   **5.** The high-low point method may be inappropriate in determining fixed and variable costs in some circumstances.

T   F   **6.** Power and utility costs are likely to be semivariable costs.

T   F   **7.** In a factory, if fixed costs per unit are $50 when 500 units are produced, the fixed costs per unit should be $20 per unit if 250 units are produced.

T   F   **8.** A flexible budget shows expected costs at several levels of production activity.

T   F   **9.** It is unusual for a company to prepare monthly budgets of manufacturing costs.

T   F   **10.** Standard costs are "ideal" costs that should generally be unattainable.

T   F   **11.** A fixed manufacturing budget is given that name because it is a budget of fixed costs.

T   F   **12.** Indirect labor costs in a factory consist of $50,000 per month of fixed costs and $10 per direct labor hour for variable costs. If 3,000 direct labor hours are used, the budget for indirect labor will be $75,000.

T   F   **13.** A materials quantity variance is computed by multiplying the difference between the standard quantity of materials and the actual quantity consumed by the actual costs per unit.

T   F   **14.** The labor rate variance is determined by multiplying the standard quantity of labor by the difference between the actual rate per hour and the standard rate per hour.

T   F   **15.** Standard costs may actually be entered into the accounts.

T   F   **16.** The human resources department should generally be held responsible for labor quantity variances.

T   F   **17.** It is possible to compute the materials quantity variance for an individual job under the job order cost accounting system if standard costs have been established.

Part B Completion

Answer each question below based on the information given for ABA Industries. ABA has set manufacturing overhead standard costs at $5 per unit, based on an expected volume of 100,000 units requiring 100,000 hours of direct labor, fixed costs of $100,000 per year, and variable costs of $4 per hour. During the year, actual production was 90,000 units requiring 96,000 hours, actual fixed costs were $110,000 and variable costs were $4.10 per hour.

_____ **1.** What are the standard manufacturing overhead costs of the units produced during the year?

_____ **2.** What are the total actual costs for the year?

_____ **3.** What is the amount of variable costs budgeted for the actual hours worked?

_____ **4.** What is the amount of variable costs budgeted for the standard hours for the work performed?

_____ **5.** What is the amount of fixed costs budgeted for the actual hours worked?

_____ **6.** What are the budgeted costs for the standard hours allowed for the work?

_____ **7.** What is the total manufacturing overhead variance for the year?

Demonstration Problem

The New Orleans Company manufactures one product. Standard costs for each unit of the product are:

Direct materials, 10 gallons @ $1.80	$18.00
Direct labor, 2 hours @ $15	30.00
Manufacturing Overhead, 1 hour @ $10	10.00
Total Standard Cost per unit	$58.00

Actual production costs for the month are given below for the 2,000 units:

Direct materials, 20,500 gallons @ $1.82	$ 37,310.00
Direct labor, 3,900 hours @ $15.10	58,890.00
Manufacturing Overhead	20,500.00
Total Actual Costs	$116,700.00

Instructions
Compute the following variances:

1. Direct material price variance.
2. Direct material quantity variance.
3. Direct labor rate variance.
4. Direct labor efficiency variance.
5. Total manufacturing overhead variance.

SOLUTION

1. **Direct material price variance:** ($1.82 − $1.80) × 20,500 gallons = $410 unfavorable

2. **Direct material quantity variance:** (20,500 − 20,000) × $1.80 = $900 unfavorable

3. **Direct labor rate variance:** ($15.10 − $15.00) × 3,900 hours = $390 unfavorable

4. **Direct labor efficiency variance:** (4,000 − 3,900) × $18.00 = $1,800 favorable

5. **Total manufacturing overhead variance:** $20,500 − $20,000 = $500 unfavorable

WORKING PAPERS

Name _____

EXERCISE 31.1

Quarter	Direct Labor Hours	Utilities Cost

EXERCISE 31.2

Percent of Budgeted Hours

EXERCISE 31.3

EXERCISE 31.4

Cost Element	Standard Cost	Actual Cost

EXERCISE 31.5

EXERCISE 31.6

EXERCISE 31.7

EXERCISE 31.8

_____
_____
_____
_____
_____
_____

EXERCISE 31.9

_____
_____
_____
_____
_____
_____

EXERCISE 31.10

_____
_____
_____
_____
_____
_____

EXERCISE 31.11

_____
_____
_____
_____
_____
_____

PROBLEM 31.1A or 31.1B

_____

_____

_____

_____

_____

_____

_____

_____

_____

_____

_____

_____

_____

_____

_____

_____

_____

_____

_____

_____

Analyze: _____

_____

PROBLEM 31.2A or 31.2B

1. _____

Flexible Budget for Manufacturing Overhead

2. _____

Manufacturing Overhead Budget Performance Report

Analyze: _____

PROBLEM 31.3A or 31.3B

1. _____

Analysis of Materials Variance

_____
_____
_____
_____
_____

2. _____
_____
_____
_____
_____
_____
_____

Analyze: _____
_____

PROBLEM 31.4A or 31.4B

1. _____

Analysis of Materials Variances

2. _____

Analysis of Labor Variances

Analyze: _____

CHAPTER 31 CHALLENGE PROBLEM

_____

_____

_____

_____

_____

_____

_____

_____

_____

_____

_____

_____

_____

_____

_____

_____

_____

_____

_____

_____

_____

_____

_____

_____

_____

_____

_____

_____

_____

_____

_____

_____

Analyze: _____

_____

CHAPTER 31 CRITICAL THINKING PROBLEM

_____

_____

_____

_____

_____

_____

_____

_____

_____

_____

_____

_____

_____

_____

_____

_____

_____

_____

_____

_____

_____

_____

_____

_____

_____

_____

_____

_____

_____

_____

_____

Chapter 31 Practice Test Answer Key

Part A True-False

1. T	10. F
2. F	11. F
3. F	12. F
4. F	13. F
5. T	14. F
6. T	15. T
7. F	16. F
8. T	17. T
9. F	

Part B Completion

1. $450,000 (90,000 units × $5/unit)
2. $503,600 [$110,000 + (96,000 × $4.10)]
3. $384,000 (96,000 × $4.00)
4. $360,000 (90,000 × $4.00)
5. $100,000
6. $460,000 [$100,000 + (90,000 × $4.00)]
7. $53,600 ($503,600 − $450,000)

740 ■ Chapter 31

STUDY GUIDE

Understanding the Chapter

Objectives	**1.** Explain the basic steps in the decision-making process. **2.** Prepare income statements using the absorption costing and direct costing methods. **3.** Using the contribution approach, analyze the profits of segments of a business. **4.** Determine relevant cost and revenue data for decision-making purposes. **5.** Apply an appropriate decision process in three situations: **(a)** Pricing products in special cases, **(b)** Deciding whether to purchase new equipment, and **(c)** Deciding whether to make or to buy a part. **6.** Define the accounting terms new to this chapter.
Reading Assignment	Read Chapter 32 in the textbook. Complete the textbook Section Self Reviews as you finish reading each section of the chapter, and the Comprehensive Self Review at the end of the chapter. Refer to the Chapter 32 Glossary or to the Glossary at the end of the book to find definitions for terms that are not familiar to you.

Activities

❏ **Thinking Critically** — Answer the *Thinking Critically* questions for DuPont, Accounting on the Job, and Managerial Implications.

❏ **Internet Application** — Complete the activity for Accounting on the Job.

❏ **Discussion Questions** — Answer each assigned discussion question in Chapter 32.

❏ **Exercises** — Complete each assigned exercise in Chapter 32. Use the forms provided in this SGWP. The objectives covered by an exercise are given after the exercise number. If you need help with an exercise, review the portion of the chapter related to the objective(s) covered.

❏ **Problems A/B** — Complete each assigned problem in Chapter 32. Use the forms provided in this SGWP. The objectives covered by a problem are given after the problem number. If you need help with a problem, review the portion of the chapter related to the objective(s) covered.

❏ **Challenge Problem** — Complete the challenge problem as assigned. Use the forms provided in this SGWP.

❏ **Critical Thinking Problem** — Complete the critical thinking problem as assigned. Use the forms provided in this SGWP.

❏ **Business Connections** — Complete the Business Connections activities as assigned to gain a deeper understanding of Chapter 32 concepts.

Practice Tests

Complete the Practice Tests, which cover the main points in your reading assignment. Compare your answers with those in the Practice Test Answer Key for Chapter 32 at the end of this chapter. If you have answered any questions incorrectly, review the related section of the text.

Part A True-False
For each of the following statements, circle T in the answer column if the statement is true or F if the statement is false.

T   F   **1.** In the decision-making process, the first step is to define the problem.

T   F   **2.** In managerial decisions, all costs can be ignored.

T   F   **3.** Historical costs are usually sunk costs.

T   F   **4.** Fixed costs are rarely controllable.

T   F   **5.** All manufacturing costs, both fixed and variable, are assigned to the cost of goods manufactured under direct costing.

T   F   **6.** Absorption costing concentrates attention on the contribution margin.

T   F   **7.** When a business decision is being made, only those costs that will change as a result of the decision are relevant.

T   F   **8.** Contribution margin is the difference between sales and variable costs.

T   F   **9.** Assuming no beginning inventory, if the units produced and the units sold are equal, both direct costing and absorption costing will yield the same net income.

T   F   **10.** In general, managerial decisions such as whether or not to purchase new equipment or to drop a product line can be made using only accounting and other quantitative data.

T   F   **11.** If a segment of a business is not producing a positive contribution margin, management should consider eliminating that segment.

T   F   **12.** Direct costing does not follow GAAP financial reporting.

T   F   **13.** It may be profitable for a company to accept an offer to sell some of its product at an amount less than the total cost per unit computed under absorption costing.

T   F   **14.** Under direct costing, all variable costs are treated as part of the cost of goods manufactured in the period when the costs are incurred.

T   F   **15.** In considering whether to replace equipment, the book value of the existing equipment is of little concern.

T   F   **16.** When one is deciding whether to drop a product, the contribution margin of the product is probably the most important factor to consider.

T   F   **17.** If the variable cost per unit remains constant, but total fixed cost increases, the contribution margin will decrease.

T   F   **18.** Income taxes can be ignored in making decisions such as to replace equipment, discontinue a product line, etc.

Part B Matching

For each numbered item, choose the matching definition from the box and write the identifying letter in the answer column.

_____	**1.** sunk	
_____	**2.** controllable	
_____	**3.** relevant	
_____	**4.** manufacturing margin	
_____	**5.** differential	
_____	**6.** incremental	
_____	**7.** common or indirect	

a. The difference in cost between one alternative and another

b. Future or expected costs that will change only as a result of a decision

c. Costs that have been incurred in the past

d. Also known as differential costs

e. Costs that depend largely on the actions of the segment manager

f. Costs not traceable to any one segment of the business

g. Excess of sales over variable cost of goods sold

Demonstration Problem

Mister Tool, Inc. distributes small tools to retail hardware stores. Early in 2007, management of the business decided to develop and market a private brand line of tools. They contracted with a manufacturer to make the products and began distribution. After several months, the board of directors is rethinking the decision and has asked you to analyze the following information for the July 2007 sales.

	Fixed Costs per Month	Percent of Selling Price per Unit
Average cost of products		38%
Average cost of packaging		5%
Average freight in		2%
Average delivery costs		7%
Sales commissions		12%
Advertising		
Variable		5%
Fixed	$2,500	
Warehousing		
Variable		2%
Fixed	$1,800	
Other		
Variable		3%
Fixed	$ 600	

July sales were $11,000. Several of the directors think the private product line should be discontinued.

Instructions

1. Based on the information provided, what is the amount of income or loss on July sales of these products?

2. Based on the accounting analysis, should the private brand be eliminated?

3. Are there other considerations that bear on this decision to eliminate or keep the product line?

SOLUTION

1.

	AMOUNTS		
Sales			11 0 0 0 00
Costs and Expenses			
Variable Expenses			
Product (38% of sales)	4 1 8 0 00		
Packaging (5% of sales)	5 5 0 00		
Freight In (2% of sales)	2 2 0 00		
Delivery Costs (7% of sales)	7 7 0 00		
Sales Commissions (12% of sales)	1 3 2 0 00		
Advertising (5% of sales)	5 5 0 00		
Warehousing (2% of sales)	2 2 0 00		
Other (3% of sales)	3 3 0 00		
Total variable expenses (74% of sales)		8 1 4 0 00	
Contribution Margin (26% of sales)		2 8 6 0 00	
Fixed Costs			
Advertising	2 5 0 0 00		
Warehousing	1 8 0 0 00		
Other	6 0 0 00		
Total fixed costs		4 9 0 0 00	
Net Income (Loss) for Month		(2 0 4 0 00)	

2.   If the board of directors considers only the net loss, it appears that the private label should be eliminated.

3.   It appears that since the product is generating a positive contribution margin, the key question is—can sales be increased to a level to cover the fixed costs? Are there any variable or fixed costs that can be reduced? Are there additional consumers to reach? Are the retail stores giving us good floor visibility? Should new advertising venues be tried? These are just a few of the questions to consider before eliminating the product line.

WORKING PAPERS

EXERCISE 32.1

EXERCISE 32.2

EXERCISE 32.3

EXERCISE 32.4

_____
_____
_____
_____
_____
_____
_____
_____
_____
_____
_____
_____
_____
_____
_____
_____

EXERCISE 32.5

1. _____
_____
_____
_____
_____
_____
_____
_____
_____
_____
_____
_____
_____
_____

2. _____
_____
_____
_____
_____
_____

EXERCISE 32.6

_____
_____
_____
_____
_____
_____
_____

EXERCISE 32.7

_____
_____
_____
_____
_____
_____
_____
_____
_____
_____
_____
_____

EXERCISE 32.8

_____
_____
_____
_____
_____
_____
_____
_____
_____
_____
_____
_____

PROBLEM 32.1A or 32.1B

1. _____

Income Statement (Absorption Costing)

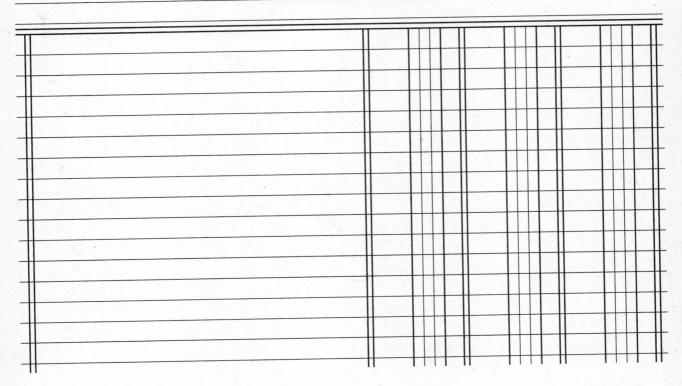

2. _____

Income Statement (Direct Costing)

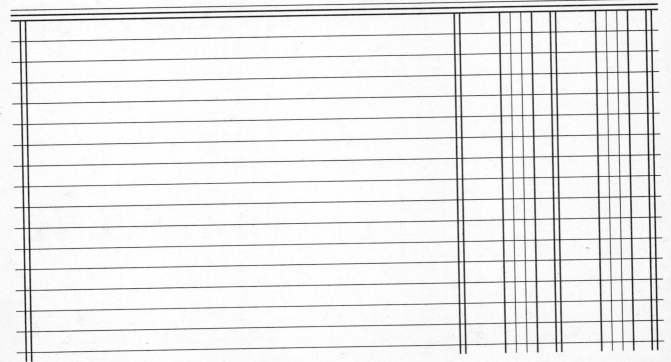

PROBLEM 32.1A or 32.1B (continued)

3. _____

_____

_____

_____

_____

_____

_____

_____

_____

_____

_____

_____

_____

_____

_____

_____

_____

_____

_____

_____

_____

_____

_____

_____

_____

_____

_____

_____

_____

_____

_____

_____

Analyze: _____

_____

PROBLEM 32.2A or 32.2B

1. _____

<u>Income Statement (Direct Costing)</u>

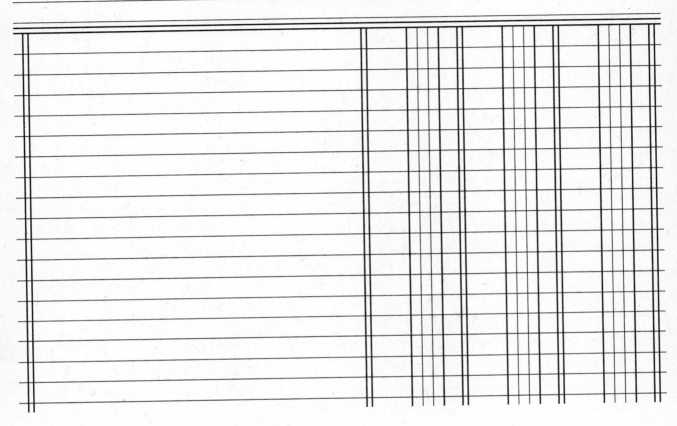

2. _____

<u>Computations</u>

Analyze: _____

PROBLEM 32.3A or 32.3B

1. ANALYSIS OF EFFECTS OF PURCHASING MACHINE

_____
_____
_____
_____
_____
_____
_____
_____
_____
_____
_____
_____
_____
_____
_____
_____
_____
_____

2. _____
_____
_____
_____
_____
_____
_____
_____
_____
_____
_____
_____
_____
_____
_____
_____
_____

Analyze: _____
_____
_____

PROBLEM 32.4A or 32.4B

1. _____

<u>Analysis of Effects of Making or Buying a Part</u>

2. _____

Analyze: _____

CHAPTER 32 CHALLENGE PROBLEM

CHAPTER 32 CHALLENGE PROBLEM (continued)

_____
_____
_____
_____
_____
_____
_____
_____
_____
_____
_____
_____
_____
_____
_____
_____
_____
_____
_____
_____
_____
_____
_____
_____
_____
_____
_____
_____

Analyze: _____

CHAPTER 32 CRITICAL THINKING PROBLEM

	ITEM 901	ITEM 902	ITEM 903	TOTAL

CHAPTER 32 CRITICAL THINKING PROBLEM (continued)

_____
_____
_____
_____
_____
_____
_____
_____
_____
_____
_____
_____
_____
_____
_____
_____
_____
_____
_____
_____
_____
_____

Chapter 32 Practice Test Answer Key

Part A True-False			Part B Matching
1. T	7. T	13. T	1. c
2. F	8. T	14. F	2. e
3. T	9. T	15. T	3. b
4. F	10. F	16. T	4. g
5. F	11. T	17. F	5. a
6. F	12. T	18. F	6. d
			7. f

EXTRA FORMS

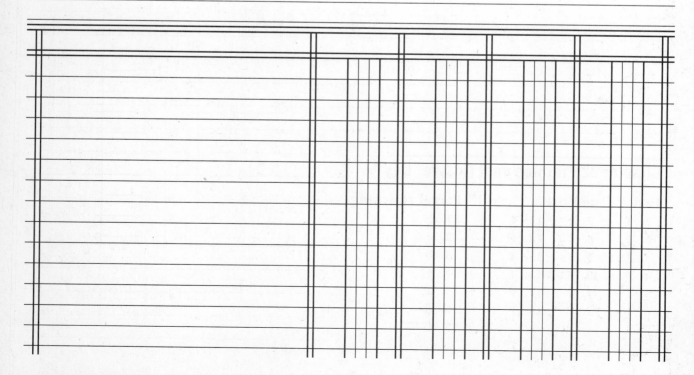

GENERAL JOURNAL

PAGE _____

	DATE	DESCRIPTION	POST. REF.	DEBIT	CREDIT	
1						
2						2
3						3
4						4
5						5
6						6
7						7
8						8
9						9
10						10
11						11
12						12
13						13
14						14
15						15
16						16
17						17
18						18
19						19
20						20
21						21
22						22
23						23
24						24
25						25
26						26
27						27
28						28
29						29
30						30
31						31
32						32
33						33
34						34
35						35
36						36
37						37

Extra Forms ■ *A1*

GENERAL JOURNAL

	DESCRIPTION	POST. REF.	DEBIT	CREDIT	
1					1
2					2
3					3
4					4
5					5
6					6
7					7
8					8
9					9
10					10
11					11
12					12
13					13
14					14
15					15
16					16
17					17
18					18
19					19
20					20
21					21
22					22
23					23
24					24
25					25
26					26
27					27
28					28
29					29
30					30
31					31
32					32
33					33
34					34
35					35
36					36
37					37

A2 ■ **Extra Forms**

GENERAL JOURNAL

PAGE _____

	DATE		DESCRIPTION	POST. REF.	DEBIT	CREDIT	
1							1
2							2
3							3
4							4
5							5
6							6
7							7
8							8
9							9
10							10
11							11
12							12
13							13
14							14
15							15
16							16
17							17
18							18
19							19
20							20
21							21
22							22
23							23
24							24
25							25
26							26
27							27
28							28
29							29
30							30
31							31
32							32
33							33
34							34
35							35
36							36
37							37

GENERAL LEDGER

ACCOUNT NO. _____

	DESCRIPTION	POST. REF.	DEBIT	CREDIT	BALANCE	
					DEBIT	CREDIT

ACCOUNT _____ ACCOUNT NO. _____

DATE	DESCRIPTION	POST. REF.	DEBIT	CREDIT	BALANCE	
					DEBIT	CREDIT

ACCOUNT _____ ACCOUNT NO. _____

DATE	DESCRIPTION	POST. REF.	DEBIT	CREDIT	BALANCE	
					DEBIT	CREDIT

ACCOUNT _____ ACCOUNT NO. _____

DATE	DESCRIPTION	POST. REF.	DEBIT	CREDIT	BALANCE	
					DEBIT	CREDIT

ACCOUNT _____ ACCOUNT NO. _____

DATE	DESCRIPTION	POST. REF.	DEBIT	CREDIT	BALANCE	
					DEBIT	CREDIT

A4 ■ **Extra Forms**

GENERAL LEDGER

ACCOUNT _____ ACCOUNT NO. _____

DATE	DESCRIPTION	POST. REF.	DEBIT	CREDIT	BALANCE	
					DEBIT	CREDIT

ACCOUNT _____ ACCOUNT NO. _____

DATE	DESCRIPTION	POST. REF.	DEBIT	CREDIT	BALANCE	
					DEBIT	CREDIT

ACCOUNT _____ ACCOUNT NO. _____

DATE	DESCRIPTION	POST. REF.	DEBIT	CREDIT	BALANCE	
					DEBIT	CREDIT

ACCOUNT _____ ACCOUNT NO. _____

DATE	DESCRIPTION	POST. REF.	DEBIT	CREDIT	BALANCE	
					DEBIT	CREDIT

ACCOUNT _____ ACCOUNT NO. _____

DATE	DESCRIPTION	POST. REF.	DEBIT	CREDIT	BALANCE	
					DEBIT	CREDIT

GENERAL LEDGER

ACCOUNT NO. _____

	DESCRIPTION	POST. REF.	DEBIT	CREDIT	BALANCE	
					DEBIT	CREDIT

ACCOUNT _____

ACCOUNT NO. _____

DATE	DESCRIPTION	POST. REF.	DEBIT	CREDIT	BALANCE	
					DEBIT	CREDIT

ACCOUNT _____

ACCOUNT NO. _____

DATE	DESCRIPTION	POST. REF.	DEBIT	CREDIT	BALANCE	
					DEBIT	CREDIT

ACCOUNT _____

ACCOUNT NO. _____

DATE	DESCRIPTION	POST. REF.	DEBIT	CREDIT	BALANCE	
					DEBIT	CREDIT

ACCOUNT _____

ACCOUNT NO. _____

DATE	DESCRIPTION	POST. REF.	DEBIT	CREDIT	BALANCE	
					DEBIT	CREDIT